THE FUTURE OF HIGH-COST CREDIT

This book proposes a new way of thinking about the controversial and complex challenge of regulating high-cost credit, with a specific focus on payday lending. These products have received significant attention in both the media and the political arena, but remain underexplored from an academic perspective. The inadequacy of regulatory interventions has created ongoing problems in the market, particularly when credit is provided to individuals who are already financially vulnerable.

Two specific gaps in the existing literature are tackled in the book. First, the inadequate analysis of the relevant philosophical concepts around high-cost credit, which can result in an oversimplification of particularly complex legal and social issues. Secondly, the lack of engagement in both the high-cost credit market and lived experience of borrowers, resulting in limited understanding of those who use these financial products.

The Future of High-Cost Credit explores the theoretical grounding, policy initiatives and interdisciplinary perspectives associated with high-cost credit, making a novel and insightful contribution to the existing literature. The problems with debt extend far beyond the legal sphere, and the book will therefore be of interest to many other academic disciplines, as well as for those working in public policy and 'the third sector'.

Hart Studies in Commercial and Financial Law: Volume 7

Hart Studies in Commercial and Financial Law
Series Editors: John Linarelli and Teresa Rodríguez de las Heras Ballell

This series offers a venue for publishing works on commercial law as well as on the regulation of banking and finance and the law on insolvency and bankruptcy. It publishes works on the law on secured credit, the regulatory and transactional aspects of banking and finance, the transactional and regulatory institutions for financial markets, legal and policy aspects associated with access to commercial and consumer credit, new generation subjects having to do with the institutional architecture associated with innovation and the digital economy including works on blockchain technology, work on the relationship of law to economic growth, the harmonisation or unification of commercial law, transnational commercial law, and the global financial order. The series promotes interdisciplinary work. It publishes research on the law using the methods of empirical legal studies, behavioural economics, political economy, normative welfare economics, law and society inquiry, socio-legal studies, political theory, and historical methods. Its coverage includes international and comparative investigations of areas of law within its remit.

Volume 1: The Financialisation of the Citizen: Social and Financial Inclusion through European Private Law
Guido Comparato

Volume 2: MiFID II and Private Law: Enforcing EU Conduct of Business Rules
Federico Della Negra

Volume 3: Reforming Corporate Retail Investor Protection: Regulating to Avert Mis-Selling
Diane Bugeja

Volume 4: The Future of Commercial Law: Ways Forward for Change and Reform
Edited by Orkun Akseli and John Linarelli

Volume 5: The Cape Town Convention: A Documentary History
Anton Didenko

Volume 6: Regulating the Crypto Economy: Business Transformations and Financialisation
Iris H-Y Chiu

Volume 7: The Future of High-Cost Credit: Rethinking Payday Lending
Jodi Gardner

The Future of High-Cost Credit

Rethinking Payday Lending

Jodi Gardner

• HART •
OXFORD • LONDON • NEW YORK • NEW DELHI • SYDNEY

HART PUBLISHING

Bloomsbury Publishing Plc

Kemp House, Chawley Park, Cumnor Hill, Oxford, OX2 9PH, UK

1385 Broadway, New York, NY 10018, USA

29 Earlsfort Terrace, Dublin 2, Ireland

First published in Great Britain 2022

A catalogue record for this book is available from the British Library.

A catalogue record for this book is available from the Library of Congress.

Library of Congress Control Number: 2022933882

ISBN: HB: 978-1-50993-935-0
ePDF: 978-1-50993-936-7
ePub: 978-1-50993-937-4

Typeset by Compuscript Ltd, Shannon

To my parents, Ian and Joy

You have always taught me to follow my dreams and fight for the underdog. Without your support, I probably would have become a rich (but miserable) lawyer or banker. As I am a happy (but underpaid) academic, I should probably *thank you.*

FOREWORD

Should the law allow moneylenders to lend money at high cost to people who lack access to mainstream credit? And if so, under what conditions? As Jodi Gardner shows in this original and important study, these are not easy questions. An instinctive response might be that lending at inflated rates of interest is exploitative and should be prohibited. A contrary argument is that to outlaw or curtail such lending further disempowers people who already have limited financial options. Are providers of high-cost credit preying on the vulnerable or increasing opportunities for the poor?

The issues which the law in this area must confront are both philosophical and intensely practical. Jodi adopts both perspectives and, along the way, explains the historical background, the judge-made and statute law currently applicable to high-cost credit in the UK, the theoretical issues raised by this subject and the results of empirical research, including her own.

She examines the philosophical issues by analysing three key concepts – freedom, regulation and the social minimum. These concepts are inter-linked. Prioritising individual freedom aligns with a regulatory approach that focuses on the process by which loan agreements are made, rather than the substance of what lenders may offer. Underpinning this process-driven approach, which has been dominant in the UK, is the ideal that, provided consumers receive accurate and adequate information about the costs and risks of high-cost loans, they should be free to decide for themselves whether to borrow on such terms.

Jodi presents arguments in favour of this approach as well as exploring its limitations. Those limitations include the ways in which poverty and urgent need restrict meaningful choice and elevate the attraction of credit that affords short-term benefit (for example, immediate escape from hunger) while leading in the longer term to even greater hardship. On the other hand, a more protectionist regime risks other forms of harm such as excluding more people from regulated credit markets and increasing illegal moneylending. A necessary part of any solution to these problems is the third concept – the provision of a social minimum – a concept which embraces not only welfare support but also means of escaping financial disaster, such as relief from bankruptcy and legal rules which prevent grossly unfair transactions from being enforced.

The deeper these issues are probed, the clearer it becomes, first, that there is no unitary solution to the problems associated with high-cost credit and, second, that the complex questions raised cannot sensibly be answered in the abstract and without empirical research. Legal policy needs to start from an accurate understanding of who actually uses high-cost credit and when and why they do so. Jodi has made an important contribution to this task by undertaking her own research project. Her findings enable her to classify borrowers into three broad categories. Each of these classes of borrower has different needs and typically uses high-cost credit for different purposes. This analysis forms the basis for some closing recommendations about what the future of high-cost credit should hold.

Reading this book has given me a valuable insight into an under-studied subject. The questions raised and the thoughts provoked have ramifications that extend more broadly to how the balance should be struck in our law and our society between freedom of contract and the protection of consumers. I have no doubt that other readers, from a variety of backgrounds and disciplines, will benefit as much as I have done from Jodi's work.

George Leggatt
Supreme Court, Parliament Square
April 2022

ACKNOWLEDGEMENTS

Studying, working and raising a family in the Oxford and Cambridge college systems truly exemplifies the concept that 'it takes a village'. Writing the acknowledgments for this book is difficult but also uplifting. It allows me to remember and recognise just how many people supported me along this long and, at times, difficult journey.

This work has been looked at by so many people and I am exceptionally grateful for their input. I have had the benefit of several friends and mentors, who kindly read and commented on my work, including The Honourable Justice Peter Applegarth AM, Paul Davies, Liz Fisher, Mia Gray, Sarah Green, Hayley Hooper, Catharine MacMillan, Josh McGeechan, Charles Mitchell, John Murphy and Sandy Steel. A significant portion of this book is based on my MPhil and DPhil theses, where I had the benefit of supportive, yet targeted, feedback from Sue Bright, John Cartwright, Sir Ross Cranston, Christopher Hodges and Iain Ramsay. I need to particularly thank Sir Ross, who continued to encourage and support me post examination, with kind but firm reminders to ensure that this book was published. I would also like to recognise the useful participant feedback received from my presentations at a wide range of conferences, where I had the opportunity to discuss different aspects of the book. The insight provided by these people and forums has undoubtedly improved the quality of the overall product. The creation and fulfillment of the consumer interviews that feature in chapter six was undertaken with Karen Rowlingson and Lindsey Appleyard, both of whom have been so important in guiding me into the exciting world of interdisciplinary and empirical research. Despite this overwhelming amount of support, all errors remain my own (but, in my defence, are likely to be linked to my four relatively young children, a global pandemic and the lack of a full nights' sleep in over nine years).

This book would not have been written without significant financial support, and I am so grateful that people saw the value in supporting and encouraging socio-legal research on high-cost credit regulation. Foremost, I would like to express my sincere gratitude to the General Sir John Monash Foundation. Without the Foundation's confidence in my project and subsequent financial assistance, I would not have been able to undertake such enlightening and meaningful research. When the length of this project was extended, my financial support was generously reinforced by the Association of Banking and Finance Lawyers. Because of the challenges of the global pandemic, St John's College's Returning Carer's Scheme kindly provided me with funding for research assistance to get the manuscript across the finishing line.

Three important people must be specifically acknowledged. My deepest gratitude goes to Mindy Chen-Wishart for her constant patience, encouragement and faith in my project. Mindy has taken every opportunity to help me grow and mature as an academic and, more importantly, as a mother; I am honoured to call you my friend. I cannot begin to recognise the patience and support of my 'work husband', Benjamin Spagnolo. You have gone above and beyond to provide me with academic, professional and personal assistance – and, when I dropped the ball as a mother – incredible birthday cakes for my children. I fear I will be forever in your debt. Finally, this book would not have been possible without the truly remarkable research assistant support of Devon Airey. She has been a constant source of support and encouragement during these final writing stages. It has been an honour to watch you grow and develop over these past few years and I cannot wait to see everything you accomplish in the future.

When I first pitched this book proposal to Hart Publishing, I expected to get a lot of pushback on the basis that this area – and my research in general – is often seen as niche, socio-legal work. I could not have been more wrong. Everyone that I have worked with has been excited, professional and supportive. The original deadline was pushed back on a number of occasions due to a combination of pandemic stresses and the birth of my fourth daughter. At every step of the journey the people at Hart were incredible, and I would specifically like to thank Roberta and Rosie for their guidance and understanding. Working with Victoria and Linda through the editing and copy editing was an absolute dream – which is an incredible feat as both Victoria and I had COVID-infected children at various stages in the process!

The most important thing in the world is family. I am forever indebted to my wonderful family who for many years have pretended, mostly convincingly, to be interested in the nuances of consumer credit law. I would particularly like to thank my eternally patient parents, Ian and Joy, who always encouraged me to follow my own path. I could not ask for more loving or supportive people in my life, and I am thankful for everything they have given me over the years. Huge levels of appreciation must go to my ever suffering, but (almost) never complaining, husband Sebastian. He has sacrificed so much of his own career to help me reach my goals and ambitions, and is the most wonderful partner in all aspects of life. My final thanks go to my daughters – all of whom were born whilst I have been writing this book – Eleanor, Margaret, Beatrice and Rosalind. You four have given me wrinkles and stretch-marks (and grey hair is probably just around the corner), but you light up my life in so many ways.

CONTENTS

TABLE OF CASES

United Kingdom

Australia

Canada

United States of America

TABLE OF ADJUDICATIONS

TABLE OF LEGISLATION AND SECONDARY LEGISLATION

United Kingdom

Commonwealth of Australia

European Union Directives

Singapore

Victoria

1

Introduction

'But I don't want comfort. I want God, I want poetry, I want real danger, I want freedom, I want goodness. I want sin.'

'In fact,' said Mustapha Mond, 'you're claiming the right to be unhappy.'

'All right then,' said the Savage defiantly, 'I'm claiming the right to be unhappy.'

'Not to mention the right to grow old and ugly and impotent; the right to have syphilis and cancer; the right to have too little to eat; the right to be lousy; the right to live in constant apprehension of what may happen to-morrow; the right to catch typhoid; the right to be tortured by unspeakable pains of every kind.'

There was a long silence.

'I claim them all,' said the Savage at last.

— Aldous Huxley, *Brave New World*[1]

1.1. Payday Problems

The collapse of Wonga, one of the largest payday lenders in Europe, sent shockwaves around the banking and finance industry and brought the regulation of these financial products back into the spotlight. Wonga was potentially worth over US$1 billion at the height of its popularity.[2] Previously the company had been a fairytale success story, winning Credit Today's Alternative Lender of the Year in 2010, providing free travel on the London Underground during New Year's Eve that year and even sponsoring Newcastle United in 2012. However, due to a run of illegal actions and irresponsible lending, the company went into liquidation in 2018. This was quickly followed by many other lenders, including other industry key players and dozens of small online companies.[3] Many people have argued that the removal of Wonga (and similar companies) from the market is a

[1] Taken from *Brave New World* by Aldous Huxley, published by Vintage. Copyright © Aldous Huxley, 1932. Reprinted with permission by The Random House Group Limited and Georges Borchardt, Inc.

[2] Kevin Peachey, 'Wonga: Where Have All the Borrowers Gone?' (*BBC News*, 30 August 2018), available at www.bbc.co.uk/news/business-45343042 (all website references cited in this chapter were last accessed on 5 January 2022).

[3] For a detailed discussion, see Sara Williams, 'The Rise and Rise of Affordability Complaints' in Gardner, Gray and Möser (eds), *Debt & Austerity: Implications of the Financial Crisis* (Edward Elgar, 2020).

good thing, as the company made its money from exploiting financially vulnerable people. Unfortunately, it is not that simple. Negative consequences can and do arise when legal (but potentially harmful) products are no longer on the market. Many questions therefore remain. Where will these customers go? Will they be better off without access to Wonga's loans (with annualised percentage rates of 1,509 per cent[4])? Is the Government required to help these borrowers? If so, how? These questions are the focus of this book. I explore the regulation of high-cost credit, and the outcomes of interest rate restrictions and consumer protection mechanisms which impact these financial products or possibly even remove them from the market. These findings are then used to make a range of recommendations to address the ongoing challenges of high-cost credit.

Complementing the analysis of high-cost credit, this book will also address the boundaries between private law and social welfare, how these concepts interact with one another, and their limitations. The focus will be on three key concepts – freedom, regulation and a social minimum – and how they relate to our legal regime. The issue of high-cost credit, particularly to people in or on the fringes of poverty, highlights the complex and sometimes conflicting nature of 'freedom'. Freedom has been the cornerstone of English law and of those systems developed from it. Contract law is premised on the freedom *to* enter into contracts, with a range of legal doctrines designed to ensure that once a contract has been formed between the parties, it is generally enforceable. The freedom to enter into high-cost credit contracts may, however, cause more harm than good, particularly for borrowers struggling with pre-existing financial difficulties. The financial implications of the pandemic and the 2022 cost of living crisis brought this issue roaring back into the spotlight, as many people scrambled to fill unexpected income gaps and/or increases in expenses.[5]

An alternative to a freedom-based approach is regulation, meaning State intervention in the market. This can involve the Government restricting or removing products from the market on the basis that they are dangerous, harmful or in some way detrimental to consumers. Whilst the motivations of the Government are generally altruistic in nature, negative consequences can arise. In the context of high-cost credit, this issue is not merely hypothetical in nature but has real consequences for large numbers of already vulnerable individuals.[6] When oversight of consumer credit in the UK was transferred from the Office of Fair Trading (OFT) to the Financial Conduct Authority (FCA),[7] the landscape changed dramatically.

[4] Wonga Group Limited, 'Short Term Loan' (*Wonga Group Limited*, August 2018), available at www.wonga.com.

[5] Some of the negative impacts of the pandemic were reduced through the enactment of The Consumer Credit (Enforcement, Default and Termination Notices) (Coronavirus) (Amendment) Regulations 2020. Despite this legislation, the pandemic enhanced existing inequalities on a number of levels: see Jodi Gardner and Mia Gray, *Covid-19, Inequality and Council Tax: A Perfect Storm* (University of Birmingham, 2020).

[6] The 2021 Woolard Review highlighted that assistance to those who are vulnerable continued to be a priority area for the Financial Conduct Authority (FCA): see FCA, *The Woolard Review – A Review of Change and Innovation in the Unsecured Credit Market*, 2021).

[7] This will be discussed in more depth in chapter two, sections 2.1.2 and 2.1.3.

The 2014 High-Cost Short-Term Credit (HCSTC)[8] reforms and the 2015 cap on the cost of credit resulted in 'pricing' certain borrowers out of the market, primarily those on low incomes or with an impaired credit history. The FCA estimated that approximately 11 per cent of the market, or around 160,000 people, would no longer be able to access HCSTC.[9]

It is assumed that these borrowers are better off because they can no longer use high-cost credit. But there was never clear evidence that this was actually the case. Questions arose, and continued to rise – where do the borrowers now go for their credit needs, and are they better off without access to this expensive and potentially harmful product? If not, how should the Government best respond to the challenges associated with high-cost credit? A freedom-based approach does not work adequately, but a regulation-based focus also raises a number of limitations and concerns. Whilst there can be no pretence that these are simple questions to answer, this book provides a taxonomy of high-cost credit borrowers and a framework for developing appropriate legal and social solutions. It presents a third approach to high-cost credit, the provision of a social minimum, and argues that freedom, regulation and a social minimum are all necessary to address the complexities of the current market. This moves the focus away from the traditional dichotomy approach and instead towards providing a certain minimum level of resources to all people to ensure an acceptable standard of living.

1.2. Why High-Cost Credit?

Freedom, regulation and the provision of a social minimum are relevant to a wide variety of legal products. This book focuses on the issues on high-cost credit, as such products provide an excellent case study for the theoretical debates raised – showing how general philosophical challenges can be applied to (and indeed, benefit from) specific case studies.[10] High-cost credit is often referred to by the colloquial

[8] Defined by FCA as credit with an interest rate of over 100% APR for a period of less than 12 months, excluding Community Development Finance Institutions and Home-Collected Credit – see FCA, *Detailed Rules for the Price Cap on High-Cost Short-Term Credit; Including Feedback on CP14/10 and Final Rules* (2014). This definition is contentious and has been subject to significant and (in the author's opinion) valid criticism.

[9] FCA, *Proposals for a Price Cap on High-Cost Short-Term Credit: Consultation Paper* (2014) para 5.15. The impact of the price cap alone was later estimated to be approximately 7% of the market: The FCA, *Detailed Rules* (n 8) 69.

[10] It is recognised that there are a number of other parties that impact the experiences of consumers in this area, including debt collectors and finance brokers, however an analysis of the legal regimes associated with these parties is beyond this book; see further Gail Pearson, 'Finance Brokers – A Regulatory Anomaly' (2003) 14 *Journal of Banking and Finance Law & Practice* 200; Gail Pearson, 'The Ambit of Unconscionable Conduct in Relation to Financial Services' (2005) 23 *Companies and Securities Law Journal* 105; Jodi Gardner and Chee Ho Tham, 'Debt Collection and Assignment of Debts: Navigating the Legal Maze' in Davies and Tan (eds), *Intermediaries in Commercial Law* (Hart Publishing, 2022).

term 'payday loan'.[11] Payday loans are a specific, and well-known, subset of high-cost credit; they are loans that are paid back in a lump sum when the borrower next receives regular income (wages or assistance from the State). High-cost credit encompasses a range of products and is not limited only to payday loans, it includes products such as loans repaid on instalment and doorstop credit. Wherever possible the term 'high-cost credit' will be used in this book, however at times it will be necessary to use 'payday loan' or a similar term.[12]

During periods of financial turbulence, consumers access short-term finance to close the gap between their income and living expenses.[13] High-cost credit is therefore used to 'make ends meet' when times get tough. This was seen during the financial crisis, because of the impacts of austerity measures and more recently as a result of the pandemic and the 2022 cost of living crisis.[14] High-cost credit is, by definition, credit that carries a high interest rate. Whilst the interest rates for these short-term loans vary dramatically,[15] after the financial crisis rates as high as 16,000 per cent APR were reported.[16] At this time, it was widely recognised that there were a range of problems with this type of financial product, including exploitative lender behaviour and harmful business models.[17] Ninety-three per cent of the population believed that further regulation was needed, with 68 per cent supporting stricter regulation of the advertising of loans, and 65 per cent supporting a cap on the total cost of credit. In contrast, only 7 per cent of people believe there is no problem with high-cost credit.[18]

After the 2008 global financial crisis, demand for high-cost credit increased dramatically over a short period of time. In 2009 the high-cost credit industry was estimated to be worth approximately £900 million annually.[19] The Competition

[11] As outlined by the FCA, 'the common term for high-cost short-term products is "payday loans"': FCA, *Detailed Proposals for the FCA Regime for Consumer Credit* (Consultation Paper CP13/10, 2013) 54–55.

[12] In line with the terminology and approach used by a variety of other bodies, unless explicitly stated otherwise, the term 'payday loan' will refer to broader high-cost credit products and not merely loans required when income is received. The distinction between high-cost instalment loans and high-cost payday loans was acknowledged by the Financial Ombudsman Service in the updated taxonomy utilised in 2020/2021 to categorise its complaints: see www.financial-ombudsman.org.uk/data-insight/how-we-categorise-data.

[13] For further discussion, see Iain Ramsay, 'Consumer Credit Regulation After the Fall: International Dimensions' (2011) 1 *Zeitschrift fur Europaisches Unternehmens – und Verbraucherrecht* 24.

[14] Mia Gray, Katharina Möser and Jodi Gardner, 'Understanding Low-Income Debt in a High-Income Country' in Gardner, Gray and Möser (eds), *Debt and Austerity: Implications of the Financial Crisis* (Edward Elgar Publishing, 2020).

[15] This is discussed in the Office of Fair Trading (OFT), *Payday Lending Compliance Review – Interim Report* (OFT, 2012).

[16] Telephone interview with David Barclay from The Contextual Theology Centre.

[17] OFT, *Payday Lending Compliance Review – Interim Report* (n 15); OFT, *Payday Lending: Final Compliance Review* (OFT, 2013); The Right Honourable Ian McCartney and Damon Gibbons, *Protecting Low Income Borrowers in the Credit Crisis*, 2008); Veronika Thiel, *Doorstop Robbery: Why the UK Needs a Fair Lending Law* (New Economics Foundation, 2009).

[18] R3: The Association of Business Recovery Professionals, 'Rein in "Payday Lenders", say 93% of GB Population', available at www.r3.org.uk/index.cfm?page=1114&element=16322.

[19] OFT, *Payday Lending Compliance Review – Interim Report* (n 15) 9.

and Markets Authority (CMA) determined in 2014 that the payday lending industry[20] was issuing around 10.2 million loans each year in a market worth £2.8 billion annually.[21] This equates to a threefold increase in five years. The FCA has provided slightly different figures based on its definition of HCSTC[22] – in 2013, 1.6 million people took out 10 million loans worth £2.5 billion.[23] Independent academic research paints an even more dramatic picture; Beddows and McAteer estimate that 'traditional payday loans and short-term cash advances' increased tenfold, from £0.33 billion in 2006 to £3.709 billion in 2012.[24] The use of these financial products then stabilised for a period, and at times even reduced slightly, but it remained at much higher rates than before the global financial crisis.[25] Unfortunately – but not unsurprisingly – the financial implications of the pandemic resulted in an increase in the use of various forms of high-cost credit, mostly to cover day-to-day expenses.[26] Many commentators believe the 2022 cost of living crisis will do the same. Despite the significant increase in the high-cost credit sector, it is still only a small percentage of the entire consumer credit market.[27] Notwithstanding this small market share, focus on the high-cost credit sector is warranted in view of the personal characteristics of borrowers, the impact that inappropriate lending can have on their financial wellbeing, and the exploitative actions of many of the lenders.[28]

The global financial crisis increased not only the number of loans, but also the severity of the problem with high-cost credit. In 2012 the OFT undertook a detailed review of the industry to determine the extent of irresponsible and exploitative behaviour. This process included a detailed review of advertisements, mystery/secret shopping,[29] and compliance inspections. The interim and final OFT reports

[20] These figures relate solely to the payday lending industry and not the high-cost credit sector in general. A number of the reports and research referred to in this book are focused solely on payday lending, however many of them mistake all forms of short-term, high-cost credit as 'payday loan'. Regardless, when a source is specifically referred to payday loans, this term will be used in the book.

[21] Competition and Markets Authority (CMA), *Payday Lending Market Investigation: Provisional Findings Report* (2014) para 2.76.

[22] See discussion of the FCA definition in n 8 above.

[23] FCA, *Proposals for a Price Cap* (n 9) para 3.8.

[24] Sarah Beddows and Mick McAteer, *Payday Lending: Fixing a Broken Market* (Association of Chartered Certified Accountants, 2014) 7. It is argued that this is the most accurate figure as it is not limited to payday loans and encompasses other forms of high-cost credit.

[25] See discussion of the market in FCA, *High-Cost Credit Review – Update* (2018) and specifically for HCSTC, see FCA, *FCA Regulation of High-Cost Short-Term Credit (HCSTC)* (2017).

[26] See FCA, *Financial Lives 2020 Survey: The Impact of Coronavirus* (2020) 44.

[27] In 2010, the consumer credit market was estimated at £200 billion, making high-cost credit less than 2% of the sector: OFT, *Review of High-Cost Credit* (2010) paras 2.1–2.4.

[28] This was discussed in Jeannie Paterson and Gerard Brody, '"Safety Net" Consumer Protection: Using Prohibitions on Unfair and Unconscionable Conduct to Respond to Predatory Business Models' (2015) 38 *Journal of Consumer Policy* 355.

[29] 'A research technique allowing businesses to evaluate the quality of the service they and their competitors provide to customers. It involves trained professional researchers posing as real customers, assessing the nature and quality of the service they receive and reporting this in aggregate form to the client': The Association for Qualitative Research, 'Mystery Shopping Definition' (2017), available at www.aqr.org.uk/glossary/mystery-shopping.

highlighted the disturbing and widespread lack of compliance with the regulatory regime.[30] There was significant evidence of irresponsible lending; too many people were given loans that they could not afford and, when they were unable to repay, were encouraged to extend them, further exacerbating their financial difficulties.[31]

One of the most alarming findings of the review was that lenders made approximately 50 per cent of their revenue from loans that were rolled over or refinanced.[32] Firms were therefore 'incentivised' to lend to people who could not afford to repay on time. The perverse effect was that lenders that undertook proper affordability assessments and lent responsibly lost out to less scrupulous businesses.[33] In light of these findings, the OFT expressed specific concerns about:

- the adequacy of affordability checks;
- the proportion of loans not repaid on time;
- the frequency and circumstances of rollovers;
- the lack of forbearance when borrowers got into financial difficulty; and
- debt collection practices.[34]

The OFT findings were strongly supported by other research. The Citizens Advice Bureau (CAB) reported that three out of four high-cost credit borrowers have some ground for an official complaint to the Financial Ombudsman Service (FOS) about their treatment. The CAB undertook an in-depth analysis of 665 high-cost loan cases between 1 January and 30 June 2013. Of these cases, 76 per cent of borrowers had at least one ground for complaint, including fraud (20 per cent), problems with Continuous Payment Authorities[35] (CPAs) (more than 33 per cent), harassment of borrowers (12 per cent), and unfair treatment of people in financial difficulties (10 per cent).[36] In a second study, Europe Economics conducted detailed research on compliance costs and firm behaviour in the high-cost credit market. Its October 2013 report outlined a number of entrenched problems, including lenders not carrying out affordability assessments, overuse of loan rollovers, exploitative and inappropriate use of CPAs, provision of unsuitable advice, unfair dealings with borrowers experiencing financial difficulties, and aggressive

[30] OFT, *Payday Lending Compliance Review – Interim Report* (n 15), the results of which were confirmed in OFT *Final Compliance Review* (n 17).

[31] OFT, *Payday Lending: Final Compliance Review* (n 17) 2.

[32] *ibid* 2.

[33] *ibid* 3.

[34] OFT, *Payday Lending Compliance Review – Interim Report* (n 15) 4.

[35] This is where the borrower gives the lender the right to take money on a regular basis from their debit or credit card without requiring further permission or authority. They give the lender more control than direct debits or standing orders and often resulted in the 'drip feeding' of funds from borrowers' accounts.

[36] Citizens Advice Bureau (CAB), 'Citizens Advice Urges Payday Loan Customers to Fight Back Against Unscrupulous Lenders' (CAB, 5 August 2013), available at www.citizensadvice.org.uk/index/pressoffice/press_index/press_office-20130805.htm.

debt collection practices.[37] A third study conducted by the Department of Business Innovation and Skills (BIS) used in-depth consumer and business surveys which confirmed that lenders were not complying with the Good Practice Charter or the relevant Codes of Practice.[38] Whilst the report highlighted a number of disturbing practices, it was particularly concerned with the unfair treatment of borrowers in financial difficulty.[39]

This extensive research has been coupled with other evidence of widespread exploitative and irresponsible behaviour of lenders. For example, the credit provider Wonga was involved in two separate regulatory actions. In late 2014, the lender was found to have breached responsible lending guidelines by providing loans to people who could not afford to repay without suffering financial hardship. The company subsequently entered into an agreement with the FCA to provide redress to over 350,000 customers, at a cost in excess of £220 million, as well as making significant changes to their lending guidelines and criteria.[40] Earlier that year, Wonga entered into an agreement with the FCA to pay over £2.6 million in compensation for unfair debt collection activities. The lender sent letters from non-existent law firms threatening legal action to customers in arrears, and some customers were even charged 'administrative' fees associated with the fraudulent correspondence.[41] In 2015, the FCA entered into an agreement with Dollar Financial (UK), another large, high-cost credit provider,[42] to provide £15.4 million of compensation to almost 150,000 customers. The regulator found that the firm was lending to people who were not in a position to repay the money without suffering financial hardship and were not carrying out adequate checks on borrowers' financial positions before approving loans.[43] These are not isolated events, with the regulator reporting similar behaviour across the industry. Many lenders in the high-cost credit industry act irresponsibly, and the business models used are often exploitative in nature.[44] These products are designed to keep borrowers 'trapped' in an expensive cycle of credit. People using high-cost credit are frequently financially vulnerable[45] and in desperate need of

[37] Europe Economics, *A New Consumer Credit Regime: Benefits, Compliance Costs and Firm Behaviour* (2013).

[38] Department of Business Innovation and Skills (BIS), *Making Consumer Credit Fairer: BIS Report on Surveys of the Payday Lending Good Practice Charter and Codes of Practice* (2013).

[39] *ibid* 13–14.

[40] FCA, *Media Release: Wonga to Make Major Changes to Affordability Criteria Following Discussions with the FCA* (2014).

[41] FCA, *Media Release: Wonga to Pay Redress for Unfair Debt Collection Practices* (2014).

[42] Trading under the names The Money Shop, Payday UK, Payday Express and Ladder Loans.

[43] FCA, *Press Release: Payday Lender Dollar to Provide £15.4 million Redress to Over 147,000 customers* (2015).

[44] OFT, *Payday Lending Compliance Review – Interim Report* (n 15), the results of which were confirmed in OFT (n 17). For further details, see FCA, *Press Release: Payday Lenders Failing Customers in Arrears, says FCA* (2015).

[45] See analysis of high-cost credit borrowers in CMA, *Research into the Payday Lending Market* (2014); FCA, *Financial Lives 2020 Survey* (n 26) and further discussion in chapter two, section 2.2.1 below.

funds, making them easy targets for businesses who offer quick cash with minimal checks and balances.

Borrowers of high-cost credit will usually be on low incomes and have limited access to alternative financial products. This means they can be desperate for money and easily taken advantage of by lenders.[46] A snapshot from the 2014 CMA empirical research highlights the extent of the problem:

- Fifty-one per cent of customers had not used any other form of credit during the previous 12 months (excluding other high-cost loans and overdrafts).[47]
- In the previous 12 months, 56 per cent of borrowers had gone into overdraft on their banking or building society account, 27 per cent had gone into unauthorised overdraft, 52 per cent had a debt problem in the last five years, and 38 per cent had a bad credit rating.[48]
- Over half the borrowers used the funds from the loan in question for 'living expenses', although this was not further defined by the CMA. In addition, 7 per cent of borrowers used it on 'general shopping' and 10 per cent on their car/vehicle, meaning these three categories of 'general expenses' relate to 70 per cent of the market.[49]
- Fifty-six per cent of people surveyed stated that they 'definitely' could not have gone without the credit.[50]
- Seventy-nine per cent of high-cost credit borrowers had taken out multiple loans, and 34 per cent had taken out ten or more loans.[51]
- Finally, four out of ten borrowers had *no access* to alternative financial products, and most of these people took the loan as a 'last resort'.[52]

Research from StepChange Debt Charity (StepChange) supports these findings, highlighting that, when people are struggling financially, they take out 'distress' credit – which is higher in cost, more damaging, and more likely to tip them into problem debt.[53] It is therefore no surprise that the financial implications of COVID-19 saw an increase in the use of high-cost, short-term credit, particularly for those who were already financially vulnerable; further reinforcing the ongoing and complex nature of these products.[54]

[46] OFT, *Payday Lending Compliance Review – Interim Report* (n 15) 2.
[47] CMA, *Research into the Payday Lending Market* (n 45) 29.
[48] *ibid* 30.
[49] *ibid* 68.
[50] *ibid.*
[51] *ibid* 32.
[52] *ibid* 80–81 (emphasis added).
[53] Stepchange Debt Charity, *Life on the Edge: Our Major New Report on the State of the Nation's Family Finances* (2014).
[54] Discussed in depth in FCA, *The Woolard Review* (n 6) Part 2 'The Impact of Covid-19'.

Even though high-cost credit is generally concerned with relatively minor amounts of money borrowed for short periods of time,[55] people often cannot repay without suffering hardship and therefore take out further loans to bridge the gap.[56] Whilst each loan is usually relatively small, the total numbers can be overwhelming to borrowers on low incomes. Consumers of high-cost credit often suffer enormously if and when their credit agreements go astray, and they cannot afford repayments. Amendments that improve the legal system are likely to make a real difference to the lives of many people who are already struggling to maintain an adequate standard of living. The current regulatory approaches are not fit for purpose. The factual matrix of these transactions calls into question the nature of the market, the role of contract law, and the limitations of our legal system. This vulnerability justifies both additional consumer protection and research on the specific challenges experienced by these borrowers.

1.3. Method, Scope and Jurisdiction

There has been a distinct and unfortunate lack of research into the characteristics, financial needs and motivations of high-cost credit borrowers. In light of the requirement for further empirical research on the topic, there are three methodologies used in this book. The first is a legal analysis of the UK high-cost credit regulatory regime. The second is a theoretical and philosophical perspective, analysing the concepts of freedom, regulation and social minimums – including the history, justifications and limitations of these concepts. The final aspect is a socio-legal one, which involves empirical research through in-depth interviews with key stakeholders to identify the most common situations where people access high-cost credit. The taxonomy developed from this process will be combined with the analysis of freedom, regulation and a social minimum to create a new paradigm for thinking about the interplay between individual private law rights and government obligations.

This book critically examines the legal approach to high-cost credit from the perspective of addressing consumer problems. It does not focus on regulatory theory, in the sense of controlling the behaviour of credit providers.[57] The book develops a taxonomy of high-cost credit borrowers and offers a framework for considering the relevant issues. It does not, however, provide specific policy

[55] For example, the average payday loan is valued between £265 and £270 and borrowed over 30 days; OFT, *Payday Lending: Final Compliance Review* (n 17).

[56] For example, a quarter of high-cost loans are for £100 or less, an indication that many borrowers have a financial safety net of less than £100 and are exceptionally financially vulnerable: BIS, *Making Consumer Credit Fairer* (n 38) para 4(a).

[57] For a very informative discussion of the latter, including engagement with empirical research on the topic, see Christopher Hodges, *Law and Corporate Behaviour: Integrating Theories of Regulation, Enforcement, Compliance and Ethics* (Hart Publishing, 2015).

advice, as further research into individual issues will be necessary before making such recommendations.

The analysis in this book is limited to high-cost credit and does not consider mainstream financial services or other forms of consumer credit. This has been done on purpose and for two key reasons. First, there has been a lack of academic attention paid to this important area in comparison to the richness of research on mainstream banking regulation. Second – as discussed above – due to the specific vulnerability of high-cost credit borrowers, it is crucial that this area is subject to rigorous academic research and scrutiny. An ineffective regulatory framework can exacerbate pre-existing hardships, while a strong, effective one can counter some of the disadvantages that exist in our society.

Responsible lending and problem debt is a universal problem. The increased financialisation of societies and focus on consumer finance to fund consumption has been seen around the globe. The pandemic has brought home how interconnected we are; we live in a shared society. Whilst this book grounds its analysis on the legal regime and lived experiences of borrowers in the UK, the framework developed can be applied more broadly. In discussing high-cost credit challenges and potential solutions, experiences from and approaches by many other countries are utilised and considered.

1.4. Outline

The book has seven chapters, which includes the current Introductory chapter. Chapter two details the history of high-cost credit, the important political issues it raises, and the consequent ongoing regulatory responses. The chapter also outlines the background of the high-cost credit market and the two regulatory approaches to high-cost credit evident in English law, the OFT's freedom-based focus and the FCA's more protective approach. While both have their advantages and disadvantages, neither approach is sufficient. This chapter concludes by deconstructing the problems associated with high-cost credit and providing the framework for the remainder of the book.

Chapters three, four and five follow the same basic structure, focusing in turn on each of the three key concepts of the book – freedom, regulation and a social minimum. The meaning of each of these concepts is complicated and subject to significant debate. For the purposes of this book, freedom is defined as government intervention limited to ensuring consent and avoiding lender exploitation or misinformation. Regulation is government intervention to avoid substantively unfair agreements and/or coercion arising from a borrowers' lack of choice. Finally, a social minimum is the provision of resources sufficient to ensure all people have a 'decent and meaningful life'.[58] Each of these key concepts will be further defined

[58] More detailed definitions of the concepts will be provided in sections 3.1, 4.1 and 5.1 of their respective chapters.

and developed in their relevant chapter. The chapters analyse the concepts in question, including their meaning, history and rationale, discuss examples of the concepts in our legal system, and finally explore their limitations. The current legal system has an 'all or nothing' approach which prioritises one concept over the others, instead of using the concepts in differing ways for the benefit of different borrowers. These chapters conclude by arguing that freedom, regulation and the provision of a social minimum are all valuable approaches to the high-cost credit market but are necessary at different times and for different borrowers.

Chapter six utilises the theoretical analyses of the preceding three chapters and applies them to the practical issues associated with high-cost credit. It develops a profile of borrowers, providing general guidance and an agenda for future research. The first part of this chapter undertakes qualitative empirical research in the form of in-depth interviews with various stakeholders and borrowers themselves. The interviews are then analysed to understand the lived experience of debt and develop a profile of high-cost credit borrowers in the UK. It identifies three distinct categories of borrowers, each with varying financial circumstances and credit needs. The second part of the chapter then applies the borrower taxonomy developed to the concepts of freedom, regulation and a social minimum, and to the current legal approach to high-cost credit.

The first six chapters of the book identify the borrower taxonomy, assess the needs of each class, and outline the current legal responses. The final chapter, chapter seven, develops these findings by proposing a range of reforms and raises questions for the future. It highlights a number of questions for further analysis and discusses what is necessary to take each forward. The chapter looks at law reform proposals, social welfare responses and required further research. It also highlights the limitations of our legal system. The solution for high-cost credit cannot be addressed merely through legislative amendments, as it is deeply rooted in issues of poverty, access to justice and financial exclusion. This chapter argues that for the law to make a positive contribution to the high-cost credit market, these societal issues need to be recognised and – where possible – addressed. The chapter also reflects on the key issues raised and concludes.

PART I

Philosophical Context: The Concepts of High-Cost Credit

2

High-Cost Credit in the UK

Debt is the slavery of the free.

— Publilius Syrus

This chapter provides an outline of the high-cost credit environment in the UK. There are two sections; the first summarises the regulation of high-cost credit, looking at the history, approaches of the Office of Fair Trading (OFT) and the Financial Conduct Authority (FCA), and direct enforcement mechanisms available to consumers. The regulatory approaches represent a complex array of considerations, and it is recognised that this discussion does not provide a detailed outline of the different approaches. The discussion can, and should, be read against the background of prevailing political philosophy. The second section analyses the challenges associated with regulating this industry – namely the tendency to blame borrowers for their own financial difficulties, inadequate engagement with the lived experiences of borrowers and the nature of the high-cost credit market. The chapter concludes by discussing what needs to be done to address these challenges.

2.1. How is High-Cost Credit Regulated?

Moneylending – and credit provision to the poor more generally – has been an ongoing challenge. It is therefore important to understand the different historic and legislative approaches taken towards high-cost credit. Whilst the history will be briefly discussed, the current section is focused on the two most recent approaches to high-cost credit, and how they represent very different underlying philosophies. It will conclude by summarising the non-regulatory enforcement mechanisms and analysing what we can learn from the different approaches to high-cost credit.

2.1.1. The History of Moneylending Regulation

From a historical perspective, lending of this kind was often labelled as 'usury'. This term is often used in an emotional or moralistic fashion, and so the definition has itself become controversial. Some texts refer to usury as the charging of *any* interest on money, whilst others limit it to only unconscionable or excessive rates of interest, and usury can alternatively be considered interest charged at an illegal rate.[1] The uncertainty between these three definitions has continued, and is highlighted by the definition of usury in the *Oxford English Dictionary* as 'The fact or practice of lending money at interest; esp. in later use, the practice of charging, taking, or contracting to receive, excessive or illegal rates of interest for money on loan'.[2] In the modern financial world, the charging of interest is generally considered a given.[3] 'Excessive' does not indicate above average market rate; it refers to setting a level of interest higher than can be reasonably justified given the lending risk posed by the specific borrower. Therefore, when 'usury' is used in this book outside of a quotation or direct reference of another source, it refers to the charging of excessive, but not illegal, rates of interest.

There is a rich and detailed history of moneylending and government-instituted caps on the cost of credit, which is far beyond the scope of this book.[4] For current purposes, discussion will commence from 1818 when a Select Committee of the House of Commons considered the effects of religiously motivated usury. It held that the laws in place were ineffective, and the techniques used by lenders to avoid the regulations increased the cost of loans. They noted that, at the time of writing, the market rate was lower than the legal rate, thus providing an opportunity to repeal the laws without fearing that borrowers would be charged extortionate levels of interest. Whilst this report had no immediate impact, it is likely to have assisted the passing of subsequent legislation reducing the limitations on usury, and the creation of 1854 17 & 18 Vict, c 90 which repealed 'all existing laws supported usury'.[5] This successful passage of the legislation was also likely to have been assisted by the 1841 Select Committee of the House of Lords, which made no concrete recommendations on this topic but did provide evidence of the harmful impact that the usury laws were having on the 'bona fide' creditors of borrowers in pecuniary distress.[6] This emphasised a focus on non-intervention and freedom of contract.

[1] This definitional issue was discussed as early as 1754 by John Erskine, *The Principles of the Law of Scotland: In the Order of Sir George Mackenzie's Institutions of that Law* (Bell & Bradfute, 1754) 532; see also discussion in Wayne AM Visser and Alistair Macintosh, 'A Short Review of the Historical Critique of Usury' (1998) 8 *Accounting, Business & Financial History* 175, 175–76.

[2] Oxford English Dictionary, '"Usury, n"', 2nd edn (Oxford University Press, 1989) 365.

[3] David Graeber, *Debt: The First 5,000 Years* (Melville House Publishing, 2013); Karl Polanyi, 'The Idea of Usury: From Tribal Brotherhood to Universal Otherhood, by Benjamin N. Nelson' (*Commentary*, 1950), available at www.commentary.org/articles/karl-polanyi/the-idea-of-usury-from-tribal-brotherhood-to-universal-otherhood-by-benjamin-n-nelson/ (all website references cited in this chapter were last accessed on 10 January 2022).

[4] Different historical aspects of high-cost credit will be discussed in the next three chapters; however, for a detailed analysis see Rosa-Maria Gelpi and Francois Julien-Labruyere, *The History of Consumer Credit: Doctrines and Practice* (Palgrave McMillan, 2000).

[5] Hugh Bellot, *The Law Relating to Unconscionable Bargains with Money-Lenders: Including the History of Usury to the Repeal of the Usury Laws* (Stevens & Haynes, 1898) 30–31.

[6] *ibid* 30. This passage of legislation is also discussed in William Selwyn, *An Abridgment of the Law of Nisi Prius* (W Clarke and Sons, 1812) 309–11.

Moneylending received further public attention at the turn of the nineteenth century, when a Select Committee was formed in 1897 to look into these issues. Significant evidence was given to the Committee about various unscrupulous activities in the market, and the harm caused by the light-touch regulation of debt agreements.[7] The full title of this group was 'The Select Committee appointed to inquire into the *alleged evils* attending Money Lending Transactions at high rates of interest, or under oppressive conditions as to Repayment, between the poorer classes and professional Money Lenders', and this provides a useful insight into how Parliament at that time viewed the moneylending profession.[8] In its later report, the Committee noted that 'the nature of the evils alleged to be attendant upon the system of money lending are well known',[9] further concluding that

> After carefully considering the evidence which has been given in regard to particular transactions and the general expressions of opinion of persons so well qualified to form a judgment .... [the] Committee have unhesitatingly come to the conclusion that the system of money lending by professional money-lenders at high rates of interest is productive of crime, bankruptcy, unfair advantage of over creditors of the borrower, extortionate from the borrower's family and friends, and other serious injuries to the community.[10]

The Committee highlighted that moneylending advertisements were often misleading in a number of ways, including stating interest rates on a monthly basis when consumers generally believed this was the annual figure.[11] High levels of interest were also charged, with one moneylender admitting his rates were sometimes as high as 3,000 per cent per annum.[12] One of the biggest apprehensions of the Committee was the fact that many borrowers obtained loans when 'default is inevitable ... such as to force him to obtain renewal after renewal at increasingly extortionate rates until he is utterly ruined'.[13] In situations such as these, moneylenders 'frequently display great cruelty and harshness'.[14]

This resulted in the *Report from the Select Committee on Money Lending*, and subsequently the Money-Lenders Act 1900 (UK) (MLA 1900). The Act introduced a variety of new duties for lenders, with severe penalties for breach – including up to two years imprisonment with hard labour.[15] It also resulted in enhanced government and contractual intervention, including the registration of lenders,

[7] The Select Committee on Money Lending, *1897 Report from the Select Committee on Money Lending; Together with the Proceedings of the Committee, Minutes of Evidence, Appendix, and Index* (19th Century House of Commons Sessional Papers, No 364, 1897).

[8] *ibid* iii (emphasis added).

[9] The Select Committee on Money Lending, *1898 Report from the Select Committee on Money Lending; Together with the Proceedings of the Committee, Minutes of Evidence, Appendix and Index* (House of Commons Papers; Report of Committees, No 260, 1898).

[10] *ibid* iv.

[11] *ibid* iii.

[12] *ibid* iv.

[13] *ibid* iv.

[14] *ibid* iv.

[15] Moneylenders Act 1900 (UK), s 4.

and the power of courts to re-open 'harsh and unconscionable' credit transactions. This represented an improvement in consumer protection but nonetheless resulted in several difficulties, since it required borrowers to personally bring actions against lenders in civil court and focused on the status of the lender rather than the type of transaction in question.[16] It also continued the focus on disclosure and consumer empowerment, as opposed to product prohibition and direct market intervention. The MLA 1900 was eventually replaced by the Moneylenders Act 1927 (UK), which introduced annual licensing of lenders and restricted the way in which creditors could seek business. This Act continued to concentrate on the status of the lender and did not provide general protection for borrowers. Such a focus became problematic, as creditors developed ways to circumvent the legislation such as installment selling, hire purchase, and the sale of goods on credit.[17]

Despite the MLA 1900, a freedom-based approach remained the predominant way of thinking until the onset of the Great Depression in the 1930s. The devastating consequences of the Depression and its potential links with the freedom-based approach to financial regulation challenged this focus, initiating a very brief return to protectionism (including interest rate restrictions) from both a practical and moral perspective. This hiatus was interrupted by the libertarian discourse of the mid-twentieth century. During this period, there was a return to individual freedom, with the attendant emphasis on respect for individual choice, negative liberty, and limited government intervention into private affairs. Many academics and policymakers rejected the previous intervention-based approach to usury and interest rate controls. Society embraced and promoted notions such as personal freedom, individual rights and acquisitiveness, and these encouraged liberal spending, consumption, and the satisfaction of immediate individual desires. At the same time, other cultural practices that tempered market activity and promoted important community values – such as charity towards those in positions of weakness, and disdain for greed and the concentration of wealth – received significantly less attention.[18]

Prior to 1974, the legal regime for consumer credit was highly unsatisfactory. Some parts of the market were regulated by a complex arrangement of different legislative and common law provisions, whilst other parts appeared to have little or no legal regulation.[19] It became clear in the 1960s that there was inadequate protection for the increasing number of people accessing consumer credit products. In 1968, Sir Geoffrey Crowther was appointed Head of a Committee to analyse the consumer credit industry, and to make recommendations for future reform.

[16] The disparity between the public enforcement regime and private redress was discussed in The Law Commission and The Scottish Law Commission, *Consumer Redress for Misleading and Aggressive Practices* (Law Com No 332 & Scot Law Com No 226, 2013).

[17] Karen Rowlingson, *Moneylenders and their Customers* (Policy Studies Institute, 1994) 13–14.

[18] Vincent D Rougeau, 'Rediscovering Usury: An Argument for Legal Controls on Credit Card Interest Rates' (1996) 67 *University of Colorado Law Review* 1, 38.

[19] For more discussion see Sir Geoffrey Crowther, *Consumer Credit: Report of the Committee* (Department of Trade and Industry, 1971) 52–60.

The resulting *Consumer Credit: Report of the Committee* (Crowther Report) was published in 1971.[20] It noted that there had been no previous attempts made by an official committee to look into consumer credit as a whole,[21] and recommended a 'sweeping review' of the existing laws.[22] The review suggested a range of reforms, including limits on advertising of consumer credit products,[23] provision of pre-contractual information,[24] mandated disclosure of the cost of credit,[25] rights of cancellation,[26] and a uniform licensing system for consumer credit.[27] It did not however recommend an interest rate cap or the prohibition of certain types of lending models.[28] The Department of Trade and Industry (DTI) considered the Crowther Report and its recommendations, and enacted the 'general approach' of the Report.[29]

2.1.2. The Office of Fair Trading

The difficulties and government processes discussed in section 2.1.1 above resulted in the Consumer Credit Act 1974 (the 1974 Act), which came into force on 31 July 1974. The stated rationale for the legislation was 'the failure of private law to protect individual rights or deter unscrupulous practices and the limited scope of existing licensing regimes'.[30] The Government was, however, reluctant to interfere with what it perceived as private agreements between individuals, and so the legislation was focused more on consumer education and 'light touch' intervention.[31] The review also resulted in the creation of the OFT, which commenced operating in 1973. The OFT had the duty to administer the licensing system, monitor persons carrying on consumer credit businesses, and take steps to enforce the Act and related regulations where necessary and expedient.[32] The Secretary of State had the power to regulate the carrying out of functions under the Act, including the drafting of specific regulations and directions.[33] As a result of the Crowther Report's recommendation for the creation of a Commission with responsibility for the consumer credit regime, the OFT was given jurisdiction over consumer credit licensing, including the administration of the licensing system, making

[20] Department of Trade and Industry (DTI), *Reform of the Law on Consumer Credit* (DTI, 1973) 6.
[21] Crowther, *Consumer Credit* (n 19) 9.
[22] *ibid* 183.
[23] *ibid* 257.
[24] *ibid* 266.
[25] *ibid* 271.
[26] *ibid* 289.
[27] *ibid* 329–34.
[28] *ibid* 79.
[29] DTI, *Reform of the Law on Consumer Credit* (n 20) 6.
[30] Iain Ramsay, *Consumer Law and Policy*, 3rd edn (Hart Publishing, 2012) 386.
[31] Rowlingson, *Moneylenders and their Customers* (n 17) 13.
[32] Consumer Credit Act 1974 (UK), s 1(1)(a) and (d).
[33] *ibid* s 2.

appropriate regulations, and educating parties on their rights and obligations.[34] It was considered preferable for this to be performed by an independent regulator, rather than as part of the Government.[35]

The 1974 Act was implemented at a time when credit cards were beginning to appear on the consumer market, and interest rates, even for short-term loans, were generally not exorbitant. For example, the Crowther Report highlighted that the interest rates for standard 'money-lender' loans were between 30 per cent and 50 per cent, with the average loan being around 40 per cent per annum.[36] As the use of consumer credit in the UK became more widespread, different types of lending emerged and the interest rates charged for short-term loans skyrocketed. It became clear in the early twenty-first century that significant amendments to the 1974 Act were required to ensure that it was appropriate and adequate to regulate the consumer credit market at the time.[37] The situation was exacerbated by the global financial crisis, as mainstream creditors generally became more risk-averse, which in turn forced more people to look to alternative lending streams.[38]

These problems prompted an in-depth examination of the consumer credit market, which resulted in the recommendation for substantial legislative amendments, particularly in relation to the enforcement of consumer rights. The Consumer Credit Act 2006 (UK) (the 2006 Act) came into force on 6 April 2007, and was the 'culmination of a three-year review of consumer credit law'.[39] The 2006 Act made significant amendments to the 1974 Act,[40] including provisions on unfair relationships between creditors and borrowers,[41] enhancing the powers of the OFT,[42] the creation of the Consumer Credit Appeals Tribunal,[43] and the increased jurisdiction of the Financial Ombudsman Service (FOS) as a redress body for users of consumer credit.[44] These changes continued the previous focus on consumer empowerment and assisting borrowers to make informed decisions, thus the freedom approach remained.[45]

[34] Crowther (n 19) 326.

[35] *ibid* 326–27.

[36] *ibid* 79.

[37] This was considered in a number of government publications. See, eg, DTI, *Fair, Clear and Competitive: The Consumer Credit Market in the 21st Century* (White Paper, 2003).

[38] The Right Honourable Ian McCartney and Damon Gibbons, *Protecting Low Income Borrowers in the Credit Crisis* (2008) 10.

[39] Julia Smith and Sandra McCalla, *Consumer Credit Act 2006: A Guide to the New Law* (Law Society (Great Britain), 2006) Introduction.

[40] See *ibid*, especially 1–91 for a full discussion of the amendments.

[41] Consumer Credit Act 2006 (UK), ss 19–23; Consumer Credit Act 1974 (UK), ss 140A–140D.

[42] Consumer Credit Act 2006 (UK), ss 38–43; Consumer Credit Act 1974 (UK), ss 1–7.

[43] Consumer Credit Act 2006 (UK), ss 55–58; Consumer Credit Act 1974 (UK), Sch A1 and Transfer of Functions of the Consumer Credit Appeals Tribunal Order 2009 (UK).

[44] Consumer Credit Act 2006 (UK), ss 59–61; Financial Services and Markets Act 2000 (UK), ss 226 and 234.

[45] See discussion in Smith and McCalla, *Consumer Credit Act 2006* (n 39).

The legislative and regulatory protection provided to high-cost credit borrowers under the Act is largely modelled on recommendations from the Crowther Report, but has been updated in an attempt to ensure its relevance to the current lending market. All providers of consumer credit must be licensed, and loans are subject to regulation. It is notable that the Act continued a freedom-based approach. An OFT review commented that 'the greatest strength of the Act is that it … explicitly *endorses freedom of contract* within a framework of rules designed to ensure openness'.[46] During this period, a combination of economic, legal and social factors resulted in an increased demand for – and supply of – high-cost credit, generally to people who were already financially disadvantaged.[47]

This section has outlined how the UK's consumer credit legislative regime underwent significant transformation in 1974, and has been amended numerous times since. Despite the reforms, the OFT's freedom-based regime remained inadequate to deal with the challenges of high-cost credit. The specific details of these issues will be discussed in more depth in the next three chapters. It is clear that the regulatory approach under the OFT focused largely on the procedural fairness of the transaction, such as disclosure and pre-contractual protection. It had several ongoing problems, which will be discussed in more detail below, including:

- a lax licensing process that did not actively exclude inappropriate lenders from the market;
- the limited utility of disclosure, particularly for those desperate to access credit;
- vague and generally unenforced responsible lending guidelines;
- a lack of engagement with the unfair terms regime and the uncertainty of the 'unfair relationship' test;[48]
- a regulator with limited resources and enforcement powers, and the inability to respond proactively to borrower detriment; and
- borrowers who were not adequately exercising their rights to obtain remedies against lenders before the FOS.

Freedom of contract remained paramount, and the regime attempted to create optimal conditions for the creation of high-cost credit contracts.[49] This approach continued until the financial crisis of 2008, when the devastating consequences of a freedom-based approach to high-cost credit started to be felt, largely by those who could afford it the least.

[46] The Office of Fair Trading (OFT), *Consumer Credit Deregulation: A Review by the Director General Of Fair Trading of the Scope and Operation of the Consumer Credit Act 1974* (OFT 1994) (emphasis added).

[47] The impact of this is further discussed in section 2.2 below.

[48] This is a mechanism which permits the court to intervene in the credit contract if the agreement is held to be 'unfair' based on a term of the contract, the way the creditor has exercised or enforced rights or 'any other thing done (or not done)'. This will be discussed more in chapter three, section 3.4.4.

[49] This type of regulatory approach is discussed in Richard Thaler and Cass Sunstein, *Nudge: Improving Decisions about Health, Wealth, and Happiness* (Yale University Press, 2008).

2.1.3. The Financial Conduct Authority

As the demand for consumer credit increased, it became clear that the existing regime posed significant difficulties and was in dire need of reform. Furthermore, the OFT compared unfavourably to the Financial Services Authority (FSA), the regulator of mainstream credit services, in terms of its resources and power to impose sanctions.[50] In addition to the limitations discussed above, the OFT did not have an adequate understanding of the high-cost credit market and assumed a false level of borrower homogeneity; the Public Accounts Committee (PAC) commented that the regulator needed 'a much better understanding of how different consumers use credit'.[51] These challenges contributed to a culture of lender non-compliance and led to significant reforms, including a transfer of jurisdiction from the OFT to the FCA, a move away from a focus on contractual freedom, and the creation of a more protective approach to regulation.

Even with the additional powers under the 2006 reforms,[52] the OFT still did not have the same authority as the FSA to monitor the behaviour of credit providers.[53] In addition, the OFT was disturbingly under-resourced, which adversely affected its ability to prevent consumer detriment. The regulator's turnover-to-expense ratio was £15,000, meaning that for every £1 spent on regulation in 2011/12, over £15,000 was lent to consumers.[54] This figure contrasted starkly with the ratios of other regulators, including those that regulate the communications, energy, post, water and rail markets, which ranged from £306 to £853.[55] Unaddressed complaints cost consumers £450 million in 2011/12 alone.[56] In 2012 it became clear that additional resources were urgently required, and consumers were suffering because of the limitations of the existing regulatory regime.[57]

The PAC review of the OFT also highlighted numerous failings of the regulator. These included a lack of information about the market which was needed to regulate it effectively,[58] a lack of understanding of the customer base,[59] and that the

[50] Report by the Comptroller and Auditor-General, *The Office of Fair Trading: Protecting the Consumer from Unfair Trading Practices* (HC57 Session 1999–20, 2000) para 2.17.

[51] Public Accounts Committee (PAC), *8th Report – Regulating Consumer Credit* (2013) Recommendation 2.

[52] See discussion at text to nns 39 to 45 above.

[53] The Financial Stability Board, *Consumer Finance Protection with Particular Focus on Credit* (FSB 2011); National Audit Office, *Office of Fair Trading: Regulating Consumer Credit* (NAO 2012); HM Treasury and Department of Business Innovation and Skills, *A New Approach to Financial Regulation: Transferring Consumer Credit Regulation to the Financial Conduct Authority* (HMT and BIS 2013).

[54] National Audit Office, *ibid* 32.

[55] The turnover-to-expense ratio spreadsheet was provided during an anonymous interview and is based on information mostly obtained from the Annual Reports of the regulators. A simple turnover-to-expense ratio was also discussed in the PAC, *8th Report* (n 51) Recommendation 4.

[56] Europe Economics, *A New Consumer Credit Regime: Benefits, Compliance Costs and Firm Behaviour* (Europe Economics 2013) para 121.

[57] National Audit Office, *Office of Fair Trading* (n 53) 32.

[58] PAC, *8th Report – Regulating Consumer Credit* (n 51) Recommendation 1.

[59] *ibid* Recommendation 2.

OFT acted in a 'passive' manner regarding breaches of regulation and exploitative business practices.[60] It was clear that further reforms were needed to strengthen consumer protection, and to ensure a proactive approach to addressing high-cost credit and the root causes of financial harm to vulnerable consumers.[61] As outlined by HM Treasury,

> [t]he Government believes that fundamental change is necessary to ensure that regulation is able to keep up with a rapidly changing market and to tackle detrimental practices more swiftly. The Government also believes that this change can best be achieved by bringing consumer credit into the same regulatory regime as other financial services, while retaining the existing consumer rights and protections in the [Consumer Credit Act].[62]

This 'fundamental change' came in the form of a new regulator – the FCA, established by the Financial Services Act 2012 (UK) with jurisdiction over credit licences and providers of consumer credit, including high-cost credit. The FCA took over responsibility on 1 April 2014 and had significantly increased resources. The jurisdiction transfer aimed to ensure that the regulator:

- was able to keep pace with a fast-growing, innovative market;
- had the powers and resources to protect consumers from actual – and potential – detriment;
- put a proportionate and manageable regulatory burden on businesses; and
- delivered a well-functioning consumer credit market, which ensured that consumers have access to the credit they need, and which supported the sustainable growth of the UK economy.[63]

The FCA declared its aim to 'step in earlier, and act faster, when we identify problems that risk harming consumers or the integrity of the market'.[64] The regulator had additional powers beyond those held by the OFT, including product governance, early intervention,[65] and the ability to completely ban misleading product promotions.[66] These all highlight a changing regulatory emphasis and an approach focused more strongly on protection, moving away from the previous approach of contractual freedom and consumer disclosure.

[60] *ibid* Recommendation 3.

[61] The Financial Stability Board, *Consumer Finance Protection* (n 53) 5–7.

[62] HM Treasury and Department of Business Innovation and Skills, *A New Approach to Financial Regulation* (n 53) para 4.18.

[63] *ibid* para 1.5.

[64] The Financial Conduct Authority (FCA), *Journey to the FCA* (FCA, 2012) 8.

[65] *ibid* 13.

[66] *ibid* 14. See also 'Annex D – A Concordat between the Office of Fair Trading and the Financial Conduct Authority' in the Financial Conduct Authority and the Office of Fair Trading, 'Memorandum of Understanding between the Office of Fair Trading and Financial Conduct Authority' (2 April 2013) 28.

The transition was, in many ways, successful. The FCA was significantly more active in the financial market than its predecessor, with a specific focus on the high-cost credit industry.[67] Nevertheless there were some causes for concern. Despite the alarming results of the OFT review,[68] the FCA highlighted its intention to adopt a 'proportionate' approach to consumer credit regulation, stating:

> the Government has worked with the [the regulator] to design *a regime where the regulatory burdens on firms are proportionate*. Broadly, fees for consumer credit activities will be lower than for other FCA regulated firms. Regulatory burdens will be also comparatively lower.[69]

Such comments are troubling. Providers of high-cost credit are obviously in a different risk category from mainstream banking institutions in that they are not classified as 'deposit taking institutions',[70] but this is not the only factor that should be considered when determining appropriate regulatory approaches.

Despite these initial comments, the FCA has been enthusiastic in its approach to the high-cost credit challenges. Since taking over the jurisdiction, the FCA has been relatively proactive – instituting a new authorisation scheme, amending responsible lending requirements, creating a number of prohibited and limited lending activities, and implementing a cap on the total cost of credit.[71] The new regulator supplemented the OFT's freedom-based disclosure approach with a regime offering a more protective focus, one that intervened in the market and actively prohibited certain conduct and products. Whilst this approach took steps to tackle the exploitation that was occurring in the industry, it raised a range of other issues. In 2014, the FCA estimated that the combination of the lending limitations and cap would result in 160,000 – or 11 per cent of the existing borrowers – being unable to access high-cost credit. The financial exclusion of such a high number of people did not seem to concern the regulator, with it reporting 'these customers will be better off not having taken out a loan'.[72]

Disturbingly, no data was given by the FCA to support these assertions, and it has not adequately followed up with these consumers to determine whether they are indeed 'better off' for not having used high-cost credit. Further research, including interviews with borrowers of high-cost credit, revealed that financial exclusion of this type can actually exacerbate pre-existing disadvantages.[73] In fact, the FCA's

[67] See discussion in Martin Wheatley, *Consumer Credit and the FCA: One Year On: A Speech Delivered by Martin Wheatley on 11 March 2015* (Financial Conduct Authorty, 2015).

[68] See discussion in section 2.1.2 above.

[69] HM Treasury and Department of Business Innovation and Skills, *A New Approach to Financial Regulation* (n 53) 12 (emphasis in original).

[70] See discussion in the Financial Conduct Authority's Practitioner Panel, 'High-Level Proposals for an FCA Regime for Consumer Credit', available at www.fs-pp.org.uk/docs/inquiry_responses/PP%20Consumer%20Credit%20FCA%20consultation%20response%2020130501%20.pdf.

[71] See discussion of the cap on the total cost of credit in chapter four, section 4.4.2.

[72] FCA, *Proposals for a Price Cap on High-Cost Short-Term Credit* (Consultation Paper, 2014) para 1.27.

[73] Karen Rowlingson, Lindsey Appleyard and Jodi Gardner, 'Payday Lending in the UK: The Regul(aris)ation of a Necessary Evil?' (2016) 45 *Journal of Social Policy* 527. Financial exclusion will be discussed in-depth in chapter four, section 4.5.3.

comments go directly against the recommendations of the PAC, which highlighted the impact of financial exclusion and the importance of supporting those who are 'credit poor' instead of merely eliminating them from the market.[74] Despite recommendations from the PAC, the FCA has not sufficiently engaged with the nuances of the high-cost credit market and its borrowers. The regulator has continued to assume a level of homogeneity, particularly in relation to borrowers who use these types of financial products. Thus, while the movement to the FCA may have improved the situation for a number of people, it is still not adequate and a more nuanced, targeted approach is necessary.

Empirical research undertaken after FCA reforms, including detailed interviews with people who were denied a loan after the lending restrictions were in place, highlights a much more complex outcome. Appleyard, Packman and Lazell reported that the most common outcome was that these individuals borrowed from family and friends, which came with a number of 'hidden costs'. Alternatively, they applied and were successful with another high-cost lender, went without, went into arrears or sought assistance from a debt management plan.[75] The UK has also seen a significant increase in the use of largely unregulated[76] 'Buy Now, Pay Later' (BNPL) products, with over five million people using these products between December 2020 and February 2021.[77] BNPL products, whilst appearing to provide consumers with helpful income-smoothing, have created their own regulatory concerns of lack of transparency for terms and conditions, no affordability assessment processes and the potential for vulnerable consumers to be exploited.[78]

People will always have income dips and unexpected increases, and businesses will continue to find ways to make money out of these situations. The FCA regulations therefore may have treated some of the symptoms of irresponsible lending in the high-cost credit market, but it did not address the underlying cause of these issues – the fact that there is an inadequate safety net and a lack of access to affordable and appropriate credit.[79]

2.1.4. Non-Regulatory Legal Enforcement

Whilst the regulators have power to commence actions against lenders, consumers themselves can also directly commence proceedings against businesses. The main way this occurs is through the FOS, which commenced in 2000 and investigates

[74] PAC, *8th Report – Regulating Consumer Credit* (n 51) Recommendation 7.

[75] Appleyard, Packman and Lazell, *Payday Denied: Exploring the Lived Experience of Declined Payday Loan Applicants* (2018) 20.

[76] At the time of writing, this lack of regulation occurred due to an exemption in Article 60F(2) of the Regulated Activities Order (RAO). The issue had however been flagged by the FCA and regulatory oversight recommended.

[77] FCA, *The Woolard Review – A Review of Change and Innovation in the Unsecured Credit Market*, 2021 para 4.18.

[78] *ibid* paras 4.25–4.45.

[79] Appleyard, Packman and Lazell, *Payday Denied* (n 75) 33–35.

complaints made by users of a range of financial services. In 2007 the jurisdiction of the FOS was expanded to cover consumer credit, including high-cost credit. Consumers can therefore make complaints about these products to the Ombudsman, and the disputes are dealt with 'fairly, reasonably, quickly and informally'.[80] The FOS service is impressively consumer-friendly; it is provided at no cost to the individual, who can choose whether or not to accept the Ombudsman's determination of the matter. If they reject the decision, the traditional court processes are still available. If the consumer accepts the Ombudsman's decision, it becomes binding on the consumer and the business involved, which has no choice but to accept the FOS determination.[81] The Personal Finance Research Centre (PFRC) conducted an in-depth review of the service provided by the FOS, and judged it 'a thoughtful, well-managed organisation that is doing a good job under difficult circumstances'.[82]

Since its inception, consumer use of the FOS has been significant. It reached a peak in 2013/14, with in excess of 2,350,000 enquiries and complaints. This was largely associated with Personal Payments Insurance and reduced slightly to just over 1,631,000 enquiries and complaints in 2015/16[83] and 1,456,396 in 2017/18.[84] Initially, high-cost credit borrowers were not making adequate use of the services provided by the FOS when compared with users of other financial services. For example, in 2011/12 there were 296 complaints to the FOS about payday loans[85] compared with 19,183 complaints about credit cards,[86] and in 2012/13 there were 542 payday lending complaints compared with 19,634 credit card complaints.[87] These numbers were grossly unbalanced, even when the complaints levels were related to the size of the market.[88]

The small number of FOS complaints about high-cost lending might be interpreted as evidence of general compliance with laws and regulation in this area, as well as consumer satisfaction with the services provided. Unfortunately, as previously outlined, this is far from the truth. The low number of high-cost credit complaints to FOS was quite surprising as it is clear that there is a substantial

[80] The Financial Ombudsman Service (FOS), *2012 Annual Review of Consumer Complaints* (2012) Key Facts About the Financial Ombudsman Service.

[81] Financial Services Market Act 2000 (UK), Part XVI especially ss 228–30.

[82] Elaine Kempson, Sharon Collard and Nick Moore, *Fair and Reasonable: An Assessment of the Financial Ombudsman Service* (Personal Finance Research Centre, 2004) 39.

[83] FOS, *Financial Ombudsman Service Annual Review 2015/2016* (2016) 19.

[84] FOS, *Financial Ombudsman service Annual Review 2017/2018* (2018) 2.

[85] FOS, *2012 Annual Review* (n 80) 24.

[86] *ibid* 53.

[87] FOS, *2013 Annual Review of Consumer Complaints* (2013) 33.

[88] There were approximately 63 million credit and charge cards in the UK at the end of 2013, compared with approximately 8.2 million payday loans (The UK Cards Association, *Summary of Key Payments Statistics: September 2013* (2013)). Extrapolating these figures, it would be expected that there would be approximately 1,540 complaints about high-cost credit loans (being 7.7% of the 19,634 credit card complaints received by the FOS). This is not factoring into account the extreme divergence in the outcomes of complaints about these two financial products (discussed in the text to nns 99 to 104 below), which should be reflected in a greater proportion of high-cost credit complaints.

and ongoing problem with exploitative business models and irresponsible lending to vulnerable consumers.[89] The underutilisation of FOS may be more related to the extreme vulnerability of high-cost credit borrowers, indicating that they have difficulties accessing even the most consumer-friendly services. It also reaffirms Lord Hunt's comments in his 2008 review, that 'the FOS still looks too much like a middle-class service, for middle-class people'.[90]

The number of FOS complaints about high-cost credit remained disproportionately small until 2015/16 (after the transfer of jurisdiction to FCA), when there was a significant increase in the use of FOS for high-cost credit, particularly payday lending. The reasons for the previous low number of complaints were unclear; however, the low numbers did not accurately reflect the reality of the short-term loan market and the extent of the problems being experienced. In an attempt to increase consumer awareness, FOS published a 2013 special issue of its update specifically focused on high-cost credit lending decisions.[91] The number of complaints about high-cost credit has increased dramatically since then, with FOS receiving 3,216 complaints about high-cost credit in 2015/16 – more than double the number received in the previous year.[92] This pattern continued, with 10,529 complaints being received in 2016/17 and 17,256 complaints received in 2017/18.[93] FOS believed that these increases are likely to be related to the high level of publicity around high-cost credit, particularly in light of the FCA's actions to tackle unfair practices in the industry.[94] The numbers continued to increase, even more dramatically, with 63,033 complaints in 2018/19.[95] At this stage, the additional FCA obligations and affordability assessment decisions saw a significant number of players leave the market and the rates of lending dropped significantly.[96] This resulted in a steep decline in complaints – to 32,864 in 2019/20[97] and 5,208 in 2020/21.[98]

There is also a dramatic divergence in the outcomes of disputes for different financial products. In 2012/13, 81 per cent of disputes for payday loans were

[89] See, eg, Collard, Finney and Crosswaite, *Facing the Squeeze: A Qualitative Study of Household Finances and Access to Credit in a 21st-Century Recession* (Personal Finance Research Centre, 2009); Sharon Collard, Andrea Finney and Sara Davies, *Working Households' Experiences of Debt Problems* (A Research Report Prepared for StepChange Debt Charity, 2012).

[90] Rt Hon Lord Hunt of Wirral MBE, *Opening Up, Reaching Out and Aiming High: An Agenda for Accessibility and Excellence in the Financial Ombudsman Service* (2008) 2.

[91] FOS, 'Ombudsman News: Payday Lending' (Issue 109, April/May 2013), available at www.financial-ombudsman.org.uk/publications/ombudsman-news/109/109-payday-lending.html. It also undertook specific staff training on these issues; FOS, *Annual Review 2015/2016* (n 83) 114.

[92] FOS, *Annual Review 2015/2016* (n 83) 48.

[93] FOS, *Annual Review 2017/2018* (n 84) 3.

[94] FOS, *Annual Review 2015/2016* (n 83) 59.

[95] Caroline Waymann, *Lessons from the Past, Ambitions for the Future: Our 2019/20 Complaints Data Analysis* (FOS, 2020).

[96] Sara Williams, 'The Rise and Rise of Affordability Complaints' in Gardner, Gray and Möser (eds), *Debt & Austerity: Implications of the Financial Crisis* (Edward Elgar, 2020).

[97] Waymann, *Lessons from the Past* (n 95).

[98] FOS, *Annual Complaints Data and Insight 2020/21* (2021).

resolved in favour of the consumer, compared with 44 per cent for credit cards and 37 per cent for personal loans.[99] This is a highly concerning statistic, as eight out of every ten loans were found to be in breach of law or professional business practices. The trend has continued, and the success rate for complaints about high-cost credit has remained significantly above the average FOS rates, with consumer success rates of 66 per cent in 2015/16,[100] 59 per cent in 2016/17,[101] 60 per cent in 2017/18,[102] 53 per cent in 2018/2019, 73 per cent in 2019/20[103] and 61 per cent in 2020/21.[104] This shows that, despite the increased regulatory oversight and attention, the market continues to experience illegal and exploitative behaviour – with more than six in 10 complaints made about high-cost credit being upheld by the Ombudsman.

In addition to the protection provided by the regulator and the FOS, consumers can make direct claims against lenders in court. In theory, consumers continue to have access to remedies under the common law, and in relation to certain statutory[105] obligations on lenders. There are, however, significant limitations on the ability of consumers to access their rights in these traditional court settings, particularly in disputes against businesses.[106] These include their inability to understand the relevant laws and the legalistic nature of the financial documents in question, the rules of evidence, the cost of litigation, as well as the complexity of the legal system and the intimidating nature of the courtroom and adversarial system in general.[107]

2.1.5. What Can We Learn?

This section has discussed the history of moneylending, focusing on the approaches of both the OFT and FCA, highlighting the dramatic changes

[99] OFT, *Payday Lending Compliance Review – Interim Report* (OFT, 2012) 10.

[100] FOS, *Annual Review 2015/2016* (n 83) 48.

[101] Ben Salisbury, 'Payday Loan Complaints to Ombudsman Triple in a Year' (*Money Saving Expert*, 13 June 2017), available at www.moneysavingexpert.com/news/loans/2017/06/payday-loan-complaints-to-ombudsman-triple-in-a-year.

[102] FOS, *Annual Review 2017/2018* (n 84).

[103] Waymann, *Lessons from the Past, Ambitions for the Future* (n 95).

[104] FOS, *Annual Complaints Data and Insight* (n 98).

[105] For eg, the unfair relationship test: OFT, *Unfair Relationships: Enforcement Action under Part 8 of the Enterprise Act 2002*, 2011 For more details on enforcement, see FCA, *Enforcement Guide, Chapter 20: Enforcement of the Consumer Credit Act 1974* (2018).

[106] See discussion in Adrian Zuckerman, *Zuckerman on Civil Procedure: Principles of Practice*, 3rd edn (Sweet & Maxwell, 2013) 454–55.

[107] Charles L Owen, Ronald W Staudt and Edward B Pedwell, *Access to Justice: Meeting the Needs of Self-Represented Litigants* (Institute of Design and Chicago-Kent College of Law, Illinios Institute of Technology, 2002) 15–17. For alternative consumer redress, see Christopher Hodges, 'Consumer Redress: Implementing the Vision' in P Cortés (ed), *The New Regulatory Framework for Consumer Dispute Resolution* (Oxford University Press, 2017); Chrisopher Hodges, 'Unlocking Justice and Markets: The Promise of Consumer ADR' in Zekoll, Bälz and Amelung (eds), *Dispute Resolution: Alternatives to Formalization Formalization of Alternatives?* (Brill, 2014).

to the regulation of high-cost credit in a relatively short period of time. Before moving forward, two key points must be highlighted. First, neither approach has worked adequately. The OFT's freedom-based focus left many borrowers vulnerable to lenders and allowed predatory lending practices to develop and prosper. Its limited resources fostered a regulatory environment that accepted disturbingly low levels of compliance in the industry. The FCA's interventionist approach, whilst providing increased protection to many people, created two unfortunate side-effects; it reduced the financial choices of borrowers, and left a number of people without any access to the (legal) credit market. Neither regulator adequately engaged with the borrower base and market. Second, the regulation of high-cost credit is a highly political issue. There have been a high number of legislative amendments and regulatory changes over a relatively short period of time.[108] There is also competing and conflicting evidence about the impact of reforms, particularly capping on the cost of credit.[109] The current dominant approach to the regulation of high-cost credit, namely enhancing freedom versus regulation, overlooks several complex issues. The problems being experienced in this area – whilst often characterised as issues of modernity[110] – are by no means new phenomena. The regulation of high-cost credit has been an ongoing problem for the State. As will be discussed in chapters three and four, there have been a variety of approaches used to tackle the problem and none have worked effectively, resulting in frequent legal changes and a swinging pendulum between freedom and regulation-based approaches.[111] This book argues that we need to better understand the nature of the high-cost credit market on an everyday and theoretical level, which requires a deeper engagement with the philosophical and practical challenges. This engagement will also highlight the importance that providing a social minimum has to the high-cost credit debate.

2.2. What are the Challenges to Regulation?

The previous section outlined the regulatory approach to high-cost credit in the UK. The system is still not working adequately, and reform is necessary. This section develops the earlier discussion, deconstructing the challenges to effective

[108] As this section has highlighted, there has been regulatory amendments to high-cost credit in 2006, 2010, 2014, 2015, 2018 and 2020.

[109] See discussion in chapter four, section 4.4.2.

[110] High-cost credit has often been referred to as 'modern day usury': see The Center for Responsible Lending, *Modern Day Usury: The Payday Loan Trap* (2010). This is strongly related to the increase in the use of technology in the lending process, including online lending or even apps developed by companies.

[111] For a detailed analysis of this pendulum approach to freedom of contract, more generally see Patrick Atiyah, *The Rise and Fall of Freedom of Contract* (Oxford University Press, 1985) and Patrick Atiyah, *Essays on Contract Law* (Oxford University Press, 1990), particularly Essay 12 'Freedom of Contract and the New Right' for discussion of a slightly later period.

regulation in the high-cost credit market. Two key issues will be discussed. First, throughout history there has been a tendency to blame users of high-cost credit for their financial difficulties. This has significantly influenced the regulatory approach and prevented borrowers from receiving adequate support. Second, the regulators have not adequately engaged with the high-cost credit market. This has resulted in a false assumption of market homogeneity for both borrowers and lenders, and over-simplistic guiding principles based on a cursory and inadequate understanding of the market. This section will analyse these two challenges and highlight how further research into the market, borrower motivations, and underlying philosophical challenges are necessary to understand and address the current challenges.

2.2.1. Victim Blaming

There has long been a tendency to blame people who use high-cost credit for their own financial misfortune. Financial regulation and intervention is often premised on the individual borrower's 'own weakness, their lack of self-discipline, or their inability to manage their finances'.[112] The majority of people who access these credit products are financially vulnerable in that they are likely to have one or more of the following characteristics – low income, limited or no savings, no access to alternative financial products, previous financial difficulties, or bad credit ratings.[113] On this basis, those who use high-cost credit can be 'blamed' for their reliance on these potentially harmful financial products. Blaming the poor is not new; it has been around since at least the Victorian period, when Mayhew discussed the 'dishonest poor' who were 'distinguished from the civilised man by his repugnance to regular and continuous employment'.[114] It is hard to imagine a more accurate portrayal of victim-blaming than debtors' prisons. Until the passing of the Debtors Act 1869, tens of thousands of people were incarcerated for not being able to repay their loans. These cruel institutions resulted in horror stories of 'shackled debtors covered with filth and vermin, and suffered to die, without pity, of hunger and jail fever', merely because they became over-indebted.[115]

Victim-blaming continued for 500 years, coming to another high-water mark with the writings of Charles Murray, who utilised Charles Darwin's 'survival of the fittest' theory to explain why Britain had developed such a distinct 'underclass'. Murray argued that people in this underclass were the 'undeserving' poor.[116]

[112] Rougeau, 'Rediscovering Usury' (n 18) 34.
[113] Rowlingson, Appleyard and Gardner, 'Payday Lending in the UK' (n 73); Competition & Markets Authority (CMA), *Research into the Payday Lending Market* (2014).
[114] Charles Murray, 'The Emerging British Underclass' in Lister (ed), *Charles Murray and the Underclass: The Developing Debate* (IEA Health and Welfare Unit in association with *The Sunday Times*, 1996) 24.
[115] David Graeber, *Debt: The First 5,000 Years* (Melville House Publishing, 2012) 334–35.
[116] *ibid* 25.

He contended that this group of people generally had no desire to be in gainful employment, were involved in crime, and had high levels of illegitimate births. The English social services system had allowed these circumstances to develop into welfare dependence, creating a strong disincentive for people to become employed and independent.[117] The appropriate response was, according to Murray, to provide these people with less state assistance in order to encourage them to become self-sufficient. This blame-the-victim mentality is frequently reflected in political approaches to poverty and welfare. Government policy often promotes self-regulation, of both borrowers and lenders, in order to produce financially responsible neoliberal subjects. The State can therefore blame individuals for their 'feckless irresponsible financial behaviours', rather than ensure sustainable employment and adequate welfare.[118]

Bentham's economic analysis also can be seen to blame victims of high-cost credit for their own struggles. In his *A Defence of Usury* manuscript, Bentham asserted that poor people were not better off, and in fact were in many ways disadvantaged, by the implementation of credit restrictions. When confronted with the protection interest rate caps provided to vulnerable borrowers, he declared they did not need any additional intervention. Bentham stated that, provided there was no 'defect' in a poor person's judgement or temper, they should be able to look after their own interests as well as someone who is better off. If they suffered from their financial decisions, it was due to their own irrationality.[119] This is the starting point of the (now largely discredited[120]) 'reasonable person' principle in economic theory.

This blame-the-victim view is still prevalent today. Fifty-nine per cent of the UK population believe that poor people are bad at managing money, and that they could cope financially if they organised their economic affairs more efficiently.[121] This belief contrasts sharply with the empirical research on the financial choices of low-income borrowers, which highlight how they often make the best possible decisions in light of their limited means and choices.[122] Political debates have used

[117] *ibid* 49.

[118] Carl Walker, '"Responsibilizing" a Healthy Britain: Personal Debt, Employment and Welfare' (2011) 41 *Neoliberalism and Health* 525, 531–33.

[119] Jeremy Bentham, *A Defence of Usury; shewing the impolicy of the present legal restraints on the terms of pecuniary bargains. In a series of letters to a friend. To which is added, a letter to Adam Smith, Esq; LL.D. on the discouragements opposed by the above restraints to the progress of inventive industry* (Messrs. D. Williams, Colles, White, Byrne, Lewis, Jones, and Moore, 1788) Letter IV.

[120] Richard Posner, 'Rational Choice, Behavioral Economics, and the Law' (1997) 50 *Stanford Law Review* 1551; Werner Hirsch, *Law and Economics: An Introductory Analysis*, 3rd edn (Academic Press, 1999) starting from 11; James Boyd White, 'Economics and Law: Two Cultures in Tension' (1987) 54 *Tennessee Law Review* 161; Alan D Miller and Ronen Perry, 'The Reasonable Man' (2012) 87 *New York University Law Review* 323. For application to high-cost credit, see Karen Francis, 'Rollover, Rollover: A Behavioral Law and Economics Analysis of the Payday-Loan Industry' (2010) 88 *Texas Law Review* 611.

[121] The Baptist Union of Great Britain and others, *The Lies We Tell Ourselves: Ending Comfortable Myths About Poverty* (2013) 19.

[122] *ibid*. See also discussion in Rowlingson, Appleyard and Gardner, 'Payday Lending in the UK' (n 73) and Maia Szalavitz, 'Why Do We Think Poor People Are Poor Because of Their Own Bad Choices?' *The Guardian* (5 July 2017), available at www.theguardian.com/us-news/2017/jul/05/us-inequality-poor-people-bad-choices-wealthy-bias.

terms such as 'welfare scroungers', welfare as a 'lifestyle choice', 'the curse of intergenerational worklessness',[123] and 'strivers and shirkers'.[124] When the extent of the lending crisis became evident, some commentators stated that 'British households that borrowed too much money must "accept responsibility" for their role in the current economic troubles'.[125]

An extreme example of victim-blaming is seen in the comments of the Conservative Peer Lady Jenkin in December 2014. During the launch of the Church of England-funded report *Feeding Britain*, examining the increasing reliance on food banks, Lady Jenkin stated 'we have lost a lot of our cookery skills. *Poor people do not know how to cook*. I had a large bowl of porridge today, which cost 4p. A large bowl of sugary cereals will cost you 25p'.[126] The combination of low-income households and porridge was actually the subject of a 1913 book, in which Reeves and Wilson highlighted that families with financial limitations have additional restraints preventing them from taking advantage of low-cost food options. When discussing the challenges associated with cooking on a low income (cleverly named 'The Gospel of Porridge'), the authors recalled how health visitors came to deprived areas of Lambeth to teach the women how to cook porridge for their families.[127] What the visitors had not taken into account was that porridge was a time-intensive dish (the working poor often have more constraints in this regard) that required the maker to have access to fresh milk, a cook top, electricity and a decent pot or pan[128] – all things to which poorer families may not have access, either in 1913 or today.[129] Lady Jenkin's comments show that many of the societal perceptions of poor families and their financial capabilities have remained largely unchanged over the last 100 years.

[123] Lindsey Macmillan, 'While there is Evidence that Workless Spells are Associated Across Generations, the 'Culture of Welfare Dependency' Argument does not Hold' (*LSE British Politics and Policy*, 2 April 2014), available at http://blogs.lse.ac.uk/politicsandpolicy/intergenerational-worklessness-the-unexplored-curse/.

[124] Juliette Jowit, '*Strivers v Shirkers*: The Language of the Welfare Debate' *The Guardian* (8 January, 2013).

[125] James Kirkup, 'Families Must Accept Share of Blame for Britain's Woes' *The Telegraph* (3 May 2012), available at www.telegraph.co.uk/finance/newsbysector/banksandfinance/9244414/Families-must-accept-share-of-blame-for-Britains-woes.html.

[126] Cited in Patrick Butler, Patrick Wintour and Amelia Gentleman, 'Tory Peer Forced to Eat her Words after Claiming Poor People can't Cook' *The Guardian* (8 December 2014), available at www.theguardian.com/society/2014/dec/08/poor-cannot-cook-peer-eats-words (emphasis added).

[127] Maud Pember Reeves and Charlotte Wilson, *Round About A Pound A Week* (G Bell & Sons, 1913) (reprinted in 1994 by Virago Books) 57.

[128] *ibid* 57–58.

[129] A report from the Department for Business, Energy & Industrial Strategy (DBEIS) highlighted that approximately 3.18 million households experienced fuel poverty in 2019, representing approximately 13.4% of all English households (p 6). Fuel poverty is measured by the Low Income High Costs definition. A household is considered to be fuel poor if they are living in a home below band C and were they to spend the required amount on fuel costs for the home, they would be left with a residual income below the official poverty line: DBEIS, *Annual Fuel Poverty Statistics Report: 2021 (2019 data)* (4 March 2021) 73. The cost of living crisis in 2022 is going to result in unprecedented numbers of people experiencing fuel poverty.

In the *Shriver Report*, Ehrenreich observes that

> pundits and politicians have bemoaned the character failings and bad habits of the poor for at least the past 50 years. In their view, the poor are shiftless, irresponsible, and prone to addiction. They have too many children and fail to get married. So if they suffer from grievous material deprivation, if they run out of money between paychecks, if they do not always have food on their tables – then they have no one to blame but themselves … sadly, this has become the means by which [countries] manage to remain complacent in the face of alarmingly high levels of poverty: by continuing to blame poverty not on the economy or inadequate social supports, but on the poor themselves.[130]

This victim-blaming provides an excuse for governments to avoid looking deeply into the issues of high-cost credit. By focusing on the individual borrowers' alleged weaknesses, instead of the complex structural and societal pressures of the high-cost credit market, governments can avoid engaging with substantive fairness and welfare issues. They do not need to actively address the fairness of the agreement, create meaningful choices, or address the reasons why so many people become dependent on these harmful financial products.

2.2.2. Inadequate Engagement with the Market

The second issue to consider is inadequate engagement with the market, especially a lack of understanding of the people using high-cost credit. It is too often assumed that lenders and borrowers in the market are largely homogeneous. In reality, the industry encompasses a wide variety of both consumers and lending models. Discussions about the need to intervene in the high-cost credit market are frequently premised on the view that users of these financial products are economically irrational and price-insensitive.[131] This is an inaccurate portrayal of the financial position of many high-cost credit borrowers. O'Connell undertook a detailed analysis of working-class debt in the UK, and 'rejects the notion that low-income consumers were feckless. Such statements emanated from a model of the rational middle-class consumer and frequently made little sense in the context of the choices available to the working-classes'.[132] It is often assumed that all people using high-cost credit products are under significant external pressures, have

[130] Barbara Ehrenreich, 'Time to Wake Up: Stop Blaming Poverty on the Poor' in Shriver (ed), *The Shriver Report: A Woman's Nation Pushes Back from the Brink* (Center for American Progress, 2014).

[131] Rowlingson, Appleyard and Gardner, 'Payday Lending in the UK: The Regul(aris)ation of a Necessary Evil?' (n 73); Lindsey Appleyard, Karen Rowlingson and Jodi Gardner, 'The Variegated Financialization of Sub-Prime Credit Markets' (2016) 20 *Competition & Change* 297; Ronald Mann, 'Nudging from Debt: The Role of Behavioral Economics in Regulation' [2011] *The Lydian Payments Journal*, available at www.pymnts.com/assets/Lydian_Journal/LydianJournalFebLawReg.pdf.

[132] Sean O'Connell, *Credit and Community: Working-Class Debt in the UK since 1880* (Oxford University Press, 2009) 286.

limited education or understanding of the financial product, cannot control their spending desires, or are so desperate for credit that they are not acting 'rationally' in their choices.[133] This view is not completely wrong – there is evidence that a significant number of borrowers do exhibit these characteristics.[134] Many borrowers are, however, not vulnerable, act rationally, and choose to use high-cost credit because of its speed and convenience.

There is also an underlying assumption that high-cost credit products are used in a similar way by individuals with comparable needs and backgrounds, reflecting a lack of understanding about the nature of the market and its borrowers. This deficiency was most accurately outlined by the PAC in its 2013 review of the OFT. Three of the eight recommendations by the PAC focused on a lack of information and engagement with the high-cost credit market.[135] Despite this report, the FCA has continued this lack of engagement.[136] There is a frequent assumption that high-cost credit is always harmful, and that consumers are better off without access to the financial product. This is not necessarily the case, as high-cost credit can actually be cheaper than many alternatives, such as going into unauthorised overdraft.[137] The high-cost credit market, like most others, has significant diversity; borrowers use credit in a wide variety of ways.[138] There is much controversy and ambiguity about who is actually borrowing, and what impact high-cost credit has on their wellbeing.[139]

There is also an assumption that high-cost lenders are uniformly exploitative, and a belief that all consumers would be better off if these products were removed from the market.[140] This is of particular concern to the media and certain political figures. An example of this approach is the 'End Legal Loan Sharking' Campaign and Petition, which was directed at high-cost credit providers in the UK.[141] Unfortunately, the approach taken by the regulators often reflects similar

[133] This can be seen in, for eg, Stella Creasy, 'Consumers Need Protection against High-Cost Moneylenders Online' *The Guardian* (1 June 2011), available at www.theguardian.com/commentisfree/2011/jun/01/consumers-protection-money-lenders-online and in numerous publications from the FCA (FCA, *Consumer Credit Firms Must Raise Advertising Standards, says FCA* (2014); FCA, *FCA Confirms Price Cap Rule for Payday Lenders* (2014)).

[134] See discussion in Competition & Markets Authority, *Research into the Payday Lending Market* (n 113), particularly the discussion at 70–87. This is also discussed in McCartney and Gibbons, *Protecting Low Income Borrowers* (n 38).

[135] PAC, *8th Report – Regulating Consumer Credit* (n 51) Recommendations 1, 2 and 5.

[136] See discussion in section 2.1.3 above.

[137] See discussion in chapter four, section 4.5.3 below.

[138] Rowlingson, Appleyard and Gardner, 'Payday Lending in the UK: The Regul(aris)ation of a Necessary Evil?' (n 73); Appleyard, Rowlingson and Gardner, 'The Variegated Financialization' (n 131).

[139] As discussed below, this topic is subject to significant disagreement between the lenders and trade associations on one hand, and the consumer advocates, politicians and charitable organisations on the other. For more discussion on this, see text of nns 152 to 160.

[140] The clearest indicator of this is the FCA's belief that the 160,000 people excluded from the high-cost credit market are better off; see discussion in chapter four, section 4.5.3 below.

[141] UK Government and Parliament: Petitions, *End Legal Loan Sharking: Cap the Total Cost of Credit Petition* (2012).

beliefs and assumptions. For example, after the OFT's Compliance Review, the regulator sent letters to the 50 largest high-cost credit providers demanding that they improve their lending practices and giving them 12 weeks to respond and explain what measures they were going to take.[142] The regulator therefore gave the appearance that all large firms were acting in the same manner. Whilst on the whole the level of compliance in the industry was inadequate, some lenders were behaving considerably better than others. This is clear from research conducted by the regulator itself. The Compliance Review Report showed that firms take very different approaches to lending, finding that some businesses were operating appropriately and in compliance with their legal obligations.[143] Further, since the release of the OFT Compliance Report and the transfer of the consumer credit jurisdiction to the FCA, many firms have either left the market or improved their practices.[144] A report commissioned by the Association of Chartered Certified Accountants (ACCA) further shows that the three biggest players in the industry (which account for 70 per cent of market share) 'are among the most responsible lenders operating in the UK'.[145]

Even the wide use of the term 'payday loan' highlights the ongoing assumptions made about this industry. As discussed above, payday loans are a specific subset of high-cost credit.[146] Many firms operating in the industry offer a variety of financial products, including payday loans; nonetheless they are more often than not referred to only as 'payday lenders', making it seem as if this is the only financial product creating difficulties. This is not the case, and all types of high-cost credit have the potential to cause consumer detriment.[147] The incorrect perception of the nature of these financial products is not just a problem in the media,[148] but also for

[142] OFT, *Payday Lending – Interim Report* (n 99).

[143] OFT, *Payday Lending: Final Compliance Review* (OFT, 2013) see esp 10 and 23.

[144] For eg, after the OFT issued notices to the 50 biggest payday lenders, 19 decided to leave the market instead of responding: Rachel Rickard Straus, 'Almost Half of Payday Lenders Quit the Market Rather than Face OFT Probe' (This is Money, 15 August 2013), available at www.thisismoney.co.uk/money/cardsloans/article-2393291/19-payday-lenders-quit-market-face-OFT-probe.html. This has also been shown empirically by the rate of lending in the industry. For example, the FCA originally predicted that a price cap would result in 11% of consumers being unable to obtain access to credit (FCA, *Proposals for a Price Cap on High-Cost Short-Term Credit* (n 72) para 5.15). This figure was, however, updated to reflect the impact of the enforcement regime and the tighter regulation of the market has resulted in less irresponsible lending, so later figures reported only 7% of the market would be unable to obtain credit (FCA, *The Financial Conduct Authority, Detailed Rules for the Price Cap on High-Cost Short-Term Credit; Including Feedback on CP14/10 and Final Rules* (2014) 69).

[145] Sarah Beddows and Mick McAteer, *Payday Lending: Fixing a Broken Market* (Association of Chartered Certified Accountants, 2014) 11. The regulatory actions against Wonga and the company's demise have however raised questions about this claim.

[146] For a discussion on the definitional issues associated with high-cost credit, see the text of nn 11 and 12 of chapter one.

[147] See, eg, the harm of doorstop credit; Andrew Falconer and Joe Lane, *Debt on Your Doorstep: Problem Debt in the Home Credit Market* (Citizen Advice, 2017); Yvonne Roberts, 'As Even the Higher Paid Fall into Debt Trap, Charities Target Money Lenders' *The Observer* (6 October 2013), available at www.theguardian.com/society/2013/oct/06/broke-britain-doorstep-lending.

[148] Amelia Gentleman, 'Wonga: The Real Cost of a Payday Loan' *The Guardian* (1 March 2012), available at www.theguardian.com/business/2012/mar/01/wonga-real-cost-payday-loan; Becky Barrow,

government bodies[149] and even for the regulators themselves.[150] Despite the fact that the FCA officially uses the definition High-Cost Short-Term Credit (HCSTC) for regulatory purposes,[151] most of the communications to the public refer only to 'payday loans', creating a misleading impression of the scope of the industry. This lack of engagement suggests that the regulator may not have an accurate comprehension of who they are regulating, and thus of the consequences of their actions.

There has been minimal research into the motivations and circumstances of people using high-cost credit.[152] Significant disagreement exists between lenders and trade associations on the one hand, and consumer advocates, debtor advisors and consumer lawyers on the other. The lenders and trade associations assert that the 'typical' high-cost borrower is employed, earns a reasonable income, and uses the loans in an educated and responsible manner for one-off expenses or discretionary purchases.[153] They also stress the favourable experiences of borrowers. At its peak, Wonga claimed that 97 per cent of customers feel 'well informed' and that 92 per cent would refer the business to a friend.[154] Further, the Consumer Finance Association (CFA) (the leading high-cost credit trade association) stated that 93 per cent of borrowers felt that they were treated with dignity and respect, and 89 per cent believed that the fees and charges were explained clearly.[155] There is also some academic support for high-cost credit. In the report *Moneylenders and their Customers*, Rowlingson identified a number of advantages to high interest, short-term credit; it supplemented the uncertainty of borrower income and stopped people from getting into long-term debt.[156] She asserted that borrowers could 'indeed act rationally since they chose between available and suitable alternatives to achieve particular goals'.[157] The PFRC also concluded that 'borrowing is not the problem *per se*: it undoubtedly helps smooth out the ebbs and flows of income and consumption'.[158]

'Britain has become "Wild West" for Payday Loan Lenders with Millions at Risk of Losing their Homes, MPs Warn' (*MailOnline*, 7 November 2012), available at www.dailymail.co.uk/news/article-2111332/Britain-wild-west-payday-loan-lenders-millions-risk-losing-homes-MPs-warn.html.

[149] CMA, *Research into the Payday Lending Market* (n 113).

[150] FCA, *FCA Confirms Price Cap Rule for Payday Lenders* (n 133).

[151] FCA, *Detailed Proposals for the FCA Regime for Consumer Credit* (Consultation Paper CP13/10, 2013) 54–55.

[152] One notable exception is Personal Finance Research Centre, *The Impact on Business and Consumers of a Cap on the Total Cost of Credit* (Department of Business and Innovation Skills, 2013). This research was focused specifically on the impact of a cap on the total cost of credit and not at developing a general borrower profile. There was some quantitative research completed by the CMA, but it was more concerned with the nature of the market and high-cost products than the motivations of the borrowers; CMA, *Research into the Payday Lending Market* (n 113).

[153] YouGov, *Consumer Finance Association: Attitudes Towards Payday Loans Amongst Payday Customers & Policymakers* (Sponsored by Consumer Finance Association, 2012).

[154] Wonga, 'Wonga.com: Straight Talking Money' (2013), available at www.wonga.com/money/about/.

[155] YouGov, *Consumer Finance Association* (n 153).

[156] Rowlingson, *Moneylenders and their Customers* (n 17) 92–95.

[157] *ibid* 78.

[158] Andrea Finney, Sharon Collard and Elaine Kempson, *Easy Come, Easy Go: Borrowing Over the Life-Cycle* (Personal Finance Research Centre, 2007) 23.

Consumer advocates, debt advisors, and consumer lawyers in the industry paint a very different picture. Research from Which? found that 69 per cent of borrowers regretted taking out a loan or other credit product in the previous year, and that 56 per cent of all borrowers had missed a payment and incurred default charges. The organisation also highlighted that creditors were regularly lending irresponsibly. As examples, 48 per cent of people who have taken out a loan could not afford the repayments, 29 per cent of people have obtained credit that they knew they could not afford to repay in full and on time, and 43 per cent of borrowers believed that it is too easy to obtain credit.[159] This information is supported by media horror stories – such as that of a 23-year-old man who borrowed £400, ended up with loans from multiple lenders totaling thousands of pounds, and committed suicide over the stress of his precarious financial position.[160]

What is still needed is an in-depth understanding of the borrowers – *who* is using these types of products and *why*, and *what* we should do to address the situation. Research already conducted by regulators, the industry, and non-governmental research bodies tells us that a variety of people access high-cost credit for different reasons. Some borrowers use these types of financial products because they value the speed and convenience that comes with the transaction, and hence are happy to pay a premium for this service.[161] These people are exercising a legitimate and valuable choice. On the other hand, many others are forced to rely on high-cost credit because they are effectively excluded from the mainstream market. They need money and do not have a meaningful choice as to how they obtain it.[162] Until this heterogeneity is recognised and responded to, it will be difficult for the Government to regulate high-cost credit in a fair and effective manner.

2.2.3. What Can We Do?

We currently have a high-cost credit market where vulnerable consumers are inappropriately blamed for their financial problems, and at the same time there is a lack of understanding of borrowers, lenders and products. The best way to respond to these two challenges is through detailed, empirical research on the problem. This book aims to take the first steps in this regard. The problems associated with the regulation of high-cost credit evolve largely from the simplistic nature of the

[159] Which?, 'Half of People with Payday Loans Cannot Afford to Pay Back their Debts' (8 November 2012), available at http://press.which.co.uk/whichstatements/half-of-people-taking-out-payday-loans-cannot-afford-to-pay-them-back/#.UYyyvMrsxn4.

[160] Ann Edwards, 'Rugby League Player, 23, Hanged Himself "After Getting into Huge Debt with Payday Loan Companies"' *The Daily Mail* (16 April 2013), available at www.dailymail.co.uk/news/article-2309797/Kenny-Davies-Rugby-league-player-23-hanged-getting-debt-payday-loan-companies.html.

[161] CMA, *Research into the Payday Lending Market* (n 113) 11; see also discussion in Rowlingson, Appleyard and Gardner (n 73); Appleyard, Rowlingson and Gardner (n 131).

[162] CMA, *Research into the Payday Lending Market* (n 113) 80–81.

regulatory debate generally.[163] We have created a dichotomy in our approach to the regulation of high-cost credit, framed as a battle between State intervention (regulation) and non-intervention (freedom).[164] This is an unrealistic and ineffective way to look at a particularly complex situation, which involves access to credit for some of the most financially disadvantaged people in our society. A valuable concept of freedom must therefore mean something more than non-intervention into the high-cost credit market. In a similar vein, if we really want to protect financially vulnerable individuals, we must do more than merely limit people's access to certain products or prohibit the most harmful aspects of the market. If we truly wish to protect borrowers, we need to understand why they are reliant on such expensive and potentially harmful credit. Taking a freedom-based approach is not bad *per se* as disclosure and consumer empowerment are both important. Taking a regulation-based and protectionist approach is also not wrong – prohibiting harmful products, limiting interest and restricting business models may be necessary to protect vulnerable borrowers. Both concepts are important and can be useful in the right situation; individually they are an inadequate response. Something more is needed. Chapters three and four provide a detailed analysis of both freedom and regulation, including the history, meaning, justifications and limitations of the two concepts. Chapter five introduces a third concept that is very important but too often overlooked – the provision of welfare and a social minimum. Having a better understanding of the key concepts and philosophical approaches to high-cost credit will provide a solid practical and theoretical basis for empirical research on the topic.

Both the current and previous regulators have recognised high-cost credit as one of the key areas needing further attention.[165] Whilst the Government is aware of *a* problem, it currently lacks sufficient information or research identifying the exact *nature* of *the* problem.[166] It therefore remains unclear exactly who is resorting to these high interest loans, why they are doing so, and the impact that this type of lending has on their general and financial wellbeing. Gibbons from The Centre for Responsible Credit notes that unlike other countries, the UK has yet to conduct a 'rigorous study of the long-term effects of a payday loan on living standards and essential budgets'.[167] Thus, during a period of immense

[163] OFT, *Consumer Credit Deregulation* (n 46); Don Pittis, 'Payday Loan Crackdown vs. the Freedom to Get Dangerously into Debt' (*CBC News*, 6 June 2016), available at www.cbc.ca/news/business/payday-lending-freedom-exploitation-1.3614559.

[164] This is discussed in Joseph Raz, *The Morality of Freedom* (Oxford University Press, 1988) 5–15. See also comments by Patrick Atiyah, 'The Liberal Theory of Contract' in Atiyah (ed), *Essays on Contract Law* (n 111) 46–147.

[165] This has been confirmed post-COVID in FCA, *Financial Lives 2020 Survey: The Impact of Coronavirus* (2020) and FCA, *The Woolard Review* (n 77).

[166] In 2010 the OFT highlighted the importance of collecting further information on the high-cost credit market to ensure accurate and useful regulation of the area: OFT, *Review of High-Cost Credit*, 2010) 52.

[167] Cited in Carl Packman, *Loan Sharks: The Rise and Rise of Payday Lending* (Searching Finance, 2012) 59.

regulatory scrutiny and legislative change, there is no accurate profile of borrowers that can pinpoint the nature and extent of the problems that need addressing. This book fills the gap by creating a profile of high-cost credit borrowers in the UK. Information of this type is crucial to understanding the nature of the problem, and to tailoring regulatory responses. It will also assist in recognising the limitations of the law and identifying what other political processes are needed to address the underlying problems.

The victim-blaming approach discussed above is strongly discredited by researchers looking at the systematic disadvantage of more vulnerable groups in our society.[168] It is not supported by academic research or empirical data, which highlights how poverty and financial disadvantage is a complex phenomenon and largely the result of systemic and structural disadvantage.[169] As one simple but clear example, there are more people living in poverty and working than there are living in poverty whilst unemployed.[170] The 2020 Financial Inclusion Annual Monitoring Report highlighted that 56 per cent of people in poverty were in a working family, compared with 39 per cent in 2000.[171] The number of people living in 'working poverty' has increased consistently and dramatically, and has been exacerbated by the pandemic. An average person in a working household is now currently 32 per cent more likely to be living in poverty in 2021 than in 1996.[172] Even so, the victim-blaming approach is still 'favoured by the political Right because it panders to their underlying belief in individual responsibility and minimum intervention by the state in welfare'.[173] The victim-blaming of those who are less fortunate is a strong political and rhetorical tool. Society cannot just blame people who are dependent on high-cost credit for their own misfortune – it is cruel, unjustified and inappropriate in a democratic welfare state. Further research on the causes of high-cost credit dependency will help to dispel the myth that people who utilise this type of financial product are to be blamed for their own debt problems. This is the aim of chapter six. Empirical research in the form of in-depth qualitative interviews with a wide range of stakeholders in the industry is used to create a profile of the key reasons why people are accessing these expensive and potentially harmful financial products. The identification of a profile of borrowers will further discredit the victim-blaming approach, as well as allow the

[168] See, eg, Alan Walker, 'Blaming the Victims' in Lister (ed), *Charles Murray and the Underclass: The Developing Debate* (IEA Health and Welfare Unit in association with *The Sunday Times*, 1996) and Ehrenreich, 'Time to Wake Up' (n 130).

[169] For a summary of this research see Walker, 'Blaming the Victims' (n 168). See Rowlingson, Appleyard and Gardner, 'Payday lending in the UK: the regul(aris)ation of a necessary evil?' (n 73) and Appleyard, Rowlingson and Gardner, Appleyard, Rowlingson and Gardner, 'The variegated financialization of sub-prime credit markets' (n 131) where the reality of high-cost credit borrowers and their financial situations is discussed.

[170] Clare McNeil and others, *No Longer 'Managing': The Rise of Working Poverty and Fixing Britain's Broken Social Settlement* (Institute for Public Policy Research, 2021).

[171] Stephen McKay and Karen Rowlingson, *Financial Inclusion Monitor 2020* (University of Birmingham, 2021) 5. Later figures have been excluded on the basis of the unprecedented impact of COVID-19 on employment.

[172] McNeil, *No Longer 'Managing'* (n 170) 13.

[173] Walker, 'Blaming the Victims' (n 168) 67.

tailoring of regulatory approaches towards the specific circumstances and needs of consumers.

2.3. Conclusion

This chapter has provided a summary of the high-cost credit environment in the UK, which will serve as background for the next three chapters. The first section in this chapter outlined how high-cost credit is regulated, looking at the historical background, as well as the differing approaches from the OFT and FCA and the direct enforcement mechanisms for consumers. It is clear that neither regulatory approach (freedom or regulation) has worked adequately, and the regulators are struggling to address the vulnerabilities of many consumers. The second section built on the work in the first by discussing the main challenges of high-cost credit, namely the ongoing victim-blaming of debtors and the lack of adequate engagement in the market. It highlights how further research, both empirical and theoretical in nature, is necessary to tackle the current situation and create an effective legal regime.

3

Freedom

> I am no bird; and no net ensnares me; I am a free human being with an independent will.
>
> — Charlotte Brontë, Jane Eyre[1]

This chapter analyses the first of the three key concepts, namely freedom. Freedom is the cornerstone of the common law, including for contracts of high-cost credit. The freedom approach is not aligned with complete non-intervention but has instead limited interference to the process of contracting and not on the content of the agreement. In the context of high-cost credit, this has meant an approach that ensures consent and avoids coercion or misinformation by lenders. The chapter has five sections. The first analyses the concept of freedom. The second highlights the history of freedom in high-cost credit, and the third analyses the justifications for taking a freedom-based approach. The fourth section outlines a variety of examples of freedom in high-cost credit contracts, including restrictions on who can lend, disclosure and advertising restrictions, cooling off rights, the unfair relationship test, and vitiating factors. The chapter concludes by discussing the limitations of the freedom approach, including the failure of disclosure, lack of meaningful choice and impact of poverty.

3.1. What is Freedom?

Before we can delve into an analysis of freedom, it is important to define what the term means, particularly in the context of high-cost credit. This is no easy task as the definition of freedom is a highly contested (but extremely important) concept that means different things in different contexts. Freedom is a central part of our legal and political system, receiving unparalleled support and respect.[2] So many of the rights that liberal societies hold dear are founded on this concept: freedom of thought, freedom of movement, freedom of speech and freedom of contract. Two things are however often overlooked when discussing what it means to be free.

[1] Charlotte Brontë, *Jane Eyre* (Smith, Elder and Co, 1847) 565.

[2] See Bramstead and Melhuish (eds), *Western Liberalism: A History in Documents from Locke to Croce* (Prentice Hall Press, 1978) ch 1, esp 1–2.

First, freedoms often come at a price, namely the favouring of an individual's choice over other factors such as the good of the community, prevention of harm, equality, protection of the vulnerable, and welfare of the individual chooser. Second, the meaning of 'freedom' is by no means self-evident. It is therefore important to define and discuss the concept before going any further.

Freedom is the starting point of the English common law on contracts. The oft-cited judgment of Sir George Jessel MR in *Printing and Numerical Registering Co v Sampson*[3] is one of the many examples[4] where freedom of contract is assumed to be the predominant factor when determining the enforceability of potentially unfair contractual arrangements. In holding that an agreement to assign all future patent rights was enforceable, His Lordship commented

> you are not to extend arbitrarily those rules which say that a given contract is void as being against public policy, because if there is one thing which more than another public policy requires it is *that men of full age and competent understanding shall have the utmost liberty of contracting*, and that their contracts when entered into freely and voluntarily shall be held sacred and shall be enforced by Courts of Justice. Therefore, you have this paramount public policy to consider – that *you are not lightly to interfere with this freedom of contract*.[5]

The primacy of freedom of contract has been the dominant value in the philosophy of contact law, the common law[6] and, until relatively recently, statute law.[7] The courts are therefore hesitant to intervene in an agreement between parties, or to impose substantive requirements of fairness of exchange. A contract will generally not be invalidated merely because of vague notions of 'justice', such as the fact that the terms were harsh, unreasonable or grossly unfair.[8] Traditionally this focus on freedom of contract also covers consumer contracts, including those for the provision of credit.[9] In the context of usury and interest rates, regulation of the relationship between lenders and borrowers arises solely from any government regulation and contractual obligations; there are very limited specific common

[3] *Printing and Numerical Registering Co v Sampson* (1875) LR 19 Eq 462 (CA).

[4] *Fender v St John-Mildmay* [1938] AC 1 (HL) 12 as per Lord Aiken *and Lancashire County Council v Municipal Mutual Insurance Ltd* [1996] 3 All ER 545 (CA) 555–56 as per Simon Brown LJ; Hugh Collins, *The Law of Contract*, 4th edn (LexisNexis, 2003) esp Ch 6.

[5] *Printing and Numerical Registering* (n 3) 465 (emphasis added).

[6] As stated by Benson, 'the common law conception of contract gives individuals an unfettered liberty to do as they please'; Peter Benson, 'The Unity of Contract Law' in Benson (ed), *The Theory of Contract Law* (Cambridge University Press, 2001) 200. This is clearly an exaggeration but makes an interesting point.

[7] Patrick Atiyah, 'Contracts, Promises and the Law of Obligations' in Atiyah (ed), *Essays on Contract Law* (Oxford University Press, 1990) 11.

[8] Jack Beatson and Daniel Friedman, 'Introduction: From "Classical" to Modern Contract Law' in Beatson and Friedman (eds), *Good Faith and Fault in Contract Law* (Oxford University Press, 1997) 8–9.

[9] *ibid* 7.

law duties of care.[10] Even in a high-cost credit setting, freedom of contract reigns supreme in the common law – regardless of the adequacy of consideration, the appropriateness of the loan, or the capacity to repay.[11]

There are many, sometimes conflicting, notions of 'freedom'. As Berlin observed, 'almost every moralist in human history has praised freedom. Like happiness and goodness, like nature and reality, it is a term whose meaning is so porous that there is little interpretation that it seems able to resist'.[12] The concept of freedom used in this book is 'negative freedom', meaning the lack of interference, obstacles or coercion – enabling a person to act unobstructed by others.[13] This can be contrasted with a positive concept of freedom, which advocates that true freedom means something more than non-intervention. Freedom and autonomy, in any valuable or meaningful sense, should equate to more than merely the right to make certain choices or enter into specific contracts.[14] A positive notion of freedom provides people with the *capability* to act upon their own free will.[15] It goes beyond a mere absence of intervention or obstacles, and requires the control of destiny and self-determination.[16]

Negative freedom allows people to enter into contracts of their choosing, on their own terms, and with whom they choose. The emphasis is on individual choice and limited government intervention into private affairs – supported by prominent libertarians including Fried,[17] Hayek,[18] Nozick[19] and Friedman.[20] This approach regards the enforcement of an individual's promise as being of the highest importance, generally outweighing other societal values such as fairness and good faith. An example of this is Mill's 'harm principle'. This principle dictates that the only legitimate reason the State can interfere with an individual's freedom is to prevent harm to others; protection of individuals from themselves, physically or

[10] Beyond those applicable to general contract law protections; Therese Wilson, 'The Bank and Customer Relationship, and *Australian Competition and Consumer Commission v Oceana Commercial Pty Ltd* (2004) 25 Queensland Lawyer 2; *Foley v Hill* (1848) 2 HL Case 28, 9 ER 1002; Lee Aitken, 'A "Duty to Lend Responsibly" – a New Terror for Lenders in a Consumer's World?' (2007) 18 *Journal of Banking and Finance Law and Practice* 18; Jodi Gardner, *The Challenges of Regulating High-Cost Short-Term Credit: A Comparison of UK and Australian Approaches* (Centre on Household Assets and Savings Management, 2014).

[11] John Cartwright, *Unequal Bargaining: A Study of Vitiating Factors in the Formation of Contracts* (Oxford University Press, 1991).

[12] Isaiah Berlin, 'Two Concepts of Liberty' in Berlin (ed), *Four Essays on Liberty* (Oxford University Press, 1958) 168.

[13] Based on the definition in *ibid* 169.

[14] Joseph Raz, *The Morality of Freedom* (Oxford University Press, 1988) 154–55.

[15] See also discussion in Martha Nussbaum, 'Women and Cultural Universals' in Martha Nussbaum (ed), *Sex and Social Justice* (Oxford University Press, 1999).

[16] Ian Carter, 'Positive and Negative Liberty' (*Stanford Encyclopedia of Philosophy*, 2003).

[17] Charles Fried, *Contract as Promise: A Theory of Contractual Obligation* (Harvard University Press, 1981).

[18] Friedrich Hayek, *The Constitution of Liberty* (University of Chicago Press, 1960).

[19] Robert Nozick, *Anarchy, State and Utopia* (Basic Books, 1974).

[20] Milton Friedman, *Capitalism and Freedom* (University of Chicago Press, 1963).

morally, is not a sufficient premise.[21] In the context of contracts 'all the law can do is to police the bargaining process, to try and ensure that contracts are indeed the result of free and voluntary ... processes; but once we have done that, the result must be accepted'.[22]

A focus on freedom does not mean a complete lack of government intervention, as that would result in the 'law of the jungle', which is clearly unsuited and unjustified for any modern society. Some restrictions and limitations are required, although negative freedom means these are limited. In the context of high-cost credit, the alignment with freedom has resulted in a focus on procedural fairness between consumers and lenders.[23] The legal restrictions are aimed at addressing the process by which parties enter into the contract, its procedure, and not the fairness of the resulting transaction, its substance.[24] There are two main aspects to procedural fairness; the first ensuring borrowers freely consent to the transaction, and the second preventing coercion by lenders.[25] The common law and legislation relevant to high-cost credit have several provisions designed to ensure procedural fairness, including restrictions on who can lend money, disclosure obligations and advertising restrictions, cooling off rights, the unfair relationship test, and vitiating factors.

3.2. The History of Freedom

This section outlines the important historical role of freedom in the development and regulation of high-cost credit. An awareness of the history of freedom of

[21] John Stuart Mill, *On Liberty* (Longman, Roberts & Green, 1859).

[22] Atiyah, *Essays on Contract Law* (n 7) Essay 11, 347.

[23] Spencer Thal, 'The Inequality of Bargaining Power Doctrine: The Problem of Defining Contractual Unfairness' (1988) 8 *Oxford Journal of Legal Studies* 17, 26. See discussion by Atiyah about the difficulties of separating the two concepts; Patrick Atiyah, 'Contract and Fair Exchange' (1985) 35 *University of Toronto Law Journal* 1, 5–6.

[24] Steven Smith, 'In Defence of Substantive Unfairness' (1996) *Law Quarterly Review* 138; Mindy Chen-Wishart, 'The O'Brien Principle and Substantive Unfairness' (1997) 56 *Cambridge Law Journal* 60. This debate then moves on to whether protection can be justified by reference only to procedural fairness, or whether substantive fairness can also be a valid aim: see discussion from an English perspective in Séverine Saintier, 'Defects of Consent in English Law' in DiMatteo and Hogg (eds), *Comparative Contract Law: British and American Perspectives* (Oxford University Press, 2016). For an American perspective on the debate, see Jeffrey L Harrison, 'Quality of Consent and Distributive Fairness: A Comparative Perspective' in DiMatteo and Hogg (eds), *Comparative Contract Law: British and American Perspectives* (Oxford University Press, 2016). It is also discussed in the context of vitiating factors in Mindy Chen-Wishart, 'The Nature of Vitiating Factors in Contract' in Saprai, Letsas and Klass (eds), *Philosophical Foundations of Contract Law* (Oxford University Press, 2014) and Thal, 'The Inequality of Bargaining Power Doctrine' (n 23).

[25] Randy E Barnett, 'A Consent Theory of Contract' (1986) 86 *Columbia Law Review* 269, esp opening comments; Raz, *The Morality of Freedom* (n 14) 88; Gillian Hadfield, 'An Expressive Theory of Contract: From Feminist Dilemmas to a Reconceptualisation of Rational Choice in Contract Law' (1998) 146 *University of Pennsylvania Law Review* 1235; Peter H Schnuk, 'Rethinking Informed Consent' (1994) 103 *Yale Law Journal* 899, 900.

contract is essential to understanding the challenges we are currently tackling. The historical aspects of freedom of contract are not merely legal and are closely linked with economic, social and political movements.[26] Whilst a detailed discussion of these issues is clearly beyond the scope of the current book,[27] a brief outline of the key historical points is necessary to illuminate the later analysis.

The early laws relating to usury and moneylending rejected notions of freedom of contract, and were strongly focused on the religious prohibition of usury. Whilst the prohibitions were the result of canon law, they clearly applied to the Christian laity and the clergy,[28] and punishment continued to be imposed by the ecclesiastical courts.[29] The protective approach was largely dominant until 1545 when the first Act to remove the cap on interest was passed.[30] Religious arguments were sidelined with the rise of commerce, and an approach favouring economic freedom was pursued.[31] This change occurred within the Enlightenment period and the corresponding increase in movement and trade, industrial progression and the creation of a more international world.[32] Money was needed to fund developments, both from commerce and from the State, and this was difficult to achieve with a religious-based prohibition on usury. New ways of thinking about these issues quickly developed to reflect the practicality of the Government's financial needs.[33]

The Enlightenment period is also strongly associated with individual and market-based freedom, with many scholars advocating against government intervention into either economic or individual affairs. This commonly resulted in a move against the historical prohibition of usury and towards freedom. It was however far from universal, and many scholars continued to endorse the religious-based moral condemnation of usury. The initial approach to usury during the Enlightenment period was to morally denounce the charging of interest but approve the practice on some other ground.[34] For example, Luther compromised

[26] As outlined in Atiyah's historical analysis, 'freedom of Contract is, at that time, by no means exclusively a legal concept or a concept of interest only to lawyers … [it] began as an economic and even political ideal, which probably had roots in the personal, religious, and intellectual freedoms': Atiyah, *Essays on Contract Law* (n 7) Essay 12, 355.

[27] See Patrick Atiyah, *The Rise and Fall of Freedom of Contract* (Oxford University Press, 1985) for this discussion.

[28] Richard Helmholz, *The Oxford History of the Laws of England. Volume I: The Canon Law and Ecclesiastical Jurisdiction from 597 to the 1640s* (Oxford University Press, 2004) 378.

[29] John Baker, *The Oxford History of the Laws of England. Volume VI: 1483–1558* (Oxford University Press, 2003).

[30] This will be discussed in more detail in chapter four, section 4.2.2.

[31] Glyn Davies, *A History of Money: From Ancient Times to the Present Day* (University of Wales Press, 1994) 221.

[32] Yaron Brook, 'The Morality of Moneylending: A Short History' (*The Objective Standard*, 20 August 2007), available at www.theobjectivestandard.com/issues/2007-fall/morality-of-moneylending/ (all websites cited in this chapter were accessed on 10 January 2022).

[33] For more discussion on this, see David Graeber, *Debt: The First 5,000 Years* (Melville House Publishing, 2012) esp ch 11.

[34] See, eg, Martin Luther, *Von Kauffshandlung vnd Wucher (On Trading and Usury)* (Durch Hans Lufft, 1524) Usury; written without page numbers: 'There are some who not only deal in little sums, but also take too much return – seven, eight, nine, ten percent. The rulers ought to look into this. Here the

by stating that, due to the economic benefits obtained from access to credit and the Crown's need for additional funds, usury should be tolerated to a limited extent. At the same time, he believed that Christianity should continue its prohibition on all forms of interest-charging, and that usury should be morally condemned in the strongest manner possible.[35] Luther justified the differences in practice and theory on the grounds of the value of freedom and the need for a strong separation between Church and State, acknowledging that different borrowers should be treated differently.[36]

The focus started to change in the eighteenth century and there was increasing emphasis on the fact that usury laws could harm 'legitimate' trade and commerce.[37] Classic free-market economic arguments prevented the imposition of interest rate caps.[38] By the end of the century almost all commentators in Britain (and the Continent) had accepted the legitimacy of interest-bearing loans, and the benefits that an open credit market had on commerce and finance.[39]

This approach to usury was not, however, universal. Smith, widely referred to as the 'Father' of free-market capitalism, was a strong advocate of laissez-faire economics. Regardless, in his seminal 1776 work *The Wealth of Nations*, Smith came out strongly in favour of an interest rate ceiling.[40] While he did not believe in a strict prohibition on usury,[41] Smith argued that the interest rate should be set only slightly higher than the market rate. Smith wanted to protect low-*risk* borrowers (as opposed to low-*income* borrowers) and allow them to continue to invest in socially useful activities. He was concerned that an unregulated market would mean valuable funds would be given to 'prodigals and projectors' as they

poor common people are secretly imposed upon and severely oppressed. For this reason these robbers and usurers often die an unnatural and sudden death, or come to a terrible end … for God is a judge for the poor and needy, as He often says in the Old Law'.

[35] The charging of interest should never be permitted in small sums and/or to the poor, as it was 'God's will that the needy shall be helped by loans or gifts'; thus the moral stance against moneylending was retained, although there was a begrudging acceptance of usury in commercial settings; *ibid* The Two Kingdoms.

[36] *ibid* God's Laws and Secular Laws.

[37] Hugh Bellot, *The Law Relating to Unconscionable Bargains with Money-Lenders: Including the History of Usury to the Repeal of the Usury Laws* (Stevens & Haynes, 1898) 28–29. See also William Hawkins, *A Treatise of the Pleas of the Crown, or, A System of the Principal Matters Relating to that Subject, Digested under Proper Heads*, vol 1 (Printed by Eliz. Nutt (executrix of J. Nutt, assignee of E Sayer) for J Walthoe, 1721) 613, ss 3–4.

[38] Vincent D Rougeau, 'Rediscovering Usury: An Argument for Legal Controls on Credit Card Interest Rates' (1996) 67 *University of Colorado Law Review* 1, 2.

[39] Joseph Persky, 'From Usury to Interest' (2007) 21 *Journal of Economic Perspectives* 227, 230. The economic benefits of interest charging were advocated by Salmasius and Turgot, with the latter also emphasising the property rights of the moneylender as a reason to permit usury: see discussion in Brook, 'The Morality of Moneylending' (n 32).

[40] Giuseppe Coco and David De Meza, 'In Defense of Usury Laws' (2009) 41 *Journal of Money, Credit & Banking* 1691, 1691.

[41] Adam Smith, *An Inquiry into the Nature and Causes of the Wealth of Nations* (The Modern Library, 1937) Book II, 4.13.

would be the ones willing to pay a higher interest rate.[42] Accordingly, the focus was not on the protection of those less fortunate, but on ensuring that there was sufficient credit available to provide funds to people who would use the money in a wealth-maximising manner.[43]

Smith's strongest concern about the capping of interest was that it had the potential to increase the cost of credit generally. The debtor would be required to pay not just for the interest, but for the 'risk' the creditor was taking in illegally lending the money (ie, any penalty they may incur from the unauthorised lending). Smith feared that the borrower 'is obliged, if one may say so, to insure his creditor from the penalties of usury'.[44] It would be the debtor who suffered the consequences of the cap, not the lender. This concern has been used relatively recently by the current regulator as a warning on the potential externalities of interest rate caps.

Smith's view on interest was further illuminated in his *Lectures on Justice, Police, Revenue and Arms*. He highlighted that the level of interest, just like any other commodity, is determined by supply and demand, and that risk must be considered in the determination of interest charge levels.[45,46] Smith's utilitarian approach to capitalism was based on the social benefits from a laissez-faire approach to economics. He therefore did not address issues of vulnerability, exploitation or lending to the poor, preferring to see interest (and the regulation of it) as just another commodity. Unfortunately, this limited focus and failure to understand the relationship between high-cost credit and social policy is an ongoing theme in the approach taken to these financial products.

Bentham strongly argued against Smith's views in his book *Defence of Usury*.[47] He believed that people were best placed to make their own decisions regarding credit and interest. Taking a laissez-faire approach to public regulation,[48] Bentham

[42] *ibid* Book II, 4.15. 'Prodigals and projectors' have been described as 'various financial promoters of highly dubious projects aimed at fleecing the public of their savings': Persky, 'From Usury to Interest' (n 39) 235.

[43] Smith also warned that an interest rate must not be set lower than the market rate or people would merely find multiple ways to evade the law, and so it would be useless to society: Smith, *An Inquiry* (n 41) 4.15.

[44] *ibid* 339.

[45] Adam Smith, *Lectures on Justice, Police, Revenue and Arms* (edited by Cannan) (Clarendon Press, 1896) 220.

[46] *ibid* 221.

[47] Jeremy Bentham, *Defence of Usury; shewing the impolicy of the present legal restraints on the terms of pecuniary bargains. In a series of letters to a friend. To which is added, a letter to Adam Smith, Esq; LL.D. on the discouragements opposed by the above restraints to the progress of inventive industry* (Messrs. D. Williams, Colles, White, Byrne, Lewis, Jones, and Moore, 1788).

[48] Bentham was a strong advocate of utilitarianism, and focused on maximising social utility and nowhere is this more obvious than in Jeremy Bentham, *A Manual of Political Economy* (McMaster University Archive for the History of Economic Thought, 1843) which is a 'direct utilitarian calculation of the likely consequences could be employed to determine the appropriateness of government action': James Crimmins, 'Political Economy and Projectors: Bentham's Defence of Usury' in Artemieva and Mikeshin (eds), *The Philosophical Age, The Science of Morality: J Bentham and Russia* (St Petersburg Center for the History of Ideas, 1999) 67.

argued against government limitations on usury. The book was universally and internationally acclaimed, but was unsuccessful in changing Smith's mind.[49] Bentham advocated that it would be better for the borrower, lender and State to have a more open credit market.[50] This included the belief that ongoing prohibition of usury may allow illegal lenders to grow and prosper.[51] He also believed that usury could not accurately be described as a 'crime', considering that the 'victim' in the scenario (ie, the borrower) had consented to the transaction. If consent for the usurious transaction was obtained improperly or exploitatively, this was an issue of fraud or duress and not the 'crime' of usury.[52] Bentham also argued that credit is the same as any other good or service, and therefore failed to see why it was appropriate to fix the cost of credit when there were no other similar restrictions in the market.[53]

One of the most famous early legal works on usury, *A Treatise upon the Law of Usury and Annuities*,[54] was written in 1797 by Plowden, then a Barrister-at-Law. This book addressed (and rejected) the religious prohibition on charging interest, explicitly declaring it to be a matter for civil law to address. Plowden argued that the regulation of usury is a legal issue, and that debate on the topic should not be overshadowed by moralist and religious stances. Whilst citing Biblical passages condemning usury,[55] he departed from the earlier work of Aristotle and Aquinas by stating that merely charging interest is not criminal or sinful.[56] Plowden reasoned that position of usury had moved beyond a religious matter and could only be held unlawful through a legal process.[57] Here we start to see movement away from religion and towards individual and economic freedom. Plowden did condemn lending to the poor, declaring that 'every species of oppression and extortion upon the poor and distressed' should be prohibited.[58] This did not mean that all acts of usury should be illegal, or that wealthy parties have an obligation to assist

[49] Smith openly approved of Bentham's work in the area but it did not change his mind on the matter. When Bentham was working on the second edition of the manuscript, he wrote to Smith asking for an open admission that Smith now favoured a more open approach to lending laws. Smith reportedly responded with a dedicated copy of *The Wealth of Nations* as a response: *ibid* 61. This is also discussed in Persky, 'From Usury to Interest' (n 39) 234.

[50] Bentham, *Defense of Usury* (n 47) Letter VI, commencing at 56, see particularly 67–71.

[51] *ibid* at, eg, 75–76.

[52] See further discussion in Crimmins, 'Political Economy and Projectors: Bentham's Defence of Usury' (n 48) 62.

[53] Bentham (n 47) Letter IX.

[54] Frances Plowden, *A Treatise upon the Law of Usury and Annuities by Francis Plowden of the Middle Temple, Barrister at Law* (Printed for J Butterworth, Fleet-Street, 1797).

[55] All Plowden quotes are cited with minor translation amendments so that they are in modern English. 'Such have at all times been the general prepossessions against Usury and Usurers, that it is scary possible to speak temperately upon the subject without given scan or offence to a large portion of mankind. If we form our opinion of Usury upon the general doctrine of divines, or the rigorous feverity with which legislators have generally punished the Usurer, we shall necessarily place it at the head of the … table of offenses against God and man. Usury has almost at every age and every civilized country been the invariable theme of censure to the moralist': *ibid* 10.

[56] *ibid* 13.

[57] *ibid* 13.

[58] *ibid* 25.

those in need. Plowden advocated instead for a prohibition on loans of money only where the agreement was obtained through corruption.[59] He argued for a system of moneylending based on legislative restrictions of interest as opposed to a complete prohibition, and limited restrictions on unconscionable loans.

Mill's 'harm principle' continued the focus on individual liberty and economic freedom.[60] The Government's role is merely to enforce contractual agreements between parties – even if they are usurious in nature. Mill was morally against usury, stating that it was absolutely appalling and the outcome of wasteful and immoral trading arrangements.[61] He proclaimed that usury allowed situations where the lender 'draws from capital which he does not possess, usurious interest, out of proportion with the capital he actually owns'.[62] Whilst this may appear to place the blame on the lender, Mill was critical of the overall system that permitted these transactions. He theorised that usury allowed people to make money solely from the ownership of money, and not from their own labour or goods.[63] Despite this, Mill did not believe that the State should regulate the cost of credit. In *Principles of Political Economy*, Book V, 'The Influence of the Government', he included usury laws under the heading 'Of An Interference of Government Grounded on Erroneous Theories'.[64] Mill believed that restrictions on usury were based on irrational religious beliefs and not on economically sound justifications.[65] He therefore saw no adequate reason for the State to intervene and undermine the individual's contractual freedoms.

The history of the freedom-based approach to high-cost credit provides a very useful insight into the current challenges associated with these financial products. The Enlightenment Period resulted in a movement away from the traditional religious prohibition of usury, and towards a focus on freedom. The early Enlightenment scholars continued to condemn usury on moral and/or religious grounds, but allowed it to continue for practical reasons associated with the freedom of economic markets and the moral importance of freedom in individual affairs. This resulted in a movement away from State intervention and, on the cusp of the twentieth century, the desire to protect people from moneylending transactions had largely disappeared. It was replaced with a belief in the rational person principle and/or overridden by the importance of individual freedom and liberty. This approach continued to be the dominant mode of regulation until the Financial Conduct Authority's (FCA) takeover and the subsequent high-cost credit reforms discussed above.

[59] *ibid* 220–21.
[60] Mill, *On Liberty* (n 21).
[61] John Stuart Mill, *On Socialism* (edited by Lewis S Feuer) (Prometheus Books, 1987) 37.
[62] *ibid* 39–40.
[63] *ibid* 9.
[64] See specifically John Stuart Mill, *Principles of Political Economy* (Longmans, Green & Co, 1891) Book V, Ch X, §2.
[65] John Stuart Mill, *Principles of Political Economy, and, Chapters on Socialism* (edited by Riley) (Oxford University Press, 1994) 306.

3.3. Justifying Freedom

The negative freedom focus has been the dominant regulatory approach for high-cost credit contracts, but why has this occurred? This section builds on previous discussion by looking at the historical explanations for a freedom-based approach. Four are put forward, namely:

- the important role of consent;
- the lack of protection for social and economic rights (when compared with protections of civil and political rights) under human rights conventions;
- the role of Thatcherism and the 'financialisation' of society after 1979; and
- the distinction between defective financial products and defective physical products.

Each of these explanations (and their limitations) will be discussed. The first two explanations are general to contract law, and the second two are more specifically focused on high-cost credit.

3.3.1. Consent

Liberal tradition has placed great importance on people's ability to voluntarily undertake obligations to one another and to rely on them once undertaken. The value placed on this has shaped the legal practice of recognising and enforcing obligations.[66] The freedom-based approach decrees that the Government's role in contract law is merely to provide a sufficient framework for the creation and enforcement of agreements between parties. This allows autonomous individuals to impose obligations on themselves as an exercise of their free will.[67] Schnuk outlines how consent is the cornerstone of English contract law, commenting that it allows individual values to be expressed and for people to be the author of their own undertakings.[68] Consent and freedom are intrinsically linked; we support a freedom-based approach because we care about the parties' consent.[69]

The current approach to contract law is strongly focused on determining the presence (or absence) of consent to legal transactions. Contracts are enforced when the parties have consented; conversely contracts are not enforced when parties do not consent, or when their consent is defective. Consent has powerful

[66] Dori Kimel, 'Neutrality, Autonomy, and Freedom of Contract' (2001) 21 *Oxford Journal of Legal Studies* 473, 473. See also Dori Kimel, *From Promise to Contract: Towards a Liberal Theory of Contract* (Hart Publishing, 2003).

[67] Fried, *Contract as Promise* (n 17). See also Brian Bix, 'Contracts' in Miller and Wertheimer (eds), *The Ethics of Consent: Theory and Practice* (Oxford University Press, 2009) 251.

[68] Schnuk, 'Rethinking Informed Consent' (n 25) 900.

[69] For a further discussion on the limitations on this link, see Alain Marciano, 'Freedom, Choice and Consent. A Note on a Libertarian Paternalist Dilemma' (2015) 32 *Homo Oeconomicus* 287.

consequences as it acts as an indication of the parties' intentions, and attributes legal responsibilities to them. For an agreement to be binding, the parties must voluntarily consent to that contract. This is not a controversial statement – it is widely accepted that valid consent is necessary for a contract to be enforceable.[70] The question is therefore not whether defective consent will prevent a contract from being enforceable, but rather *what is* defective (or valid) consent in the context of high-cost credit?

Consent is a complex phenomenon and subject to external influences. Hadfield contends that behaviour is driven by various influences beyond an individual's control, including biological, psychological and sociological factors.[71] If an individual's voluntary and informed consent is unacceptably limited, the mere notion of 'choice' is not sufficient to ground contractual obligations.[72] It is therefore important to recognise that choice and consent are not as clear-cut as they are often presented. Consent and capacity are 'constitutive of who we are and how we develop as individuals and as communities'.[73]

The limited approach often taken to the definition of consent under the common law is not sufficient for high-cost credit borrowers. Consent, without enquiring why or how it was given, has been described as 'a barren thing', and it is important for the legal system to consider what reasons are behind the giving of consent.[74] We need to go beyond narrow questions of negating contracts on the basis of 'defective' consent, and focus on a more meaningful definition of consent. True consent requires more than mere acquiescence to the promise or agreement in question; the promisee must be able to make an informed judgement on their own situation and best interests.[75] A meaningful concept of consent requires people to have a range of worthwhile choices from which to pick.[76] As previously discussed,[77] a number of common factors in high-cost credit scenarios undermine borrowers' ability to validly consent, including the use of legalistic and complex standard form contracts, provision of easy credit to vulnerable consumers, and the inequality of bargaining power.

3.3.2. Human Rights Approaches

The second explanation for a negative freedom approach is based on society's approach to human rights. The majority of human rights protections are focused

[70] Barnett, 'A Consent Theory of Contract' (n 25) esp opening comments; Raz, *The Morality of Freedom* (n 14) 88.

[71] Hadfield, 'An Expressive Theory of Contract' (n 25).

[72] *ibid* 1251.

[73] *ibid* 1260.

[74] Atiyah commented that it 'can easily become formalistic if not fetishistic, to insist that consent must bind': Atiyah, *Essays on Contract Law* (n 7) Essay 11, 353. See also discussion in Chen-Wishart, 'The Nature of Vitiating Factors in Contract' (n 24) 295–296.

[75] Raz, *The Morality of Freedom* (n 14) 155.

[76] *ibid* 151–55; Schnuk, 'Rethinking Informed Consent' (n 25) 900.

[77] See discussion in chapter one, section 1.2.

on civil and political rights, and not on basic economic rights. This comes from a largely Western perception regarding which rights are of paramount importance.[78] The predominant human rights instrument, the Universal Declaration of Human Rights (UNDHR), includes the right to:

- equal protection and freedom from discrimination (Article 7);
- effective court or tribunal remedies (Articles 8, 10 and 11);
- freedom of movement (Article 13);
- a nationality (Article 16);
- own property (Article 17);
- freedom of thought, opinion and assembly (Articles 18, 19 and 20);
- take part in democratic processes (Article 21);
- work (Article 23); and
- rest and leisure (Article 24).

Only one Article in the UNDHR provides protection for economic rights.[79] Article 26(1) states that all people should have 'the right to a standard of living adequate for the health and well-being of himself and of his family'. This was, however, followed by Article 26(2), which focuses on the civil right of equality between children born in and out of wedlock. The one human right that protects economic rights was not considered important enough to be a free-standing right on its own and was instead linked with political issues of family and prevention of child marriage. This puts the right to an adequate standard of living in context, highlighting that it is implicitly limited to issues of family living standards and not a right in and of itself.

Whilst political and civil rights are valid and worthy of protection, the UNDHR reflects a predominately Western approach to what is considered important. Posner argues that one of the reasons why there was such hesitation to enshrine economic rights was the disagreement between the United States and the Soviet Union on what rights should be protected. The United States favoured civil and political rights, whereas the Soviet Union focused more on social and economic rights. Hence the former was associated with libertarian democracies and the latter with socialist states. Many Asian countries have chosen to restrict political and civil rights in favour of economic progression. For example, China and India – two countries responsible for lifting almost one billion people out of

[78] Emily Badger, 'Are Economic Rights Fundamental Human Rights?' *PacificStandard*, updated 14 June 2017), available at https://psmag.com/are-economic-rights-fundamental-human-rights-524ede71ed88#.3wmf7jymh.

[79] Fredman has however questioned whether there is any difference between social and economic rights when compared with civil and political rights; Sandra Fredman, *Human Rights Transformed: Positive Rights and Positive Duties* (Oxford University Press, 2007) esp chs 7 and 8.

extreme poverty[80] – have come under significant criticism for their approaches to human rights and for preferring economic development to political liberalism.[81] It took another 18 years after the UNDHR to develop a treaty that provided anything close to adequate recognition of social and economic rights, namely the 1976 International Covenant on Economic, Social and Cultural Rights.[82]

This Westernised approach to human rights is reflected in the libertarian focus of the English legal system, which is much more comfortable protecting people's negative liberty than actively promoting positive concepts of freedom.[83] A connection can be drawn between civil/political rights and the negative freedom approach.[84] This provides a degree of justification for the lack of regulation of financial products, including high-cost credit. It is, however, ultimately unconvincing. Research has increasingly highlighted the importance of providing people with both social/economic rights and civil/political rights – as Satz and Green show, the two are inherently linked.[85] The global financial crisis, the 2022 cost of living crisis and the pandemic have confirmed the importance of social and economic rights, with increasing numbers of people in some of the most privileged and economically developed countries struggling to provide themselves with basic food and shelter.

The positive and negative notions of freedom do not conflict or compete with each other. There needs to be some scope for negative freedom and protections for civil and political rights, but this must be bounded to some extent by protection of economic and social rights. Intervening and limiting vulnerable people's right to access potentially harmful financial products does undermine people's negative liberty, but it also enhances their ability to contribute actively to our society and to live meaningful lives. The benefits can therefore outweigh the detriments.

[80] The Economist, 'Towards the End of Poverty' *The Economist* (1 June 2013), available at www.economist.com/news/leaders/21578665-nearly-1-billion-people-have-been-taken-out-extreme-poverty-20-years-world-should-aim.

[81] Badger, 'Are Economic Rights Fundamental Human Rights?' (n 78). See also, discussion in Eric Posner, 'Human Rights – the Long Read: The Case Against Human Rights' *The Guardian* (4 December 2014), available at www.theguardian.com/news/2014/dec/04/-sp-case-against-human-rights.

[82] Posner, 'Human Rights', *ibid.*

[83] See discussion in chapter four, section 4.1 of this book.

[84] There is also a connection between substantive fairness and protection of social and economic rights.

[85] Debra Satz, *Why Some Things Should Not Be For Sale: The Moral Limits of Markets* (Oxford University Press, 2010) 100–105; Thomas Green, 'Liberal Legislation and Freedom of Contract' in Harris and Morrow (eds), *Lectures on the Principles of Political Obligation and Other Writings* (Cambridge University Press, 1986); See also quote from Messer and Cohen: 'Country case studies across the developing world demonstrate that those denied civil liberties suffer disproportionately from social injustices and material deprivations, including food insecurity, hunger-related disease, malnutrition, and preventable child mortality. The significance of freedom of speech, a free press, and freedom of assembly for the protection of economic rights, including the right not to starve, connects food security to democracy and good governance': Ellen Messer and Marc J Cohen, *Approaches to Food and Nutrient Rights, 1976–2008* (World Hunger Education, 2009). This will be further discussed in chapter five, section 5.3.1.

3.3.3. Responsibilisation and Financialisation

Since 1979, the UK has undergone a process of 'responsibilisation', where individuals are expected to become increasingly responsible for their own financial wellbeing, as opposed to relying on the State for assistance. This is closely linked to the victim-blaming discussed in chapter two,[86] as it places accountability for financial decisions on individuals, consequently allowing them to be blamed if and when things go wrong. Governments from the 1980s onwards have increasingly promoted the idea of an active welfare state to replace the supposedly passive welfare system. Such ideas were accepted by New Labour's Third Way approach, which supported the idea of a modern, active welfare state based on welfare-to-work, and the development of skills and flexibility to support those in work or those actively seeking work.[87] The 1997 New Labour (and more recently the Coalition and Conservative) governments extended this notion of obligations alongside rights through the personalisation of welfare and the strengthening of responsibility agendas, identifying the root causes of poverty with the individual problems rather than any structural issues. For example, Tony Blair suggested in 2002 that welfare reform is essential to restore civic responsibility by making a 'new contract between citizen and state, a contract that says with rights come responsibilities and obligations'.[88]

Under New Labour, the Gregg Review and the Department for Work and Pensions (DWP) proposals for welfare reform aimed to reward responsibility. The welfare system adopted an active, personalised role to widen the obligations on people to both work and save. Labour continued the reforms begun by the Thatcher and Major Conservative governments by further implementing pension reforms, which were marketed as providing the public with greater information and choice, and to encourage individual responsibility for savings and borrowing behaviour.[89] This focus was also evident in Tony Blair's modernising agenda, which aimed to create a market-oriented 'third way' of delivering welfare by removing the responsibility from the Government and transferring it to other agencies.[90] These changes have reconfigured the relationship between individuals and the State so that citizens actively participate in their own social and economic wellbeing. The responsibility of providing credit to low-income people was transferred from

[86] See discussion in chapter two, section 2.2.1.

[87] Fran Bennett and Jane Millar, 'Social Security: Reforms and Challenges' in Millar (ed), *Understanding Social Security: Issue for Policy and Practice* (Policy Press, 2003) 20.

[88] Tony Blair, 'My Vision for Britain: by Tony Blair' *The Guardian* (10 November 2002), available at www.guardian.co.uk/politics/2002/nov/10/queensspeech2002.tonyblair?CMP=email.

[89] Neil Gilbert, *Transformation of the Welfare State: The Silent Surrender of Public Responsibility* (Oxford University Press, 2002).

[90] John Clarke, Mary Langan and Fiona Williams, 'Remaking Welfare: The British Welfare Regime in the 1980s and 1990s' in Cochrane, Clarke and Gewirtz (eds), *Comparing Welfare States*, 2nd edn (Sage, 2001) 101.

government bodies (through the social fund) to commercial entities by deregulation and the opening of the lending market.[91]

The responsibility discourse emerged alongside the 'financialisation' of everyday life, with increased access to the private financial market.[92] Successive British governments encouraged and expanded the financial services sector from the mid-1980s onwards through de-regulation and the introduction of 'light-touch' regulation. This approach to regulation facilitated an expansion of personal lending from the 1970s onwards. Whilst mortgage lending has declined since 2008, there has been a corresponding increase in other types of borrowing, particularly high-cost credit.[93] This financialisation of personal lending facilitated the changed regulatory approaches towards disclosure, consent and competition – further emphasising the State's focus on negative freedom. As will be discussed in section 3.4 below, regulation in the UK is largely focused on the registration of lenders and on disclosure obligations, continuing to put responsibility on borrowers to ensure they read and understand the agreement.[94]

The State's response towards lending has been to decrease government assistance while increasing access to financial markets, in order to create more individually responsible citizens. These two concepts – responsibilisation and financialisation – are the constant impetus behind the regulation most affecting vulnerable groups in our society. These political movements help to explain the ongoing hesitation to engage with the market and take a more active approach to addressing the problems associated with high-cost credit. They do not, however, provide anything close to a justification. The opening of the financial markets for high-cost credit allowed lenders to develop unfair business practices, and consumers in desperate need of funds have become dependent on these products.

3.3.4. Differing Approaches to Financial and Physical Products

The different approaches taken to defective financial products compared with those for defective physical products further facilitated the negative freedom approach to high-cost credit. There are strong justifications for holding the manufacturers of dangerous products strictly liable for any harm caused, or for going a

[91] *ibid* 40.

[92] Alan Finlayson, 'Financialisation, Financial Literacy and Asset-Based Welfare' (2009) 11 *The British Journal of Politics and International Relations* 400, 403.

[93] See discussion in Jodi Gardner, Karen Rowlingson and Lindsey Appleyard, 'Responsible Borrowing and Lending' (2018) 2 *Journal of International Consumer Law and Practice* 16.

[94] Karen Fairweather, 'Apples and Oranges? Responsible Mortgage Lending in the UK and Australia' in O'Shea, Fairweather and Grantham (eds), *Credit, Consumers and the Law: After the Global Storm* (Routledge (Markets and the Law Series, 2016)).

step further and completely preventing the product from entering the market.[95] Financial products have been treated differently from physical items throughout history, although it is not at all clear if the distinction is defensible. States have generally actively intervened to ensure the safety of tangible products, and it is arguable that this approach should be replicated with credit products. In the words of Warren, 'consumers can enter the market to buy physical products confident that they won't be tricked into buying exploding toasters and other unreasonably dangerous products … Consumers entering the market to buy financial products should enjoy the same protection'.[96] Unfortunately this is not the case, and governments are often hesitant to intervene in the financial market to the same extent as for physical products.

Consumers frequently use high-cost credit in a dangerous manner, resulting in financial hardship or a debt spiral.[97] Grossly unfair contracts are often considered unfair precisely because of their potential for adverse long-term impacts on the autonomy of the individual in question.[98] The Government can (and arguably should) restrict a person's short-term freedom of choice in order to ultimately provide them with greater autonomy, or prevent harm to their future autonomy. This includes removing dangerous financial products from the market if and when necessary.[99] Whilst high-cost credit may deliver temporary relief to individuals, the significant repayment burden is likely to limit future autonomy and choices and can result in extreme financial hardship. The negative impact that these products can have on borrowers and their future autonomy therefore justifies a movement away from the traditional focus of negative freedom. It is important to recognise that harmful financial products can cause just as much damage as dangerous tangible products.[100]

This distinction between physical products and financial products may be defended on the ground that defective credit products cause financial/economic losses, compared with dangerous physical products which have the potential to cause physical harm. The tort laws in numerous countries[101] have limited the ability of people to claim damages for pure economic loss compared with damages for physical injury and mental distress. There are varying reasons for this, but

[95] Roger Traynor, 'The Ways and Meanings of Defective Products and Strict Liability' (1965) 32 *Tennessee Law Review* 363.

[96] Elizabeth Warren, 'Unsafe at Any Rate' [2007] *Democracy: A Journal of Ideas* 8.

[97] See the case studies in Sarah Beddows and Mick McAteer, *Payday Lending: Fixing a Broken Market* (Association of Chartered Certified Accountants, 2014).

[98] Chen-Wishart, 'The Nature of Vitiating Factors in Contract' (n 24) 12.

[99] Raz, *Essays on Contract Law* (n 14) 419. See also Chen-Wishart, 'The Nature of Vitiating Factors in Contract' (n 24).

[100] Luke Nottage, 'Innovating for "Safe Consumer Credit": Drawing on Product Safety Regulation to Protect Consumers of Credit' in Wilson (ed), *International Responses to Issues of Credit and Over-indebtedness in the Wake of Crisis* (Ashgate Publishing Ltd, 2013).

[101] *Hedley Byrne & Co Ltd v Heller & Partners Ltd* [1964] AC 465, [1963] UKHL 4; *Perre v Apand* (1999) 198 CLR 180, [1999] HCA 36; Bussani and Valentine Palmer (eds), *Pure Economic Loss in Europe* (Cambridge University Press, 2003); Herbert Bernstien, 'Civil Liability for Pure Economic Loss under American Tort Law' (1998) 46 *American Journal of Comparative Law* 111.

they largely revolve around economic loss being seen as a less important interest to protect,[102] concerns of indeterminate liability, and the focus on compensating physical and psychiatric damage over financial loss. None of these explanations are adequate in the context of high-cost credit.

Despite the widespread problems associated with these financial products, they focus on a specific group in society and are limited in both the size of loan and number of loans given.[103] There are few, if any, concerns of indeterminate liability for products that can cause physical damage such as contaminated food, defective household appliances, and flammable clothing, even though all these products are significantly more common in our society than high-cost credit loans. Also, whilst the immediate harm caused by defective high-cost credit products is financial in nature, the consequences of these types of credit products can go significantly further than mere economic loss. StepChange highlights the harmful nature of high-cost credit products on children's development and family structure,[104] Shelter comments that it can contribute to homelessness and rough housing,[105] and research from the Glasgow Centre for Population Health states that these products are contributing to physical and mental health problems for the most vulnerable groups in our society.[106]

3.4. Examples of Freedom

This section sets out some examples of how negative freedom has been incorporated into the legal system. In the context of high-cost credit, negative freedom has resulted in a focus on procedural fairness between consumers and lenders.[107] The legal restrictions are aimed at addressing the process by which parties enter into the contract, and not on the underlying fairness of the resulting transaction.[108] There are two main aspects of procedural fairness; first, ensuring borrowers consent to the transaction[109] and second, preventing active coercion by lenders.

[102] See discussion in *Canadian National Railway v Norsk Pacific Steamship Co* [1992] 1 SCR 1021, (1992) 91 DLR (4th) 289, 383.

[103] See Beddows and McAteer, *Payday Lending* (n 97) for statistics on both.

[104] StepChange Debt Charity, 'Life on the Edge: Towards more Resilient Family Finances' (2014), available at www.stepchange.org/portals/0/stepchangelifeontheedgereport.pdf.

[105] See discussion in H Osborne, 'Millions Use Payday Loans to Cover the Mortgage and Rental Costs' The Guardian (4 January 2012), available at www.theguardian.com/money/2012/jan/04/payday-loans-cover-mortgage-costs?CMP=twt_gu.

[106] Glasgow Centre for Population Health, *Public Health Implications of Payday Lending* (Briefing Paper 48, 2016). For example, 'public health has a responsibility to recognise payday lending as a contemporary socioeconomic determinant of health and wellbeing': 16–17.

[107] Thal, 'The Inequality of Bargaining Power Doctrine: The Problem of Defining Contractual Unfairness' (n 23) 26. See discussion by Atiyah about the difficulties of separating the two concepts; Atiyah, 'Contract and Fair Exchange' (n 22) 5–6.

[108] See discussion in n 24 above.

[109] Barnett, 'A Consent Theory of Contract' (n 25) esp opening comments; Raz, *The Morality of Freedom* (n 14) 88; Hadfield, 'An Expressive Theory of Contract' (n 25); Schnuk, 'Rethinking Informed Consent' (n 25) 900.

The common law and the legislation relevant to high-cost credit have several provisions designed to ensure procedural fairness, including restrictions on who can lend money, disclosure obligations and advertising restrictions, cooling-off rights, the unfair relationship test, and vitiating factors. Each will be discussed in turn.[110]

3.4.1. Restrictions on Who Can Lend

In an attempt to prevent exploitation or coercion, the Consumer Credit Act 1974 (the Act) makes it an offence for a lender to enter into a consumer credit agreement[111] without a licence.[112] To obtain a licence, the creditor must make an application and satisfy the regulator that they are a 'fit person' to carry on a consumer credit business.[113] If the Office of Fair Trading (OFT) wanted to refuse a licence, it would need to provide reasons for the refusal and give the applicant an opportunity to provide supporting information for the application.[114] The requirement that all parties involved in consumer credit lending be licensed was recommended by the Crowther Report,[115] and is arguably its most significant contribution[116] (at least, in principle). The OFT published guidance on how it determined whether a person is 'fit' to obtain a licence.[117] The guidelines were disturbingly vague; they focused on the creditor's 'personal integrity'[118] and 'credit confidence' without providing adequate clarification of these requirements.[119] The guidelines also provided

[110] For an interesting perspective on these rights under the Consumer Credit Act 1974 (UK), see Atiyah, *Essays on Contract Law* (n 7) Essay 12, 361–63. Atiyah discusses how these provisions are in line with freedom of contract and 'the New Right'.

[111] Defined as 'an agreement between an individual ("the debtor") and any other person ("the creditor") by which the creditor provides the debtor with credit in any amount': Consumer Credit Act 1974 (UK) s 8(1).

[112] *ibid* s 21(1) and definition of 'consumer credit business' in s 189. The only exceptions to this are public authorities (s 21(2)) and 'A body corporate empowered by a public general Act naming it to carry on a business' (s 21(3)).

[113] *ibid* s 25(1); see also s 25(1B). To determine whether this criterion is satisfied, the regulator shall have regard to the skills, knowledge and experience of the applicant and other persons participating in the business, and any practices or procedures that the applicant proposes to implement in connection with the business; *ibid* s 25(2).

[114] *ibid* s 27.

[115] Sir Geoffrey Crowther, *Consumer Credit: Report of the Committee* (Department of Trade and Industry, 1971) 52–60. Named after Sir Geoffrey Crowther who, in 1968, was appointed Head of a Committee to analyse the consumer credit industry and to make recommendations for future reform (hereinafter referred to as the 'Crowther Report').

[116] This includes the provision of financial advice and debt management services, *ibid* Part 7.2.

[117] Consumer Credit Act 1974 (UK) s 25A. This obligation has now been passed to the Financial Conduct Authority (FCA).

[118] The Office of Fair Trading (OFT), *Consumer Credit Licensing: General Guidance for Licensees and Applicants on Fitness and Requirements* (2008) 3–4.

[119] *ibid* 6. The OFT denied licences to three debt management companies on the basis that the organisations 'lacked the necessary skills, knowledge and experience to operate a compliant consumer credit businesses' (OFT, 'OFT Refuses to Licence Three Debt Management Companies in Ongoing Drive to Push Up Standards', available at www.oft.gov.uk/news-and-updates/press/2013/13-13#.URj3H2fz6So).

'examples of the kind of evidence that may involve integrity issues' as opposed to a list of prohibited activities.[120] This can be contrasted with the stricter, more prescriptive requirements for determining whether a private landlord is a fit and proper person to be a licence-holder under the Housing Act 2004 (UK).[121]

There were significant concerns with the licensing system under the OFT, and evidence that it did not provide a sufficient safety net for borrowers. As an example of a potential oversight, Olivier Larholt was given a consumer credit licence despite the fact he had served 20 days in jail for possessing a flare pistol with intent to cause fear of violence.[122] Larholt went on to establish Toothfairy Finance, which continued to lend for a number of years despite numerous allegations of harassment,[123] being the subject of a dedicated Consumer Action Group fraud warning webpage,[124] and official action from the OFT to address its unsatisfactory business practices.[125]

The Public Accounts Committee (PAC) reviewed the OFT in May 2013 and was scathing of its regulation of the industry, particularly the regulator's lax licensing regime. It reported that

> The OFT told us that it *ran a 'licensing regime' rather than a 'supervisory regime'* meaning that it didn't look at the firms' activities regularly. Instead the OFT relied on information received from customer complaints and other third parties such as Citizen's Advice, the FSA and the Financial Ombudsman Service. Although it relied on others to supply it with intelligence the OFT claimed that it was also able to be proactive by picking up emerging themes from this information. However the OFT acknowledged that this approach was not picking up all the problems in the market. The OFT recognised that many people who had problems did not come forward to complain, and we were also concerned that many local Citizens Advice Bureaux did not have the resources to pick up all debt issues and look into debt problems so information they supplied would be incomplete.[126]

Between its inception in 1973 and transfer of the jurisdiction to the FCA in 2015, the OFT only revoked 25 licences, representing approximately 0.03 per cent of the 72,000 licences awarded.[127] In addition, firms were able to continue trading whilst being investigated and if they appealed the OFT decision against them.[128]

[120] OFT, *Consumer Credit Licensing* (n 118) 4.

[121] Helen Carr and others, *The Housing Act 2004: A Practical Guide* (Jordan Publishing Ltd, 2005) 88–89; see also Housing Act 2004 (UK) ss 88–89.

[122] Carl Packman, *Loan Sharks: The Rise and Rise of Payday Lending* (Searching Finance, 2012) 69.

[123] Carl Packman, 'OFT Writes to 240 Payday Lenders to Warn Them Over Poor Practices: The Legal Loan Sharks Have Been Cautioned' *The New Statesman* (21 November 2012), available at www.newstatesman.com/economics/2012/11/oft-writes-240-payday-lenders-warn-them-over-poor-practices.

[124] Consumer Action Law Group, 'Consumer Action Group Fraud Warning: Toothfairy Finance Limited' (2013), available at www.consumeractiongroup.co.uk/forum/forumdisplay.php?334-Toothfairy-Finance-Limited.

[125] OFT, 'OFT Acts to Improve Lending Practices' (Press Release, 9 November 2010), available at www.oft.gov.uk/news-and-updates/press/2010/116-10#.UjsIuj8ygmY.

[126] Public Accounts Committee (PAC), *8th Report – Regulating Consumer Credit* (2013) para 2.8.

[127] *ibid* para 2.9.

[128] *ibid* para 2.10.

The revocation process took up to two years, during which the firm continued to lend.[129] The licensing regime therefore provided limited assistance in avoiding exploitation, and allowed numerous unscrupulous lenders to continue operating.

The OFT had power to take action against lenders that breached their obligations under the 1974 Act. Lenders, however, had various rights to appeal against decisions made by the OFT regarding licences and the imposition of civil penalties. The 2006 Act included the creation of the Consumer Credit Appeals Tribunal,[130] which has jurisdiction over appeals from these OFT decisions. The system underwent significant changes when the Consumer Credit Appeals Tribunal was replaced with a First Tier Tribunal (Consumer Credit), which can be appealed to the Upper Tribunal.[131] The Crowther Report recognised the difficulties of enforcement through the court system. It did not, however, make any specific recommendations for the creation of a dedicated tribunal or any alternative dispute-resolution process.[132] The Tribunals were exceptionally under-utilised; between 2008 and 2013 a total of 59 cases were heard by the First Tier Tribunal (Consumer Credit), of which only four have been allowed in full or in part, the vast majority being dismissed, struck out or withdrawn by the licence-holder.[133] This is likely to be related to the OFT's resource difficulties discussed above, as there were so few decisions from which to appeal. The regulator's enforcement actions were limited to only the most heinous breaches, meaning that those businesses were unlikely to appeal the decision and even less likely to be successful on appeal. The under-utilisation of the Tribunal was likely a factor in its closure in 2013.

The authorisation regime under the FCA is significantly more proactive than the OFT's approach. The basic conditions of authorisation are found in the Financial Services and Markets Act 2000 (Threshold Conditions) Order 2013 (UK).[134] This sets out a range of 'threshold conditions' that firms must meet. These conditions involve a wide range of requirements, including locating an office in the UK,[135] undertaking activities and providing products that can be effectively supervised by the FCA,[136] ensuring that the business has adequate financial and non-financial resources,[137] and ensuring that the individual is a fit and proper person with adequate skills and experience.[138] These reflect the OFT's licensing

[129] *ibid* Recommendation 3.

[130] Consumer Credit Act 2006 (UK) ss 55–58; Consumer Credit Act 1974 (UK) Sch A1.

[131] The Transfer of Functions of the Consumer Credit Appeals Tribunal Order 2009 (UK).

[132] Crowther Report (n 115) see especially 303–307.

[133] HM Courts & Tribunals Service, 'First-tier Tribunal (Consumer Credit): Case Register as at 3rd June 2013' (2013), available at http://consumercreditappeals.decisions.tribunals.gov.uk/. The HM Courts & Tribunals Service does not appear to have released a Case Register since this time.

[134] This Order amends the Financial Services and Markets Act 2000 (UK) and came into effect on 1 April 2013.

[135] Financial Services and Markets Act 2000 (UK) Sch 6, Part 1B, r 2B.

[136] For further discussion, see FCA, *FCA Handbook, COND Threshold Conditions*, COND 2.3 'Effective Supervision'.

[137] Financial Services and Markets Act 2000 (UK) Sch 6, Part 1B, r 2D.

[138] *ibid* Sch 6, Part 1B, r 2E.

regime, but provide more detail on what is required by the firm and the individuals involved in lending. The FCA also states that the firms' 'business model (that is ... strategy for doing business) must be suitable for a person carrying on the regulated activities'.[139] Factors that the FCA will consider in determining whether the business model is suitable include whether the model is being conducted in a sound and prudent manner, the interests of consumers, and the integrity of the financial system.[140] The threshold conditions have also been incorporated into the FCA's Handbook.[141]

All firms licensed under the OFT were required to apply for authorisation under the FCA. Out of the 72,000 licences given by the OFT, only 19,533 applied to be authorised under the new regime by June 2015.[142] Out of these, 93.3 per cent were approved, 6.5 per cent were withdrawn (usually after requests for further information by the FCA), and 0.2 per cent were refused.[143] The numbers continued to grow and in 2021, there were 38,000 firms regulated by the FCA. Since the authorisation process was completed, the FCA has continued to be strongly proactive. In the first two years, the regulator revoked the authorisations of 40 consumer credit firms – compared with just 25 revoked by the OFT in approximately 40 years. In addition, over 1,400 firms have had their authorisation refused or have decided to withdraw their application.[144] The FCA is therefore taking a more rigorous approach to preventing active exploitation and ensuring procedural fairness.

3.4.2. Disclosure Obligations and Advertising Restrictions

Disclosure obligations and advertising restrictions aim to ensure the borrowers' informed consent to the transaction, and to prevent lenders targeting vulnerable consumers. Disclosure requirements are a keystone of the Act, and creditors have several obligations in this regard.[145] These include the provision

[139] *ibid* Sch 6, Part 1B, r 2F.

[140] *ibid* Sch 6, Part 1B, r 2F(2)(a)–(e).

[141] See FCA, *FCA Handbook, COND Threshold Conditions* (n 136) COND 2.1.

[142] These statistics are the latest available as at 9 August 2016. It is likely that a small number of firms have sought authorisation since June 2015. If firms do not seek authorisation under the FCA, they are excluded from lending; thus the authorisation process has resulted in a significant reduction in the number of licensed firms.

[143] FCA, *Consumer Credit: Authorisations Data Bulletin* (June 2015) 7.

[144] Tracey McDermott, 'Consumer Credit Regulation: The Journey So Far' (Speech Delivered at the Credit Summit 2016 on 7 April 2016).

[145] The disclosure requirements largely follow the Crowther Report recommendations. The Report outlined a number of basic principles that should be observed when prescribing the formalities of a consumer credit contract, including that: (a) any requirements should be easy to understand and comply with, (b) relevant information should be made prominent, and (c) the sanctions when lenders breach these formalities should be tailored to the gravity of the offence. The Report also provided specific details about what should be included in different types of loan agreements; it explicitly made reference to the disclosure of the interest rate and recommended that the 'debtor should be told the

of adequate pre-contractual explanations of important terms[146] and a copy of the consumer credit agreement.[147] This area is further regulated by the Consumer Credit (Disclosure of Information) Regulations 2010 (UK).[148] When oversight of consumer credit was transferred to the FCA, the regulator increased disclosure obligations, including requiring a financial warning to be included in advertisements[149] and requiring lenders to provide borrowers who rollover a loan with an information sheet including how to access free debt advice.[150] This sheet is, however, provided to the borrower after the rollover has occurred, thereby limiting the opportunity for it to inform the borrower's decisions. In the light of economic and psychological evidence on the impact of bounded rationality and cognitive bias, the protective potential of consumer disclosure and the impact it has on the decision-making abilities of consumers, without further regulatory action, this approach is subject to significant and valid criticism.[151] Despite this, the FCA has continued to focus on increasing borrowers' awareness[152] as a way of preventing exploitative lending. For example, in its 2018 *Review of High-Cost Credit*, the regulator recommended further contractual disclosure for 'Buy Now Pay Later' products.[153]

Procedural fairness requires all communications and advertisements to be fair, clear and not misleading. The Act gives power to the Secretary of State to make regulations on the form and content of advertisements for consumer credit products.[154] The resulting Regulations, produced in 1989, 2004 and 2010,

cost of borrowing in terms of a rate per cent per annum'; Crowther Report (n 115) 271. It was however despondently noted that this may not have much influence on consumer actions, particularly on borrowers in lower income brackets, *ibid* 272.

146 Consumer Credit Act 1974 (UK) s 55A.

147 *ibid* s 55C.

148 See specifically, Consumer Credit (Disclosure of Information) Regulations 2010 (UK) Sch 1, created under Consumer Credit Act 1974 (UK) s 55.

149 FCA, *FCA Handbook, Consumer Credit Sourcebook (CONC)*, para 3.4.

150 *ibid* 6.7.20. See also HM Treasury and Department of Business Innovation and Skills, *A New Approach to Financial Regulation: Transferring Consumer Credit Regulation to the Financial Conduct Authority* (2013) 54.

151 Bix, 'Contracts' (n 67) 265–66.

152 FCA, *Detailed Proposals for the FCA Regime for Consumer Credit* (Consultation Paper CP13/10, 2013) 175.

153 FCA, *High-Cost Credit Review: Feedback on CP18/12 with Final Rules and Guidance and Consultation on Buy Now Pay Later Offers* (December 2018) paras 4.18–4.20. Interestingly enough, the regulator has emphasised the limitations of disclosure stating that 'We are unable to predict the impact of this disclosure without trialling it. We therefore use a wide range for our assumptions about the proportion of consumers that respond to the proposed disclosure': para 21.

154 Consumer Credit Act 1974 (UK) s 44. The protection given to borrowers prior to entering into contracts is strongly in line with the suggestions of the Crowther Report. The Report recognised the importance of providing borrowers with protection against unfair practices before they enter into contracts with potential creditors; Crowther Report (n 115) Part 6.4. This includes making it an offence to issue advertisements of consumer credit products that are false or misleading (*ibid* 259) and requiring that relevant financial information (including, but not limited to, the overall cost and effective interest rate of the credit) be published in advertisements (*ibid* 260).

provide detailed rules on the general form of advertisements,[155] as well as specific information about the disclosure of the total cost of credit.[156] The Advertising Standards Authority (ASA) has been active in preventing the publication of potentially misleading high-cost credit advertisements. It upheld a number of complaints about advertising, including text messages sent to customers encouraging borrowing to fund social activities,[157] on-screen advertisements that did not display APRs and other required information[158] or did not display it prominently enough,[159] and on-screen text that was not legible.[160] The ASA upheld a number of complaints made against Cash Lady regarding its 'fast cash for fast lives' advertisements using Kerry Katona, a celebrity famous partly because of her widely-publicised financial difficulties and subsequent bankruptcy.[161] The advertisement was found to be irresponsible as it encouraged people in similar situations to Ms Katona to borrow money from high-cost credit lenders,[162] and the lender advertised itself as a legitimate alternative to banks, despite charging interest of over 2,000 per cent APR.[163] It also held that the phrase 'fast cash for fast lives' may give the impression that high-cost loans are not a financial commitment that required consideration and planning.[164] Under the FCA, the ASA continued to ban high-cost credit advertisements in breach of the relevant guidelines.[165] This included an action against Pounds to Pocket for an advertisement encouraging people to borrow high-cost credit to fund birthday celebrations, and giving a discount for people who applied for loans over £2,000.[166]

The Consumer Credit (Advertisements) Regulations 2010 were repealed when the oversight of consumer credit was transferred to the FCA. This area is now regulated by the Consumer Credit Sourcebook (CONC). Under these rules, all lenders must ensure that communications are clear, fair and not misleading.[167] The

[155] Consumer Credit (Advertisements) Regulations 1989 (UK) reg 2; Consumer Credit (Advertisements) Regulations 2004 (UK) reg 3; Consumer Credit (Advertisements) Regulations 2010 (UK) reg 3.

[156] Consumer Credit (Advertisements) Regulations 1989 (UK) Sch 3; Consumer Credit (Advertisements) Regulations 2004 (UK) Sch 2; Consumer Credit (Advertisements) Regulations 2010 (UK) Sch 1.

[157] Advertising Standards Authority (ASA), *ASA Adjudication on First Financial (UK) Ltd* (19 June 2013).

[158] ASA, *ASA Adjudication on CashEuroNet UK LLC* (7 October 2009).

[159] ASA, *ASA Adjudication on CashEuroNet UK LLC* (31 July 2013).

[160] ASA, *ASA Adjudication on SRC Transatlantic Ltd* (11 September 2013).

[161] Jessica Winch, 'Kerry Katona Payday Loan Advert Banned' *The Telegraph* (8 May 2013), available at www.telegraph.co.uk/finance/personalfinance/borrowing/10041767/Kerry-Katona-payday-loan-advert-banned.html.

[162] ASA, *ASA Adjudication on PDB UK Ltd* (31 July 2013).

[163] ASA, *ASA Adjudication on PDB UK Ltd* (8 May 2013).

[164] ASA, *ASA Adjudication on PDB UK Ltd* (n 162). On the other hand, the ASA has also upheld a complaint from Provident (the largest doorstep lender in the UK) against a credit union for sending out printed flyers labelling doorstep lenders as 'loan sharks who charge extortionate levels of interest': ASA, *ASA Adjudication on Stevenage Homes* (13 April 2011)).

[165] It continued to consider complaints received prior to 1 April 2014.

[166] ASA, *ASA Ruling on CashEuroNet UK LLC* (n 158).

[167] FCA, *CONC* (n 149), *Financial promotions and communications with customers*, para 3.3.1(1).

FCA expects firms to comply with the Consumer Protection from Unfair Trading Regulations 2008 (UK), which make it an offence to engage in unfair practices, including misleading actions.[168] In addition, all communications must:

- be balanced and, in particular, not emphasise any potential benefits of a product or service without also giving a fair and prominent indication of any relevant risks;
- be sufficient for, and presented in a way that is likely to be understood by, the average member of the group to which it is directed, or by which it is likely to be received; and
- not disguise, omit, diminish or obscure important information, statements or warnings.[169]

The FCA has been proactive regarding the advertising of high-cost credit, reviewing 500 different advertisements and commencing 108 cases against lenders within seven weeks of becoming the regulator.[170] Of the cases commenced, 75 firms agreed to withdraw or amend the offending advertising.[171] These actions highlight the ongoing attempts to ensure procedural fairness in high-cost credit transactions by limiting exploitative and potentially misleading advertisements.

Despite the ASA and FCA activity, advertising by high-cost lenders is still a significant concern, particularly when aimed at vulnerable low-income borrowers.[172] What was particularly concerning was that C2DE ('working class') adults were being exposed to nearly double the number of advertisements for high-cost credit as ABC1 ('middle class') adults.[173] A 2013 study by Ofcom on the advertising of high-cost credit reported that almost 400,000 high-cost credit advertisements were shown annually.[174] Adults are watching on average 152 advertisements a year, and children between 70 and 84 (depending on the age group),[175] including some advertisements being shown during programmes specifically designed for children.[176]

[168] Consumer Protection from Unfair Trading Regulations 2008 (UK), see esp regs 3–5. The Act also makes it an offence to 'canvass debtor-creditor agreements off trade premises' (Consumer Credit Act 1974, s 49(1)) unless in response to a written request from the borrower (Consumer Credit Act 1974, s 49(2)).

[169] FCA, *CONC* (n 149) para 3.3.1A(c)–(e).

[170] This included 38 cases against payday lenders, 19 cases against other unsecured lenders, five against home-collected credit and four against pawnbrokers: FCA, *Consumer Credit Firms Must Raise Advertising Standards, Says FCA* (2014).

[171] *ibid.*

[172] Department of Business Innovation and Skills, *Making Consumer Credit Markets Fairer: Payday Lending Advertising Research Conducted for BIS by Ipsos MORI Social Research Institute* (2013) 9–10, 42–46.

[173] Ofcom, *Trends in Advertising Activity – Payday Loans* (2013) 16. These classes are developed from Office of National Statistics; C2DE adults are generally categorised as 'working class' and ABC1 are 'middle class': see discussion in James Dobson, *Measuring Social Class* (Bright Blue, 2016).

[174] Ofcom, *ibid* 4.

[175] *ibid* 4.

[176] *ibid* 19.

3.4.3. Cooling-Off Rights

The cooling-off rights under the Consumer Credit Act allow consumers an opportunity to change their mind. They aim to ensure borrowers have properly consented to the credit contract. The Act gives consumers who change their minds after entering into certain consumer credit agreements the right to cancel the contract within 14 days,[177] and requires lenders to inform borrowers of this cancellation right. This was designed to curb abusive or aggressive sales tactics, and to ensure consumers consent to the transaction.[178] Whilst these provisions have the potential to provide an escape route for consumers who experience 'borrowers' remorse', consumers must be aware of their rights and therefore have read and understood the information provided to them. More importantly, the speed and convenience of high-cost loans means that the funds are provided and most likely spent before the consumer has had the opportunity to consider exercising their cancellation rights, strongly undermining the effectiveness of this regulatory provision.

3.4.4. Unfair Relationship Test

A further mechanism to ensure procedural fairness is the 'unfair relationship test'.[179] This gives consumers the right to take direct action against lenders, and allows the court to look at the general relationship between the lender and borrower, including 'any other thing done (or not done) by, or on behalf of, the creditor'.[180] Whilst there is no specific reference to responsible lending in the legislation, it was explicitly stated that the duty to lend responsibly was included in the unfair relationship test.[181] Ramsay observed that the broad scope of the unfair relationship test gave it the potential to be used as an effective private law

[177] Consumer Credit Act 1974 (UK) ss 66A. This section was inserted by Directive 2011/83/EU of the European Parliament and of the Council of 25 October 2011 on consumer rights, amending Council Directive 93/13/EEC and Directive 1999/44/EC of the European Parliament and of the Council and repealing Council Directive 85/577/EEC and Directive 97/7/EC of the European Parliament and of the Council [2011] OJ L304/64. See also Consumer Credit Act 1974 (UK) ss 67 and 69–73.

[178] Consumer Credit Act 1974 (UK) s 64(1). In addition, there is a five-day cooling-off period for contracts entered into off trade premises: *ibid* ss 63 and 68. The borrower obligations associated with the cancellation right and cooling-off period are slightly different, see *ibid* ss 67–68. This post-contractual protection largely reflected the Crowther Report recommendation that if a consumer credit agreement is entered into other than at an appropriate trade premises, consumers should have the right to cancel the agreement even if there is a binding contract (Crowther Report (n 115) 289). The Committee also recognised that many consumers would have difficulties writing 'even the simplest letter', and therefore recommended that in these circumstances lenders be required to provide the debtor with a cancellation slip that could simply be signed and posted.

[179] *ibid* s 140A as implemented by the Consumer Credit Act 2006.

[180] Consumer Credit Act 1974 (UK) s 140A(1)(c).

[181] Parliamentary Under-Secretary of State for Trade and Industry Responding to suggested amendments in Grand Committee (8 November 2005); HL Deb 8 November 2005, vol 675, cols GC160–GC162.

method to respond to irresponsible lending activities.[182] This could be an effective approach to regulation of the market, as it will allow the courts to set definite limits on what is acceptable and unacceptable lender behaviour.

There has been limited judicial consideration of the scope of the protection afforded by the unfair relationship test. It therefore remains unclear how the courts will approach the interpretation of the test and its connection with responsible lending obligations or substantive unfairness issues. The Court of Appeal analysed the unfair relationship test in *Harrison v Black Horse Ltd*.[183] It applied the test narrowly, holding that a relationship will not be 'unfair' unless the lender has breached a legal duty. This case did not refer to responsible lending obligations, and in fact stated that the wording of the legislative provision 'offers no guidance in respect of the factors which either may or must be regarded as rendering the relationship unfair'.[184] The outcome of *Harrison* was effectively overruled in the Supreme Court case of *Pelvin v Paragon Personal Finance Ltd*,[185] which held that a relationship can be unfair without the creditor breaching a legal duty. *Pelvin* considered the application of the unfair relationship test in relation to a credit agreement where the lender obtained a large commission from the sale of Personal Protection Insurance (PPI), and therefore did not consider issues related to irresponsible lending.[186] The case did, however, increase the scope and role of the unfair relationship test, which will be a positive outcome if a high-cost credit or irresponsible lending case is brought before the courts.

The cases referring to the unfair relationship test have largely related to procedural issues, and therefore continued the focus on negative freedom.[187] The direction of the court in these matters has included the right to amend pleadings to introduce a claim of an unfair relationship,[188] and an application to appeal against forfeiture out of time on the grounds that the credit was obtained through an unfair relationship.[189] There has been a handful of cases considering the scope of the test. An unfair relationship was not found in *Shaw v Nine Regions*[190] in the context of a £3,000 loan at 119.16 per cent APR for 36 months, which created total repayments of £13,724.88. This was on the basis that the borrower, despite having bad financial judgement, was considered a 'sophisticated, articulate and intelligent man'.[191]

[182] Iain Ramsay, *Consumer Law and Policy* (Bloomsbury, 2012) 440.
[183] *Harrison v Black Horse* Ltd [2011] EWCA Civ 1128, [2012] Lloyd's Rep IR 521.
[184] Lord Justice Tomlinson in *ibid* [38].
[185] *Pelvin v Paragon Finance Ltd* [2017] UKSC 23, [2018] 1 All ER 292.
[186] Lord Sumption did however mention responsible lending obligations when discussing voluntary codes of conduct; *ibid* [36].
[187] The Queen's Bench has considered the unfair relationship test in the context of a credit card agreement and held that a breach of the Consumer Credit Act 1974 (UK) s 78(1) (duty to give information to debtor under running-account credit agreement) does not on its own give rise to an unfair relationship: *Carey v HSBC Bank Plc* [2009] EWHC 3417 (QB).
[188] *Barnes v Black Horse Ltd* [2011] EWHC 1416 (QB), [2011] 2 All ER (Comm) 1130.
[189] *Barons Finance Ltd v Makanju* [2013] EWHC 153 (QB), [2013] All ER (D) 87 (Feb).
[190] *Robert Shaw v Nine Regions* [2009] EWHC 3553 (QB).
[191] *ibid* [29].

In contrast, an unfair relationship was held to exist in *Morrison v Betterplace Ltd (t/a Log Book Loans)*.[192] In this case two loans of £1,500 were entered into, one at 343.4 per cent APR with Mr Morrison and the second one approximately two and a half years later at 485.25 per cent APR, but this time with Mrs Morrison. Both were repayable over 58 weeks. The judge held that the second loan was out of the ordinary as Mrs Morrison was essentially taking over responsibilities of the first loan, but at a significantly higher rate. His Honour therefore varied the rate of the second loan to that of the first. He also held that sending multiple default letters each month at a cost of £12 per letter was unfair, and limited this to one letter per month. The judge did not directly consider whether 485.25 per cent APR was unfair and did not make a finding on this point.

An unfair relationship was also held to exist in *Patel v Patel*, where a number of loans totalling £56,450 between two friends had snowballed after 30 years into over £6 million owed, despite the borrower making repayments totalling £72,336. The unfair relationship was found for a variety of reasons, including the parties' personal relationship, a lack of any written terms of the loans, the borrower not being provided with a copy of the agreements, repayment sums only being made on request of the creditor, and a lack of account information provided to the borrower.[193]

There have been later cases emphasising that the wording of the tests allows the courts to look at the 'whole relationship'[194] and stating that 'the reference to "including" is important in ensuring that the court's enquiry is not foreclosed and limited only to matters directly attributable (in the strict legal sense) to one party or the other to the transaction'.[195] Despite the disturbing practices in the cases on unfair relationships and the broadness of the test, the courts have not focused on whether the lender's actions breached responsible lending obligations, or any substantive unfairness issues. In *Bank of Beirut (UK) Ltd v Moukarzel*, the borrower's allegation that the bank failed to undertake an adequate investigation of his creditworthiness was not sufficient, on the basis that he was already indebted to the bank as a third party's personal guarantor.[196] The exact meaning of 'unfair relationship' remains unclear, as does its relationship to responsible lending; further clarification from the courts is urgently required. It does show that the courts have largely focused on procedural aspects of contract, the law intervenes when there are issues with how the contract was entered into and not when there was substantive unfairness. The test, as currently applied, therefore continues the freedom-based approach to high-cost credit.

[192] *Morrison v Betterplace Ltd (t/a Log Book Loans)* 1 September 2009 (County Court at Lowestoft).
[193] *Patel v Patel* [2009] EWHC 3264 (QB), [2010] 1 All ER (Comm) 864.
[194] *Doran and Doran v Paragon Personal Finance Ltd* [2018] GCCR 16077 at [60].
[195] *Pilgrim Rock Ltd v Iwaniuk* [2019] EWHC 203 (Ch) at [75].
[196] *Bank of Beirut (UK) Ltd v Moukarzel* [2021] 10 WLUK 210.

3.4.5. Vitiating Factors

Several common law and equitable doctrines can potentially protect the procedural fairness of high-cost credit contracts. These include misrepresentation and non-disclosure, incapacity, mistake of fact, duress, unfairness, undue influence and unconscionable bargains.[197] Whilst a detailed analysis of the nature of vitiating factors is clearly beyond the scope of this book,[198] their focus on ensuring valid consent and avoiding coercion and exploitation of the vulnerable provide potential protection for high-cost credit borrowers. The specific circumstances of these financial products however mean that vitiating factors provide limited assistance. As an example, economic duress is unlikely to provide any sort of protection for users of high-cost credit. As the UK Supreme Court has taken a restrictive approach to lawful act duress in *Times Travel v Pakistan International Airline Corporation*,[199] the borrower would need to show either an unlawful threat or exceptionally reprehensible conduct for the contract to be rescinded on the grounds of duress.[200]

The major advantages of high-cost credit are the speed and convenience of the transaction,[201] with some lenders advertising that the 'money will be in your bank within 15 minutes',[202] 'no credit checks',[203] and 'get a loan with just two simple texts'.[204] These types of limited processes open the door for potential issues of misrepresentation and non-disclosure, capacity, and mistakes of fact. In addition, many borrowers are vulnerable to exploitation due to their desperate situations, and so the common law vitiating factors of undue influence and unconscionable bargains may assist these consumers.[205] These vitiating factors require personal dealings between the parties, so would generally only be of assistance to borrowers who have taken loans out in person, and provide limited use for the majority who use the online process.

One doctrine that could be particularly relevant is unconscionability. This, however, generally requires a specifically identifiable characteristic or 'disadvantage'

[197] For more information, see Edwin Peel and G.H. Treitel, *The Law of Contract*, 13th edn (Sweet & Maxwell, 2011), chs 8–10, 12; Mindy Chen-Wishart, *Contract Law*, 7th edn (Oxford University Press, 2022) chs 5, 7–9; Hugh Beale and Joseph Chitty, *Chitty on Contracts*, 34th edn (Sweet & Maxwell, 2021) chs 5–8.

[198] For very insightful analysis of these issues, see Chen-Wishart, 'The Nature of Vitiating Factors in Contract' (n 24).

[199] *Times Travel v Pakistan International Airline Corporation* [2021] UKSC 40.

[200] For further analysis, see Iona Branford and Jodi Gardner, '"Cause I Gotta" Have (Bad) Faith: *Times Travel v Pakistan International Airlines Corporation*' [2022] LMCLQ 64–69.

[201] This was one of the major findings in Competition & Markets Authority (CMA), *Research into the Payday Lending Market* (2014).

[202] Mobile Quid, 'Quick 'n Easy Cash', available at https://mobilequid.com/.

[203] Cobra Payday Loan, 'Apply Now', available at www.cobrapaydayloans.co.uk/small-loans/no-credit-check/.

[204] Toothfairy Finance, 'Fast Track: Instant Money' (2013), available at www.toothfairyfinance.com/.

[205] For a discussion of the vulnerability of payday borrowers, see Jeannie Marie Paterson and Gerard Brody, '"Safety Net" Consumer Protection: Using Prohibitions on Unfair and Unconscionable Conduct to Respond to Predatory Business Models' (2015) 38 *Journal of Consumer Policy* 331.

such as a disability, having English as a second language, or literacy problems.[206] The protection provided by this doctrine was stretched to include lower income and less educated parties in *Cresswell v Potter*, which may benefit borrowers of high-cost credit.[207] Despite this extension to the notion of 'disadvantage', financial difficulties in and of themselves remain insufficient to warrant legal protection through the doctrine of unconscionability. In Lord Templeman's words, 'unequal bargaining power [without further abuse] … provide[s] no basis for equitable interference'.[208]

The Canadian Supreme Court's approach in *Heller v Uber Technology*[209] provides some potential protection for borrowers of high-cost credit. In this case, the majority emphasised both inequality of bargaining power and substantial unfairness as a basis for severing an Arbitration Clause in Uber's downloaded Terms and Conditions with its drivers. There is the potential for an analogy to be drawn between this case and, in particular online, high-cost credit contracts. They both involve potentially substantively unfair terms entered into on the basis of standard form contracts with people in financial need.[210] *Heller v Uber Technology*, whilst providing some potential protection for borrowers, has received significant criticism for inappropriately expanding the notions of unconscionability and potentially creating 'a standard so malleable that it may, in certain contexts, be virtually meaningless'.[211]

Further, the use of any general law doctrine is dependent on the consumer obtaining access to expensive court processes and remedies, meaning the doctrines are under-utilised. Therefore, the ability of vitiating factors to provide meaningful assistance to high-cost credit borrowers is clearly limited. To conclude this section, the English approach to credit regulation has largely focused on negative freedom – avoiding intervention where possible and, when it was required, emphasising procedural over substantive fairness.

3.5. Limitations of Freedom

The range of potential explanations for the focus on freedom and limiting intervention in the high-cost credit market to matters of procedural fairness has been

[206] *Boustany v Pigott* (1993) 69 P & CR 298 (PC); *Commercial Bank of Australia v Amadio* (1983) 151 CLR 447 (HCA).

[207] *Cresswell v Potter* [1978] 1 WLR 255 (Ch D).

[208] *Boustany v Pigott* (1993) 69 P & CR 298 (PC), 303. See also Mindy Chen-Wishart, 'Undue Influence: Beyond Impaired Consent and Wrongdoing towards a Relational Analysis' in Burrows and Rodger (eds), *Mapping the Law: Essays in Memory of Peter Birks* (Oxford University Press, 2006) 203.

[209] *Heller v Uber Technology* 2020 SCC 16.

[210] For further analysis, see Jodi Gardner, 'Being Conscious of Unconscionability in Modern Times: *Heller v Uber Technologies*' (2021) 84 *The Modern Law Review* 874.

[211] Chris Hunt, 'Unconscionability in the Supreme Court of Canada: *Uber Technologies Inc v Heller*' (2021) 80 *Cambridge Law Journal* 25, 28.

discussed. None of these have been adequate, they are necessary but not sufficient. There is an innate value in consumer choice and freedom of contractual affairs. We need to go beyond a lack of justification and consider whether the negative freedom approach *creates* any problems. This section will therefore discuss three concrete limitations of freedom – the failure of disclosure, lack of consumer choice, and impact of poverty.

3.5.1. Failure of Disclosure

As previously discussed, disclosure is one of the key aspects of procedural fairness.[212] It is easy to over-estimate the effectiveness of mandatory disclosure.[213] The Crowther Report recognised the limited impact of such disclosure on the decision-making of low-income borrowers,[214] and this is supported by a large body of academic literature.[215] For disclosure to be an effective form of consumer protection, borrowers have to: (a) read the material disclosed, (b) understand the information provided, and (c) respond to the information in a rational way.[216] Unfortunately 'humans can be short-sighted, impulsive, inert and optimistic',[217] and a large number of consumers do not undertake these steps, act in a rational manner, or have financial options.[218] In addition, many borrowers of high-cost credit often have limited financial choices but urgent financial

[212] *Baker v Canada* [1999] 2 SCR 817 (SCC); In the context of administrative decisions, see Kristina Stern, 'Procedural Fairness – Its Scope and Practical Obligation' (2008) 56 *AIAL Forum* 2.

[213] See the comprehensive critique of the impact of mandatory disclosure in Omri Ben-Shahar and Carl E Scheider, 'The Failure of Mandated Disclosure' (2011) 159 *University of Pennsylvania Law Review* 647, esp 665–67.

[214] Crowther Report (n 115) 272.

[215] See further, Amartya Sen, 'Rational Fools: A Critique of the Behavioral Foundations of Economic Theory' (1977) 6 *Philosophy & Public Affairs* 317; Hillel Einhorn and Robin Hogarth, 'Behavioural Decision Theory: Processes of Judgment and Choice' (1981) 19 *Journal of Accounting Research* 1; Gordon Foxall, 'A Behaviouralist Perspective on Purchase and Consumption' (1993) 27 *European Journal of Marketing* 8; Justin Malbon, 'Shopping for Credit: An Empirical Study of Consumer Decision-Making' (2001) 29 *Australian Business Law Review* 44; Wim Dubbink, *Assisting the Invisible Hand: Contested Relations Between Market, State and Civil Society* (Kluwer Academic Publishers, 2003); Larry DiMatteo and others, *Visions of Contract Theory: Rationality Bargaining and Interpretation* (Carolina Academic Press, 2007); Richard Wiener and others, 'Consumer Credit Card Use: The Roles of Creditor Disclosure and Anticipated Emotion' (2007) 13 *Journal of Experimental Psychology* 32; Ren Essene and William Apgar, *Understanding Mortgage Market Behaviour: Creating Good Mortgage Options for All Americans* (Joint Centre for Housing Studies, Harvard University, 2007); Karen Francis, 'Rollover, Rollover: A Behavioral Law and Economics Analysis of the Payday-Loan Industry' (2010) 88 *Texas Law Review* 611; Ronald Mann, 'Nudging from Debt: The Role of Behavioral Economics in Regulation' [2011] *The Lydian Payments Journal* www.pymnts.com/assets/Lydian_Journal/LydianJournalFebLawReg.pdf.

[216] Hadfield, 'An Expressive Theory of Contract' (n 25) 1247.

[217] David Evans, 'The Behavioral Economics of Paying and Borrowing' [2010] *The Lydian Payments Journal*, available at http://pymnts.com/assets/Lydian_Journal/LydianJournalJanuaryEconomics.pdf.

[218] Richard Thaler, 'Toward a Positive Theory of Consumer Choice' (1980) 1 *Journal of Economic Behaviour and Organisation* 39.

needs, meaning that this approach will have a minimal impact on their lending decisions.[219]

Disclosure will only be effective if the consumer can adequately understand the contractual obligations into which they enter. Financial education and awareness is a significant concern for high-cost credit users, and can significantly undermine the effectiveness of disclosure. As outlined by Raz,

> Autonomy is opposed to a life of coerced choices. It contrasts with a life of no choices, or of drifting through life without ever exercising one's capacity to choose. Evidently the autonomous life calls for a certain degree of self-awareness. To choose *one must be aware of one's options ... he must be capable of understanding how various choices will have a considerable and lasting impact on his life.*[220]

Clearly, not all high-cost credit borrowers are impacted by a lack of financial awareness. Research shows that many borrowers make financially responsible decisions,[221] and use this type of financial product because it is the best option available to them.[222] To some extent this validates the imposition of disclosure requirements on lenders, although they are insufficient. There is still a significant group of people whose inability to fully understand the operation of high-cost credit leaves them open to exploitation,[223] and challenges the value of disclosure.[224] Even if they understand the agreement, unless they have financial options, they are unable to utilise the information to make more appropriate choices. The high-cost credit industry was referred to the Competition & Markets Authority (CMA)

[219] Marianne Bertrand and Adair Morse, *Information Disclosure, Cognitive Biases and Payday Borrowing* (Chicago Booth Research Paper No 10-01, 2009). Because of this, Plymouth Council went a step further and banned lenders from advertising on billboards and bus stops, as well as blocking the 50 most popular high-cost credit websites on all council computer networks, including libraries and schools; Steven Morris, 'Plymouth Council becomes First to Ban Payday Loan Ads on Billboards' *The Guardian* (23 July 2013), available at www.theguardian.com/uk-news/2013/jul/23/plymouth-council-bans-payday-loans.

[220] Raz, *The Morality of Freedom* (n 14) 15 (emphasis added).

[221] See, eg, discussion in Maud Pember Reeves and Charlotte Wilson, *Round About A Pound A Week* (G Bell & Sons, 1913 (reprinted in 1994 by Virago Books)) and again Sendhil Mullainathan and Eldar Shafir, *Scarcity: Why Having Too Little Means So Much* (Allen Lane, 2013). Amazingly, these books were originally published exactly 100 years apart – highlighting the importance of understanding the historical aspect to these challenges.

[222] Karen Rowlingson, Lindsey Appleyard and Jodi Gardner, 'Payday Lending in the UK: The Regul(aris)ation of a Necessary Evil?' (2016) 45 *Journal of Social Policy* 527, 530.

[223] OFT, *Payday Lending Compliance Review – Interim Report* (OFT, 2012); Citizens Advice Bureau, 'Citizens Advice Urges Payday Loan Customers to Fight Back against Unscrupulous Lenders' (Citizens Advice Bureau, 5 August 2013), available at www.citizensadvice.org.uk/index/pressoffice/press_index/press_office-20130805.htm; Europe Economics, *A New Consumer Credit Regime: Benefits, Compliance Costs and Firm Behaviour* (2013).

[224] See FCA, *Consumer Credit and Consumers in Vulnerable Circumstances* (2014). This lack of understanding is part of the wider phenomenon of information asymmetry that exists with consumer transactions and standard form contracts; Mindy Chen-Wishart, 'Regulating Unfair Terms' in Gullifer and Vogenaur (eds), *English and European Perspectives on Contract and Commercial Law: Essays in Honour of Hugh Beale* (Hart Publishing, 2015) and Margaret Radin, *Boilerplate: The Fine Print, Vanishing Rights, and the Rule of Law* (Princeton University Press, 2012).

for review in 2013.[225] A 20-month long investigation found that the industry was not working adequately, the key issue being that borrowers were focused more on the speed and ease of getting credit and not on the interest, fees and charges that may be incurred.[226] The law must therefore go beyond disclosure when trying to respond to these challenges.

Individuals can be denied the opportunity to live an autonomous life through the working of social institutions, without any active overriding or violation of their rights.[227] This is particularly obvious in the way in which high-cost credit contracts are trivialised in advertisements (in that they are portrayed as minor or unimportant decisions), and are aimed at particularly vulnerable audiences.[228] Entering into a high-cost credit contract gives the borrower immediate gratification, pushing their financial problems to another day. This type of advertising takes advantage of the lack of understanding and financial awareness of many high-cost credit borrowers. Such advertising makes getting a high-cost credit loan seem like a very simple, straight-forward exercise as opposed to a serious financial commitment, and thus can prey on people in desperate times. The extent of advertising is also a serious concern. In 2011 Wonga spent £16 million on television advertising alone, approximately £1 million more than the entire annual budget of the OFT.[229] These challenges undermine the benefits of disclosure obligations and highlight the need to focus beyond procedure to issues of substantive fairness.

3.5.2. Lack of Meaningful Choice

The second limitation is the lack of meaningful choice available for consumers. To validly consent to a contractual arrangement, the promisee must have a genuine choice whether or not to enter into the agreement. Raz believed that having a range of acceptable options is of intrinsic value and is a requirement to live an autonomous life.[230] A similar approach exists in the analysis of market intervention. There is a widely held belief that strong competition can correct existing market failings, and therefore benefit consumers.[231] As a result, consumer protection

[225] FCA, *Detailed Proposals for the FCA Regime for Consumer Credit* (n 152) 53.

[226] See discussion in CMA, *Payday Lending Market Investigation: Provisional Findings Report* (2014) especially paras 12–20.

[227] Raz, *The Morality of Freedom* (n 14) 247.

[228] Committee of Advertising Practice, *Trivialisation in Short-Term, High-Cost Credit Ads* (2015); Ofcom, *Trends in Advertising Activity* (n 173); Broadcasting Committee of Advertising, *BCAP Payday Loans Consultation Regulatory Statement* (2015).

[229] Amelia Gentleman, 'Wonga: The Real Cost of a Payday Loan' *The Guardian* (1 March 2012), available at www.theguardian.com/business/2012/mar/01/wonga-real-cost-payday-loan.

[230] Raz, *The Morality of Freedom* (n 14) 205.

[231] Joshua Gans, 'Protecting Consumers by Protecting Competition: Does Behavioural Economics Support this Contention?' (2005) 13 *Competition and Consumer Law Journal* 1; Department of Trade and Industry, *A Fair Deal for All – Extending Competitive Markets: Empowered Consumers, Successful Businesses* (2005).

regimes, particularly those related to the provision of consumer credit, have largely focused on increasing competition in the marketplace.[232] True competition creates a choice of *suppliers* and a choice of *products*. The high-cost credit market is lacking in both aspects.[233] The absence of effective competition and adequate consumer options allows lenders to charge customers more than they would in an adequately competitive market, adding between £5 and £10 to the average cost of a loan.[234] Freedom implicitly assumes that people have a range of meaningful choices from which to pick. In high-cost credit, borrowers often have limited options,[235] and in these situations, procedural fairness is unlikely to produce a useful or fair result.

Borrowers of high-cost credit products generally have little choice of financial products. The majority of consumers are using these high-cost products because they have an impaired credit history, and therefore limited access to mainstream products.[236] The CMA review found that four out of every ten high-cost credit borrowers had no access to alternative financial products.[237] Due in large part to government austerity measures, there is currently insufficient access to alternative financial products, including Community Development Financial Institutions (CDFIs) and Credit Union products, both of which provide affordable and safe credit to borrowers who are financially marginalised or on low incomes. The government-run Social Fund – widely considered the lender of last resort – has been dismantled and replaced with *ad hoc* council-based schemes.[238] Because of this lack of choice and competition, borrowers who use high-cost credit products are more likely to accept a (fully disclosed) loan that may be detrimental to them in the long run, such as one with extremely high interest rates, financial repayments that they will be unable to meet without substantial hardship, or high default fees and charges.[239]

The current state of the high-cost credit market highlights that a narrow concept of freedom is not appropriate, and often results in extreme consumer detriment. Atiyah contends that despite the emphasis on individual free choice in Western societies, there are many countervailing values that need to be considered. He comments that pursuit of collective goals and 'paternalistic beliefs' can, in certain circumstances, be favoured over an individual's own judgement. The legal system

[232] Ian Manning and Alice de Jonge, *Regulating the Cost of Credit* (Consumer Affairs Victoria, 2006) 13.

[233] See findings in CMA, *Payday Lending Market Investigation: Final Report* (2015).

[234] *ibid*, Overall Findings.

[235] Raz, *The Morality of Freedom* (n 14) 152.

[236] Department of Business Innovation and Skills, *Making Consumer Credit Markets Fairer* (n 172); Keith Ernst, Debbie Bocian and Wei Li, *Steered Wrong: Brokers, Borrowers, and Subprime Loans* (Centre for Responsible Lending, 2008).

[237] CMA, *Research into the Payday Lending Market* (n 201) 80–81.

[238] Damon Gibbons, *Where Now for Local Welfare Schemes?* (Centre for Responsible Credit, 2015) 20 and 30–33.

[239] See discussion in Lynden Griggs, 'The [Ir]rational Consumer and Why We Need National Legislation Governing Unfair Contract Terms' (2005) 13 *Competition and Consumer Law Journal* 1.

in many countries and for a significant part of history has determined that pure autonomy and complete freedom of contract is unjust and should not be allowed at the expense of other values.[240] A negative freedom approach is over-simplistic in light of these challenges. Whilst disclosure and consumer empowerment are important concepts, it is clear that many high-cost credit borrowers require more. Any truly valuable concept of freedom would engage with the context of the decision being made, something which the regulators have not done in any meaningful sense.

The UK is experiencing a difficult employment market that has been made significantly worse by the gig economy and the impacts of COVID-19,[241] and a movement away from State-provided assistance towards individual financial empowerment.[242] The multiple economic and social pressures on high-cost credit borrowers have a significant impact on the value of freedom.[243] The choice between expensive debt and hunger is not a worthwhile option. The dramatic consequences of the limited financial choices for many borrowers call into question the utility of emphasising on procedural fairness. People in these situations will not benefit from a focus on the bargaining process. We need to move beyond limited questions of procedural fairness to tackle issues of fairness of outcome, and the causes of the increasing demand for high-cost credit.

3.5.3. Poverty

The third limitation to consider is the role of poverty, as the weight of hardship will undermine the utility of procedural fairness. If people are teetering on the brink financially, they will struggle to make free and informed decisions, particularly around accessing credit. Loans (especially high-cost ones) provide short-term benefits, but potentially create long-term problems for people struggling to make ends meet. As outlined by Raz, 'harsh … conditions can reduce the degree of autonomy of a person to a bare minimum just as effectively as systematic coercive intervention'.[244] He provides the example of hunger, stating that a person who is forced to take a job they do not like out of necessity to eat has no 'free choice'. Whilst the action of taking the job was free, the person was not really free to do

[240] Patrick Atiyah, 'The Liberal Theory of Contract' in Patrick Atiyah (ed), *Essays on Contract* (Oxford University Press, 1990) 146.

[241] See discussion in Stephen McKay and Karen Rowlingson, *Financial Inclusion Monitor 2020* (University of Birmingham, 2021), which highlights the impact of both unemployment and underemployment and the significant impact of 'zero-hours contracts': 12–17.

[242] As discussed in Rowlingson, Appleyard and Gardner, 'Payday Lending in the UK' (n 222), since 1979 the UK Government has increasingly encouraged people to engage in the financial markets as opposed to seeking assistance from the State. This has occurred in conjunction with reduced regulation of many sectors; CMA, *Research into the Payday Lending Market* (n 201) 80–81.

[243] Hadfield, 'An Expressive Theory of Contract' (n 25) 1251.

[244] Raz, *The Morality of Freedom* (n 14) 156.

anything else.[245] In the context of employment, the State moved beyond the mere bargaining process and has implemented a range of substantive protections to limit the opportunity for exploitation, including minimum wage, workplace safety laws, and working time regulations. The same type of approach can therefore be justified for high-cost credit.

The focus on freedom and procedural fairness does not engage with the challenges posed by poverty, nor give guidance on an appropriate way to improve the situation. This is not, however, a new challenge. As discussed in chapter two, section 2.2, historically, these issues have significantly impacted the State's approach to high-cost credit. These concerns were raised in 1973 by Cayne and Treblicock, who stated 'consumer problems of the poor are an inherent consequence of paucity of resources and can only be remedied by augmenting these resources, that is by making the poor not poor'.[246] Poverty is a central cause of the current challenges.[247] O'Connell's investigation into working-class debt in the UK further highlights the fact that high-cost credit[248] increased largely due to the rise in inequality, and in the growth of lone-parent families.[249] These challenges were reiterated by Landsley and Lack in *Breadline Britain: The Rise of Mass Poverty*, which discusses the links between poverty and the use of high-cost credit.[250]

The liberal economic approach assumes that people only enter into credit contracts above market rates if they are acting irrationally.[251] In truth, the increasing dependency on this type of financial product appears to have more to do with the underlying socio-economic status of borrowers. As Rowlingson states,

> poverty is the underlying reason why some people lack access to suitable, low-cost credit. The improved provision of social lending schemes will be a help. But … these

[245] *ibid* 15.

[246] David Cayne and MJ Treblicock, 'Market Considerations in the Formulation of Consumer Protection Policy' (1973) 23 *University of Toronto Law Journal* 396, 430 (similar comments are also made at 407). This quotation finishes by saying that 'we have too often in the past yielded to the temptation to look for scapegoats to whom to attribute the unpleasant consequences of poverty. The somewhat unromantic and visible figures of the ghetto merchant, slum land-lord, peddlar, and loan shark, have proved easy, although irrelevant, targets'. I strongly disagree with the last few words and believe that lenders are definitely *relevant* targets for government regulation.

[247] The authors, for example, discuss how, due to the lack of liquidity, the poor pay more for a variety of goods and services, which has a strong impact on their credit need; *ibid* 397–98. See also David Caplovitz, *The Poor Pay More* (Free Press, 1967).

[248] In the era O'Connell was analysing, door-stop lending (also known as home-collected credit) was the most common form of high-cost credit.

[249] Sean O'Connell, *Credit and Community: Working-Class Debt in the UK Since 1880* (Oxford University Press, 2009) 186–87.

[250] Stewart Lansley and Joanna Mack, *Breadline Britain: The Rise of Mass Poverty* (OneWorld Publications, 2015) 59–60.

[251] Anthony Ogus, *Regulation: Legal Form and Economic Theory* (Clarendon Law Series, 1994); see also discussion of efficient market hypobook in relation to the credit market; Ray Ball, 'The Global Financial Crisis and the Efficient Market Hypobook: What Have We Learned?' (2009) 21 *Journal of Applied Corporate Finance* 8 and analysis of rational choice theory and credit cards: Richard Posner, 'Rational Choice, Behavioral Economics, and the Law' (1997) 50 *Stanford Law Review* 1551, esp 1574.

schemes will just be papering over the cracks of the much more fundamental problem of poverty.[252]

This is further supported by Ramsay who summarises the situation by declaring that the central problem *is* poverty.[253] Responding to the impact of deprivation remains a challenge for policy makers and, in the context of high-cost credit, this is particularly concerned with creating affordable and safe credit products for people on low incomes.[254]

The question of regulation of high-cost credit is therefore exceptionally complex. As outlined by O'Connell, 'working-class consumer credit is a subject where it is difficult to separate the social from the economic, the commercial from the cultural'.[255] Mullainanthan and Shafir further highlight the complexities of low-income borrowers' need for further credit in their ground-breaking book *Scarcity: Why Having too Little Means so Much*.[256] The majority of people who use these products are financially vulnerable, and a significant minority are living in or on the fringe of poverty. Whilst a solution to increasing levels of poverty is clearly beyond the scope of this book, the importance of this issue must be recognised. Until these challenges are addressed, a mere focus on ensuring procedural fairness is unlikely to make any substantial impact on the lives of vulnerable borrowers.

3.6. Conclusion

Freedom is and will continue to be a cornerstone of the English legal system. It is an important philosophical concept and has a strong historical grounding. This approach is generally limited to negative freedom, focusing on the freedom *to* enter into contracts. There is inherent value in this approach, but in the context of high-cost credit, it is severely inadequate. A freedom-based approach is useful for people who have multiple options and are choosing to use high-cost credit for the convenience and speed of these products. In these circumstances, the current legal protections focused on procedural fairness will generally be sufficient.

[252] Karen Rowlingson, *Moneylenders and their Customers* (Policy Studies Institute, 1994) 166.

[253] Iain Ramsay, '"To Heap Distress Upon Distress": Comparative Reflections of Interest-Rate Ceilings' (2010) 60 *University of Toronto Law Journal* 707, 708.

[254] Rowlingson, *Moneylenders and their Customers* (n 252) 166.

[255] O'Connell, *Credit and Community* (n 249) 3.

[256] For example, they outline how one in every six families in the lowest income quintile pay at least one bill late per year; 18% of the poorest families have had their phones disconnected and 10% have had their utilities shut off. Nearly 5% of the annual income of the poor is spent on debt servicing, reconnection charges, and late fees: Mullainathan and Shafir, *Scarcity* (n 221) 107. These are statistics from the US, however similar issues have been reported in the UK, see Sharon Collard, Andrea Finney and Sara Davies, *Working Households' Experiences of Debt Problems* (A Research Report Prepared for StepChange Debt Charity, 2012) and Sarah Bridges and Richard Disney, 'Use of Credit and Arrears on Debt Among Low-Income Families in the United Kingdom' (2004) 25 *Fiscal Studies* 1.

A large number of people who rely on high-cost credit are entering into these agreements from vulnerable situations and with limited options. This personal situation impacts their ability to utilise their contractual freedom in a meaningful way. The negative-freedom approach does not adequately address the needs of these borrowers, and allows them to enter into potentially harmful contracts including ones with Continuous Payment Authorities that provide automatic access to bank accounts, high interest rates, and significant penalty fees. Sometimes the law has to go beyond negative freedom and procedural fairness, and instead protect people from substantively unfair contracts.

4

Regulation

> These men ask for just the same thing, fairness and fairness only.
> This, so far as in my power, they, and all others, shall have.
>
> — Abraham Lincoln, letter to Hon L Swert on 30 May 1860

Chapter three outlined how freedom is a guiding principle in the law's approach to high-cost credit contracts. Freedom is not, however, absolute. Complete negative freedom and lack of government intervention is clearly not a suitable concept for a functioning society. We need to maintain a balance between different values. This chapter therefore moves away from freedom to discuss the role of regulation in the challenges presented by high-cost credit. It has five sections and follows the same structure as the previous chapter. The first section considers the role of regulation in high-cost credit, explaining that regulation prevents both substantively unfair agreements and coercion through lack of choice. The second outlines the history of regulation, specifically focusing on the role of religion in the approach to these issues. The third section develops this analysis by outlining the historical justifications for regulation, namely preventing harmful outcomes, stopping unconscionable behaviour, and defending the vulnerable. The fourth discusses the examples of regulation that already exist in the UK legal system, including interest rate restrictions, responsible lending, unfair terms legislation, and various common law doctrines. The chapter finishes by highlighting the limitations of a regulation-based approach, providing evidence for the need to look beyond the freedom versus regulation dichotomy.

4.1. What is Regulation?

Freedom, particularly negative freedom, is associated with *non*-intervention into private arrangements and economic markets. Regulation is, by contrast, linked with intervention into laws and markets, largely to ensure that these systems are not used in an unfair or unacceptable manner. Freedom and regulation are inherently connected. Berlin highlights the relationship between the two concepts, stating,

> to avoid glaring inequality or widespread misery I am ready to sacrifice some, or all, of my freedom: I may do so willingly and freely; but it is freedom that I am giving up for the sake of justice or equality or love of my fellow men.[1]

So many aspects of life that we take for granted are impositions on our freedoms for the greater good – the development of government and democracy, health and safety requirements to ensure people are not injured unnecessarily, traffic and road rules to prevent avoidable accidents, the wearing of masks during a global pandemic to stop the spread of an infectious disease, employment laws to give workers rights against potentially exploitative employers, the list goes on.[2] These restrictions (and many more) are highly valued and ingrained in our society. We are surrounded by limitations on our negative freedom that are designed to protect ourselves and those around us. The question then becomes not whether society should enact regulations that impinge on some freedoms, but more 'where should we draw the line'?

Enacting regulation to protect parties means, by definition, intervening with the market or legal system. This type of intervention can be criticised on the basis that the Government is not acting fairly or 'neutrally'; it favours one party over another. There are two types of neutrality discussed in this book – neutrality between competing notions of 'the good', and neutrality between individuals.[3] Both types of neutrality are relevant. When the State limits or prohibits certain types of contracts on the ground of potential danger or harm, it appears to be choosing a particular concept of 'good' financial products and contracts.[4] When intervening in a contractual dispute to protect a vulnerable individual, the State can also appear to favour the weaker party over the stronger, and consequently not remain neutral.[5]

This concern for neutrality assumes two things; first, the State should not intervene into contracts for the purpose of ensuring its version of 'good' or a 'good life',

[1] Isaiah Berlin, 'Two Concepts of Liberty' in Berlin (ed), *Four Essays on Liberty* (Oxford University Press, 1958) 174.

[2] See discussion in Anthony Ogus, *Costs and Cautionary Tales: Economic Insights for the Law* (Hart Publishing, 2006).

[3] 'In invoking neutrality in the context of examining the liberal attitude to the freedom of contract, the basic thought is that most forms of intervention in the freedom of contract represent a deviation from a policy of neutral concern. When the law protects the relatively vulnerable party against the strong, for instance, it is not neutral; it helps the former and hinders the latter': Dori Kimel, 'Neutrality, Autonomy, and Freedom of Contract' (2001) 21 *Oxford Journal of Legal Studies* 473, 477.

[4] John Rawls, *A Theory of Justice* (Harvard University Press, 1971); See also Samuel Freeman, *Rawls* (Routledge, 2007).

[5] Dori Kimel, *From Promise to Contract: Towards a Liberal Theory of Contract* (Hart Publishing, 2003) 121–22; Kimel, 'Neutrality, Autonomy, and Freedom of Contract' (n 3) particularly 477–79.

and second, that all parties come to the transaction on an equal footing. Neither of these assumptions is valid in the context of high-cost credit. Chapter two discussed the real concerns about how these products are working, and the harm that is being caused to borrowers. The State has strong justifications to intervene in the market to create its version of a 'good' credit and lending environment. Sandel stresses the need for society to have a richer and more morally engaged discourse about what is a 'good life,' and how this should impact the products available on the market.[6] Government intervention is allowed, even required, to prevent harm to a borrower's ability to live a 'good life'.[7] This discourse should also take into account the context in which the lending is occurring, and therefore be influenced by social values, conventions and norms.[8] A 'good life' is multi-faceted, encompassing notions of success, happiness and most importantly, meaningfulness.[9] Having a situation where many low-income individuals regularly resort to loans with thousands of per cent interest[10] challenges society's norms about minimal living standards. These situations negatively impact many people's ability to live a good life and raise serious questions about provision of financial products specifically and contractual freedom more generally. A regulation-based approach is readily justified.

Second, there are inequalities in the high-cost credit market that have a significant impact on the way that 'freedom' operates in practice. If extreme inequalities already exist between contracting parties, a strong adherence to neutrality will support the status quo and therefore favour the stronger party.[11] Freedom and neutrality are supported on the ground that they allow for a 'fair contest' between parties. Providing high-cost credit to vulnerable individuals is far from a fair contest. These loans can be harmful and cause the borrower to go into financial hardship or a debt spiral. Borrowers are frequently unable to meet the repayments and can therefore be subjected to default fees and/or 'roll-overs' of the original loan. Lenders are aware of this vulnerability and can utilise it to their own advantage.[12] Lending to people who cannot afford to repay without suffering financial hardship is therefore beneficial for the lender.[13] Whilst many high-cost credit borrowers are an increased risk and therefore there is justification for higher costs, it should not be used as tool for exploitation. These extreme inequalities and the lack of a 'fair contest' between lenders and borrowers show that, for the State to

[6] Michael Sandel, *What Money Can't Buy: The Moral Limits of Markets* (Penguin, 2013). See also Margaret Radin, 'Market-Inalienability' (1987) 100 *Harvard Law Review* 1849.

[7] Joseph Raz, *The Morality of Freedom* (Oxford University Press, 1988) 417.

[8] Michael Sandel, *Liberalism and the Limits of Justice*, 2nd edn (Cambridge University Press, 1998).

[9] Susan Wolf, 'Happiness and Meaning: Two Aspects of the Good Life' (1997) 14 *Social Philosophy and Policy* 207.

[10] The current interest rate cap in the UK is 1,270% APR, see discussion in section 4.4.2 below.

[11] Kimel, *From Promise to Contract* (n 5) 122. See also Raz, *The Morality of Freedom* (n 7) Ch 9.

[12] As outlined in chapter one, section 1.2, lenders make approximately 50% of their revenue from the loans that are rolled over or refinanced at least once: Office of Fair Trading (OFT), *Payday Lending: Final Compliance Review* (OFT, 2013) 2.

[13] See economic analysis in Sarah Beddows and Mick McAteer, *Payday Lending: Fixing a Broken Market* (Association of Chartered Certified Accountants, 2014).

be acting in a truly neutral fashion, it must intervene on behalf of the weaker party – in this case the borrower.[14]

The State has a strong justification for intervention to 'level the playing field'. There are many accepted and uncontroversial examples of this happening. For example, sports such as boxing are often run with weight classifications to ensure that contestants are not placed in grossly unfair competitions. In criminal trials, prosecutors (the stronger party) are required to hand over relevant evidence to defendants, who are weaker, in order to level the playing field. The negative freedom approach discussed in the previous chapter results in legal processes being limited to ensuring a framework for the creation and enforcement of agreements between parties. When there are power imbalances, the law needs to go further; as stated by Kimel

> by defining the framework in a way which enables a certain 'strong' party to capitalise on the vulnerability of a certain 'weak' party, the state – the law – does not merely fail to help the latter; it plays an active role in creating the conditions of its fall.[15]

If the State wishes to act in a truly neutral fashion it should not avoid intervention. Such situations will often require active intervention by the Government to ensure that power imbalances are not manipulated.

A regulation-focused approach can also be criticised on the grounds of consent. By intervening into a contract between two parties, the State can appear to be undermining the value of consent.[16] There are, however, many interventions which cannot be explained by a narrow concept of consent. Many limitations placed on people in our society are imposed in situations where full and informed consent can be and is given by the parties involved. There are multiple examples of these, including the limitations on the purchase and consumption of cigarettes and alcohol, the requirement for passengers of motor vehicles to wear seat belts, and the inability for people to limit potential liability for personal injury and death. These all reduce the choice and freedom of the parties involved. Our current approach limits or prohibits certain actions, even if people involved have consented to the transaction or risk.[17] Consent is therefore an insufficient rationale for stopping regulation and State-based protection of borrowers.

Like freedom, regulation can mean a wide variety of different things. For the purpose of this book, regulation is associated with government, or on occasions

[14] Raz, *The Morality of Freedom* (n 7); Robert Nozick, *Anarchy, State and Utopia* (Basic Books, 1974); Rawls, *A Theory of Justice* (n 4).

[15] Kimel, 'Neutrality, Autonomy, and Freedom of Contract' (n 3) 480.

[16] Examples of this can be seen in John Adams and Roger Brownsword, *Understanding Contract Law*, 5th edn (Sweet & Maxwell, 2007) and comments in *Zamet v Hyman* [1961] 1 WLR 1442 (UKCA), where the Court focuses on whether there has been 'full, free and informed' consent (at 1444). For a full list of the Orthodox defective consent approach, see Mindy Chen-Wishart, 'The Nature of Vitiating Factors in Contract' in Saprai, Letsas and Klass (eds), *Philosophical Foundations of Contract Law* (Oxford University Press, 2014) fns 3–22.

[17] The most well-known example of this is the infamous criminal law case, *R v Brown* [1993] UKHL 19, [1994] 1 AC 212.

judge-based, intervention into the contractual affairs of individuals. This means restricting liberty in some cases to promote other important values including equality, social or moral norms, justice and protection of the weak.[18] In the context of high-cost credit, this book will focus on two main types of regulation. The first, which is grounded on Kantian respect and concerns for distributive justice,[19] is regulation preventing substantively unfair agreements – meaning preventing enforcement of grossly one-sided contracts.[20] The second type of regulation is focused on preventing coercion that arises from a borrowers' lack of choice. This goes further than avoidance of coercion by lenders discussed in chapter three, as many factors can undermine choice. Atiyah believes that, in these situations, the weaker party should be able to challenge the transaction, drawing a comparison with fraud and duress, as they had no effective option but to consent.[21] This type of regulation therefore also aims to provide assistance when borrowers are coerced through social structures, the environment, or any other impairment that may impact the transaction in question.

The negative freedom approach discussed in the previous chapter is based on concern for an individual's autonomy. The mere theoretical right to freedom is hollow if it cannot be utilised in a way that improves a person's life. If we value autonomy in a meaningful sense, the State is required to do more to protect parties. For example, Kimel highlights that law should play an active role in shaping how freedom of contract can be exercised to enhance the well-being of parties and make a positive contribution on their ability to lead valuable and successful lives.[22] Sometimes the only way we can do this is by moving away from a freedom focus to a more regulation-based approach.

4.2. The History of Regulation

This section will briefly outline the historical development of a regulatory approach to high-cost credit. It will commence with a discussion of the link between usury, religion and high-cost credit, followed by an analysis of the

[18] See Ian Carter, *Positive and Negative Liberty* (Stanford Encyclopedia of Philosophy, 2003) discussing Berlin.

[19] Chen-Wishart, 'The Nature of Vitiating Factors in Contract' (n 16) 304; Anthony Townsend Kronman, 'Contract Law and Distributive Justice' (1980) 89 *Yale Law Journal* 472; Séverine Saintier, 'Defects of Consent in English Law' in Larry DiMatteo and Martin Hogg (eds), *Comparative Contract Law: British and American Perspectives* (Oxford University Press, 2016); for an American perspective on the debate, see Jeffrey L Harrison, 'Quality of Consent and Distributive Fairness: A Comparative Perspective' in Larry DiMatteo and Martin Hogg (eds), *Comparative Contract Law: British and American Perspectives* (Oxford University Press, 2016).

[20] Patrick Atiyah, *Essays on Contract Law* (Oxford University Press, 1990) Essay 11; Steven Smith, 'In Defence of Substantive Unfairness' (1996) *Law Quarterly Review* 138; Mindy Chen-Wishart, 'The O'Brien Principle and Substantive Unfairness' (1997) 56 *Cambridge Law Journal* 60.

[21] Atiyah, *ibid* Essay 11, 353.

[22] Kimel, 'Neutrality, Autonomy, and Freedom of Contract' (n 3) 493.

religious basis of regulation. The section will conclude with a summary of what the historical approach can teach us about current high-cost credit challenges.

4.2.1. Usury, Religion and High-Cost Credit

The regulation-based approach to moneylending has a strong religious grounding in the prohibition of usury. Every major religion has criticised usury, favouring restrictions on lending practices.[23] This book will however focus on Judeo-Christian beliefs, as they have had a significant impact on the current legal system. There are four references to moneylending and usury in the Old Testament.[24] These four passages have been subject to significant analysis and debate as to their exact meaning, given that they contain ambiguous and contested phrases such as 'thy brother', 'waxen poor', and 'my people'.[25]

The most direct prohibition of usury is in *Deuteronomy*, where lending of money to 'thy brother' is prohibited but is allowed 'unto a foreigner'.[26] Passages from *Exodus*[27] and *Leviticus*[28] clearly apply usury restrictions to the 'poor' without any other limitations. The *Leviticus* passage further extends the obligations outlined in *Exodus*, applying restrictions on both money and food stuff or grain.[29] Whilst all four references prohibit the charging of any interest, there is a significant variation when it comes to those to whom the restrictions apply.[30] The exclusion of usury is

[23] This section focuses on regulation-based approaches to usury in Judeo-Christian practices. It should however be noted that historically there has been hostility to usury in all major religions, including Hinduism and Buddhism; Vincent D Rougeau, 'Rediscovering Usury: An Argument for Legal Controls on Credit Card Interest Rates' (1996) 67 *University of Colorado Law Review* 1, 25. In fact, some of the oldest references to usury are in the Vedic texts from Hinduism; Wayne AM Visser and Alistair Macintosh, 'A Short Review of the Historical Critique of Usury' (1998) 8 *Accounting, Business & Financial History* 175, 175.

[24] *Exodus* XXII, 25–27; *Leviticus* XXV, 35–37; *Deuteronomy* XXII, 19–20; *Ezekiel* XVIII, 8 and 13.

[25] Also known as the 'Old Testament' or 'Torah' and consists of the first part of the Christian Bible.

[26] 'Thou shalt not lend upon usury to thy brother; usury of money, usury of victuals, usury of any thing that is lent upon usury: Unto a foreigner thou mayest lend upon usury; but unto thy brother thou shalt not lend upon usury: that the Lord thy God may bless thee in all that thou settest thine hand to in the land whither thou goest to possess it': King James Bible, *Authorised Version* (Cambridge Edition) *Deuteronomy* XXII, 19–20.

[27] 'If thou lend money to any of my people that is poor by thee, thou shalt not be to him as an usurer, neither shalt thou lay upon him usury. If thou at all take thy neighbour's raiment to pledge, thou shalt deliver it unto him by that the sun goeth down: For that is his covering only, it is his raiment for his skin: wherein shall he sleep? and it shall come to pass, when he crieth unto me, that I will hear; for I am gracious': *ibid Exodus* XXII, 25–27.

[28] 'And if thy brother be waxen poor, and fallen in decay with thee; then thou shalt relieve him: yea, though he be a stranger, or a sojourner; that he may live with thee. Take thou no usury of him, or increase: but fear thy God; that thy brother may live with thee. Thou shalt not give him thy money upon usury, nor lend him thy victuals for increase': *ibid Leviticus* XXV, 35–37.

[29] Bernard J Meislin and Morris L Cohen, 'Backgrounds of the Biblical Law against Usury' (1964) 6 *Comparative Studies in Society and History* 250, 262.

[30] Whether 'foreigner' in the *Deuteronomy* passage is the same as 'stranger' referred to in *Leviticus* is highly contentious; however Meislin and Cohen strongly argue that they have very different meanings as, during the period of *Deuteronomy*, a 'foreigner' was a non-resident alien who was only temporarily present in the land and therefore could be charged interest: *ibid* 264–265.

continued in a dramatic fashion in *Ezekiel*,[31] which clearly prohibits the charging of interest in any form and includes vivid indications of the consequences of usury. The Old Testament passages imply that there were strong concerns about the impact of moneylending on their communities, and on the exploitative actions of lenders.

The situation in the New Testament is not however as straightforward. There are passages that continue to criticise or forbid the charging of usury, but the message is significantly weaker and sometimes conflicted.[32] Despite this, there are a number of specific references to Jesus speaking out against usury and encouraging Christians to lend to those who are less fortunate without the charging of interest. For example, in *Luke* Jesus told his disciples 'But love ye your enemies, and do good, and lend, hoping for nothing again; and your reward shall be great.'[33] Jesus also famously went into Temple where the moneychangers operated and cast them out, calling them 'thieves'.[34]

Despite the very clear condemnations in the Old Testament of the charging of interest, moneylending continued to be widely practiced by Jewish communities during Biblical times and beyond. There is evidence from the fifth century BC that Jewish moneylenders in Egypt charged interest on loans as a standard practice.[35] It also represents a widespread interpretation of the usury limitations only applying to people in the same religious or cultural group, leading to the creation of the 'Jewish moneylender' stereotype. In the New Testament, the concept of usury was something that was 'most fervently taken up as a cause by the institutions of the Christian Church',[36] at least on a theoretical level. On a practical level, commercial credit and debt has become widely accepted, and almost unquestionably forms part of the commercial market. Hudson summarises that 'nowhere has this ideology moved further away from that of Biblical times than in its tolerance of … interest-bearing debt regardless of their polarizing economic consequences'.[37]

[31] 'He that hath not given forth upon usury, neither hath taken any increase, that hath withdrawn his hand from iniquity, hath executed true judgment between man and man' and later 'hath given forth upon usury, and hath taken increase: shall he then live? he shall not live: he hath done all these abominations; he shall surely die; his blood shall be upon him'; King James Bible (n 26) *Ezekiel* XVIII, 8 and 13.

[32] The most famous of these is the Parable of the Talents, discussed in John Duncan and Martin Derrett, 'Law in the New Testament: The Parable of the Talents and Two Logia' (1965) 56 *Zeitschrift für die neutestamentliche Wissenschaft* 184.

[33] King James Bible (n 26) *Luke* VI, 35.

[34] *ibid Matthew* XXI, 12–18.

[35] This has led Visser and MacIntosh to consider that 'the prohibition on interest suggests that its violation was regarded not as a criminal offence with penal sanctions attached but as a moral transgression': Visser and Macintosh, 'A Short Review of the Historical Critique of Usury' (n 23) 178.

[36] *ibid* 178.

[37] Michael Hudson, *The Lost Tradition of Biblical Debt Cancellations* (Hentry George School of Social Science, 1992) 44.

4.2.2. The Development of Regulation

Religion has a strong influence on the way we look at credit and usury. Judeo-Christian beliefs were the basis of the State's approach to usury and protection of borrowers throughout much of early history. By the fourth century AD, the Roman Catholic Church had prohibited the clergy from charging interest.[38] Usury was declared to be a criminal offence by the eighth century, and this approach continued until the 'high water' mark in 1311 when Pope Clement V made a bar on usury absolute, abolishing all secular law on the topic.[39] There was little analysis of the reasons why usury was no longer allowed, merely control by the Church and a belief that because the Bible opposed usury, it should be prohibited.[40]

One of the first philosophers to consider the role of usury in a secular manner was Aristotle. He argued that, whilst the creation and accumulation of wealth was something that should be encouraged, money should not be loaned merely for the purpose of making money, as this was not good for society.[41] He fought against moneylenders, as their trade was merely focused on making money as an end to itself.[42] In his book *The Politics*, Aristotle argued that usury is unproductive and unnatural, and therefore unjust. He later commented that there can be virtue in the good use of wealth, but people in this position should exercise both temperance and generosity.[43]

The impact of religion was particularly evident during the Middle Ages, where society reverted to earlier views on money and exchange, as well as there being a strong reliance on the Bible for guidance and teaching and thus the law.[44] This impacted the stance on usury as well as the justifications used for its prohibition. There was a movement away from a freedom-based approach that allowed interest to be charged, and towards Judeo-Christian based prohibition on usury in all forms. Nearly 1,500 years later, Thomas Aquinas further developed the concept of

[38] Visser and Macintosh, 'A Short Review of the Historical Critique of Usury' (n 23) 178.

[39] *ibid* 178.

[40] Glyn Davies, *A History of Money: From Ancient Times to the Present Day* (University of Wales Press, 1994) 219. Unsurprisingly, various avoidance mechanisms were adopted by lenders to get around those provisions. To combat these issues, all previous usury laws were repealed in 1545 by 37 Hen VIII, c 9. This Act fixed the legal rate of interest at 10% for commercial and real estate transactions, and enacted a range of anti-avoidance provisions. Penalties also increased, so that if a person was found guilty of usury they forfeited treble the value of the loan and treble the value of profit obtained, half which went to the King and half to the plaintiff or informer. The usurer was also subject to imprisonment and a fine: Hugh Bellot, *The Law Relating to Unconscionable Bargains with Money-Lenders: Including the History of Usury to the Repeal of the Usury Laws* (Stevens & Haynes, 1898) 20–21.

[41] Jean Roberts, *Routledge Philosophy Guidebook to Aristotle and the Politics* (Routledge Philosophy Guidebooks, Routledge, 2009) 69–70.

[42] *ibid* 70.

[43] *ibid*.

[44] 'The Bible was the most studied book of the middle ages. Bible study represented the highest branch of learning': Beryl Smalley, *The Study of the Bible in the Middle Ages*, 3rd edn (Blackwell, 1983) 1.

fairness in an exchange raised by Aristotle.[45] He argued that money was developed for promoting exchanges; hence the proper and principled use of money was as an intermediary of exchange for goods and services as opposed to being a wealth-creating resource in and of itself. The use of money to create more money (ie, the charging of interest) was an unnatural use. Aquinas also advocated strongly for the fairness of exchange, stating

> a man with money is not in every case bound to lend it … he who is not bound to lend may receive compensation for what he has done in lending, but ought not to exact more. But compensation is given him according to the equality of justice, if the exact amount is returned to him that he has lent. Hence if he exacts more for the use of a thing that has no other use than the consumption of the substance, he exacts a price for that which has no existence, and so the exaction is unjust.[46]

Despite drawing on the Bible to support his position on usury, Aquinas clearly felt that there was no duty on the wealthy to lend money.[47]

A similar approach to usury is evident in the writings of Enlightenment scholar Francis Bacon, who in 1601 wrote one of the earliest known detailed academic texts on usury. In his piece *De Usura sive Foenore*,[48] Bacon approached usury from a religious perspective, but justified the charging of limited and strictly enforced levels of interest on the basis of the potential benefits this could have for society. He outlined the many negative aspects of freedom of contract and the charging of interest – it was a 'lazy trade' that unfairly disadvantaged the poor, centralised wealth into the hands of a few, impacted the price of land, and dampened industry and development. Lastly and potentially most importantly, interest had the potential to create 'the canker and ruin of many men's estates; which, in process of time, breeds a public poverty'.[49] Bacon argued that society needed to be protected from these practices. This highlights a very early understanding of the harmful impact that exploitative loans can have on society.

Bacon recognised the limited benefits of usury, including the encouragement of new industry and trade, particularly for young merchants. It could provide people with access to funds to get through difficult periods, so that they would not have to sell their possessions, and finally it had a practical value, as people need to charge some level of interest for their lending services.[50] After weighing up the positive and negative aspects of usury, Bacon suggested a two-tiered approach to the law. First, anyone could lend money, but only at a maximum rate of five per cent

[45] Saint Thomas Aquinas, *Aquinas Ethicus, or, The Moral Teaching of St Thomas: A Translation of the Principal Portions of the Second Part of the 'Summa Theologica'*, 2nd edn (edited by Rickaby) (Burns and Oates, 1896) especially Question LXXVI.

[46] *ibid* Question LXXVII, § 5.

[47] See, *ibid* Question LXXVII, § 2.

[48] Francis Bacon, *The Essayes or Covnsels Civill and Morall of Francis Bacon: Baron of Verulam, Viscount St. Alban, and Lord High Chancellor of England* (translated by Judy Boss in 1998) (Renascence Editions, 1625), written in Latin and translated without page numbers.

[49] *ibid* 'Of Usury'.

[50] Stating 'whereas usury doth but gnaw upon them, bad markets would swallow them quite up'; *ibid.*

per annum. Second, a category of licensed moneylenders would be created. These people would be allowed to charge higher rates of interest (up to ten per cent per annum) but would then be subject to regulation and limitations.[51] When faced with criticism that his plan allowed or encouraged unconscionable behaviour, Bacon adopted a practical approach stating 'that it is better to mitigate usury, by declaration, than to suffer it to rage'.[52]

As discussed in chapter three, the Enlightenment created a variety of practical needs and philosophical justifications for the charging of interest, and for a freedom-based approach to credit. At the end of the nineteenth and beginning of the twentieth centuries, the full extent of moneylending (and its damaging impact) was becoming apparent. In response, the regulatory approach began to change and there was a return to a more protective stance.[53] This resulted in a further Select Committee being designated in 1897 to investigate the issues associated with moneylending, resulting in the Money-Lenders Act 1900.[54] This Act improved some consumer protections, but still focused largely on economic and contractual freedom of borrowers by advocating non-intervention into debt agreements where possible.[55]

Influenced by the work of Marx, twentieth century thinking on usury changed significantly with a focus on the harmful effects of an open credit market on society.[56] Marxist theory emphasised the importance of labour, and the artificial impact usury had on the market.[57] Both of these benefitted the lenders, who obtained profits without undertaking any productive work; merely making money from the manipulation of capital and the desperation of others. Marx describes usury as 'like a parasite … it sucks out its blood, enervates it and compels reproduction to proceed under ever more pitiable conditions'.[58]

Keynes' work on interest rates and monetary policies built on these foundations. Whilst disagreeing with a significant proportion of Marxist theory, Keynes had similar approaches to usury and moneylending. He described the acceptance of interest during the Enlightenment as one of the 'pseudo-moral principles which have hag-ridden us for two hundred years, by which we have exalted some

[51] *ibid*. This is highly reflective of the approach taken in the Crowther Report (Sir Geoffrey Crowther, Consumer Credit: Report of the Committee (Department of Trade and Industry, 1971)) and the Consumer Credit Act 1974 (UK).

[52] Bacon, *The Essayes or Covnsels Civill and Morall of Francis Bacon* (n 48) 'Of Usury'.

[53] Chesterton's book was written in 1933 but was only published in 1943 after his death.

[54] The Select Committee on Money Lending, 1897 Report from the Select Committee on Money Lending; Together with the Proceedings of the Committee, Minutes of Evidence, Appendix, and Index (19th Century House of Commons Sessional Papers, No 364, 1897).

[55] See discussion in section 4.2.1 above.

[56] Rougeau, 'Rediscovering Usury: An Argument for Legal Controls on Credit Card Interest Rates' (n 23) 3.

[57] Karl Marx, *Capital Volume III: The Process of Capitalist Production as a Whole* (Institute of Marxism-Leninism, translated by Marxists Internet Archive, 1894) Ch 36, 'Pre-Capitalist Relationships, Division of Profit into Interest and Profit of Enterprise. Interest-Bearing Capital'.

[58] *ibid*.

of the most distasteful of human qualities into the position of the highest virtues'.[59] Keynes was against opening the credit market because it created 'distasteful and unjust' outcomes that were accepted because they were very useful in promoting the accumulation of wealth.[60] He commented that the 'Medieval' practices forbidding usury were one of the most ancient economic practices on record. In addition to their moralistic arguments, limitations on credit had a positive impact on economic growth. If the credit market was allowed to run without restriction, it would impede industrial growth and those with money would focus on exploitative moneylending instead of useful investments.[61]

The devastating consequences of the Great Depression saw a sharp return to protectionism, which included statutory controls on lending and interest rates. When writing shortly after the Depression, Chesterton advocated for a return to an Aquinas-based approach to usury.[62] He believed that the Bentham method of trade and finance[63] was not only morally bankrupt, but was also the cause of the largest 'universal commercial collapse of our time'.[64] This argument has some justification, and indeed open monetary policies and laissez-faire economic approaches had a clear impact on the Great Depression[65] (although the specific causes are strongly contested and beyond the scope of this book). What is clear is that, after the Depression, society was more skeptical of the financial system and more willing to accept government intervention into the market, including the limitation of interest rates.[66] There was also an increasing concern about the need to assist the less fortunate – poverty, inequality and under-consumption all played a role in the creation and impact of the Great Depression.[67] This period saw a movement away from the traditional thoughts of regulation to a more consumer-focused consideration of the issues.

The Marx/Keynes approach to usury and interest rate restrictions clearly had a significant impact on both ongoing academic work and government policy. For example, Franklin D Roosevelt cited moneylending and usury as a cause of the Great Depression in his First Inaugural Address in 1933.[68] The analogies that

[59] John Maynard Keynes, 'Economic Possibilities for our Grandchildren' in Keynes (ed), *Essays in Persuasion* (W. W. Norton & Company, 1963) 362.

[60] *ibid* 362–63.

[61] John Maynard Keynes, *The General Theory of Employment, Interest and Money* (MacMillan Cambridge University Press, 1936) Ch 23: 'Notes on Mercantilism – The Usury Laws, Stamped Money and Theories of Under-Consumption', Section V.

[62] Joseph Persky, 'From Usury to Interest' (2007) 21 *Journal of Economic Perspectives* 227, 235.

[63] Discussed above in chapter three, section 3.2.

[64] Gilbert Keith Chesterton, *St. Thomas Aquinas* (Hodder & Stoughton, 1943) 225.

[65] See discussion in Peter Temin, *Did Monetary Forces Cause the Great Depression?* (Norton, 1976).

[66] See discussion in Yaron Brook, 'The Morality of Moneylending: A Short History' (*The Objective Standard*, 20 August 2007), available at www.theobjectivestandard.com/issues/2007-fall/morality-of-moneylending (all websites cited in this chapter were last accessed on 14 January 2022).

[67] Elisabeth Allgoewer, *Underconsumption Theories and Keynesian Economics: Interpretations of the Great Depression* (University of St. Gallen, Department of Economics: Research Paper 2002–14, 2002) especially 24–26.

[68] 'Because the rulers of the exchange of mankind's goods have failed, through their own stubbornness and their own incompetence, have admitted their failure, and abdicated. Practices of the unscrupulous money changers stand indicted in the court of public opinion, rejected by the hearts

lenders have 'fled from their high seats in the temple of our civilization' and of the need to restore 'ancient truths' are particularly interesting, appearing to reference the Christian perspectives on moneylending (discussed in chapter three, section 3.2 above). Rougeau outlined that 'most usury prohibitions are grounded in deep ethical and religious condemnations'.[69] The approach taken by Roosevelt signalled a strong movement away from the free market approach to monetary principles, and towards government intervention to ensure a system that reflected 'social values'. The religious prohibition on usury remained a strong underpinning of the regulatory approaches to high-cost credit.

4.2.3. What Can We Learn?

The historical discussion of high-cost credit effectively highlights the dynamic nature of credit regulation. Throughout history many people have been unable to access mainstream credit, and so were reliant on sub-prime lenders – whether that be the moneychangers from the Bible, moneylenders of Shakespearean times, the doorstop lenders of the early 1900s, or the online payday lenders of today. Whilst the forms of lending have changed dramatically with the evolution of technology, the problems have largely stayed the same. There has been an ongoing pendulum approach, swinging between freedom and regulation.

Religious grounding resulted in the prohibition of usury throughout much of early history. At the end of the Middle Ages, moneylending was still considered morally reprehensible but was also becoming economically beneficial. Indeed, precept did follow practice – when the Enlightenment arrived, so did new justifications allowing for the charging of interest. The religious stance was swept away in favour of a more practical focus which emphasised personal and economic freedom. The Benthamite approach to usury[70] remained predominant for almost a century, and during this time most lawyers, economists and political commentators advocated against what they perceived as undue restrictions on the access to credit.[71] The post Great Depression period saw a temporary return to

and minds of men. True they have tried, but their efforts have been cast in the pattern of an outworn tradition. Faced by failure of credit they have proposed only the lending of more money. Stripped of the lure of profit by which to induce our people to follow their false leadership, they have resorted to exhortations, pleading tearfully for restored confidence. They know only the rules of a generation of self-seekers. They have no vision, and when there is no vision the people perish. The money changers have fled from their high seats in the temple of our civilization. We may now restore that temple to the ancient truths. The measure of the restoration lies in the extent to which we apply social values more noble than mere monetary profit': Franklin D Roosevelt, 'First Inugural Address' (*History Tools*, 4 March 1933), available at www.historytools.org/sources/froosevelt1st.html.

[69] Rougeau, 'Rediscovering Usury: An Argument for Legal Controls on Credit Card Interest Rates' (n 23) 25.

[70] Discussed above in section 4.2.2.

[71] See, eg, discussion in Persky, 'From Usury to Interest' (n 62) and Brook, 'The Morality of Moneylending' (n 66). Hume added to the jurisprudence on this topic by analysing the connection between high mercantile profits and high interest levels, 'No man will accept of low profits where he can

a regulation-focused approach towards moneylending and usury. This hiatus was, however, short-lived. The mid-twentieth century resulted in the rise of libertarianism and a focus on individual freedom, choice and limited government intervention. The high-water mark was hit in the Thatcher era of 'responsibilisation', and the opening of the economic and credit markets. The financial crisis and explosion in harmful forms of consumer credit highlighted the failure of this disclosure-focused, freedom-based regime, and the Financial Conduct Authority (FCA) instituted the protective regime discussed in chapter two. Thus, the pendulum approach between freedom and regulation continued.

4.3. Explanations for Regulation

The discussions in chapter three showed that freedom is almost uniformly considered the starting point of English law.[72] Actions by the Government to 'protect' people from certain types of credit mean taking options away from borrowers. Justification is therefore needed to move away from this basis to a more regulatory approach.[73] In the context of high-cost credit, there are three potential justifications for regulation that will be discussed – preventing harmful outcomes, stopping unconscionable behaviour, and defending the vulnerable.[74]

4.3.1. Preventing Harmful Outcomes

The first explanation to consider is regulation as a means of preventing harmful outcomes. There are two strands to this justification, the first focusing on the harm caused to society in general and the second based on harms to the individual borrower. Both are highly relevant for the regulation-based approach to high-cost credit contracts.

We as a society have a general dislike of (and distrust towards) people engaging in usurious activities. These types of products are often seen as destructive in the community. Intervention can therefore be justified by the impact that these financial agreements have on our society. The 'protection' given is not only to specific individuals, but more importantly to notions of what are acceptable and palatable

have high interest; and no man will accept of low interest where he can have high profits': David Hume, *The Philosophical Works of David Hume* (Adam Black and William Tait, 1826) Book III, 343; general discussion at 340–45.

[72] See discussion above in section 4.2.2.

[73] Rougeau, 'Rediscovering Usury: An Argument for Legal Controls on Credit Card Interest Rates' (n 23) 19.

[74] It is recognised that there are a number of other justifications for regulation available, see, eg, Debra Satz, *Why Some Things Should Not Be For Sale: The Moral Limits of Markets* (Oxford University Press, 2010) and Chen-Wishart, 'The Nature of Vitiating Factors in Contract' (n 16).

aspects of society. Intervention of this type in the context of high-cost credit is largely associated with the general disdain for usury. The charging of extortionate levels of interest is widely criticised, arising from the historical religious prohibitions. As has been discussed in section 4.2.1 above, there is a long and complex history of multiple religions prohibiting usury.[75] This has had a strong impact on the way our society views high-cost credit. These products, in particular payday lending, have been widely referred to as 'modern day usury',[76] and there is frequent discussion on their evil nature.[77] In these extreme cases, the contracts made are 'offensive to decency' and intervention is appropriate.[78]

Many commentators throughout history have justified regulation on the grounds of harm to society, for example Aristotle, Aquinas and Bacon.[79] This approach is an example of moral-based paternalism,[80] where intervention is justified on the belief that society will be better without the activity in question. It is not concerned with the outcome for the individual impacted, only the state of the community as a whole. This notion of 'harm' is linked with ideas of the moral limits of markets, and what types of contractual transactions can and should be

[75] See discussion in section 4.2.1 above. It is also discussed in Charles R Geisst, *Beggar Thy Neighbor: A History of Usury and Debt* (University of Pennsylvania Press, 2013).

[76] See discussion in The Center for Responsible Lending, *Modern Day Usury: The Payday Loan Trap* (2010).

[77] See, eg, Amelia Gentleman, 'Wonga: The Real Cost of a Payday Loan' *The Guardian* (1 March 2012), available at www.theguardian.com/business/2012/mar/01/wonga-real-cost-payday-loan; Becky Barrow, 'Britain has become "Wild West" for Payday Loan Lenders with Millions at Risk of Losing their Homes, MPs Warn' *MailOnline* (7 March 2012), available at www.dailymail.co.uk/news/article-2111332/Britain-wild-west-payday-loan-lenders-millions-risk-losing-homes-MPs-warn.html; Ann Edwards, 'Rugby League Player, 23, Hanged Himself "after Getting into Huge Debt with Payday Loan Companies"' *The Daily Mail* (16 April 2013), available at www.dailymail.co.uk/news/article-2309797/Kenny-Davies-Rugby-league-player-23-hanged-getting-debt-payday-loan-companies.html.

[78] Charles Fried, *Contract as Promise: A Theory of Contractual Obligation* (Harvard University Press, 1981) 11.

[79] These historical commentators are discussed in section 4.2.2 above.

[80] Gerald Dworkin, 'Moral Paternalism' (2005) 24 *Law and Philosophy* 305, 307–10. The contrast between these moral and welfare-based paternalism can be seen in the regulation of prostitution. A strict moral-based paternalistic approach would outlaw the activity, enforcing punishments on both the prostitute and their clients. Hence the immoral act has been prevented and the regulatory goal has been fulfilled. In contrast, a welfare-based paternalistic approach would focus on the harm caused by prostitution, ie, the damage that is suffered when people are in such potentially degrading and harmful situations. A regulatory response may therefore outlaw the activity but is unlikely to punish the 'victims' of prostitution – the prostitutes themselves – and instead focus on the clients. It would also organise rehabilitation programmes designed to prevent people from falling into this profession. Alternatively, a welfare-based response may recognise that outlawing these activities often pushes the activities underground, making the situation more dangerous for the people involved. Thus, it could legalise prostitution providing that certain requirements are met, ensuring that the activity occurs in a safe and secure manner: For more details on the different regulatory approaches to prostitution, see Jane Scoular and Maggie O'Neill, 'Regulation Prostitution: Social Inculsion, Responsibilisation and the Politics of Prostitution Reform' (2007) 47 *British Journal of Criminology* 764. It is beyond the scope of this book to consider the different forms of paternalism in any depth, however further reading can be found at Christian Coons and Michael Weber (eds), *Paternalism: Theory and Practice* (Cambridge University Press, 2013).

enforced by our society.[81] A similar distinction is raised by Satz, who uses the extreme harm that noxious markets can have on society as a justification for government intervention.[82]

The second type of harm to consider is the damage that these products can cause to borrowers. In the context of high-cost credit, the focus is not on the state of the lender or the characteristics of the borrower, but on how the lending impacted the debtor.[83] There is strong evidence to support this justification which has been discussed in-depth earlier in this book.[84] Inappropriate lending of high-cost credit clearly has the ability to cause significant and long-lasting harm to borrowers.[85]

We have created an economic and social situation where many people enter into these potentially harmful contracts just to 'get by'. This is unacceptable – as outlined by Chen-Wishart, 'voluntarily undertaking something repugnant is worse than undertaking it under coercion'.[86] As an example, having a society where people choose to be enslaved (or sell their children into slavery) due to lack of viable alternatives is in many ways worse than forcing people into slavery.[87] The outcome is the same, but because a 'choice' was apparently made, responsibility is taken away from the State and blame placed on the individual. As discussed above in chapter two, section 2.2.1, victim-blaming is an ongoing problem in the high-cost credit market. Raz highlights that a more meaningful understanding of freedom can justify the restriction of a person's rights for the sake of providing them with greater autonomy or preventing harm to their future autonomy.[88] Such contracts need not and should not be upheld; they are not worthwhile choices that the law should facilitate.

4.3.2. Stopping Unconscionable Behaviour

The second explanation to consider in the context of high-cost credit is the prevention of unconscionable lender behaviour and exploitative actions. This concept focuses on the actions of lenders, and states that, when a certain threshold of

[81] See Satz, *Why Some Things Should Not Be For Sale* (n 74) especially 98, Table 1: What Makes a Market Noxious.

[82] See Gerald Dworkin, 'Paternalism' (*Stanford Encyclopedia of Philosophy*, 2016) Parts 2.1–2.5, available at https://plato.stanford.edu/entries/paternalism/. It is beyond the scope of this book to consider the different forms of paternalism in any depth, however further reading can be found at Coons and Weber, *Paternalism* (n 80).

[83] See Dworkin, *ibid*, Parts 2.1–2.5. See further Coons and Weber, *Paternalism* (n 80).

[84] See the discussion in chapter one, section 1.2.

[85] Carl Packman, Author and Consumer Advocate, Telephone interview; David Barclay, The Contextual Theology Centre, Telephone interview.

[86] Chen-Wishart, 'The Nature of Vitiating Factors in Contract' (n 16) 26. See also Raz, *The Morality of Freedom* (n 7).

[87] Satz, *Why Some Things Should Not Be For Sale* (n 74) 100.

[88] Raz, *The Morality of Freedom* (n 7) 419.

unconscionability is reached, the law is entitled (and possibly even obligated) to intervene in the market to protect borrowers. A freedom of contract approach is not concerned with advantage-taking by parties. Financial difficulties in and of themselves remain insufficient to warrant legal regulation.[89] The liberal version of contract law is generally associated with a rigid concept of freedom of contract. It is a freedom to make contracts and have them enforced, even in circumstances where considerations of fairness and substantive equality may justify otherwise.[90] A regulatory approach has a different focus; exploitation and unconscionability are key reasons for active intervention.

Unconscionable lender conduct has been an ongoing theme of moneylending. The condemnation of usury and 'villainous' moneylenders is prevalent throughout most of history, and even appears in writings by Dante and Shakespeare.[91] In Dante's poem *The Inferno*, usurers were condemned to the seventh rung of Hell, where they were punished by having a heavy bag of money placed around their neck for eternity and so were forever weighed down by their own greed.[92] One of the most famous examples of the 'evil moneylender' is in the Shakespearean play *The Merchant of Venice*. The moneylender Shylock is described as acting with 'extreme cruelty'[93] when he lends money to the Merchant of Venice.[94] The condemnation of usury and moneylenders was also evident in the courts. In 1913 a judge in New York sent a moneylender to jail for six months, stating:

> Poor people must be protected from such sharks as you, and we trust that your conviction and sentence will be a notice to you and all your kind that the courts have found a way to put a stop to usury. Men of your type are a curse to the community, and the money they gain is blood money.[95]

This distaste towards usury and high-cost credit was further reflected in literature, with many prominent authors such as Dickens and Dostoyevsky including villainous moneylenders as characters in their works.[96]

[89] *Boustany v Pigott* (1993) 69 P & CR 298 (PC), 303. See also Mindy Chen-Wishart, 'Undue Influence: *Beyond* Impaired Consent and Wrongdoing towards a Relational Analysis' in Burrows and Rodger (eds), *Mapping the Law: Essays in Memory of Peter Birks* (Oxford University Press, 2006) 203. This was also outlined in Lord Templeman's words 'unequal bargaining power … provide[s] no basis for equitable interference', which is discussed in chapter three, section 3.4.5 above.

[90] Kimel, *From Promise to Contract* (n 5) 117. Iain Ramsay, 'Consumer Law, Regulatory Capitalism and the "New Learning" in Regulation' (2006) 28 *Sydney Law Journal* 9; Ogus, *Costs and Cautionary Tales* (n 2); Anthony Ogus, *Regulation: Legal Form and Economic Theory* (Clarendon Law Series, 1994).

[91] Brook, 'The Morality of Moneylending' (n 66).

[92] Dante Alighieri, The Inferno, Canto XVII, lines 51–54.

[93] William Shakespeare, *The Merchant of Venice* (Printed by IR for Thomas Heyes, 1600) Title Page.

[94] See, eg, Barbara K Lewalski, 'Biblical Allusion and Allegory in "The Merchant of Venice"' (1962) 13 *Shakespeare Quarterly* 327.

[95] James Grant, *Money of the Mind: Borrowing and Lending in America from the Civil War to Michael Milken* (Farrar Straus Giroux, 1992) 83.

[96] Brook, 'The Morality of Moneylending: A Short History' (n 66).

There is much evidence of modern-day lender unconscionability. Chapters one[97] and two[98] of this book provided numerous further examples of lenders acting in a reprehensible manner that justifies State interference in any resulting contracts. There is clearly ample evidence of inappropriate lender actions, and to such an extent that a more regulatory approach is strongly justified, and indeed necessary.

4.3.3. Defending the Vulnerable

The final historical explanation to consider is the defence of vulnerable parties. Intervention on this basis is justified because the borrower in question is in such an impaired situation that they could not have provided sufficient consent to the contract in question. A 'defending the vulnerable' approach can be seen in *Earl of Aylesford v Morris*[99] and *Fry v Lane*,[100] where the courts set aside the transactions on the basis that one of the parties was 'poor, ignorant or illiterate'.[101] The approach was continued in *Cresswell v Potter*, where Megarry J applied the test in *Fry v Lane* to find that a telephone receptionist without any understanding of property transactions and conveyancing 'may fairly be described as falling within whatever is the modern equivalent of "poor and ignorant"'.[102] The interpretation placed on these words in the modern context has been expanded generously to provide assistance to a wide range of potentially vulnerable parties.[103] A modern example of this focus is the Supreme Court of Canada's decision in *Heller v Uber Technologies*, where the various judgments reiterated the Court's important role in protecting vulnerable parties against improvident bargains.[104]

This justification focuses on the context of the lending situation and recognises that the multiple economic and social pressures experienced by borrowers can justify regulation. The discussions in chapter three identify that people should have a range of meaningful choices from which to pick. If these choices are not present, there is sufficient ground for intervention.[105] Protecting the vulnerable

[97] See discussion in the text in chapter one, nns 29 to 45.
[98] See discussion in chapter two, section 2.1.2.
[99] *Earl of Aylesford v Morris* (1872–73) LR 8 Ch App 484 (CA).
[100] *Fry v Lane* (1888) 40 Ch D 312 (Ch D).
[101] *ibid* in particular the statement from Kay J that there 'are clear authorities that a purchase at an undervalue from a poor, ignorant, or illiterate person, having no independent advice, cannot be sustained' (at 319).
[102] *Cresswell v Potter* [1978] 1 WLR 255 (Ch D), 257.
[103] In fact, Atiyah goes further and comments that 'the interpretation placed on these words … is so generous that they seem to have virtually disappeared as independent requirements of the principle': Atiyah, *Essays on Contract Law* (n 20) Essay 11, 344–45.
[104] *Heller v Uber Technologies* 2020 SCC 16 at, for eg, [60], [61], [74], [81], [89] (Abela and Rowe JJ), [166], [170] (Brown J); see also analysis in Jodi Gardner, 'Being Conscious of Unconscionability in Modern Times: *Heller v Uber Technologies*' (2021) 84 *The Modern Law Review* 874, 883.
[105] Raz, *The Morality of Freedom* (n 7) 152.

focuses on personal autonomy[106] and engages with the specific characteristics of borrowers. As discussed by Kimel, it is possible for people to make decisions that will reduce their overall autonomy. Restricting these choices can be justified on the basis of protecting individuals and preventing them from compromising their future options because of a 'rash or ill-calculated, albeit free, decision'.[107]

In the context of high-cost credit, an analogy can be drawn between regulation to protect borrowers and justifications for indirect discrimination prohibition. They are both concerned with preventing 'compounding injustice'[108] to an already vulnerable group of individuals.[109] It does, however, mean that legal intervention can be justified, not because the lender caused the borrower's vulnerability, but because their actions exacerbated or increased the harm suffered by that individual. There is also severely unequal bargaining power between the parties involved in the high-cost credit market.[110] Exchanges between individuals with vast differences in wealth can often include some form of advantage-taking due to the superior bargaining position of the wealthier party. They are less likely to be in a position that forces them to make an agreement on unfavourable terms.[111] They can be compared to impecunious parties who are conversely almost always at some sort of disadvantage.[112]

The emphasis on freedom, particularly relating to the economic market, is often based on unrealistic assumptions about individuals. One of these is the fiction that all parties are rational beings who can look out for their own interests.[113] Several characteristics of high-cost credit borrowers challenge this libertarian perspective of contractual relations. Many borrowers have attributes that place them in a vulnerable position where they can be easily exploited by lenders, although determining when a consumer is sufficiently 'vulnerable' can be difficult.[114] High-cost credit products are often not an active choice for some people and may be the only option for many desperate consumers to 'get by' each month. These borrowers will usually be unable to access mainstream products due to

[106] Personal autonomy is discussed also in *ibid.*

[107] Kimel, 'Neutrality, Autonomy, and Freedom of Contract' (n 3) 485.

[108] Defined as 'an action that exacerbates the harm caused by the prior injustice because it entrenches the harm or carries it into another domain'; Deborah Hellman, 'Indirect Discimination and the Duty to Avoid Compounding Injustice' in Collins and Khaitan (eds), *Foundations of Indirect Discrimination Law* (Hart Publishing, 2018) 107. I am very grateful to Sandy Steel for bringing this material to my attention.

[109] *ibid* 108.

[110] Justin Malbon, 'Predatory Lending' (2005) 33 *Australian Business Law Review* 224, 235.

[111] Kronman, 'Contract Law and Distributive Justice' (n 19) 496.

[112] See comments by Justice Posner in *Selmer Co v Blakeslee-Midwest Co* 704 F 2d 924 (7th Cir 1983) 928.

[113] Daniel Farber, 'Contract Law and Modern Economic Theory' (1983) 78 *Northwestern University Law Review* 303.

[114] Fred Morgan, Schuler Drue and Jeffrey Stoltman, 'A Framework for Examining the Legal Status of Vulnerable Consumers' (1995) 14 *Journal of Public Policy & Marketing* 267; Craig Smith and Elizabeth Cooper-Martin, 'Ethics and Target Marketing: The Role of Product Harm and Consumer Vulnerability' (1997) 61 *Journal of Marketing* 1.

their previous interactions with the credit system.[115] This financial vulnerability means that high-cost credit borrowers will continue to need these potentially harmful products, justifying government regulation and intervention into the market.

4.4. Examples of Regulation

The law has used a number of tools to protect borrowers from substantively unfair agreements and lenders' coercive tactics. In the context of high-cost credit, five key examples of regulatory-based intervention will be discussed: (1) amending or restricting contract terms; (2) interest rate restrictions; (3) responsible lending requirements; (4) unfair terms legislation; and (5) common law protections. The first three are specifically related to high-cost credit and, whilst the final two are general provisions they are highly relevant to the current issues.

4.4.1. Amending or Prohibiting Contract Terms

The first legal mechanism that can be used to protect borrowers is amending or prohibiting harmful terms in the loan contract. Prohibitions are amongst the strongest types of regulations as they directly restrict the choices that can be made by consumers. The regulation of credit contract terms in this manner was loosely supported in the Crowther Report. Its recommendations included making a number of 'objectionable terms' void, such as terms seeking to exclude or limit borrowers' rights or to accelerate borrowers' obligations, and the imposition of interest on default at a rate higher than the contract interest rate.[116] These were largely implemented in the Consumer Credit Act 1974 (UK),[117] creating a range of contractual restrictions and prohibitions that apply specifically to high-cost credit contracts.

Prior to the transfer of jurisdiction, the FCA announced a further range of limitations and prohibitions that would apply to these financial products. These proposals expanded the existing Office of Fair Trading (OFT) regulation, complementing them with increased supervision and enforcement powers.[118] The regulations

[115] Department of Business Innovation and Skills, *Making Consumer Credit Markets Fairer: Payday Lending Advertising Research Conducted for BIS by Ipsos MORI Social Research Institute*, 2013).

[116] Crowther Report (n 51) 286.

[117] See, eg, Consumer Credit Act 1974 (UK) ss 86F, 87 and 93.

[118] HM Treasury and Department of Business Innovation and Skills, *A New Approach to Financial Regulation: Transferring Consumer Credit Regulation to the Financial Conduct Authority*, (2013) Parts A4, 11, 12.

took a more interventionist approach, recognising the considerable problems being experienced.[119] The contractual limitations included:

- permitting a maximum of two rollovers[120] of the loan amount;[121]
- allowing for a maximum of two unsuccessful attempts at Continuous Payment Authorities (CPAs) to pay off the loan in full;[122] and
- a prohibition on the use of CPAs for part payments.[123]

The purpose of these reforms was to protect borrowers by removing some of the most harmful aspects of high-cost credit, and prohibiting businesses from lending to consumers who could not afford the loan.[124] These legal provisions attempt to stop relatively small and short-term loans of money from snowballing into largely unmanageable debts, and to prevent lenders from being able to 'drip-feed' money from borrowers' accounts without their awareness or approval (and before priority debts are paid). It highlights a movement away from the OFT's freedom-based approach, and towards a more interventionist focus where specific business practices or lending models are prohibited.

4.4.2. Prohibiting or Limiting Interest

Another key way the law regulates high-cost credit contracts is through the prohibition or restriction on the interest that can be charged. After significant consideration, the Crowther Report decided not to recommend an interest rate cap. It agreed instead with the approach already in place, where an interest rate in excess of 48 per cent would be considered by the court to be *prima facie* excessive, and the transaction harsh and unconscionable.[125] As the use of consumer credit in the UK became more widespread, different types of lending emerged and the interest rates charged for short-term loans skyrocketed. It became clear in the early 2000s that significant amendments to the 1974 Act were required to ensure that it was appropriate and adequate to regulate consumer credit in the twenty-first century.[126] The situation was exacerbated by the global financial crisis, as mainstream creditors generally became more risk-averse in lending, which in

[119] *ibid* 53–54.

[120] Defined as the automatic extension of the loan after its initial due date, thus incurring further interest.

[121] Financial Conduct Authority (FCA), *FCA Handbook, Consumer Credit Sourcebook (CONC)* 6.7.23.

[122] *ibid* 4.6.2(2)(j).

[123] *ibid* 7.6.12(1).

[124] HM Treasury and Department of Business Innovation and Skills, *A New Approach to Financial Regulation* (n 118) 54.

[125] Crowther Report (n 51) 274.

[126] This was considered in a number of government publications. See, eg, Department of Trade and Industry, *Fair, Clear and Competitive: The Consumer Credit Market in the 21st Century* (White Paper, 2003); HM Treasury and Department of Business Innovation and Skills, *A New Approach to Financial Regulation* (n 118).

turn pushes people out of the market and forces them towards alternative lending streams.[127]

The explosion of high-cost credit from 2011 created a renewed focus on restricting the total cost of credit,[128] and the interest rate cap debate received increased levels of media and academic interest.[129] Interest rate caps are not unusual; England had interest caps at a number of points during history.[130] A number of jurisdictions have caps, including Japan,[131] Germany, Greece, France, Ireland, Malta[132] and more recently Australia.[133] There is strong evidence that interest rate caps have had a positive impact in other jurisdictions, as they ensure loans can be provided only at a socially agreed maximum rate, and consequently force unscrupulous lenders out of the (legal) market.[134] Limitations on the cost of credit can be justified on the grounds of substantive fairness[135] or distributive justice.[136] The 'horror stories' from chapter two[137] citing interest repayments that quickly spiral out of control also make these reforms seem an appropriate response. Implementing interest rate caps is not, however, the straightforward fix many people believe it to be; banning high-cost credit will not stop people on low incomes experiencing financial difficulties.[138]

[127] The Right Honourable Ian McCartney and Damon Gibbons, *Protecting Low Income Borrowers in the Credit Crisis* (2008) 10.

[128] See Iain Ramsay, '"To Heap Distress Upon Distress": Comparative Reflections of Interest-Rate Ceilings' (2010) 60 *University of Toronto Law Journal* 707, which comments 'All groups believe that they are acting in the best interests of lower-income consumers. They agree that the poor pay more for credit but differ on the effective means of responding to this problem … These differences may reflect deeper ideologies about the market and consumers, with more concern in France than in the United Kingdom to protect consumers from the market rather than the presumption in favour of consumer choice or access' (at 714).

[129] See, eg, Chris Deeming, Sharon Collard and David Hayes, *Affordable Credit: Lessons from Overseas* (Personal Finance Research Centre, 2011); Damon Gibbons, *Taking on the Money Lenders: Lessons from Japan* (Centre for Responsible Credit, 2012).

[130] See discussion above in sections 4.2.1 and 4.2.2.

[131] See discussion in Gibbons, *Taking on the Money Lenders* (n 129).

[132] Udo Reifner, Sebastien Clerc-Renaud and RA Michael Knobloch, *Study on Interest Rate Restrictions in the EU, Final Report for the EU Commission DG Internal Market and Services* (Institute for Financial Services, Hamburg, 2010).

[133] On 1 July 2013, the Consumer Credit Legislation Amendment (Enhancements) Act 2012 (Cth) came into force. This Act made significant amendments to the National Consumer Credit Protection Act 2009 (Cth) and the National Credit Code 2009 (Cth) limiting interest to 48% per annum and providing strict restrictions on fees and charges for loans: National Credit Code 2009 (Cth) ss 31A, 32A. Note that this is subject to some exemptions for Authorised Deposit Taking Institutions. Discussed in detail in Nicola Howell, 'Small Amount Credit Contracts and Payday Loans' (2015) 41(3) *Alternative Law Journal* 174.

[134] See analysis of Japan in Gibbons, *Taking on the Money Lenders* (n 129), and Australia in Marcus Banks and others, *Caught Short: Exploring the Role of Small, Short-Term Loans in the Lives of Australians* (Social Policy Unit, The University of Queensland, Brisbane, 2012).

[135] See discussion of substantive unfairness in chapter three, section 3.4.4.

[136] See Harrison, 'Quality of Consent and Distributive Fairness' (n 19); Kronman, 'Contract Law and Distributive Justice' (n 19); Iain Ramsay, 'Consumer Credit law, Distributive Justice and the Welfare State' (1995) 15 *Oxford Journal of Legal Studies* 177.

[137] See text attached to chapter two, nns 159 to 161.

[138] Marie Burton, *Keeping the Plates Spinning: Perceptions of Payday Loans in Great Britain* (Consumer Focus, 2010).

Under the OFT, there was a debate about the merits of enforcing some sort of cap on the total cost of credit, particularly as reports came to light of interest rates of 8,000 per cent[139] and 16,000 per cent[140] APR. The OFT did not implement any sort of restriction on the cost of credit. The Personal Finance Research Centre (PFRC) at Bristol University released a report in 2013 highlighting the lack of empirical evidence on the potential impact of a cap in the UK. The FCA itself also commented that owing to the lack of credit alternatives for low income consumers, a restriction on the total cost of credit could exacerbate the financial difficulties of some borrowers.[141] Consumer organisations themselves are divided about whether restricting access to credit, particularly in the form of interest rate caps, is the best way to protect borrowers.[142] Whilst the exact outcome of a cap on credit is difficult to determine, it is clear that due to the high upfront costs and the short-term nature of the loans, any substantial cap on the cost of credit will price the vast majority of payday lenders out of the market. A report produced by the Joseph Rowntree Foundation estimated that, because of the significant costs involved in short-term lending, a not-for-profit home lending business would have to charge customers approximately 129 per cent per annum merely to cover costs.[143] Any significant limitation on the cost of credit will therefore result in less access to high-cost credit products, particularly for low-income individuals, as businesses may not to lend to higher risk borrowers at the statutory rate.

[139] McCartney and Gibbons, *Protecting Low Income Borrowers in the Credit Crisis* (n 127) 8.

[140] Barclay, The Contextual Theology Centre (n 85).

[141] The Regulator stated 'Many consumers use payday loans because, despite high APRs, that is the only source of credit available to high-risk borrowers in emergencies. They might be made worse off by caps on APRs or restrictions on how often they can borrow if they reduce availability to some consumers. Indeed, usury laws and similar provisions have been cited as an example of regulatory failure driven by regulators' own behavioural biases.' See further discussion in Tara Evans, 'No Cap on Payday Loan Interest Rates Hints New Government Watchdog' (*This Is Money*, 12 April 2013), available at www.thisismoney.co.uk/money/cardsloans/article-2308191/No-cap-payday-loan-rates-hints-new-government-watchdog.html. The comments about behavioural bias of regulators reflects the discussion in section 4.5 below, which highlights the potential for regulators to overlook the negative impact caps can have on people who can no longer access credit. This is further discussed by Porres in disturbingly similar wording – 'In this respect, usury laws have been denounced as a "regulatory failure" driven by the regulators' own behavioural biases': Eva Porres, *Bubbles and Contagion in Financial Markets: An Integrative View* (Palgrave MacMillan, 2016) 87.

[142] The complex nature of this question is elegantly outlined by the conflicting messages in an article by Rougeau analysing usury laws. The potential negative impact of increased restrictions on consumer lending is discussed by the author, who states consumer protection reforms can 'constrict the supply of credit in the economy and the ability of consumers of credit to make economic choices. Such laws hurt the poorer members of society because they are least likely to get credit … If one assumes that the major purpose of usury laws are to protect lower income borrowers, then the economic analysis suggests that the laws harm exactly those people they are supposed to help' (Rougeau, 'Rediscovering Usury: An Argument for Legal Controls on Credit Card Interest Rates' (n 23) 17). He does however comment later in the same article that a restriction in the supply of credit can have positive consequences for borrowers and society at large, stating that 'consumers might have less access to credit, but that is not necessarily a negative development. Less unsecured consumer credit in the economy may have socially beneficial effects, such as promoting savings, lowering indebtedness, discouraging impulse buying, and encouraging more community-based and mutual-aid type lending' (*ibid* 43).

[143] Elaine Kempson and others, *Is a Not-For-Profit Home Credit Business Feasible?* (Joseph Rowntree Foundation, 2009).

Despite these reservations, the Government announced a cap on the total cost of credit in November 2012. An amendment to the Financial Services (Banking Reform) Act 2013 required the FCA to restrict the charges applicable to High-Cost Short-Term Credit (HCSTC) by 2 January 2015. After the results of the research by Bristol University and the FCA, this move took a large number of stakeholders by surprise and appeared to be a highly politicised reaction to the public backlash against high-cost credit.

The FCA published proposals for the cap on 15 July 2014,[144] and confirmed the details on 11 November 2014.[145] It consisted of the following:

- the initial cost of credit capped at 0.8 per cent per day;[146]
- default fees limited to £15 and default interest to 0.8 per cent per day;[147] and
- a 100 per cent repayment cap, meaning that the borrowers will not repay more than double the amount they borrowed.[148]

The impact of the cap means that the 'average' 30-day loan will cost consumers £24 per £100 lent. This is still expensive credit, equating to a rate of 1,270 APR. Prior to the implementation of a cap, the OFT reported that the average loan was costing £25 per £100 lent.[149] This suggests that, for some loans, the impact of the cap will be relatively small. This is not uniform, and the cap will have more of an impact in certain parts of the industry and for certain lenders. As an example, prior to the cap Wonga charged £37.15 to borrow £100 over a month.[150]

The FCA cap has reduced the cost of credit for many borrowers in the market, but removed others from the high-cost credit market completely. The FCA estimated that the combination of the lending limitations (discussed in section 4.4.1 above) and cap would result in 160,000 – or 11 per cent of the existing borrowers[151] – being unable to access high-cost credit. The regulator commented that these borrowers would be 'better off', although no data was given by the FCA to support these assertions. The regulator also continued to enact price caps on other types of products, such as the Rent-to-Own market.[152] Further research, including interviews with borrowers of high-cost credit, highlights financial exclusion of this

[144] FCA, *Proposals for a Price Cap on High-Cost Short-Term Credit: Consultation Paper* (2014).

[145] FCA, *Detailed Rules for the Price Cap on High-Cost Short-Term Credit; Including Feedback on CP14/10 and Final Rules* (2014).

[146] FCA, *FCA Handbook* (n 121) 5A.2.3.

[147] *ibid* 5A.2.14.

[148] *ibid* 5A3.2.

[149] OFT, *Payday Lending Compliance Review – Interim Report* (The Office of Fair Trading, 2012) 4.

[150] Website checked 30 June 2014.

[151] FCA, *Proposals for a Price Cap on High-Cost Short-Term Credit: Consultation Paper* (n 144) para 5.15. The impact of just the price cap was later estimated to be approximately 7% of the market; FCA, *Detailed Rules for the Price Cap on High-Cost Short-Term Credit* (n 145) 69.

[152] FCA, *Rent-to-Own Price Cap – Feedback on CP18/35 and Final Rules* (March 2019) para 1.19.

type can exacerbate pre-existing disadvantages.[153] This will be discussed further in section 4.5.3 below.

4.4.3. Responsible Lending Obligations

The third regulatory mechanism is the introduction of responsible lending obligations, arguably the most important aspect of the current legislative regime for high-cost credit. Responsible lending protects borrowers by providing a legal imperative ensuring that (a) lenders act in an accountable and safe manner when contracting with borrowers and (b) the loan repayments are appropriate and affordable for borrowers. There were no explicit references to responsible lending obligations in the 1974 Act. Under the Act as passed, the requirement to lend responsibly was included in the fitness test for licensees; the OFT required creditors to engage in responsible lending in order to obtain and continue to hold a consumer credit licence.[154] There were also indications of responsible lending requirements in the duty to explain the 'nature and consequences' of credit,[155] and the duty to make a creditworthiness assessment.[156] The Consumer Credit Act 2006 introduced section 25(2B), stating that the OFT required creditors to lend 'responsibly' as a licence condition – although again no definition of 'responsible lending' was provided under the Act.

Prior to the FCA amendments in this area, the duty on the lender was merely a requirement to explain the nature and consequences of the credit. The lender had an obligation to provide the borrower with a sufficient explanation of the credit contract so that the *borrower* could determine whether the agreement was suitable for their needs and financial situation.[157] Effectively, this put the obligation on the consumer to *borrow* responsibly. There was no obligation for the lender to enquire about the borrower's intended use, requirements or objectives of the credit sought.[158] It was, however, a breach of the guidance to promote the sale of a credit product which was 'clearly unsuitable' for the specific borrower and their financial situation and/or intended use (but only if this information was known by the lender).[159] As there was no obligation on the lender to enquire about this

[153] Lindsey Appleyard and Carl Packman, *Payday Futures: Sub-Prime Credit Markets in Transition?* (Centre for Business in Society, Toynbee Hall and Barrow Cadbury Trust, 2018).

[154] See references to the requirement to lend responsibly in Office of Fair Trading, *Consumer Credit Licensing: General Guidance for Licensees and Applicants on Fitness and Requirements*, 2008) 4, 6, 8, 9 and 30.

[155] Consumer Credit Act 1974 (UK) s 55A.

[156] *ibid* s 55B.

[157] *ibid* s 55A(1).

[158] This was discussed in Karen Fairweather, 'Apples and Oranges? Responsible Mortgage Lending in the UK and Australia' in O'Shea, Fairweather and Grantham (eds), *Credit, Consumers and the Law: After the Global Storm* (Routledge (Markets and the Law Series) 2016).

[159] OFT, *Irresponsible Lending – OFT Guidance for Creditors* (2010) 15.

information, it was unclear if and how this provision could be enforced by the regulator. It effectively encouraged lenders to not enquire about the borrower's financial situation or intended use, thereby putting a premium on lender ignorance. In addition, the reference to 'clearly unsuitable' laid down a high threshold for a breach of the obligation.

It became evident that many lenders were not following these requirements, and in 2011 the OFT produced 'Irresponsible Lending – OFT Guidance for Creditors' (ILG). Lenders needed to comply with this guidance as part of determining fitness for their consumer credit licence, taking 'reasonable steps' to ensure that borrowers could meet their credit repayments in a sustainable manner (ie credit can be repaid without undue difficulty, over the life of the specific credit agreement, and without the borrower having to release any assets).[160] The specific requirements of 'reasonable steps' were proportionate to[161] and dependent upon a number of different factors, including the type of credit product, the amount of credit provided, the borrower's financial situation, existing and future financial commitments, and credit history.[162] Unfortunately, the OFT did not lay down any guidance on the steps that may be required in this regard, indicating that it was left to the discretion of the business to determine what was reasonable in the specific circumstances of the loan. Huge discretion was given to the lender, despite clear evidence of exploitative activities and business models.

The legal enforceability of the ILG was also uncertain, as outlined in its Foreword:

> The primary purpose in producing this guidance is to provide greater clarity for businesses and consumer representatives as to the business practices that the Office of Fair Trading (OFT) considers may constitute irresponsible lending practices for the purposes of section 25(2B) of the Consumer Credit Act 1974. It indicates types of deceitful or oppressive or otherwise unfair or improper business practices which, if engaged in by a consumer credit business, could call into consideration its fitness to hold a consumer credit licence. Whilst this guidance represents the OFT's view on irresponsible lending, it is not meant to represent an exhaustive list of behaviours and practices which might constitute irresponsible lending.[163]

The 'guidance' appeared to have been treated as such, with several Trade Association Codes of Conduct previously stating that members merely need to 'have regard to'[164] the ILG; it was not considered to provide specific enforceable

[160] *ibid* 14, 36.

[161] Proportionality was clearly a key concept for the OFT guidelines on Irresponsible Lending, as it was referred to 17 times in the Guidance, including the aim of a 'fair, effective and proportionate enforcement' regime. However, what this phrase meant in the context of responsible lending and how the test would be applied was never specified by the regulator.

[162] OFT, *Irresponsible Lending – OFT Guidance for Creditors* (n 159) 36, 40–42.

[163] *ibid* Foreword.

[164] For eg, the Consumer Finance Association, which no longer operates but had previously been the leading trade organisation representing credit providers, used this phrase in its 'Code of Conduct for FCA Members'.

requirements. The guidance also appeared to have little, if any, impact on the actions of lenders. This is despite the fact that it could be 'taken into account' by the Financial Ombudsman Service (FOS) in its decision-making process.[165] The OFT Compliance Review in 2013 found that unacceptably high levels of irresponsible lending continued in the industry.[166]

There were also inadequate sanctions for irresponsible lending. The potential sanctions that were available to the OFT were fines for breaches of licence requirements,[167] revocation or suspension of a credit licence,[168] or the imposition of additional obligations on a licence holder.[169] The regulator did not have the power to remove the firm from the market instantaneously, meaning lenders were able to continue trading during investigations and appeals against OFT decisions.[170] All of these factors undermined the ability for responsible lending obligations to provide useful protection for borrowers of high-cost credit.

With the movement of consumer credit oversight to the FCA, the ILG has been supplemented by the FCA's Consumer Credit Source Book (CONC 5) *Responsible Lending*. The underlying obligations remain very similar. Under CONC 5, lenders are expected to conform to general principles of fair business practice and must make 'reasonable creditworthiness assessment' to ensure that borrowers can meet their credit repayments in a sustainable manner.[171] How this varies from the OFT's obligation to take 'reasonable steps' is unclear.[172] CONC 5 does, however, provide slightly more guidance for lenders, including suggestions for useful documentation to request from borrowers.[173]

Despite the 2006 amendments to the responsible lending regime and the transfer of oversight to the FCA, the process in the UK continues to focus on responsible *borrowing*. The UK regime puts the onus on consumers to ensure that the loan is suitable for their needs. This creates a situation where borrowers are not given adequate protection and can be exploited by lenders who have limited regard for responsible lending requirements and are happy to exploit their vague and discretionary nature. Unfortunately, the 2014/2015 FCA proposals largely transposed the current ILG into the new FCA regime. Parts of the guidance became binding rules (including the requirement for firms to lend only where the loan is affordable, and to only refinance a loan at the consumer's request and where the firm

[165] The Financial Ombudsman Service (FOS), *Terms of Reference* (2010) Term 8.1.

[166] OFT, *Payday Lending Compliance Review – Interim Report* (n 149); OFT, *Payday Lending: Final Compliance Review* (n 12).

[167] Consumer Credit Act 1974 (UK) s 39A.

[168] *ibid* s 32.

[169] *ibid* s 33A. There is however the potential for enforcement action under the Enterprise Act 2002 (UK), Part 8 but it must be shown that the collective interests of consumers have been harmed.

[170] Public Accounts Committee, *8th Report – Regulating Consumer Credit* (2013) para 2.10.

[171] FCA, *FCA Handbook* (n 121) *Responsible Lending* 5.2.2.

[172] *ibid* 5.2.4.

[173] *ibid* 5.2.4(3).

reasonably believes it is in the consumer's best interests), but mostly it remains as mere guidance.[174]

Whilst the FCA did not drastically change the approach to responsible lending, from 2014 onwards the FOS seriously engaged with affordability complaints from consumers and this had significant consequences. Williams, author of the debt advice website www.debtcamel.co.uk, discussed the situation in a 2020 book chapter, emphasising the key role that responsible lending and affordability decisions had in shaping the high-cost credit market. She outlined the significant increase in complaints to FOS about high-cost credit, growing from 40 in 2009/10 to 542 in 2012/13 and 17,256 in 2017/18. From 2015 onwards more than two-thirds of these complaints were about irresponsible lending and lack of adequate affordability assessments. In October 2014 a FOS decision against Wonga required the lender to write-off 330,000 loans at a cost of £220 million and started the downfall of Europe's largest payday lender, followed quickly by a number of other key players in the industry.[175]

4.4.4. Unfair Terms Legislation

The next example of regulation is unfair terms legislation. This is a general mechanism but has the potential to be applied to high-cost credit contracts. When enforced effectively by the regulator, limitations of unfair terms have the potential to 'advance the interests of consumer protection in an effective and controlled manner'.[176] Credit contract terms were previously subjected to a 'fairness' test under the Unfair Terms in Consumer Contracts Regulations 1999 (UK) (UTCCR). Directly restricting unfair terms is a controversial issue, and the OFT has provided significant additional guidance and information on what it considered an 'unfair term'.[177] This has included the creation of the 'Unfair Terms Hub', a website which provided assistance to business and consumers on the UTCCR, and specific guidance for a range of different industries including package holidays, tenancies and fitness clubs.

This area is currently regulated by the Consumer Rights Act 2015 (UK) (CRA) Part 2. The legislation has the potential to protect high-cost credit borrowers, as it strikes out unfair terms in contracts between traders[178] and consumers.[179] A term

[174] FCA, *Detailed Proposals for the FCA Regime for Consumer Credit* (Consultation Paper CP13/10, 2013) 56.

[175] Sara Williams, 'The Rise and Rise of Affordability Complaints' in Gardner, Gray and Möser (eds), *Debt & Austerity: Implications of the Financial Crisis* (Edward Elgar, 2020).

[176] Susan Bright, 'Winning the Battle Against Unfair Contract Terms' (2000) 20 *Legal Studies* 331, 352.

[177] OFT, *Unfair Contract Terms Guidance: Guidance for the Unfair Terms in Consumer Contracts Regulations 1999* (2008).

[178] Defined as a 'person acting for purposes relating to that person's trade, business, craft or profession': Consumer Rights Act 2015 (UK) s 2(1). A high-cost credit lender will generally meet this definition.

[179] Defined as 'an individual acting for purposes that are wholly or mainly outside that individual's trade, business, craft or profession': Consumer Rights Act 2015 (UK) s 2(1). A person borrowing high-cost credit not for professional circumstances will generally meet this definition.

'is unfair if, contrary to the requirement of good faith, it causes a significant imbalance in the parties' rights and obligations under the contract to the detriment of the consumer'.[180] Whilst there are likely to be significant imbalances in high-cost credit contracts, the price and main subject matter of the contract is excluded from the fairness requirement, provided these terms are 'transparent and prominent'.[181]

The underlying assumption in the unfair terms regime is that individuals are aware of the price of goods, but underestimate the importance of other terms. The key issues associated with high-cost credit contracts tend to be the interest rate payable, and default fees and charges.[182] This information is generally provided in a clear and transparent fashion, and therefore will be excluded from the fairness assessment.[183] For example, there are detailed rules on disclosure for consumer credit contracts in the *FCA Handbook*, including sections focused on 'Financial Promotions and Communications with Customers'[184] and 'Pre-Contractual Disclosure and Adequate Explanations'.[185] These requirements are highly likely to ensure that the information on costs fulfils the definition of 'transparent and prominent'. As the interest rates and fees are excluded from a fairness analysis, the CRA is of limited application to high-cost credit contracts.

No specific guidance has been created in relation to unfair terms in consumer credit or high-cost credit agreements. These types of contracts have continued to receive little attention in relation to unfair contract terms.[186] This may be because high-cost credit is thought to have its own legislation and consumer protection regime under the Consumer Credit Act 1974, which is more suited to respond to borrowers' needs than the unfair terms legislation.

[180] Consumer Rights Act 2015 (UK) s 62(4).

[181] Transparent means 'expressed in plain and intelligible language' (Consumer Rights Act 2015 (UK) s 64(3)) and prominent means 'brought to the consumer's attention in such a way that an average consumer would be aware of the term' (*ibid* s 64(4)). It is however contended that the 'average' consumer is not, in fact, the 'average' consumer as defined by *ibid* s 64(5) which requires them to be 'reasonably well-informed, observant and circumspect'. This juxtaposition between theory and practice will have serious ramifications on how the test of prominence is defined.

[182] This is discussed in, for example, the OFT, *Final Compliance Review* (n 12).

[183] See *The Office of Fair Trading v Abbey National Plc & Ors* [2009] UKSC 6, [2009] 3 WLR 1215 where it was held that the unplanned overdraft of an account was a 'core term' and thus excluded from the fairness assessment. A similar analysis was provided by Immanuel Kant, *Anthropology from a Pragmatic Point of View* (Cambridge University Press, 2006).

[184] FCA, *FCA Handbook* (n 121) CONC 3.

[185] *ibid* CONC 4.2.

[186] For example, there are only three references to consumer credit contracts in the Unfair Contract Terms Guidance: Guidance on the unfair terms provisions in the Consumer Rights Act 2015 (UK) (Competition & Markets Authority, *Unfair Contract Terms Guidance: Guidance on the Unfair Terms Provisions in the Consumer Rights Act 2015* (2015). The first one relates to cancellation of a credit contract (para 5.18.4). The second one is a general discussion on the unfair relationship test under the Consumer Credit Act 1974 (UK) (paras 6.31–6.32). The third are two footnotes discussing statutory provisions governing cancellation rights (fns 96 and 103). There was a similar lack of attention to consumer credit contracts under the previous guidance.

4.4.5. Common Law Protections

High-cost credit borrowers could also be protected by a range of common law doctrines. As discussed in chapter three, freedom is generally associated with procedural fairness. The 'standard view' of contract law is that the courts refuse to intervene solely on the grounds of substantive unfairness, as this would be too great a threat to contractual freedom. Whilst this is the prevailing perspective of the role of contract law, it is by no means universal. Atiyah in his essay *Contract and Fair Exchange* provides numerous examples of ways that the law looks beyond the procedural issues to the substantive outcome.[187] In light of the detailed analysis that has already been made on this point, it is unnecessary to go into detailed discussion, although a number of brief points can be made.

Vitiating factors, whilst generally seen to be focused on ensuring procedural fairness,[188] often look behind these issues and analyse the fairness of the subsequent agreement. In this manner they can be concerned with regulating behaviour and protecting the fairness of outcome. The law does this in numerous ways, but the starting point is that 'there is a reasonable presumption of fact that a very unfair or imbalanced contract was the result of procedural improprieties'.[189] The unfairness is then merely used as evidence of a procedural fault, and so the courts still appear to be concerned with procedure and not substance. There are however numerous other instances where the court clearly goes beyond this and invalidates a contract because the unfairness of outcome is so severe that it 'shocks the conscience of the court'.[190] An example of this regulation-based approach is the recent decision in *Heller v Uber Technologies*, where the Supreme Court of Canada commented that 'unconscionability's substantive inquiry must consider the entire bargain – that is, the entire exchange of value between the parties.'[191]

A protective approach was also seen in the third-party undue influence case of *Royal Bank of Scotland v Etridge (No 2)*.[192] In this case, legal intervention was warranted on the basis that, even though the bank had not done anything actively wrong, it should have been more aware of the guarantor's vulnerability and lack of meaningful choice. Despite this vulnerability, the bank protected its own interests and was a party to a grossly unequal bargain between the borrower and guarantor. The House of Lords held that these circumstances and the bank's knowledge justified intervention.[193] There is a parallel between this situation and high-cost credit

[187] Patrick Atiyah, 'Contract and Fair Exchange' (1985) 35 *University of Toronto Law Journal* 1, 14–15.

[188] See discussion in chapter three, section 3.4.5 above.

[189] Atiyah, *Essays on Contract Law* (n 20) Essay 11, 334. See also discussion at 343–44.

[190] Chen-Wishart, 'The Nature of Vitiating Factors in Contract' (n 16) 303–304; Atiyah, *Essays on Contract Law* (n 20) Essay 11.

[191] *Heller v Uber Technologies* 2020 SCC 16 at [172] referring to Benson's academic analysis.

[192] *Royal Bank of Scotland v Etridge (No 2)* [2001] UKHL 44, [2002] 2 AC 773.

[193] See further Mindy Chen-Wishart, *Contract Law*, 7th edn (Oxford University Press, 2022) ch 9; Malcolm Cope, *Duress, Undue Influence and Unconscientious Bargains* (The Law Book Company Ltd,

transactions. Due to the obligation to undertake an affordability assessment, the lender will (or at the very least *should*) have actual knowledge of the borrower's precarious financial situation, the fact that they are unlikely to have viable credit alternatives, and the very realistic prospect of financial hardship. When providing a loan at thousands of per cent interest in these instances, the lender is making a grossly unequal bargain. Intervention in high-cost credit transactions can therefore be justified without actual lender wrongdoing; passive victimisation of the borrower is sufficient.

The common law can also be used to protect people from contracts that were entered into because of the coercion arising from lack of choice. This is evident in salvage duress cases. The court will set aside or amend a salvage agreement if the ship in distress was so desperate that they had no alternative but to consent to a salvage agreement that was inequitable, disproportionate or exorbitant.[194] In *The Cargo Ex Woosung*, a ship was wrecked on a reef and the captain entered into an agreement with the salvage boat to give over half the value of any items saved. This was significantly more than standard salvage agreements, but it was unlikely that any other ship would reach the *The Woosung* in time to assist. After the salvage was completed, the captain refused to pay the agreed amount and offered an amount closer to standard salvage agreements. When this case was litigated, the Court of Appeal held the transaction to be unenforceable. Even though the captain of *The Woosung* was 'perfectly capable of understanding' the nature and consequences of the salvage agreement,[195] the agreement was not enforced. This was justified on the basis that the captain had no choice but to accept 'the lesser evil of losing a portion of the profit and property being submitted to rather than the greater evil of losing all'.[196] This type of reasoning can be applied to high-cost credit transactions, where borrowers (who are desperate for credit and limited alternatives) accept loans of over 1,000 per cent. A number of common law provisions can therefore hypothetically be used to regulate high-cost credit contracts.

4.5. Limitations of Regulation

Analogous to the freedom-based approach, the regulatory focus also has limitations that undermine its ability to respond adequately to the challenges posed by

1985); Malcolm Cope, 'The Review of Unconscionable Conduct Bargains in Equity' (1983) 57 *The Australian Law Journal* 279. A similar approach was taken in Australia through the use of unconscionable bargains, where a stronger party takes advantage of a special disadvantage of the weaker party for their own benefit: see *Commercial Bank of Australia v Amadio* (1983) 151 CLR 447 (HCA) and Competition and Consumer Act 2010 (Cth) Sch 2, pt 2.2 'Unconscionable Conduct'.

[194] See discussion in John Reeder (ed), *Brice on Maritime Law of Salvage*, 5th edn (Sweet & Maxwell, 2012) paras 5-121–5-127.

[195] *The Cargo Ex Woosung* (1876) 1 PD 260 (CA) 265 (Sir Phillimore, with whom the Court of Appeal agreed).

[196] *ibid.*

high-cost credit. In addition to the limitations already discussed in chapter three, section 3.5, this section will discuss the issues of illegal lending and financial exclusion.

4.5.1. Overlap with Limitations of Freedom

Chapter three discussed three limitations of the freedom-based approach to high-cost credit contracts, namely failure of disclosure, lack of meaningful choice, and poverty. These are also limitations to a regulatory approach. Increased regulation aims to exclude or limit potentially unfair or injurious contracts or remove harmful terms from agreements. These actions have significant benefits for borrowers, but (similar to a freedom-based approach) do not address disclosure limitations, provide consumers with additional choices, or address ongoing poverty concerns.

4.5.2. Illegal Lending

The potential relationship between illegal lending and increased regulation must also be considered. The claim that decreased access to high-cost legal credit is likely to result in increased use of illegal credit is one of the main arguments against an interventionist approach to regulation.[197] A highly regulated high-cost credit market is likely to decrease access to legal products for certain high-risk borrowers, and this may in turn push people towards illegal lending. During his 2015 prosecution for illegal lending, Samuel Hayes defended his actions by arguing that he was merely providing a valuable service to 'people payday lender Wonga wouldn't touch'.[198] Whilst clearly anecdotal evidence only, the case highlights the potential for strongly protective laws to make previous borrowers of (legal) high-cost credit turn to illegal lenders.

The claim that decreased access to legal credit is likely to result in increased use of illegal credit is a highly contentious matter that assumes people desperate for credit will turn to unlawful activities. Research on illegal lending levels is notoriously difficult to conduct, as people are unlikely to volunteer that they have engaged in this unlawful industry. Whilst all figures are estimates, the PFRC and think-tank Policis conducted research into the market in 2006 (the 2006 Report), and stated that approximately 165,000 households in the UK used illegal

[197] Gibbons, *Taking on the Money Lenders: Lessons from Japan* (n 129); Russell Hamblin-Boone, *Industry Response to FCA Regulation* (Consumer Finance Association, 2014).

[198] See National Trading Standards, 'Manchester Loan Shark Sentenced to Twelve Months in Prison' (*National Trading Standards*, 30 September 2015), available at www.nationaltradingstandards.uk/news/manchester-loan-shark-sentenced-to-twelve-months-in-prison/, for accurate details on the case and prosecution, see also Paul Britton, 'Loan Shark who Claimed he was Cheaper than Wonga Ordered to Pay Back £43,000 – or Go to Jail' *Manchester Evening News* (29 February 2016), available at www.manchestereveningnews.co.uk/news/greater-manchester-news/loan-shark-samuel-hayes-manchester-10964426, for comments from Hayes.

moneylenders.[199] This figure was increased to 310,000 in a 2010 Policis report prepared for the Department of Business, Innovation & Skills ('the 2010 Report'), representing two per cent of all low-income households and six per cent of households in the most deprived areas.[200] Both reports observed that the majority of borrowers were based in the most deprived communities, and were people who usually could not access credit from other forms of high-cost lending.[201] The 2010 Report focused particularly on the strong links between financial exclusion and illegal moneylending, stating that:

> The high cost of certain types of sub prime and non standard lending products may not be a socially desirable feature of these models. However the modus operandi of legal, regulated lenders is surely less detrimental to the interests of disadvantaged consumers than that of unregulated illegal lenders. Resorting to illegal lenders will be not only to incur a much higher cost than any form of legal credit but is also deeply damaging in a number of other respects.
>
> Clearly, there are a range of consumer protection considerations in this context. However, against this background, *perhaps the single most important element in containing illegal money lending and moderating the damage done to victims and communities arising from it, is the maintenance of a regulatory environment that maximises the availability of legal, regulated credit, albeit that this may come at a high cost for some.*[202]

This concern appears to be reasonably widespread. In 2010 Ramsay noted that many mainstream UK consumer organisations (Which?, Consumer Focus and Citizens Advice Bureau) were opposed to interest rate caps because of the potential to push already struggling people into the hands of illegal loan sharks.[203]

There is some empirical support for this concern. StepChange surveyed clients who had taken out high-cost credit, and found that five per cent of those who had been refused a loan would consider using an illegal lender and that two per cent had actually used (or attempted to use) one.[204] A particularly concerning finding from this survey was the lack of government support; if unable to use high-cost credit products, over twice as many people would access credit from an illegal lender than from the Social Fund or government services.[205] These figures are obviously conservative, as many people would not want to admit either considering or using an illegal activity.

[199] Personal Finance Research Centre and Policis, *Illegal Lending in the UK: Research Report* (2006) 5.

[200] Anna Ellison and others, *Interim Evaluation of the National Illegal Money Lending Projects* (Department of Business, Innovation & Skills and Policis, 2010) (hereinafter '2010 Report') 10.

[201] Personal Finance Research Centre and Policis, *Illegal Lending in the UK* (n 199) 7; 2010 Report *ibid* 10–11.

[202] 2010 Report *ibid* 105 (emphasis added).

[203] This can be compared to the equivalent French organisations, which focused on the importance of ceilings to limit over-indebtedness: Ramsay, "To Heap Distress Upon Distress" (n 128).

[204] This can be compared with 60% of people who stated that if their application was refused, they would not borrow money at all: Stepchange Debt Charity, *StepChange Debt Charity Response to the Financial Conduct Authority Consultation: CP10/14: Proposals for a Price Cap on High-Cost Short-Term Credit* (2014) 4.

[205] Based on figures from CMA, *Research into the Payday Lending Market* (2014) 71.

Even though these do sound like small numbers, data from the FCA[206] estimates that 8,000 people would consider using illegal lenders, and 3,200 would use or attempt to use an illegal lender as a result of the new restrictions on high-cost credit. In its 2020 Financial Lives survey, the FCA noted that 0.5 per cent of people surveyed admitted to borrowing from an illegal lender – but stated that this is likely to be a significant underreporting. The regulator noted an overlap between high-cost credit and illegal lending, commenting that 82 per cent of adults who had used an unlicensed moneylender in the last year had also used an overdraft and/or high-cost credit.[207] These figures differ sharply with The Centre for Social Justice's 2022 report *Swimming with Sharks*, which estimates as many as 1.07 million people are borrowing from an illegal lender – over 700,000 more than identified previously. The relationship between high-cost credit and illegal lending is therefore worthy of further research and is something that the regulator must be aware of before enacting additional regulation.

4.5.3. Financial Exclusion

The final limitation to consider is the impact of financial exclusion[208] on high-cost credit borrowers. Financial exclusion and vulnerability remain significant – and in many ways growing – problems in the UK,[209] and one that has been exacerbated by COVID-19. There is legitimate concern that increased regulation (and subsequent decreased access to high-cost credit) could exclude increasing numbers of people desperate for credit from the (legal) financial market completely. As previously discussed, the FCA estimated that its legal reforms will result in approximately 11 per cent of the market, or around 160,000 people, no longer being able to access high-cost credit.[210] The financial exclusion of such a high number of people did not seem to concern the regulator, with it reporting:

> we believe that for most of these people [high-cost credit] is not the best outcome for them due to the high cost, particularly if they are unable to pay back on time. The effect

[206] FCA, *Financial Lives 2020 Survey: The Impact of Coronavirus* (2020) 42. The 160,000 borrowers are no longer using legal high-cost credit: FCA, *Proposals for a Price Cap on High-Cost Short-Term Credit: Consultation Paper* (n 144) para 5.15.

[207] The Centre for Social Justice, *Swimming with Sharks* (2022).

[208] There is no agreed definition of financial exclusion, although the European Commission defines it as 'a process whereby people encounter difficulties accessing and/or using financial services and products in the mainstream market that are appropriate to their needs and enable them to lead a normal social life in the society in which they belong': Social Affairs and Equal Opportunities Inclusion Directorate-General for Employment, Social Policy Aspects of Migration, Streamlining of Social Policies, *Financial Services Provision and the Prevention of Financial Exclusion* (European Commission, 2008) 9; See also Social Affairs and Equal Opportunities Directorate-General for Employment, *Towards a Common Operational European Definition of Over-Indebtedness* (European Communities, 2008).

[209] Charlie Cadywould, *Banking for All* (Demos, 2016) 15–17.

[210] FCA, *Proposals for a Price Cap on High-Cost Short-Term Credit: Consultation Paper* (n 144) para 5.15. The impact of just the price cap was later estimated to be approximately 7% of the market; FCA, *Detailed Rules for the Price Cap on High-Cost Short-Term Credit; Including Feedback on CP14/10 and Final Rules* (n 145) 69.

> of our cap will prompt more people in financial difficulty to seek other ways of handling their situation, such as by seeking debt advice. Apart from a short initial period we believe *these customers will be better off not having taken out a loan*.[211]

Paradoxically, the FCA's comments in this regard go directly against the recommendations of the Public Accounts Committee (PAC), which highlighted the impact of financial exclusion and the importance of supporting those who are 'credit poor' instead of merely eliminating them from the market.[212]

Regulation, including caps on the cost of credit, are likely to result in financial exclusion, which can exacerbate pre-existing financial problems, as opposed to solving them. As Rougeau states, regulation can

> constrict the supply of credit in the economy and the ability of consumers of credit to make economic choices. Such laws hurt the poorer members of society because they are least likely to get credit … If one assumes that the major purpose of usury laws are to protect lower income borrowers, then the economic analysis suggests that the laws harm exactly those people they are supposed to help.[213]

This thinking is by no means new. Bentham asserted in 1788 that poor people were not better off, and in fact were in many ways disadvantaged by the implementation of credit restrictions. When confronted with potential regulation of moneylending, he declared that borrowers did not need any additional protection. Bentham stated that provided there is no 'defect' in a poor person's judgement or temper, they should be able to look after their own interests as well as someone who is better off; 'he knows what is his interests as well as they do, and is well disposed and able to pursue it as they are'.[214] Bentham's assertions are largely supported by more recent empirical research.

Enacting regulation will prevent many borrowers from accessing high-cost credit products. This may benefit people who are using the funds for discretionary expenses, although it will disadvantage those who urgently need money or who are reliant on the funds for everyday living expenses. A significant portion of borrowers have no access to alternative financial products and are using the funds for everyday expenses that they 'definitely' could not have gone without.[215] If access

[211] FCA, *Proposals for a Price Cap on High-Cost Short-Term Credit: Consultation Paper* (n 144) para 1.27 (emphasis added).

[212] Public Accounts Committee, *8th Report – Regulating Consumer Credit* (n 170) Recommendation 7.

[213] Rougeau, Rediscovering Usury: An Argument for Legal Controls on Credit Card Interest Rates' (n 23) 17. He does however comment later in the same article that a restriction in the supply of credit can have positive consequences for borrowers and society at large, stating that 'consumers might have less access to credit, but that is not necessarily a negative development. Less unsecured consumer credit in the economy may have socially beneficial effects, such as promoting savings, lowering indebtedness, discouraging impulse buying, and encouraging more community-based and mutual-aid type lending': 43.

[214] Jeremy Bentham, *Defence of Usury; shewing the impolicy of the present legal restraints on the terms of pecuniary bargains. In a series of letters to a friend. To which is added, a letter to Adam Smith, Esq; LL.D. on the discouragements opposed by the above restraints to the progress of inventive industry* (Messrs. D. Williams, Colles, White, Byrne, Lewis, Jones, and Moore 1788) Letter IV.

[215] Fifty-nine per cent of payday borrowers used the money for purchases they 'definitely' could not have gone without; Competition & Markets Authority, *Research into the Payday Lending Market* (n 205) 68.

to high-cost credit was reduced or severely limited for these people, their alternatives include pawnbroking, unauthorised overdrafts, borrowing from family or friends, and (as discussed above) possibly illegal lending. These have the potential to further disadvantage an already marginalised and financially excluded group of people.[216] The unauthorised overdraft option may be even more expensive than high-cost credit, due to the crippling nature of current bank fees.[217] This analysis is supported by the borrowers themselves, with one in 15 using high-cost credit because the alternatives were *more* expensive.[218] Similar concerns exist in other countries. Comments of a similar type were made by the United States Federal Reserve Board Governor Martha Seger, when contemplating imposing a federal cap on credit card charges. Seger stated that a cap 'would likely reduce the amount of credit made available, forcing consumers to rely instead on less convenient and possibly more expensive substitutes, or to lose access to credit at any rate'. She further commented that this impact would be most severe on lower-income borrowers.[219] A strongly protective regulatory approach to high-cost credit will undoubtedly leave significant gaps, particularly for those who are unable to access other forms of credit.

Quantitative research undertaken by the Competition & Markets Authority (CMA) has been supported by empirical research commissioned as part of Arts and Humanities Research Council's (AHRC) *FinCris Research* Project, which analysed responsibility and ethics in the financial crisis. As part of this project, Appleyard, Gardner[220] and Rowlingson interviewed borrowers of a variety of short-term credit about their experiences and attitudes to credit use. These discussions revealed that most people understood they were using an expensive form of credit, but due to their financial position it was unavoidable.[221] The findings of

[216] Karen Rowlingson, Lindsey Appleyard and Jodi Gardner, 'Payday Lending in the UK: The Regul(aris)ation of a Necessary Evil?' (2016) 45 *Journal of Social Policy* 527, see especially 540–43.

[217] Which? Investigated the cost of short-term borrowing and found that going into unauthorised overdraft can often be significantly more expensive than using payday lenders. As an example, borrowing £100 over a month would cost the borrower £36.72 with Wonga.com and £186.00 with NatWest or Royal Bank of Scotland. For more detail, see www.which.co.uk/news/2011/09/payday-loans-and-bank-overdrafts-compared-266802/. The FCA has recognised this problem and required banks to more clearly explain the cost of these charges, however at the time of writing no substantive regulation had been implemented; see the FCA's 22 January 2020 Press Release 'New Overdraft Rules Mean 7 out of 10 People will be Better off or See No Change'.

[218] CMA, *Research into the Payday Lending Market* (n 205) 84. Considering this, the regulator has made it clear that further changes are needed to the fee structure for bank accounts, as well as proposals to increase competition and consumer confidence in the sector: OFT, 'OFT says Major Change Still Needed in Personal Current Account Market' (Press Release, 25 January 2013), available at www.oft.gov.uk/news-and-updates/press/2013/10-13#.UY4pCsrsxn4. This will benefit consumers who may otherwise turn to high-cost credit when in desperate need of funds, due to the astronomically high cost of certain bank fees.

[219] Martha Seger, 'Fed Opposes Legal Cap on Credit Card Interest Rates' (*LA Times*, 22 April 1987), cited in Rougeau, Rediscovering Usury: An Argument for Legal Controls on Credit Card Interest Rates' (n 23) 14.

[220] The author of this book.

[221] Rowlingson, Appleyard and Gardner, 'Payday Lending in the UK' (n 216) 536.

this project were published in the *Journal of Social Policy*, with the authors' commenting that

> We are not seeking to deny … that payday lending is an extremely expensive form of credit which can lead people into highly problematic debt situations. We do, however, argue that a more critical analysis of the root causes of the growth of payday lending, along with a better understanding of the 'lived reality' of payday borrowing provides an important basis for a robust analysis of policy options. We have shown that the regula(risa)tion of payday lending will do nothing to tackle the root causes of demand for this form of credit.[222]

Many users of high-cost credit may benefit from enhanced regulation of high-cost credit, whilst others – usually those who are already the most vulnerable – could be worse off.[223] The financial exclusion experienced by these borrowers can exacerbate their pre-existing disadvantages. High-cost credit and subsequent debt spirals can result in other types of exclusion, such as homelessness or rough housing, children being kept from school as they cannot afford books, fees and uniforms, and adults being unable to hold down jobs as they cannot afford car repayments or public transportation costs. This type of situation severely limits people's long-term choices and their ability to pursue freely chosen goals and relationships. It is therefore critically important to address how and why such large numbers of people have become financially excluded from the mainstream credit system and need to use loans in such a dangerous way, and attempt to stop the demand for this type of credit. Without engaging with the welfare system, any type of protective regulatory response is going to increase the financial exclusion of some borrowers, potentially exacerbating their already precarious financial situation.

4.6. Conclusion

Regulating potentially unfair contracts is important, and there is a long history of a protective approach to high-cost credit, commonly associated with usury and religious concerns regarding these products. There are already a number of regulations under both statute and common law, but this type of approach has significant limitations. The complexity of high-cost credit justifies a more nuanced approach than simply 'should we restrict access to certain products?' or 'should we implement an interest rate cap?'. Merely regulating credit does not deal with the underlying difficulties that many households face. The Government needs to understand and recognise the reasons *why* people use such expensive and potentially harmful credit products, and the impact that financial exclusion can have on their wellbeing. Chapters three and four have discussed the

[222] *ibid* 540.
[223] *ibid.*

competing and often conflicting notions of freedom and regulation. Neither of these approaches is adequate by itself. Freedom has not worked, as the vulnerable have continued to be exploited, and regulation creates limited choices for people already struggling with financial exclusion. This tension is evident in the political, social and legal attitudes to the regulation of high-cost credit. The pendulum has continually swung between the two dominant theories, with neither providing a sustainable solution. When one fails, the other comes to the forefront and the cycle continues endlessly. All the while, vulnerable people are financially excluded or mistreated. The next chapter therefore introduces a third concept, a social minimum, which can address some of the limitations posed by both freedom and regulation.

5

A Social Minimum

A decent provision for the poor is the true test of civilization.

— Samuel Johnson

This chapter introduces a third concept – the provision of a social minimum.[1] Unlike the two concepts already discussed, freedom and regulation, the role of a social minimum has not previously been considered in relation to high-cost credit. The debate on how to address these financial products is usually characterised in terms of a tension between freedom and regulation. This dichotomous approach has not yielded effective results for tackling the problems associated with high-cost credit. The current chapter moves away from this dichotomy to consider the role that the provision of a social minimum can play in the response to high-cost credit challenges. There are five sections, following the same structure as the previous two chapters. The first section examines the concept of a social minimum, including why it is an important consideration in high-cost credit markets. This is followed by an analysis of the history of social minimum provision and the development of the Welfare State. The third section analyses three justifications for the State's responsibility to provide a social minimum. The fourth section summarises how this concept is already incorporated into the legal and regulatory system, including welfare support, bankruptcy processes, and vitiating factors. The final part considers various limitations of a social minimum.

5.1. What is a Social Minimum?

The modern notion of a social minimum has been around since Rawls' *A Theory of Justice* in 1979. This concept recognises the importance of providing a certain level of resources to all people to ensure a minimally acceptable

[1] The discussion in this book will use 'a social minimum', but it is recognised that the term 'social minima' is also used in the existing literature to refer to the same concept.

standard of living.[2] This has been pivotal in how we approach issues of poverty and inequality, and is linked to the provision of welfare by the State.[3] Academics and philosophers have framed the social minimum in a variety of ways.[4] For the purpose of this book, the focus is identifying what is necessary for people to have a 'decent and meaningful life' in the society in which they live. This approach is largely based on Rawls' analysis[5] and supported by Nussbaum, who framed the concept of a social minimum by identifying central functional capabilities that people need to live a life which is truly 'human'.[6]

Precisely pinpointing the appropriate level of a social minimum is a difficult task, and a highly political one.[7] The Beveridge Report itself stated that 'any estimate of subsistence income' could not be scientifically determined but had to be 'to some extent a matter of judgment'.[8] Throughout modern history there have been many attempts to determine the poverty level and/or social minimum. This started with the ground-breaking work of Rowntree, whose surveys on the living standards in York shocked the nation when they highlighted the extent of 'in work' poverty. Rowntree was the first person to coin the term 'poverty line', which for a long period formed the basis of the social minimum in the UK.[9] This research was followed by the Breadline Britain surveys, which identified what society believed to be the basic necessities for all citizens. These surveys were first conducted in

[2] For a sample of the literature on this topic, see John Rawls, *A Theory of Justice* (Harvard University Press, 1971); Amartya Sen, *Inequality Reexamined* (Harvard University Press, 1992); Amartya Sen, *The Standard of Living* (Cambridge University Press, 1987); Jeremy Waldron, 'John Rawls and the Social Minimum' (1986) 3 *Journal of Applied Philosophy* 21. An excellent introductory writing by Stuart White, 'Social Minimum' (*Stanford Encyclopedia of Philosophy*, 2004), available at http://plato.stanford.edu/entries/social-minimum/ (all websites cited in this chapter were last accessed on 19 January 2022).

[3] See discussion in Kotkas, Leijten and Pennings (eds), *Specifying and Securing a Social Minimum in the Battle Against Poverty* (Hart Publishing, 2019) in general and specifically Michael Alder's chapter, 'The Social Minimum in the Context of Inequality'; Stewart Lansley and Joanna Mack, *Breadline Britain: The Rise of Mass Poverty* (OneWorld Publications, 2015) specifically chs 1 and 2.

[4] The definition of protection of a social minimum is also open for debate. For example, Waldron defines it as a 'level of material well-being beneath which no member of society should be allowed to fall' (Waldron, 'John Rawls and the Social Minimum' (n 2) 21), Sen talks about the need for people to be 'happy and satisfied' (Sen, *The Standard of Living* (n 2)), and White states it is 'the bundle of resources that a person needs in order to lead a minimally decent life in their society' (White, 'Social Minimum' (n 2)).

[5] Rawls, *A Theory of Justice* (n 2) 127–28.

[6] These are: (1) the capability for physical survival; (2) the capability for bodily health; (3) the capability for bodily integrity; (4) the capability for the exercise of imagination; (5) the capability for emotional response and exploration; (6) the capability for practical reason; (7) the capability for love and friendship; (8) the capability for connection with nature and other species; (9) the capability for play; and (10) the capability for the exercise of control over environment, including political control; Martha Nussbaum, 'Women and Cultural Universals' in Nussbaum (ed), *Sex and Social Justice* (Oxford University Press, 1999). Whilst the majority are reasonable uncontentious, the last few capabilities are clearly up for debate, particularly their application to developing countries.

[7] See, eg, discussion in Lansley and Mack, *Breadline Britain* (n 3) 25–31.

[8] Rodney Lowe, *The Welfare State in Britain since 1945*, 2nd edn (MacMillan Press Ltd, 1999) 136.

[9] Benjamin Seebohm Rowntree, *Poverty: The Study of Town Life* (MacMillan and Co Ltd, 1908); these surveys were repeated decades later and similar results obtained: Benjamin Seehohm Rowntree, *Poverty and Progress: A Second Social Survey of York* (Longmans, Green and Co, 1941); Lowe, *ibid* 136.

1983, and have been repeated numerous times since – most recently in 2012.[10] Later a social minimum focused on identifying a 'Minimum Income Standard'.[11] As Boyle has recognised, outlining a core obligation to provide a social minimum is a starting point from which all relevant bodies – the legislature, the executive and the judiciary – cannot depart.[12] Whilst the questions are important, the answer is far from clear. These challenges must be acknowledged, but they do not in any way minimise the importance of a social minimum for both the current high-cost credit debate and society in general.

The role of a State-provided social minimum has developed at great speed in the UK. Minimum wages were first set a little over 100 years ago with the protection of the 'sweated trades' in 1909.[13] The National Health Service (NHS) provides all people in England with access to a minimum level of health care, and was founded less than 70 years ago.[14] It was a mere 25 years ago that the Labour Party and Liberal Democrats both promised – if elected – to institute a country-wide minimum wage, thus starting a political, economic and philosophical debate on the topic.[15] This was followed by the implementation of child and working tax credits in 2003,[16] which supplemented the minimum wage and were again designed to ensure that families in the UK did not fall below a certain designated level of income. The ongoing political focus on living wages versus minimum wages[17] has again reignited the discussion of a social minimum, and what, if any, role they play in the UK's political system – especially during times of austerity.

The chapter does not attempt to define what is an appropriate level for a social minimum (a quantitative issue that is constantly changing with political, social and economic movements, and is beyond the scope of the current book).[18] The task here is to establish its necessity and relevance to the issues currently being discussed. Before moving forward to analyse the concept, three key points must be

[10] For details see Lansley and Mack, *Breadline Britain* (n 3) Ch 1.

[11] Centre for Research in Social Policy, 'Minimum Income Standards' (Department of Social Sciences, Loughborough University) accessed 14 June 2016. Analysis of this Standard has been performed by Abigail Davis and others, *A Minimum Income Standard for the UK in 2016* (Joseph Rowntree Foundation, 2016); Abigal Davis, Donald Hirsch and Matt Padley, 'The Minimum Income Standard as a Benchmark of a "Participatory Social Minimum"' (2018) 26 *Journal of Poverty and Social Justice* 19.

[12] Katie Boyle, 'Constitutionalising a Social Minimum as a Minimum Core' in Kotkas, Leijten and Pennings (eds), *Specifying and Securing a Social Minimum in the Battle Against Poverty* (n 3).

[13] Stephen Machin and Alan Manning, 'Employment and the Introduction of a Minimum Wage in Britain' (1996) 106 *The Economic Journal* 667, 668. These trades were known for their long hours and poor rates of pay, in particular clothing and boot making.

[14] National Health Service Choices, 'The History of the NHS in England' (*National Health Service*, 2015), available at www.nhs.uk/NHSEngland/thenhs/nhshistory/Pages/NHShistory1948.aspx.

[15] David Greenway, 'Economic Aspects of Minimum Wages' (1996) 106 *Economic Journal* 637.

[16] Tax Credits Act 2002 (UK). See discussion of family poverty in Tony Atkinson, *The Economics of Inequality* (Oxford University Press, 1975) 216–18.

[17] Heather Stuart, 'No 10 to Proceed with "National Living Wage" Despite Pressure' *The Guardian* (8 August 2016); See, eg, the London Assembly's Economy Committee investigation into low pay in London and London's living wage (final report available at www.london.gov.uk/sites/default/files/london_assembly_-_economy_committee_-_low_pay_and_in-work_poverty_.pdf).

[18] See however the detailed analysis of these issues in Kotkas, Leijten and Pennings, *Specifying and Securing a Social Minimum in the Battle Against Poverty* (n 3).

made about high-cost credit and the social minimum: (1) to be effective it must be provided *and* maintained; (2) it is a relative and not an absolute concept; and (3) it fluctuates over time and societies.

First, for the concept to be effective and valuable, the State needs to focus on both the provision and maintenance of a social minimum. This is particularly relevant in the context of high-cost credit. The current concept is usually focused on the *provision* of an adequate bundle of resources. It does not tackle the question of the *maintenance* of these resources.[19] Despite the significant impact a social minimum has had on the way many people think about protecting the vulnerable, it has yet to be discussed in the context of debt and credit obligations.[20] A consideration of these issues can therefore be used to develop new approaches to high-cost credit regulation, particularly the importance of maintaining the social minimum. These financial products work in a manner that requires individuals, many of whom are already on low incomes, to repay loans at exceptionally high interest rates. A social minimum will only achieve its aim of providing a decent and meaningful life if the individual in question does not have any unforeseen or emergency expenses that necessitate obtaining credit. This is often not the case. The majority of people using high-cost credit are doing so because of an unforeseen change in circumstances.[21] This means that even if people are initially provided with a social minimum, unexpected outgoings and high-cost credit contracts have the potential to put borrowers below the level of resources needed to live a decent and meaningful life. This is not acceptable; people should not be required to agree to contracts that push them below the social minimum because they have no other options. To truly tackle the problems with high-cost credit, the Government needs to develop a welfare system that not only provides but also *maintains* the social minimum of vulnerable borrowers.

The second point is the general acceptance that a social minimum and welfare provision are relative notions; they are not absolute 'lines in the sand'. Many people believe it is inappropriate to talk about 'poverty' in today's advanced countries, as even the most deprived individuals are significantly better off than the general population during most of history, and possibly better off than many people in developing countries.[22] However, as Galbraith explains,

> People are poverty-stricken when their income, even if adequate for survival, falls markedly behind that of their community. Then they cannot have what the larger community regards as the necessary minimum for decency, and they cannot wholly

[19] White, 'Social Minimum' (n 2) Pt I.

[20] See, however, Torry's discussion of the important role that 'modes of delivery' has on the social minimum; Malcolm Torry, 'An Essential Dimension of the Social Minimum' in Kotkas, Leijten and Pennings, *Specifying and Securing a Social Minimum in the Battle Against Poverty* (n 3).

[21] See discussion in Competition & Markets Authority, *Research into the Payday Lending Market* (2014) 70 and confirmed more recently in Financial Conduct Authority, *Financial Lives 2020 Survey: The Impact of Coronavirus* (2020) 44.

[22] Atkinson, *The Economics of Inequality* (n 16) 186. See also discussion in Sen, *Inequality Reexamined* (n 2) 114–16.

> escape therefore, the judgment of the larger community that they are indecent. They are degraded for, in a literal sense, they live outside the grades or categories which the community regards as acceptable.[23]

The exact level of a social minimum will therefore depend on the community in which the individual is based. Richer communities will have a higher standard of living, thus a higher social minimum.[24]

The relativity of a social minimum is widely accepted across the political spectrum in the UK,[25] and by economists,[26] philosophers[27] and academics alike.[28] It was even acknowledged by the Conservative Government, which claimed that those who are in poverty should still 'share in [the] increasing national prosperity'.[29] Townsend concludes that 'poverty' should be relative to the standards and amenities 'customary' to the society in question.[30] Whilst it is generally perceived that the social minimum increases as society becomes more affluent, the relationship is not linear.

The final point to note is that the social minimum can and does fluctuate. Given that this concept is itself a reflection of the values that exist in a specific community at that specific time, the minimum will increase or decrease depending on the values of that society. Items that may be considered a 'necessity' at one period of time may become less important later on. One of the best illustrations of this fluctuation is the Breadline Britain/Poverty and Social Exclusion surveys.[31] These surveys provide a very useful and unique insight into a community-defined social minimum. A selection of the responses has been included below in Table 1. During specific years (1983, 1990, 1999 and 2012), adults in Britain were given a list of items or experiences and asked whether these items were 'necessities' or were 'widespread and may be desirable but are not necessities'.[32]

[23] John Kenneth Galbraith, *The Affluent Society* (Penguin, 1958) 261.

[24] Sen, *The Standard of Living* (n 2) specifically 38–40.

[25] Lansley and Mack, *Breadline Britain* (n 3) 4–8. Save for a short period under the Thatcher administration: see discussion in *ibid* 6.

[26] Adam Smith, *An Inquiry into the Nature and Causes of the Wealth of Nations* (The Modern Library, 1937) Book 5, Ch 2, art IV.

[27] Sen, *Inequality Reexamined* (n 2) 39: the social minimum can vary 'from such elementary things as being adequately nourished, being in good health, avoiding escapable morbidity and premature mortality, etc., to more complex achievements such as being happy, having self-respect, taking part in the life of the community'; also discussed in Sen, *The Standard of Living* (n 2) and Nussbaum, 'Women and Cultural Universals' (n 2).

[28] Peter Townsend, 'The Meaning of Poverty' (1962) 13 *British Journal of Sociology* 225. Even Raz has highlighted the importance of relativism, stating that 'a person's well-being depends to a large extent on success in social defined and determined pursuits and activities': Joseph Raz, *The Morality of Freedom* (Oxford University Press, 1988) 309.

[29] Lowe, *The Welfare State in Britain since 1945* (n 8) 143.

[30] *ibid* 141.

[31] The surveys were called Breadline Britain in 1983 and 1990, but were renamed Poverty and Social Exclusion Surveys in 1999 and 2012: Lansley and Mack, *Breadline Britain* (n 3) 16–17.

[32] *ibid* 17.

The surveys show that whilst the UK financial situation has improved significantly in the 30 years between the first and last survey, there has not been a universal increase in what is considered a 'necessity'. Many social activities have seen an increase, whereas other 'traditional' aspects of life have seen sharp decreases.[33] Even the gross average has not increased in a uniform manner. In 1983 the average determination of the items and experiences as necessities was 64 per cent, this increased in 1990 (73 per cent) and 1999 (74 per cent), but then decreased sharply in 2012 (67 per cent).[34] Technological developments also mean some items that were not envisioned at the commencement of the surveys, and were once thought of as luxuries, are now considered necessities.[35]

Table 1 Breadline Britain Surveys[36]

	1983	**1990**	**1999**	**2012**
Heating to keep home adequately warm	97%	97%	95%	96%
Damp free home	94%	98%	94%	94%
Two meals a day	64%	90%	91%	91%
Fresh fruit and vegetables every day			86%	86%
Washing machine		88%	87%	83%
Celebrations on special occasions	69%	73%	77%	82%
Warm waterproof coat	87%	91%	87%	83%
Telephone	43%	56%	72%	77%

(continued)

[33] For example, having a roast joint or equivalent once a week was considered a necessity by 67% of people in 1983, but by 2012 this had decreased to 36%. There has also been a decrease in the number of people who believe that a washing machine, keeping the home in a decent state of decoration, household contents insurance, a warm waterproof coat, and an annual holiday are necessities.

[34] Using figures from Table 1 to determine percentages but removing items/experiences that had only been surveyed twice.

[35] This was discussed by Lord Knight who said the Government used to have 'a scheme where people on tax credits could apply for a pre-charged visa card which could be used in a number of high street stores to buy a laptop. As a result, 500,000 low-income families buy a computer. It delivered for a lot of kids and the government is continuing to fund it for children with special educational needs but not for everyone. People may think it is a luxury and times are hard, but the times are changing, and the next generation need to know how to use the latest technology': quoted in Daniel Boffey, 'Children with Internet Access at Home Gain Exam Advantage, Charity says' *The Guardian* (21 May 2011), available at www.theguardian.com/education/2011/may/21/children-internet-access-exam-advantage. One of the clearest examples of this is access to a computer-like device and the internet at home. Increasing research is highlighting that children who do not have access to these perform significantly worse at school (Jessica Shepherd, 'No Web Access at Home for 2m Poor Pupils, Warns Charity' *The Guardian* (28 December 2010), available at www.theguardian.com/technology/2010/dec/28/uk-children-home-computer-access. This is one of the key causes of inequality of educational outcomes: Boffey, *ibid*.

[36] This information was obtained from consumer surveys conducted around Britain during the specified years. Participants were given a list of items and asked if the list was considered a 'necessity' for life in Britain. The table is exerted from information in Lansley and Mack, *Breadline Britain* (n 3) 19.

Table 1 ***(Continued)***

	1983	1990	1999	2012
Meat, fish or protein source every other day	63%	77%	81%	76%
Hobby or leisure activity	64%	67%	79%	70%
Enough money to keep home in decent state of decoration		88%	80%	69%
Household contents insurance		92%	83%	69%
Two pairs of all-weather shoes	67%	74%	67%	54%
Regular savings (of at least £20 month[37]) for rainy days		68%	67%	54%
Television	51%	58%	58%	51%
Friends or family around for meal or drink at least monthly	32%	37%	65%	45%
Holiday away from home (not staying with relatives)	63%	54%	56%	42%
Roast joint or equivalent once a week	67%	64%	58%	36%
Going out socially once a fortnight	36%	42%	41%	34%
Total average	64%	73%	74%	67%

5.2. The History of A Social Minimum

The term 'social minimum' is relatively new, although the underlying concept of welfare provision has strong historical grounding. This section briefly summarises the history of a social minimum and welfare, particularly in relation to high-cost credit. It will consider religious and charitable obligations, the Victorian Poor Laws, the Beveridge Report, and the post 'Welfare State' period.

5.2.1. Religious and Charitable Obligations

The provision of welfare was historically a voluntary or charitable obligation, rather than a duty of the State.[38] There is a strong historical link between high-cost credit and religious-based provision of welfare. The prohibition on lending for profit in the Old Testament – discussed in chapter four, section 4.2.1 above – was

[37] This was £10/month in 1990 and 1999.

[38] David Gladstone, 'Welfare before the Welfare State' in Gladstone (ed), *Before Beveridge: Welfare before the Welfare State* (IEA Health and Welfare Unit, 1999) 2–3. Self-help was also an important factor, with 'friendly societies' being the largest working-class organisation in Britain at the end of the nineteenth century: David G Green, 'The Friendly Societies and Adam-Smith Liberalism' in Gladstone (ed), *ibid* 18. See also William P Quigley, 'Five Hundred Years of English Poor Laws, 1349–1834: Regulating the Working and Nonworking Poor' (1997) 30 *Akron Law Review* 73, 78–82.

coupled with an obligation to give charitably (or potentially lend at no cost) to the poor. This is explained in Bible passages addressing usury.[39] First, *Exodus* states that 'gracious' people are to provide financial assistance to those who are suffering.[40] The religious obligation is reinforced in *Leviticus*, where Jewish people were forbidden by Moses to practice usury among themselves.[41] These Bible passages clearly apply to the 'poor' without any other limitations. Thus, in Biblical days,[42] moneylending to people already suffering from financial hardship went against religious dogma; instead, there were charitable obligations. The *Leviticus* passage further extends the obligations outlined in *Exodus*, applying restrictions on both money and food stuff or grain. The nature of these loans therefore appears to be related to aiding the poor for short-term agricultural needs, or generally to relieve hardship.[43]

There are also several references to debt forgiveness in the New Testament, and this forms a strong part of the teachings of Jesus:

> Lending is put forth as the characteristic test for admission to heaven, for it is the most prevalent mode of exerting either coercive power or generosity with regard to one's fellow beings. Luke 6:35 cites Jesus' admonition to 'lend, without expecting to be repaid.' Centuries of commentary on this passage by medieval Churchmen elaborated how this exhortation meant that *a creditor should not demand to be repaid if the debtor cannot do so without injuring himself*.[44]

The Parable of the Unmerciful Servant further encourages people to forgive the debts of the poor.[45] The historical tradition of forgiving debts and freeing debt-servants every seventh year[46] further highlights the interesting juxtaposition

[39] The other two bible passages discussed in chapter four, section 4.2.1 do not address the moral obligation to assist the poor that was evident in the *Exodus* and *Leviticus* passages. Despite this, it is widely accepted that Jewish (and later Christian) approaches to lending involved charitable responsibilities to those who were less fortunate.

[40] 'If thou lend money to any of my people that is poor by thee, thou shalt not be to him as an usurer, neither shalt thou lay upon him usury. If thou at all take thy neighbour's raiment to pledge, thou shalt deliver it unto him by that the sun goeth down: For that is his covering only, it is his raiment for his skin: wherein shall he sleep? and it shall come to pass, when he crieth unto me, that I will hear; for I am gracious': King James Bible, *Authorised Version* (Cambridge Edition) *Exodus* XXII, 25–27. All emphasis (ie italics and bolding) are from this version and not included by the author. See further discussion in Bernard J Meislin and Morris L Cohen, 'Backgrounds of the Biblical Law against Usury' (1964) 6 *Comparative Studies in Society and History* 250, 260.

[41] 'And if thy brother be waxen poor, and fallen in decay with thee; then thou shalt relieve him: *yea, though he be* a stranger, or a sojourner; that he may live with thee. Take thou no usury of him, or increase: but fear thy God; that thy brother may live with thee. Thou shalt not give him thy money upon usury, nor lend him thy victuals for increase': King James Bible (n 40) *Leviticus* XXV, 35–37.

[42] For example, Deuteronomy was probably written approximately 1000 BC: Meislin and Cohen, 'Backgrounds of the Biblical Law against Usury' (n 40) 254.

[43] *ibid* 262.

[44] Michael Hudson, *The Lost Tradition of Biblical Debt Cancellations* (Hentry George School of Social Science, 1992) 47 (emphasis added).

[45] *ibid* 46.

[46] This year has special importance in Jewish tradition. As outlined in King James Bible (n 40) *Deuteronomy* XXXI, 10, Moses commanded that the laws be read out to all people 'at the end of *every* seven years, in the solemnity of the year of release, in the feast of tabernacles'. The 'year of release' refers to *shemitta* – the forgiving of debts: Hudson, *The Lost Tradition of Biblical Debt Cancellations* (n 44) 7.

between two related but strongly conflicting phenomena. The widespread practice of moneylending in Jewish communities, even during Old Testament times, and the fact that debt forgiveness was enforced, continued Jesus' teachings about assisting those who were less fortunate and the importance of welfare.[47]

5.2.2. The Poor Laws

The provision of welfare was generally considered a voluntary or charitable obligation until the passing of the Elizabethan Poor Law Act of 1598,[48] where welfare duties to the poor were transferred from religious organisations to local parishes.[49] The Act developed 'the first comprehensive English system of poor relief'.[50] It created an obligation on local authorities to put able-bodied people to work, and to provide for those who were unable to work.[51] The Act[52] imposed obligations on the local authorities to give 'outdoor' relief to the poor, in the form of basic necessities or possibly money to make their own purchases.[53] The amount given was very little (merely enough to 'prevent death or utter destitution'), and was only provided to those who were deemed unfit to work.[54] Despite these rather extreme limitations, the provision of Poor Laws was an early form of social minimum provision and is often referred to as transitioning from individualism to collectivism – represented by AC Dicey's famous analysis of this period.[55]

From the 1800s, a wave of 'New Liberalism' stressed the importance of a laissez-faire approach. This resulted in an increased role of the State to ensure that vulnerable people were not overly disadvantaged, whilst also promoting individual responsibility.[56] An example of this thinking was the passing of the 1834 Poor

[47] For a full discussion on debt forgiveness in Jewish tradition, see *ibid*.

[48] There were some state-based attempts to alleviate the circumstances of the poor prior to this law, however they tended to be piecemeal and short-lived: see Quigley, 'Five Hundred Years of English Poor Laws' (n 38) 82–92. One important piece of legislation was the Statute of Artificers 1563, which created a legal obligation for every person to be employed (see *ibid* 94). Beggars who were deemed to be fit for work were subject to punishment, including arrest, imprisonment and whipping (first offence) and having an ear cut off (second and third offence). This was a statutory obligation for local parishes: *ibid* 94–95.

[49] *ibid* 82.

[50] *ibid* 92.

[51] John F Sleeman, *The Welfare State: Its Aims, Benefits and Costs* (George Allen & Unwin Ltd, 1973) 9. The law was further developed by the Act of Settlement in 1662, which declared that people had a right to be assisted by their 'parish of settlement'. This created a system where local parishes would remove the poor and send them back to their original parish, as they were obliged to provide the support: Quigley, 'Five Hundred Years of English Poor Laws, 1349–1834' (n 38) 104–106.

[52] In addition to the frequent amendments in 1723, 1756 and 1782.

[53] For example, this happened in the 1790s when the cost of bread rose significantly and it was easier to provide poor relief in the form of money: Sleeman, *The Welfare State* (n 51) 10.

[54] Quigley, 'Five Hundred Years of English Poor Laws, 1349–1834' (n 38) 81, citing Backer.

[55] Jose Harris, 'Political Thought and the Welfare State 1870–1940: An Intellectual Framework for British Social Policy' in Gladstone, *Before Beveridge* (n 38) 45.

[56] John Stewart, 'The Twentieth Century: An Overview' in Page and Silburn (eds), *British Social Welfare in the Twentieth Century* (Palgrave, 1999) 23.

Law Amendment Act, which was designed to address and reduce homelessness in Britain. It abolished 'outdoor' relief (ie the provision of basic necessities to the poor) and created a system of 'indoor relief' where the poor were required to live in workhouses. The standard of living in these houses was specifically designed to be less favourable than the lowest form of paid labour, to discourage people from unnecessarily utilising the system.[57]

Even with the passing of the Poor Laws, voluntary organisations and individual philanthropy still provided significant assistance to those who were vulnerable and/or financially struggling.[58] As government intervention increased in 1908 (with the provision of old-age pensions) and again in 1911 (with social insurance), the concepts of charity and the volunteer sector changed to ones that complemented or supplemented government support.[59]

5.2.3. The Beveridge Report

Social minimum provision as we know it and the true 'Welfare State'[60] were developed post World War II (WWII). There were, however, significant steps taken in this direction decades earlier. Numerous government welfare schemes were enacted after World War I. These included statutory social insurance schemes for the unemployed, sick, elderly, widows and orphans. Local authorities started to run publicly funded health services, including maternal and infant welfare clinics, treatments for specific diseases (mainly venereal diseases, tuberculosis and infectious diseases) and mental health conditions. These were limited to the poor and working classes, whilst middle-class consumers were expected to cover their own medical expenses and were excluded from the social insurance schemes.[61]

This all changed after WWII, as the impact of the War led to a 'profound rethinking and reorganisation' of Britain's social services.[62] Society had become used to two novel aspects; first, a significant increase in government provision of services, and second, a higher level of taxation – to cover the costs of the War.

[57] Norman Barry, 'Neoclassicism, the New Right and British Social Welfare' in Page and Silburn, *ibid* 64. It therefore encompassed the concept of moralistic judgementalism: Robert M Page, 'The Prospects for Social Welfare' in Page and Silburn, *ibid* 302.

[58] Jane Lewis, 'The Voluntary Sector in the Mixed Economy of Welfare' in Gladstone, *Before Beveridge* (n 38) 13; Harris, 'Political Thought and the Welfare State' (n 55) 43, 47.

[59] Lewis, *ibid* 15–16.

[60] It is noted that there is considerable debate and disagreement on how 'welfare state' should be defined and whether, in fact, Britain was ever a pure welfare state: see, eg, Stewart, 'The Twentieth Century' (n 56) 26–31; Barry, 'Neoclassicism, the New Right and British Social Welfare' (n 57) 66–68; Sleeman, *The Welfare State: Its Aims, Benefits and Costs* (n 51) ch 1. This book does not intend to enter this debate.

[61] Noel Whiteside, 'Private Provision and Public Welfare: Health Insurance Between the Wars' in Gladstone, *Before Beveridge* (n 38) 27. Details on the health care provided can be found at 28–32. See also Sleeman (n 51) ch 3.

[62] Sleeman, *The Welfare State: Its Aims, Benefits and Costs* (n 51) ch 3.

These two issues were key to the development of a social services network in Britain.[63] The Beveridge Report (formerly known as the Social Insurance and Allied Services Report)[64] used the post-War experience in Britain to recommend a complete reshaping of the welfare system into a single comprehensive scheme to cover the entire population.[65]

The Beveridge Report is considered the 'founding document' of the Welfare State.[66] It provided several key policies for post-war Britain to improve welfare in the country and was aimed to address the 'Five Giants' in the community – Want, Disease, Ignorance, Squalor and Idleness.[67] Beveridge believed that the Government had three key welfare duties:

- the introduction of a family allowance to limit poverty in large families;
- the introduction of a comprehensive, nationwide health service; and
- governmental responsibility for maintaining a high and stable level of employment in the country.[68]

This represented the development of a clear social minimum, a 'defining moment' in English history, and a transition to an institutional Welfare State.[69] The Report resulted in the passing of several key pieces of legislation, including the Education Act 1944, the Family Allowances Act 1945, The National Health Service Act 1946, and the National Insurance Act 1946.[70] The aim of these reforms was to expand the role of the State. The social minimum provided by the Government was no longer limited to relieving the most extreme cases of poverty or inequality; it was now designed to positively promote the welfare of all citizens.[71]

5.2.4. After the 'Welfare State'

In the 1970s the Welfare State in Britain was widely perceived to be in crisis, largely because the social minimum provided to citizens was considered (by some parties) to be excessively generous. This view was precipitated by a range of political and economic factors, including the election of a Conservative Government, the quadrupling of oil prices creating an unprecedented level of annual inflation, the slowing down of economic growth, an actual fall in GDP, and an unprecedented increase in unemployment.[72] As a result, the 'New Right' started a campaign to roll

[63] For specific details of the impact of WWII on social service provision, see *ibid* 39–41.
[64] Sir William Beveridge, *Social Insurance and Allied Services* (HMSO London, 1942).
[65] Sleeman, *The Welfare State: Its Aims, Benefits and Costs* (n 51) 41.
[66] Stewart, 'The Twentieth Century: an Overview' (n 56) 17.
[67] Sleeman, *The Welfare State: Its Aims, Benefits and Costs* (n 51) 41.
[68] *ibid* 43.
[69] Gladstone, 'Welfare before the Welfare State' (n 38) 3.
[70] Louise Warwick-Booth, *Social Inequality* (Sage Publishing, 2013) 170–71.
[71] Sleeman, *The Welfare State: Its Aims, Benefits and Costs* (n 51) 1.
[72] Lowe, *The Welfare State in Britain since 1945* (n 8) 305.

back the Welfare State and decrease the government social minimum, particularly through the promotion of the private sector for the delivery of social services, and requiring family provision of assistance previously delivered by the State. This was continued and enhanced when Margaret Thatcher came to power in 1979.[73] The gradual erosion of the social minimum continued for the next 15 or so years.[74] In May 1996 *The Guardian* published a now-infamous frontpage article titled 'The End of the Welfare State'. This article discussed the ways in which both Labour and the Conservatives had chipped away at the welfare safety net created decades earlier.[75] During this process, the State began to view charity and voluntary organisations as not just complementary services, but as an alternative to government welfare provision.[76]

When elected in 2010, the UK Coalition Government set about making significant changes to the welfare system, mainly in the form of large cuts to its funding.[77] This culminated in the Spending Review 2010 Command Paper (Spending Review 2010), which aimed to make 'net welfare savings of £7 billion a year'.[78] This was largely a response to the global financial crisis and the savings were mainly made through a reduction of the social minimum. Many argued that this focus was quite unfair, as the poorest in society had seen very little, if any, of the benefit of the financial boom, but were the ones who suffered the most from the crash.[79] As well as reduced welfare spending, the financial crisis resulted in difficulties obtaining credit (particularly for borrowers classed as 'higher risk') and job insecurity and/or instability for many people.[80] A similar programme was announced in 2013, when the Government proposed its 'big bang' package of benefits reforms, which aimed to further reduce spending by around £20 billion.[81] The 'Big Society' and 'Shared Society' notions promoted by the Conservative Party[82] further indicated an erosion of the Welfare State in favour of individual responsibility.

Whilst there has been movement away from the classic Welfare State envisioned by the Beveridge Report, some level of political inheritance remains, despite changes in government.[83] The Beveridge reforms were so universally popular that subsequent Conservative governments have been reluctant to significantly curb

[73] Stewart, 'The Twentieth Century: an Overview' (n 56) 24.
[74] For details of this see Lowe, *The Welfare State in Britain Since 1945* (n 8) ch 12, particularly 305–29; Lawrence M Mead, 'The Rise of Paternalism' in Mead (ed), *The New Paternalism: Supervisory Approaches to Poverty* (Brookings Institution Press, 1997) 17–20.
[75] Stewart, 'The Twentieth Century: an Overview' (n 56) 15.
[76] Lewis, 'The Voluntary Sector in the Mixed Economy of Welfare' (n 58) 16.
[77] Lansley and Mack, *Breadline Britain* (n 3) 121–25.
[78] HM Treasury, *Spending Review 2010* (Cm Paper 7942, 2010) 8.
[79] Warwick-Booth, *Social Inequality* (n 70) 177–78.
[80] *ibid* 177–78.
[81] Lansley and Mack, *Breadline Britain* (n 3) 130.
[82] This is discussed further in section 5.5.2 below.
[83] The 'path dependency' theory highlights that significant policy mechanisms shape political interests for many years: Page, 'The Prospects for Social Welfare' (n 57) 303.

these advances. Even the Spending Review 2010, which was aimed at making severe reductions in welfare spending, confirmed the importance of many pillars of the Beveridge Report, including the NHS,[84] adequate state pensions, and the provision of free education for all.[85] The key aspects of the Beveridge Report and provision of a social minimum have endured, albeit damaged, for numerous decades and across many political changes.[86] Politicians are careful to ensure that new reforms are not seen as taking away the social minimum, but rather as shifting the emphasis or limiting its application to those deemed 'not worthy' of State assistance. Commentators have therefore optimistically noted that 'the Welfare State is here to stay'.[87]

5.3. Explanations for a Social Minimum

The provision of a social minimum requires the redistribution of assets; the State must remove property from businesses and higher earning individuals and give it to those on a lower income.[88] This type of action requires justification. Three potential explanations for the provision of a social minimum will be discussed – equality and liberal democracy, general government obligations, and the happiness of society. These three justifications are inherently linked, but each focuses on a different aspect of a State's obligations to its citizens.

5.3.1. Equality and Liberal Democracy

The first explanation for a social minimum is the fact that a certain level of equality is needed for a functioning democratic system. The provision of a social minimum is intrinsically connected to the social and economic rights of individuals, and these rights are key elements of a working democratic system. Developing on

[84] NHS England, 'New Research – Public NHS Satisfaction Levels Rise with Dissatisfaction Levels at All Time Low' (NHS England, 29 January 2015), available at www.england.nhs.uk/2015/01/nhs-satisfaction-levels-rise/. The societal pride of this system was highlighted in the London Olympics opening ceremony in 2012, which had a large part specifically dedicated to the NHS and Great Ormond Street Hospital, and their impact on English history.

[85] HM Treasury, *Spending Review 2010* (n 78) 6–7. The education assistance has specific benefits to those most in need, including 15 hours a week for young children and the introduction of a £2.5 billion pupil premium to assist the most disadvantaged.

[86] Although the Beveridge Report findings were broadly subscribed into the principles of the Labour Party, the majority of the practical development of these principles actually occurred under the Conservative Party which has continued to 'cautiously praise' the communitarian aspects of the Welfare State: Stewart, 'The Twentieth Century: an Overview' (n 56) 17; Barry 'Neoclassicism, the New Right and British Social Welfare' (n 57) 55; Warwick-Booth, *Social Inequality* (n 70) 171.

[87] Sleeman, *The Welfare State: Its Aims, Benefits and Costs* (n 51) 187.

[88] David Bilchitz, 'What is the Relationship between the Minimum Thresholds and Distributive Justice?' in Kotkas, Leijten and Pennings, *Specifying and Securing a Social Minimum in the Battle Against Poverty* (n 3). This is discussed in more detail at section 5.5.1.

TH Marshall's influential work on citizenship, Satz outlines the importance of equal status in a functioning democracy, stating that:

> an equal right to vote has little effective meaning if some voters are too badly educated to read a ballot; citizenship means little for the destitute if society is so structured that they have no opportunity to share in society's benefits … Someone who is desperately poor might agree to an exchange that requires her to function as an around-the-clock domestic servant or to *bond her labor to obtain a loan at usurious rates that she can never hope to repay*. The fate of such a person may be little different from that of a serf under feudalism.[89]

Satz advocates 'positive liberty'[90] as a fundamental tenant of democracy. If we believe in a democratic society, people need to be given a social minimum in order to exercise their democratic choice as 'co-deliberants and co-participants' in society.[91] This is further confirmed by Badger, who states 'what good is the right to vote, they ask, if you starve on the way to the ballot box? Or the right to an independent media if you can't read what it's printing?'.[92] The provision of a social minimum allows people to participate in society, thus in government and democratic processes.[93]

Correspondingly, inequality is 'divisive and socially corrosive', and undermines the democratic structures of our society.[94] It creates a range of negative outcomes, including health and social problems, political instability, delayed economic growth, negative impacts on subjective well-being, and exclusion of the most vulnerable.[95] The greater the level of inequality, the lower the trust in the Government.[96] The achievement of complete equality is clearly impossible, although we can (and should) aim to reduce inequalities between citizens. People need to participate on an equal footing when deciding the laws that will govern them.[97] A certain level of resources, in the form of a social minimum, is therefore necessary for individuals to participate in democracy.

[89] Debra Satz, *Why Some Things Should Not Be For Sale: The Moral Limits of Markets* (Oxford University Press, 2010) 100 (emphasis added).

[90] Acting in a way to have more meaningful control over one's life; see discussion of positive freedom in chapter three, section 3.1.

[91] Satz, *Why Some Things Should Not Be For Sale* (n 89) 96, see also 100–105. This is not a new concept, see also Thomas Hill Green, 'Liberal Legislation and Freedom of Contract' in Paul Harris and John Morrow (eds), *Lectures on the Principles of Political Obligation and Other Writings* (Cambridge University Press, 1986).

[92] Emily Badger, 'Are Economic Rights Fundamental Human Rights?' (*Pacific Standard*, updated 14 June 2017), available at https://psmag.com/are-economic-rights-fundamental-human-rights-524ede71ed88#.3wmf7jymh.

[93] This can be applied more specifically to markets for goods and services. Markets are designed to allow a person to participate in society. Intervention into the market is therefore justified if it is harmful for the standing of parties as equal citizens in a democracy; Satz, *Why Some Things Should Not Be For Sale* (n 89) 95.

[94] Warwick-Booth, *Social Inequality* (n 70) 21.

[95] See discussion that statistic evidence outlined in *ibid* 18–21.

[96] Richard Wilkinson and Kate Pickett, *The Spirit Level: Why Equality is Better for Everyone* (Penguin, 2010) 52–53. This may be linked to the impact of oxytocin on the body; see discussion in 213–14.

[97] Satz, *Why Some Things Should Not Be For Sale* (n 89) 102.

5.3.2. Government Duty

The second explanation is that providing a social minimum is a *duty* of government. Political institutions must be justified – by the will, choices or decisions of people over whom they have authority.[98] The State should act for the good of its citizens, thus promoting their interests and allowing for human flourishing.[99] In a modern democracy, this equates to a government obligation for the provision of a social minimum to those in need. Communitarians[100] believe that the State has a duty to redistribute property in favour of the poor to create greater equality within society. Goodin argues that the Government is responsible for the consequences that its actions and choices have on those affected. Since the State's job is to protect the public interest, it must attempt to do good, or at the very least to prevent harm.[101] There is a duty to assist those who are dependent on State resources and have nowhere else to turn.[102] These people are vulnerable and dependent on the Government, which has a special obligation to protect the group – this is the primary purpose of welfare.[103] More recently, O'Cinneide has linked these obligations with social and economic rights.[104]

Even between communitarians, there are clear differences in opinions on the level of support that should be provided. Dworkin argues for a strict notion of equality of resources, where inequality is only legitimate if it arises from the decisions or intentions of the individuals concerned.[105] In a slightly less extreme claim, Rawls believes that the State should play an active role in promoting equality of all people. He advocates in *A Theory of Justice*[106] that each person should have an equal right to basic liberties (The Liberty Principle),[107] and that social and economic inequalities should be arranged to give the greatest benefit to the least advantaged (The Difference Principle).[108] He argues for the presumption of

[98] Jonathan Wolff, *An Introduction to Political Philosophy* (Oxford University Press, 2016) vol 3, 35.

[99] See Joseph Raz, 'Liberalism, Autonomy, and the Politics of Neutral Concern' (1982) 7 *Midwest Studies in Philosophy* 89, 112–13.

[100] For discussion on definitional issues, see Stephen Mulhall and Adam Swift, *Liberals and Communitarians*, 2nd edn (Blackwells, 1996) xiii–xiv.

[101] Robert E Goodin, *Protecting the Vulnerable: A Reanalysis of Our Social Responsibility* (The University of Chicago Press, 1985) 142; see also Charles Fried, *Contract as Promise: A Theory of Contractual Obligation* (Harvard University Press, 1981) 106.

[102] Goodin, *ibid* 147.

[103] *ibid* 150–51.

[104] Colm O'Cinneide, 'Giving Legal Substance to the Social Minimum' in Kotkas, Leijten and Pennings, *Specifying and Securing a Social Minimum in the Battle Against Poverty* (n 3).

[105] Ronald Dworkin, *Soverign Virtue: The Theory and Practice of Equality* (Harvard University Press, 2000) Ch 2.

[106] Described as the 'single most important stimulus to the renaissance of political theory' for decades: Mulhall and Swift, *Liberals and Communitarians* (n 100) 1.

[107] Rawls, *A Theory of Justice* (n 2) 176–80. There is also a third principle 'The Fair Opportunity Principle', which will not be discussed here.

[108] *ibid* 65–68.

equality, famously declaring that 'all social values – liberty, opportunity, income and wealth and the bases of self-respect – are to be distributed equally unless an unequal distribution of any, or all, of these values is to everyone's advantage'.[109] Rawls therefore sees an inherent link between justice and equality, considering injustice as simply inequalities that are not for the benefit of society.

There are two further potential reasons that the duty to provide a social minimum falls on the State. First, it is a responsibility of the moral community, and democratically elected governments are the embodiment of the moral community.[110] Second is the 'deep pockets' theory; the Government is in the best financial position to provide such assistance.[111] Whilst morally justified and in light of the State's obligations to its citizens, in the 'age of austerity' it is less convincing on a practical level. Others believe that the primary role of the State is to promote 'social justice'. This concept arose over 2,000 years ago from Plato's *Republic* and his enquiry into the 'true nature' of justice, including the role of the State.[112] It is generally accepted that social justice includes the provision of a social minimum (although the level is often subject to significant dispute).[113]

5.3.3. Social Minimum and Happiness

The final explanation to consider is the relationship between providing a social minimum and a happy, functioning society. A wide range of research highlights that the provision of a social minimum is beneficial not just for the recipients, but also for society as a whole.

In contrast to the theoretical analyses of the earlier section, this proposition is grounded in utilitarianism. A key aim of societies should be to maximise people's happiness. Government intervention promotes happiness more effectively than the state of nature.[114] A natural extension of this is that the State should redistribute property and provide welfare in a way that maximises happiness in society. Analysing the social minimum from a basic economic perspective should indicate that people 'losing' resources would be strongly against the concept.[115] By extension,

[109] *ibid* 54.
[110] Goodin, *Protecting the Vulnerable* (n 101) 152.
[111] *ibid* 152–53.
[112] Norman P Barry, *An Introduction to Modern Political Theory*, 3rd edn (The MacMillan Press Ltd, 1995) 148.
[113] *ibid* 149–50. See also discussion at 166 on the difficulty of distinguishing between welfare and justice in the framework of Western morality.
[114] Wolff, *An Introduction to Political Philosophy* (n 98) 52.
[115] The standard claim is that 'collective delivery of the familiar welfare services does not normally result in an increase in social well-being because particular individuals will be harmed, especially those compelled to pay for them, and because compulsion reduces freedom of choice': Barry, 'Neoclassicism, the New Right and British Social Welfare' (n 57) 59.

this would mean that the provision of a social minimum is unlikely to fulfil the utilitarian test for State regulation. Surprisingly this does not play out in practice, and societies with strong welfare systems are generally the happiest.[116]

In their book *The Spirit Level: Why Equality is Better for Everyone*, Wilkinson and Pickett argue that, once a country reaches a certain level of economic achievement, further unequal financial gains do not improve happiness levels and, in fact, are likely to decrease the levels in that society.[117] The authors reviewed a wide range of indicators, including community life and social relations, trust, mental health and drug use, physical health (including life expectancy and obesity), educational performance, violence and imprisonment, and social mobility to determine what makes the happiest society. They concluded that the majority of the population benefitted from increased equality, not just the recipient of the welfare.[118]

Table 2 highlights further compelling links between welfare and happiness. It outlines the top ten countries in terms of highest levels of happiness, lowest poverty rates, and highest levels of equality.[119] Whilst it is difficult to obtain an objective measure of a social minimum, two indicators have been used; the lowest poverty rate and the highest levels of equality. Both factors are indicative of a government system that is redistributing resources from those who have the most to those who have the least.[120] As discussed above, absolute equality is not achievable – but society can take steps to reduce pre-existing inequalities. There is a significant overlap between these factors. Six countries, Denmark, Iceland, Norway, Finland, the Netherlands and Sweden (all underlined), appear in the top ten for all three indices, and a further two, the Czech Republic and Switzerland (both italicised), appear in two out of the three categories.

[116] When determining what makes an individual 'happy', the following aspects were considered: GDP per capita, social support available, healthy life expectancy at birth, freedom to make choices, generosity and perceptions of corruption: John Helliwell, Richard Layard and Jeffrey Sachs, *World Happiness Report 2016, Update* (Sustainable Development Solutions Network, 2016) 16 (with a detailed summary of each aspect at 17).

[117] Wilkinson and Pickett, *The Spirit Level* (n 96) 8.

[118] *ibid* 275. This is particularly evident in health. In developed nations, inequality has a much bigger impact on health than the national average income. Health and social problems are closely related to inequality in more prosperous nations; they are however only weakly related to national average income in these countries: *ibid* 20–21. The authors note that this trend is repeated within US states: 22. These health problems are not linked to only those who are negatively impacted by the inequality, but spread across all spectrums of society, indicating that in the context of health, equality is better for everyone; *ibid* 175–77.

[119] Due to the unprecedented impact that COVID-19 and its consequences have had on issues of equality and happiness, the figures for this section are purposefully kept before 2019. The World Happiness Report 2020 focuses specifically on the impact that COVID-19 has had on happiness and, whilst important, is not central to the current analysis.

[120] For a critique of this connection, see Barry, 'Neoclassicism, the New Right and British Social Welfare' (n 57) 66–68.

Table 2 Happiness, Poverty and Equality Rates

Rank	Highest Levels of Happiness[121]	Lowest Poverty Rates[122]	Highest Levels of Equality[123]
1.	Denmark	Iceland	Iceland
2.	*Switzerland*	Denmark	Norway
3.	Iceland	*Czech Republic*	Denmark
4.	Norway	Finland	Slovenia
5.	Finland	Norway	*Czech Republic*
6.	Canada	Netherlands	Finland
7.	Netherlands	France	Belgium
8.	New Zealand	Luxembourg	Austria
9.	Australia	*Switzerland*	Netherlands
10.	Sweden	Sweden	Sweden

The link between equality and happiness also appears to be reflected in the UK. Inequality in this country generally increased from 2000 to 2015,[124] with the most significant changes occurring in the period 2012–2015.[125] The combination of austerity measures and the pandemic resulted in further – and in many cases drastic – inequality increases from 2015 to 2021.[126] Over the same period, happiness levels in the UK have decreased. In 2012 the country was ranked the 18th happiest country in the world.[127] This dropped significantly over the subsequent three years, where it has been ranked 21st,[128] 22nd[129] and 23rd[130] happiest country. In 2016 it received its worst relative happiness rating, behind Mexico, Singapore,

[121] John Helliwell, Richard Layard and Jeffrey Sachs, *World Happiness Report 2016, Update* (Sustainable Development Solutions Network, 2016) 20. It is recognised that Australia and New Zealand are amongst the happiest countries, but do not have low poverty rates or highest levels of equality. The antipodean author's personal (and biased) perspective on this are the benefits of the good weather and excellent people.

[122] Organisation for Economic Co-operation and Development Data, 'Poverty Rate: Chart' (*Organisation for Economic Co-operation and Development*, 2016), available at https://data.oecd.org/inequality/poverty-rate.htm#indicator-chart.

[123] Organisation for Economic Co-operation and Development Data, 'Income Inequality: Chart' (*Organisation for Economic Co-operation and Development*, 2016), available at https://data.oecd.org/inequality/income-inequality.htm.

[124] For a discussion on austerity, see Adam Corlett and Stephen Clarke, *Living Standards 2017: The Past, Present and Possible Future of UK Incomes* (Resolution Foundation, 2017) 8–9.

[125] For statistics, see *ibid* 11. This is also discussed in Lansley and Mack, *Breadline Britain* (n 3) Ch 2, particularly 51–55.

[126] Stephen McKay and Karen Rowlingson, *Financial Inclusion Monitor 2020* (University of Birmingham, 2021).

[127] John Helliwell, Richard Layard and Jeffrey Sachs, *World Happiness Report 2012* (United Nations Sustainable Development Solutions Network, 2012) 30.

[128] John Helliwell, Richard Layard and Jeffrey Sachs, *World Happiness Report 2015* (Sustainable Development Solutions Network, 2015) 26.

[129] John Helliwell, Richard Layard and Jeffrey Sachs, *World Happiness Report 2013* (Sustainable Development Solutions Network, 2013) 22.

[130] Helliwell, Layard and Sachs, *World Happiness Report 2016, Update* (n 116) 17.

Brazil and the United States.[131] Quantitative happiness levels in the UK have also dropped significantly.[132]

The link between equality and happiness has also been endorsed by both mainstream UK political parties. David Cameron said in 2009

> that among the richest countries, it's the more unequal ones that do the worst according to almost every life indicator ... We all know, in our hearts, that as long as there is deep poverty living systematically with ... great riches, we all remain poorer.[133]

The following year, Ed Miliband stated in his first speech as the leader of the Labour Party,

> I do believe that this country is too unequal and the gap between rich and poor doesn't just harm the poor, it harms us all ... if you look around the world – at the countries that are healthier, happier and more secure – they are the more equal countries.[134]

The connection between happiness and equality is so strong that the 2016 *Happiness Report* specifically addressed the relationship.[135] The Report stated that 'there are arguments both ethical and empirical suggesting that humans are or at least ought to be happier to live where there is more equality of opportunities and generally of outcomes as well'.[136] Initial research conducted by the United Nation's Sustainable Development Solutions Network highlights a number of connections between equality and happiness, including the fact that inequality reduces social trust,[137] and that there is a correlation between increased income equality and general well-being.[138] Similar comments were made in the 2018 *Happiness Report*, indicating that it is an ongoing theme.[139] Despite these comments, 'much further research is needed' to fully understand and utilise the initial findings.[140] It is, however, clear that a social minimum is beneficial for those who technically 'lose' from the redistribution of assets, as well as for those who are recipients of the welfare.

[131] *ibid* 17. There has however been a slight increase since then and the UK is now ranked the 19th happiest country; see John Helliwell, Richard Layard and Jeffrey Sachs, *World Happiness Report 2018* (Sustainable Development Solutions Network, 2018). This is however an increase relative to other countries. There has still been a general decrease in absolute happiness in the country: *ibid* 26.

[132] Helliwell, Layard and Sachs, *World Happiness Report 2016, Update* (n 116) 26.

[133] Cited in Wilkinson and Pickett, *The Spirit Level* (n 96) 298.

[134] *ibid.*

[135] Helliwell, Layard and Sachs, *World Happiness Report 2016, Update* (n 116) 4–6, 9–10, 29–41.

[136] *ibid* 29–30. This Report goes on to state 'Beyond such direct links between inequality and subjective well-being, income inequalities have been argued to be responsible for damage to other key supports for well-being, including social trust, safety, good governance, and both the average quality of and equal access to health and education, – important, in turn, as supports for future generations to have more equal opportunities': *ibid* 30.

[137] *ibid* 31.

[138] *ibid* 32.

[139] Helliwell, Layard and Sachs, *World Happiness Report 2018* (n 131) 14–15.

[140] Helliwell, Layard and Sachs, *World Happiness Report 2016, Update* (n 116) 41.

5.4. Examples of a Social Minimum Provision

The provision of a social minimum is incorporated into our current regulatory system in several ways. This section will discuss three examples, government welfare, bankruptcy relief processes and vitiating factors.

5.4.1. Welfare Provision

The main way in which a social minimum is delivered to individuals is through State-based social welfare. Ensuring a minimum level of resources to live a decent and meaningful life is an important obligation of the political system. A detailed discussion of the welfare system and its different benefits is not necessary, and is clearly beyond the scope of this book.[141] The provision of a social minimum is, however, evident in a number of areas such as benefits payments, including sickness and disability assistance,[142] access to education,[143] minimum wage,[144] social housing initiatives,[145] the NHS,[146] and tax credits.[147] The impact of a social minimum on the political outlook in the UK should therefore not be underestimated.

Poverty is often measured solely in monetary terms, but this does not capture the full extent of deprivation.[148] As has been discussed above,[149] the Government first took responsibility for social minimum provision on the premise that it was merely basic resources (ie food and possibly shelter). Our understanding of welfare has developed further, and it is now recognised that it must move beyond the mere avoidance of starvation or destitution. It is widely believed that income inequality as a concept is too narrow, as it does not reflect the range of social disadvantages

[141] For more information, see Sleeman, *The Welfare State: Its Aims, Benefits and Costs* (n 51); Lowe (n 8); Carl Walker, '"Responsibilizing" a Healthy Britain: Personal Debt, Employment and Welfare' (2011) 41 *Neoliberalism and Health* 525. For a historical discussion, see Gladstone, 'Welfare before the Welfare State' (n 38); Harris, 'Political Thought and the Welfare State 1870–1940' (n 55); Pat Lane, 'The Working Class and State "Welfare" in Britain, 1880-1914' in Gladstone (n 38); John Clarke, Mary Langan and Fiona Williams, 'Remaking Welfare: The British Welfare Regime in the 1980s and 1990s' in Cochrane, Clarke and Gewirtz (eds), *Comparing Welfare States*, 2nd edn (Sage 2001).

[142] Lawrence H Summers, 'Some Simple Economics of Mandated Benefits' (1989) 79 *The American Economic Review* 177.

[143] See discussion in White, 'Social Minimum' (n 2) Pt 3.3.

[144] Machin and Manning, 'Employment and the Introduction of a Minimum Wage in Britain' (n 13); Greenway, 'Economic Aspects of Minimum Wages' (n 17).

[145] Summers, 'Some Simple Economics of Mandated Benefits' (n 142).

[146] See discussion of health care provision in the USA in Richard B Freeman, 'The Minimum Wage as a Redistributive Tool' (1996) 106 *The Economic Journal* 639.

[147] Summers, 'Some Simple Economics of Mandated Benefits' (n 142).

[148] Warwick-Booth, *Social Inequality* (n 70) 7–8.

[149] See chapter five, section 5.2.2.

that may be experienced by people.[150] Social inequality encompasses a great range of disadvantages, including loneliness, vulnerability, disenfranchisement, and the denial of dignity.[151] Rawls outlined that equality is not just about money, emphasising both the importance of 'fair equality of opportunity' and the complicated nature of a social minimum.[152] It goes beyond merely preventing death or utter deprivation, and instead focuses on addressing multiple forms of social exclusion.[153] The social minimum level should identify what it means to be a human and to live a life of dignity within a given society. If we truly believe in addressing social exclusion and inequality, the social minimum must include other important aspects of society including education, health, and opportunities to achieve. An example of this broader concept is the Scottish approach to welfare.[154]

The social minimum in the UK is clearly designed to go beyond the provision of basic resources. There are multiple examples of government services and assistance that highlight the State's desire for people, even those on the lowest incomes or in some way vulnerable, to live a meaningful and fulfilled life. The Government provides various allowances so that people can afford to heat their homes adequately;[155] certain groups have access to free or significantly subsidised television licences;[156] others receive assistance with the cost of public transport;[157] free education is provided for all children; and early education is free for children whose parents earn below a certain level.[158] Government assistance has even been extended to provide free access to public swimming pools for all children under 16

[150] Warwick-Booth, *Social Inequality* (n 70) 2.

[151] See Amartya Sen, *Development as Freedom* (Oxford University Press, 1999) and *ibid* (n 70).

[152] Rawls, *A Theory of Justice* (n 2) 73–77.

[153] Warwick-Booth discusses three potential dimensions of social exclusion: (1) Resources – material and economic, access to private and public services; (2) Participation – economic (by employment), social, education and political participation (voting); and (3) Quality of life – health and well-being, the environment and crime levels; Warwick-Booth, *Social Inequality* (n 70) 6, drawing on research from Ruth Levitas and others, *The Multi-Dimensional Analysis of Social Exclusion* (University of Bristol, 2007) 117.

[154] Six dimensions of social exclusion have been identified – low incomes, access to employment, house quality and availability, education, health and fertility, and citizenship and community participation; Scottish Parliament, *Measuring Social Exclusion Research Paper 99/11* (Scotland Information Centre, 1999) 7. These categories are still – by large – applied when determining issues of social exclusion; see Peter Kenway and others, *Monitoring Poverty and Social Exclusion in Scotland 2015* (Joseph Rowntree Organisation, 2015) especially Ch 1.

[155] GOV.UK, 'Winter Fuel Payment' (*GOV.UK*, 8 February 2017), available at www.gov.uk/winter-fuel-payment; GOV.UK, 'Cold Weather Payment' (*GOV.UK*, 28 December 2016), available at www.gov.uk/cold-weather-payment; GOV.UK, 'Warm Home Discount Scheme' (*GOV.UK*, 28 December 2016), available at www.gov.uk/the-warm-home-discount-scheme.

[156] GOV.UK, 'Get a Free or Discounted TV Licence' (*GOV.UK*, 23 September 2016), available at www.gov.uk/free-discount-tv-licence.

[157] Department of Transport and HM Treasury, *Support to Help with the Cost of Transport: Policy Paper* (GOV.UK, 2013).

[158] GOV.UK, 'Help Paying for Childcare' (*GOV.UK*, 8 November 2016), available at www.gov.uk/help-with-childcare-costs/free-childcare-and-education-for-2-to-4-year-olds.

years of age, and free swimming lessons to children whose parents receive certain benefits.[159] It is not, however, all positive. As discussed in section 5.2.4 above, there has been a shift towards a more conservative approach to social security and a reduction in social welfare spending since the 2008 global financial crisis and economic downturn. This declining welfare provision and social minimum coincides with stagnating wages, increased unemployment and higher costs of living, occurring at a time when people most need the extra support.[160] Welfare provision has therefore decreased just at the time when people need it the most.

5.4.2. Bankruptcy Relief

Bankruptcy can be considered the ultimate social minimum maintenance.[161] It gives borrowers an opportunity to 'wipe the slate clean' and have existing debts forgiven, whilst still providing them with a socially-agreed minimum standard of living. Bankruptcy is also an instrument of distributive justice. It aims to achieve a 'fair division of wealth among members of society',[162] and has the effect of shifting wealth from one group of people (the creditors) to another (the debtors).[163]

Whilst it is very important to have bankruptcy 'protection', its role in the social minimum debate should not be overstated. Bankruptcy is not an appropriate response in most cases where people are pushed below the social minimum. The poverty rate in the UK before the impact of the pandemic was 16.7 per cent, meaning – even without the devastating impacts of COVID-19 – approximately one in six people live below the social minimum.[164] In addition, 7.3 per cent of people[165] in the country were in 'persistent poverty'.[166] Income instability and financial insecurity are also significant problems, with 30 per cent of people in the UK at risk of falling into poverty.[167] The situation has worsened considerably since the pandemic.[168]

[159] Oxford City Council, 'Free Swimming for Young People Aged 16 and Under' (*Oxford City Council*, 2017), available at www.oxford.gov.uk/info/20029/leisure_centres_and_swimming_pools/811/free_swimming_for_young_people_aged_16_and_under.

[160] See Karen Rowlingson, Lindsey Appleyard and Jodi Gardner, 'Payday Lending in the UK: The Regul(aris)ation of a Necessary Evil?' (2016) 45 *Journal of Social Policy* 527.

[161] Anthony Kronman, 'Contract Law and Distributive Justice' (1980) 89 *Yale Law Journal* 472, 473.

[162] *ibid* 472.

[163] *ibid* 473.

[164] Dominic Webber and Callum Clark, *Persistent Poverty in the UK and EU* (Office of National Statistics, 2017) 5.

[165] *ibid* 5.

[166] Persistent poverty is defined as 'being in relative income poverty in the current year and at least two of the three preceding years': *ibid* 2. Relative poverty occurs if the individual lives 'in a household with an equivalised disposable income that falls below 60% of the national median in the current year. This is a relative low-income measure also referred to as the "at risk of poverty" rate, which measures income compared with other people'. For 2020, the poverty threshold in the UK was £13,156.

[167] *ibid* 7.

[168] David Taylor-Robinson, Margaret Whitehead, and Ben Barr, 'Poverty, Health, and COVID-19: Yet Again, Poor Families will be Hardest Hit by the Pandemic's Long Economic Fallout' (2021) *British Medical Journal* 372.

In light of the high numbers of people struggling to maintain a social minimum, bankruptcy cannot shoulder the entire burden.

Bankruptcy is also not an appropriate solution to high-cost credit challenges. There is no evidence of a link between the two, as ironically those who are struggling with problem debt often cannot afford the £680 fee required for bankruptcy relief.[169] This means that a number of people who are repaying these loans are living significantly below the social minimum, but cannot afford the one thing that would provide them with a financial lifeline.[170] Bankruptcy therefore offers a certain level of protection for middle-income earners, but is of limited utility to low-income individuals struggling under the weight of high-cost credit.

There are other potential arrangements for people with problem debt that are not as drastic as bankruptcy, including Debt Management Plans (DMPs), Individual Voluntary Arrangements (IVAs), and Debt Relief Orders (DROs). None of these options is as costly as bankruptcy, but they are still inadequate responses to the current issues. Most providers of DMPs will charge the consumer fees to implement the agreement.[171] The DMP is also not binding on all creditors, so the borrower may continue to be contacted by parties demanding repayment of existing debts. Consumers under an IVA will repay their loan over five or six years, and at the end of the period the remaining debt is written off. IVAs are binding on all creditors,[172] and therefore provide a greater level of coverage, but involve both a nominee and ongoing supervisor fee. Similar to bankruptcy, the IVA and DRO will be recorded on the public register and the borrower's credit rating will be adversely impacted, as will their ability to access credit during the IVA period.

Each of these debt repayment options has its own advantages and disadvantages, although none are an adequate solution for social minimum maintenance.[173] Bankruptcy and other debt relief processes are a drastic response to indebtedness and are at the far end of the outcome spectrum. As well as impacting the individual involved, bankruptcy has a number of detrimental impacts on society. It undermines commercial stability and lowers consumer confidence in the enforceability of financial arrangements.[174] It is therefore not something that should be used regularly for maintaining a social minimum. High-cost credit borrowers need programmes that will prevent them from getting into financial difficulties in the first place, as opposed to expensive 'escape routes' when they become overburdened with problem debt.

[169] Applications currently cost £680; GOV.UK, 'Guide to Bankruptcy: Costs' (*Crown Copyright*, 2018), available at www.gov.uk/bankruptcy/overview.

[170] Telephone interview with Carl Packman, Author and Consumer Advocate.

[171] A notable exception to this is StepChange Debt Charity.

[172] Not including family court proceedings, student loans, court fines or debt relating to fraud, or any debts incurred after the IVA was in place.

[173] For further discussion of this see Joseph Spooner, 'Seeking Shelter in Personal Insolvency Law: Recession, Eviction and Bankruptcy's Social Safety Net' (2017) 44 *Journal of Law and Society* 374.

[174] Michelle White, 'Personal Bankruptcy under the 1978 Bankruptcy Code: An Economic Analysis' (1988) 63 *Indiana Law Journal* 1.

5.4.3. Vitiating Factors

Providing a social minimum is generally considered the responsibility of government policies, as opposed to the results of common law rules and doctrines. The welfare system provides a social minimum, and the bankruptcy regime maintains it. Whilst the law can consider and respond to the procedural and, at times, substantive unfairness of a transaction in question, it is much harder for it to address underlying issues of poverty and welfare. There is, however, one area of law where the financial situation of the vulnerable party can be relevant. This section will discuss how vitiating factors are beginning to recognise and respond to the challenges associated with social minimum.

Vitiating factors are relevant in a wide range of situations. Chapter three of this book highlighted how they can be used to ensure the procedural fairness of the agreement in question, and chapter four discussed how vitiating factors can prevent grossly unfair transactions being enforced. There are also indications that the courts look beyond the agreement between the parties and consider the impact the contract would have on the social minimum of the vulnerable party. For example, this concern is evident in the test for whether a threat to breach a contract will be classified as economic duress. If the party threatens to breach a contract because performance would risk putting them into bankruptcy or financial difficulties (and thus below a social minimum), this is generally considered a 'warning' and not a threat sufficient for a finding of economic duress.[175] An example of this is *Williams v Roffey Brothers*, where the Court of Appeal held there was no economic duress when the claimant was unable to perform the contract at the originally agreed price.[176]

One of the key examples of social minimum maintenance is the infamous undue influence case, *Allcard v Skinner*.[177] In this case the Court of Appeal set aside gifts given to the Catholic Church by Ms Allcard, a postulant[178] at the time. It is difficult to explain the outcome of this case on any other basis apart from the maintenance of a social minimum and avoidance of poverty. The decision cannot be justified because of the wrongful actions of the defendant; the judges were very careful not to make any allegations of misconduct by the Mother Superior in taking the gifts.[179] Neither can it be explained through protecting a vulnerable claimant. Ms Allcard was categorised by the Court as 'a woman well-informed

[175] *ibid* 326–27 citing J Beatson, *The Use and Abuse of Unjust Enrichment* (Clarendon Press, 1991).

[176] *Williams v Roffey Brothers & Nicholls (Contractors) Ltd* [1991] 1 QB 1 (CA) at 6 where it was held 'that the agreed price of £20,000 was too low to enable the plaintiff to operate satisfactorily and at a profit'.

[177] *Allcard v Skinner* (1887) LR 36 Ch D 145 (CA).

[178] A novice nun who is asking for admission to the convent.

[179] *Allcard v Skinner* (n 177), for example in the original decision as per Kekewich J at 158; and appeal as per Cotton LJ at 170.

respecting the matter in hand, and capable of appreciating and forming a decision on matters of business'[180] and 'a well-educated lady'.[181] As Ms Allcard handed over all her worldly positions to the Church, she would have suffered from severe poverty when leaving the sisterhood.[182] The Court returned her gifts to prevent this from happening. The decision can therefore be rationalised on the grounds that the judges were concerned with preventing the claimant from going into poverty, thus maintaining a social minimum.

Other undue influence cases demonstrate a similar concern for avoidance of poverty and maintenance of a social minimum. For example, in *Hammond v Osborn*[183] the defendant (Ms Osborn) was given a gift of £297,005 from Mr Pritler's estate. He was a frail, elderly man who was living alone when the defendant had befriended him. The Court of Appeal required Ms Osborn to repay the money, even though she 'was not guilty of any reprehensible conduct',[184] and that Mr Pritler had 'sufficient ability to comprehend fully what he was going'.[185] The gift given by Mr Pritler constituted over 90 per cent of his estate and left him without sufficient assets to pay for his future care. Only £30,000 remained, which would not have been enough to pay for the capital gains tax bill. A similar situation arose in *Randall v Randall*, where the Court set aside a number of gifts from an elderly woman to her nephew.[186] In this case, the Court was concerned that the donor would not have been able to afford her additional nursing home care when she left the hospital.[187] *Royal Bank of Scotland v Etridge (No 2)*[188] also shows concerns about the maintenance of a social minimum, in this case the matrimonial or family home. When determining whether the surety was valid, the House of Lords emphasised that the applicants' 'home may be her only substantial home, as well as the family's home … she could be made bankrupt'.[189] If the property in question was one of numerous assets held by the applicants, it is likely that the Court would have been less concerned with protecting their financial interests from the bank.

The maintenance of a social minimum is also important in unconscionable conduct cases. The entire basis of unconscionable dealing is premised on protecting people who have a special disadvantage, which includes people who are (or who at risk of falling) below the social minimum. In the UK it is designed to

[180] *ibid*, Kekewich J at 166.
[181] *ibid* at 167.
[182] This transfer was referred to as one that could not 'be reasonably accounted for on the ground of friendship, relationship, charity, or other ordinary motives on which ordinary men act'; *ibid*, Lindley LJ at 185. It is expressed doctrinally as a transaction that 'calls for an explanation'.
[183] *Hammond v Osborn* [2002] EWCA Civ 885, [2002] 2 P & CR D41 [61].
[184] *ibid* [61].
[185] *ibid* [59].
[186] *Randall v Randall* [2004] EWHC 2258 (Ch).
[187] *ibid* [55].
[188] *Royal Bank of Scotland Plc v Etridge (No 2)* [2002] 2 AC 773 (HL).
[189] *ibid* 808.

protect those who are 'poor, ignorant or illiterate'.[190] This type of approach was seen as early as 1787 in *Evans v Llewellin*.[191] In this case, the Court of Chancery protected a desperate man who sold his share of an estate, which was his only real asset, at a significant undervalue. In Australia, the beneficiaries of unconscionable conduct were defined by Fullagar J as individuals who had a range of 'weaknesses', including 'poverty or need of any kind'.[192] This does not only protect people who are below the social minimum, but those who are at risk of going into poverty because of the transaction in question.

This approach can be seen in the Australian case of *Louth v Diprose*.[193] In this case Mr Diprose became infatuated with Ms Louth, giving her significant gifts and eventually buying her a house. When the relationship deteriorated, Mr Diprose requested Ms Louth return the property. The High Court ordered Ms Louth to transfer the house back to Mr Diprose. The judges were concerned that the house was a 'substantial gift' and Mr Diprose had children to support. He 'had only limited assets, that the mortgage moneys were his principal asset'.[194] Similar to *Etridge*, it is likely that the courts would have been less interested in protection had Mr Diprose had other significant assets, and the social minimum was not a concern. The majority decision of the Canadian Supreme Court in *Heller v Uber Technologies* shows similar concerns when considering the impact of a restrictive Arbitration Clause on the rights of an UberEats driver. Abella and Rowe JJ emphasised that when determining what constitutes a weakness or vulnerability, the courts should consider the impact of the contract on the individual's ability to freely enter or negotiate a contract, or compromise their ability to understand the impact of a contract they have entered into.[195]

Whilst not explicitly taking the matter into account, a range of vitiating factor cases are concerned with preventing the vulnerable party from going into poverty. This is best seen as the maintenance of a social minimum. There are strong justifications for this type of approach. As stated by Chen-Wishart,

> The law should not facilitate undertakings that can have the effect of unduly reducing an individual's overall autonomy; hence it should be reluctant to enforce contracts that will push the complainant below some social minimum. Grossly unfair contracts are often objectionable precisely because they have an adverse long-term effect on the autonomy of the complainant. This is but an extension of the facility of bankruptcy, which renders contracts unenforceable in order to give the bankrupt a fresh start rather than require her to live the life of quasi-indentured servitude.[196]

[190] *Fry v Lane* (1888) 40 Ch D 312 (Ch D), in particular the statement from Kay J that there 'are clear authorities that a purchase at an undervalue from a poor, ignorant, or illiterate person, having no independent advice, cannot be sustained' (at 319). This was discussed in more detail in chapter three, section 3.4.5 above.

[191] *Evans v Llewellin* (1787) 1 Cox 334 (Ct of Ch).

[192] *Blomley v Ryan* [1956] HCA 81; (1956) 99 CLR 362 at 405.

[193] *Louth v Diprose* [1992] HCA 61; (1992) 175 CLR 621.

[194] *ibid* [9]–[10].

[195] *Heller v Uber Technologies* 2020 SCC 16 at [78].

[196] Mindy Chen-Wishart, 'The Nature of Vitiating Factors in Contract' in Saprai, Letsas and Greg Klass (eds), *Philosophical Foundations of Contract Law* (Oxford University Press, 2014) 304.

Whether the maintenance of a social minimum is an appropriate factor for judges to consider, and whether the courts should be concerned with avoiding poverty, are very interesting questions that unfortunately need to be left for another day.

5.5. Limitations of a Social Minimum

Despite its many positives – equality, respect, protection of the vulnerable, happiness of society and adherence to a valuable notion of democracy – maintaining a social minimum is not entirely without controversy. This section will consider three limitations of the concept – the impact on property rights, difficulties with responsibility and moral hazards.

5.5.1. Impact on Property Rights

Providing a social minimum means removing the property of some without their express permission and giving it to others. The way money is taxed and spent inherently highlights the State's values. All people enjoy the benefits of the State, and therefore must contribute to the costs involved in running it.[197] Everyone who is earning a salary (over a certain level) is required to pay income tax. The Government then uses these resources and the tax system in general to support the activities and programmes that it believes worthy.[198] Taxes are, however, unequally distributed, with a larger share generally going to people who are recipients of the social minimum. The higher the provision of welfare, the more property must be taken from the wealthy and redistributed to those in need. Despite the strong justifications already discussed,[199] the impact on property rights has made the welfare system a highly contentious issue. Libertarians[200] argue that, because of the importance of property rights, redistribution should be kept as minimal as possible.[201] For example, Nozick believes that the State should only tax for the defence of citizens against each other, and for protection from foreign aggressors. It would therefore be an unjustified violation of property rights to provide tax-based welfare to the poor.[202]

[197] Wolff, *An Introduction to Political Philosophy* (n 98) 55–56. It is recognised that taxes can be collected in a variety of non-income related manners, including Value Added Tax on expenditure, excise duties, company tax and stamp duty.

[198] As an example of this value-system, people who spend their time gambling (which is subject to significant levies and duties) are subsidising the life of those who visit museums or art galleries, which are supported by government funds; Mulhall and Swift, *Liberals and Communitarians* (n 100) 26. See also discussion in Raz, *The Morality of Freedom* (n 28) 161.

[199] See discussion in section 5.3.

[200] It is acknowledged that terms such as 'liberals', 'libertarians' and 'communitarian' often have competing definitions: see Mulhall and Swift, *Liberals and Communitarians* (n 100) xiii–xiv.

[201] See discussion on the individualist prerogative and the right to private property in Eric Mack, 'Individualism and Libertarian Rights' in Christiano and Christman (eds), *Contemporary Debates in Political Philosophy* (Blackwell Publishing, 2009) 130–34.

[202] Robert Nozick, *Anarchy, State and Utopia* (Basic Books, 1974).

Providing welfare to individuals in need is a restriction on the actions of others; it can be justified on many grounds, including equality, protection of the vulnerable, and compassion.[203] The impact on property rights is therefore not sufficient to prevent the Government from providing a social minimum. Raz advocates that 'a government whose responsibility is to promote the autonomy of its citizens is entitled to redistribute resources, to provide public goods and to engage in the provision of services'.[204] The aim of a social minimum is to create a fairer and more egalitarian society, which can override concerns for the property rights of certain individuals.[205] Dworkin famously stated that 'no government is legitimate that does not show equal concern for the fate of those citizens over whom it claims dominion and from whom it claims allegiance'.[206]

Debates on property rights and social welfare are often categorised as one between 'libertarian versus communitarian'. Libertarians believe that individual property rights are of paramount importance, whereas communitarians focus on issues of social good and fairness. This book argues that it does not have to be an either/or proposition. As outlined in section 5.3.3, all groups in society benefit from the provision of a social minimum. Property rights are valued, and in fact protected by the promotion of equality and fairness. People who own property generally do not want social unrest and destabilisation, as this would negatively impact their property rights. As Chamberlain notes, 'the foundations of property are made more secure when no real grievance is felt by the poor against the rich'.[207] Despite the fact that the property of some people is taken without their express permission, the Government duty for the provision (and maintenance) of a social minimum is justified on the grounds of both property rights and fairness.

5.5.2. Responsibility for the Social Minimum

The second difficulty to consider is who should have the responsibility for social minimum provision. As discussed in section 5.2, there is an ongoing historical debate on the obligations of welfare and protection of the vulnerable. There has been a gradual movement from welfare provision by religious or charitable organisations towards a stronger role for the State, but this has not been complete or linear.[208] Without a clear understanding of who is responsible for the social minimum to be provided, those in need could easily slip through the cracks of the welfare system.

[203] See discussion in section 5.3 above. Mill famously stated 'all that makes existence valuable to anyone depends on the enforcement of restraints upon the actions of other people': John Stuart Mill, *On Liberty* (Longman, Roberts & Green, 1859) 9.

[204] Raz, *The Morality of Freedom* (n 28) 417.

[205] Page, 'The Prospects for Social Welfare' (n 57) 301.

[206] Dworkin, *Soverign Virtue: The Theory and Practice of Equality* (n 105) 1.

[207] Lane, 'The Working Class and State "Welfare" in Britain" (n 141) 91.

[208] It is however recognised that this movement has not been linear: see Lewis, 'The Voluntary Sector in the Mixed Economy of Welfare' (n 58); Stewart, 'The Twentieth Century: an Overview' (n 56) 31–32.

As discussed above, social welfare provision was initially the duty of religious institutions, and there is a strong historical link between moneylending and social welfare. The religious prohibition on lending for profit in the Old Testament was coupled with an obligation to give charitably (or potentially lend at no cost) to the poor.[209] Providing this financial assistance was generally considered a charitable obligation to be performed by the church, which has a proud history of assisting those in need.[210] Writing shortly after the Depression, Chesterton advocated for a return to religious and Aquinas-based beliefs on usury – namely that 'loans were a manifestation of charity. Usury was a sin precisely because it took advantage of the needs of others'.[211]

Even with the development of the Welfare State, charities and religious organisations have continued to assist in providing a social minimum to the most vulnerable in our society. When the danger of high-cost credit were recognised and publicised, the church took steps to minimise the harm caused by these products, highlighting the relevance of connections between Christianity, usury and protection of the poor.[212] The charging of excessive interest, particularly to the poor, continues to be something that the church[213] is fighting against. This includes the creation of the organisation Christians Against Poverty, which aims to help people 'crippled by debt'.[214] The condemnation of usury by Christianity also had important implications for the high-cost credit debate. In 2013, the Archbishop of Canterbury stated in the House of Lords that the industry was preying on the 'most disadvantaged' in our society. He further stated that 'my own group, the church, can play a part' in solving these problems, and that 'the church is in a unique position up and down the country'.[215] The Archbishop also created a taskforce chaired by the previous Chair of the Financial Services Authority (FSA), Sir Hector Sants, to 'compete payday lenders out of business'.[216]

[209] 'If thou lend money to any of my people that is poor by thee, thou shalt not be to him as an usurer, neither shalt thou lay upon him usury. If thou at all take thy neighbour's raiment to pledge, thou shalt deliver it unto him by that the sun goeth down: For that is his covering only, it is his raiment for his skin: wherein shall he sleep? and it shall come to pass, when he crieth unto me, that I will hear; for I am gracious': King James Bible, *Authorised Version* (n 40) *Exodus* XXII, 25–27.

[210] Meislin and Cohen, 'Backgrounds of the Biblical Law against Usury' (n 40) 260; Martin Charlesworth and Natalie Williams, *The Myth of the Undeserving Poor: A Christian Response to Poverty in Britain Today* (Grosvenor House Publishing Ltd, 2014); Mead, 'The Rise of Paternalism' (n 74) 10.

[211] Joseph Persky, 'From Usury to Interest' (2007) 21 *Journal of Economic Perspectives* 227, 235.

[212] Charlesworth and Williams, *The Myth of the Undeserving Poor* (n 210); Justin Welby, The Archbishop of Canterbury, *Payday Loans: Archbishop's Speech in the House of Lords on 20 June 2013* (2013).

[213] For example, Christians Against Poverty, the Salvation Army, Compassion International and Samaritan's Purse.

[214] Christians Against Poverty, 'The CAP Story: How it all Started', available at https://capuk.org/about-us/the-cap-story.

[215] The Archbishop of Canterbury, *Payday Loans* (n 212).

[216] Michael Klimes, 'CoE Bolsters Crusade Against Payday Loans with Hector Sants Hire' (*International Business Times*, 16 January 2014), available at www.ibtimes.co.uk/coe-eyes-crusade-against-payday-loans-hector-sants-hire-1432514.

Whilst these are all excellent steps, and the Church should be commended for its work in this area, significant difficulties arise when social minimum provision is left to religious and/or charitable organisations. Beyond the theoretical questions about whether these institutions should be responsible for welfare, it raises concerns about whether all individuals would receive equal assistance. Leaving responsibility for welfare in the hands of the Church may create a real fear that people of other faiths or non-religious individuals would not receive the help they may clearly need. There are much stronger practical and philosophical justifications for social minimum provision to be an obligation on the State.

Despite these justifications, the current Conservative Government is trying to limit its responsibility for social minimum provision. The Beveridge Report is largely considered the 'high water mark' of the Welfare State; since the 1970s, there has been a marked decrease in the willingness of the State to address social minimum issues.[217] Unsurprisingly, poverty has continued to be a significant concern, and the need for assistance remains. The Conservative Government has attempted to address these issues by pushing responsibility for social minimum provision from the State to the general public. This approach can be seen in David Cameron's (failed) creation of 'A Big Society'. Cameron's 2010 speech outlined this policy, stating 'whether it is in building affordable housing, tackling youth unemployment, *inviting charities to deliver public services* … the people in Britain worked out the answer to the big social problems. A big part of that answer is the Big Society'.[218] The emphasised section is highly telling, indicating a desire for the Government to move away from benevolent public services, and instead put them in the hands of charities and other social organisations. This concept has been highly criticised; the Big Society discourse has been dismissed by many commentators as merely a cynical attempt to allow cuts in public spending by the Government.[219] The concept is highly reminiscent of Thatcher's 'responsibilisation' of society,[220] although it also adds a further requirement that in addition to being responsible for their own individual welfare needs, people have a moral obligation to volunteer for the general betterment of their society.[221]

The problem with the Big Society concept goes deeper than government malaise – it is highly contradictory. As outlined by Kinsby,

> given that the conservative critique of the state usually rests on a deeply negative and pessimistic view about human nature – with individuals viewed as selfish utility-maximisers in conflict with others, and that since they themselves know best what they want, their needs ought to be met through market rather than state mechanisms – it seems

[217] For details of this, see sections 5.2.3–5.2.4.
[218] David Cameron, *Speech on the Big Society* (A Speech Delivered in Liverpool on 18 July 2010) (emphasis added).
[219] Ben Kinsby, 'The Big Society: Power to the People?' (2010) 81 *The Political Quarterly* 484, 485.
[220] Analysed in chapter three, section 3.3.3.
[221] Kinsby, 'The Big Society' (n 219) 486.

> odd that Cameron is appealing to human altruism, albeit not an altruism expressed through state redistribution of resources, to prop up public services.[222]

Unsurprisingly, the Big Society concept was widely considered a disappointment that disproportionately impacted the most vulnerable.[223] An independent review completed by The Civil Exchange and DHA Communications concluded that the Big Society has 'largely failed'.[224] One of the most negative aspects of the movement was the transfer of government services to the voluntary sector, and the subsequent reduction of funding. As a result, the voluntary sector lost £1.3 billion of State funding in the 2011–12 financial year alone. Whilst this had negative outcomes across the board, smaller organisations and services to disadvantaged groups were impacted to the greatest extent.[225] These drastic cuts were not replaced by an increase in contribution from voluntary or charitable organisations. Prior to the Big Society, these organisations were already frequently struggling to meet the demands of the public[226] and, post Big Society, formal volunteering and community social action actually declined.[227]

Despite more recent attempts by governments to reduce their responsibility for delivering a social minimum, the obligation for this important task should remain with the State. The Government is trying to get the best of both worlds; advocating the importance of a social minimum whilst also reducing its practical obligations in this regard. This approach was continued in Theresa May's vision of a 'shared society', despite the demonstrable lack of prior success.[228] The reliance on the Church to fill these gaps, despite having a strong historical grounding, raises significant theoretical and practical challenges. Using a concept of the Big Society is also an inadequate and inappropriate response, particularly when these organisations are already stretched to fulfil the current demands on their services. Until the State recognises its responsibility to ensure that a social minimum is provided and maintained, significant problems will continue to exist and the welfare system will not be able to adequately address the challenges posed by high-cost credit.

[222] *ibid* 485.

[223] Caroline Slocock, Ruth Hayes and David Harker, *Whose Society? A Final Big Society Audit* (Civil Exchange and DHA, in conjunction with Joseph Rowntree Charitable Trust and the Barrow Cadbury Trust, 2015) 57. Slocock et al comment that 'the poorest in society have paid disproportionately for efforts to reduce the government deficit … cuts in public services have hit the poorest particularly hard'.

[224] *ibid* 8.

[225] *ibid* 32, with further discussion at 33; 'The loss of statutory income will be significantly greater each year until at least 2017–18 and there is no sign of income from other sources filling the gap. Moreover, nongovernmental funding is less likely to reach those causes which in the past have been funded by government and where needs may be greatest'.

[226] See statistics discussed in *ibid* 25.

[227] *ibid* 11. For interesting comparison, see discussion of reciprocity and undertakings in the communal domain in Mindy Chen-Wishart, 'In Defence of Consideration' (2013) 13 *Oxford University Commonwealth Law Journal* 209, 236–37.

[228] Theresa May, *The Shared Society: Prime Minister's Speech at the Charity Commission Annual Meeting on 9 January 2017* (Gov.UK, 2017), see specifically her comment 'The shared society is one that doesn't just value our individual rights but focuses rather more on the responsibilities we have to one another … And it's a society that recognises the obligations we have as citizens – obligations that make our society work'.

5.5.3. Moral Hazards

One of the most intractable concerns arising from the provision of a social minimum is the potential for a 'moral hazard' to develop.[229] This occurs 'when a measure designed to deal with the problem of a deprived group encourages the size of that group to grow'.[230] It is difficult to provide an appropriate level of assistance for those who need State help without creating a system that encourages 'opportunism' by others. This is not a new challenge. When the social security provisions in the Beveridge Report were first enacted, there was a remarkable increase in the number of people claiming invalidity benefit (which was higher than unemployment benefits), despite the fact that the general health of the population was improving significantly at that time.[231] As social minimum provision is a State obligation, taxpayers will ultimately bear the cost.[232] To avoid a floodgates situation, assistance should only be provided to those who are legitimately at risk of falling into poverty.[233]

The private market has developed several incentives to reduce the impact of moral hazards, for example the use of deductibles and increased premiums for claims under insurance policies. It is more difficult for the State, as it risks hurting or excluding people who need the assistance.[234] Attempts have been made, but these often fall under significant scrutiny. There is a certain level of acceptance of the consequences of moral hazards if an attempt to remove the assistance provided would victimise or harm those in need. There are, however, limits to how much this will be tolerated.[235] If, for example, the State were to abolish all commercial high-cost credit and instead institute a government system of small-amount loans, many people who could afford to pay for these financial products would utilise the system, with the taxpayer covering the cost. Whilst universal coverage may be acceptable in some circumstances and has been embodied in the approach to health care and education, it is unlikely to be considered appropriate in the context of the financial sector.[236]

Moral hazards are a particular concern when dealing with users of high-cost credit. The British model of welfare is largely based on means-testing and the idea that welfare policies should not be widespread or all-embracing but instead focused on the genuinely needy.[237] The standard form of means-testing assistance

[229] Jonathan Klick and Greg Mitchell, 'Infantilization by Regulation' (2016) 39 *Regulation* 36, 39.
[230] Barry, 'Neoclassicism, the New Right and British Social Welfare' (n 57) 63.
[231] *ibid.*
[232] See discussion in section 5.5.1 above.
[233] Sleeman, *The Welfare State* (n 51) 2–4.
[234] *ibid.*
[235] *ibid* 65.
[236] See, eg, discussion of language in Juliette Jowit, '*Strivers v Shirkers*: The Language of the Welfare Debate' *The Guardian* (8 January 2013) and means-testing benefits in Barry, 'Neoclassicism, the New Right and British Social Welfare' (n 57) 69–72.
[237] Barry, 'Neoclassicism, the New Right and British Social Welfare' (n 57) 68.

uses income levels and family size.[238] This approach cannot be applied to providing a social minimum for high-cost credit users. Whilst there is some link between income and dependence on these financial products, it is only one of many relevant factors.[239] Not all borrowers of high-cost credit are financially vulnerable and in need of State support. To develop an appropriate solution for providing and maintaining the social minimum of high-cost credit users, we first need to identify the differing profile and needs of these borrowers. As outlined in chapter two, section 2.2.2, there has been limited engagement in the market and therefore it is difficult to understand accurately who is using these products and why. Before any recommendations on social minimum provision can be made, further research into the high-cost credit market must be undertaken.

5.6. Conclusion

Whilst freedom and regulation are both important concepts, we must move beyond a focus on contract law and legal rights. The State should encourage self-authorship, with people pursuing valuable goals and relationships.[240] This is a richer conception of 'a decent and meaningful life',[241] going beyond both procedural and substantive fairness. In the context of high-cost credit, we need a legal and social welfare system that allows all people access to a robust and meaningful social minimum which is not imperiled by high-cost credit contracts. Providing and maintaining this social minimum can justify coercive government action, including overriding contractual obligations and the redistribution of assets via the tax and welfare system.[242] The legal and political systems have already instituted several processes to provide and maintain the social minimum, although in the context of high-cost credit these are not adequate, and further work is necessary. The provision of a social minimum is not without its difficulties. Whilst questions about interference with property rights and the relative responsibilities of the State or non-State sectors for delivering the social minimum can be dealt with reasonably easily, the concern about how to respond appropriately to moral hazards is more complicated. The challenges related to social minimum provision and moral hazards make it imperative that further research into the high-cost credit market be undertaken. Until this occurs, it will be difficult to make any valid and helpful recommendations on how social minimum maintenance can deal with the challenges of high-cost credit.[243]

[238] Atkinson, *The Economics of Inequality* (n 16) 219–27.

[239] Competition & Markets Authority, *Research into the Payday Lending Market* (n 21) 12, 25.

[240] Joseph Raz, 'Promises in Morality and Law' (1982) 95 *Harvard Law Review* 916; Chen-Wishart, 'In Defence of Consideration' (n 227).

[241] The definition of a social minimum is discussed in section 5.1.

[242] Chen-Wishart, 'In Defence of Consideration' (n 227) 214; Raz, *The Morality of Freedom* (n 28) 157, 416.

[243] This will be discussed further in chapter seven, section 7.2.

PART II

The Social Context: Identifying High-Cost Credit Borrowers

6

The Lived Experience

> True freedom requires the rule of law and justice, and a judicial system in which the rights of some are not secured by the denial of rights to others.
>
> — Rabbi Lord Jonathan Sacks[1]

The preceding chapters have highlighted the need for further empirical research on the circumstances of high-cost credit borrowers in the UK. This chapter fills the information and research void previously identified by analysing the result of interviews with stakeholders and borrowers themselves. Chapter two suggested that although lenders insist that there is no real problem and therefore no need for major reform, the overwhelming evidence (from borrowers themselves, consumer advocates, debt advisors, parliamentarians, and lawyers working in the industry) points to the contrary. Both the Office of Fair Trading (OFT) and Financial Conduct Authority (FCA) have recognised high-cost credit as one of the key areas needing further attention, including the collection of additional information on the market to ensure evidence-based and effective regulation.[2] Whilst it is widely accepted that there is *a* problem, the Government lacks adequate information or research that identifies the exact nature of *the* problem.[3] There have been multiple different reviews by the FCA and other bodies, but the regulator has yet to undertake detailed qualitative empirical research in this area. As a result of this, despite this area being subject to immense scrutiny and legislative change, there is no accurate profile of high-cost credit borrowers that can pinpoint the nature and extent of the problem being addressed by the regulator.

The first part of this chapter fills the information gap by creating a profile of high-cost credit users. Information of this type is crucial for the FCA to understand

[1] I would like to thank The Rabbi Legacy Trust for permission to use this quote.

[2] The Office of Fair Trading (OFT), *Review of High-Cost Credit* (2010) 52; The Financial Conduct Authority (FCA), *Detailed Rules for the Price Cap on High-Cost Short-Term Credit; Including Feedback on CP14/10 and Final Rules* (2014) esp 69; FCA, *Financial Lives 2020 Survey: The Impact of Coronavirus* (2020); FCA, *The Woolard Review – A Review of Change and Innovation in the Unsecured Credit Market* (2021) para 3.50 specifically for open banking.

[3] Gibbons from the Centre for Responsible Credit summarises that unlike other countries, the UK has not conducted a 'rigorous study of the long-term effects of a payday loan on living standards and essential budgets': cited in Carl Packman, *Loan Sharks: The Rise and Rise of Payday Lending* (Searching Finance, 2012) 59.

the nature of the lending problems, and to tailor its regulatory response in the light of the findings. There are two sections: the first outlines the methodology used during the empirical research process; the second provides a summary of the research results, outlining three 'classes' of high-cost credit borrowers. The second part of the chapter engages with the findings from chapters three, four and five in light of the profile developed. It highlights the complexity of the high-cost credit market, and the need to address borrowers in a fair and appropriate manner.[4] The concepts of freedom, regulation and a social minimum are important for the three classes of borrowers identified, but in differing ways. There is an additional dimension to these categories, as the legal regime has very different responses to the three borrower classes, which will also be explored in the chapter. It is recognised that COVID-19 and the financial consequences of the pandemic have significantly impacted the demand and supply of high-cost credit. This chapter does engage in the relevant aspects of the pandemic and its impact, but the focus is on identifying general longer-term trends on the use of these financial products. Some of the later empirical data is therefore not utilised in the analysis, as it relates specifically to the consequences of the pandemic and not the general trends.

6.1. Research Method and Results

Empirical qualitative research was collected through a series of in-depth interviews with people involved in the high-cost credit industry. Empirical research is 'the systematic collection of information ("data") and its analysis according to some generally accepted method'.[5] Bright and Whitehouse observe that empirical legal studies are generally associated with the scientific or positivist tradition, meaning that quantitative work tends to dominate.[6] The aim of this book is to develop a general profile of the motivations of users of high-cost credit, and to identify the circumstances in which they access these financial products. Whilst this type of research could be interpreted as quantitative, given that the results are placed into a table and counted, it is more aligned with qualitative research processes. As outlined by Kirk and Miller, 'a "qualitative observation" identifies the presence or

[4] The basis of this chapter is 'personalised paternalism', which is where the Government creates differentiated approaches for people in different circumstances, rather than having a single blanket approach that applies to everyone: see Cass R Sunstein, 'The Storrs Lecture: Behavioral Economics and Paternalism' (2013) 122 *The Yale Law Journal* 1826, 1871.

[5] Peter Cane and Herbert Kritzer, 'Introduction' in Cane and Kritzer (eds), *The Oxford Handbook of Empirical Legal Research* (Oxford University Press, 2010) 4. For a discussion on the use of empirical research in the social sciences, see Christopher McCrudden, 'Legal Research and the Social Sciences' (2006) 122 *Law Quarterly Review* 632, 632–50.

[6] Susan Bright and Lisa Whitehouse, 'The Opportunities and Challenges of Empirical Work: Housing Possession in Theory and in Practice' in Akkermans, Ramaekers and Marais (eds), *Property Law Perspective II* (Intersentia, 2013).

absence of something, in contrast to a "quantitative observation" which involves measuring the degree to which some feature is present'.[7]

There were two aspects of the qualitative research. The first (stakeholder interviews) was undertaken solely by the author and was with people involved in the high-cost credit industry as opposed to borrowers themselves. The second (borrower interviews) was part of a joint Art & Humanities Research Council (AHRC) funded project and was undertaken by the author in conjunction with Karen Rowlingson and Lindsey Appleyard.

6.1.1. Methodology of Stakeholder Interviews

The stakeholder interview recruitment, process and questions received full ethical approval from the University of Oxford. The interview development was based on the requirements of a high-quality empirical research project, as suggested by Webley in her paper 'Qualitative Approaches to Empirical Legal Research'.[8] First, the most appropriate method was identified to answer the research question within the relevant constraints.[9] In this case, the main constraints were limitations on access to high-cost credit borrowers, ethical difficulties of working with vulnerable consumers,[10] and financial restrictions. The required information was obtained from a series of interviews with different stakeholders instead of from the borrowers themselves. The interviewees included consumer advocates, debt advisors, consumer lawyers, lenders, parliamentarians, trade associations, credit unions and researchers. By interviewing a wide range of people, I obtained a broad portrayal of the lending situation, which could be cross checked against responses from different stakeholders. Second, the subjects needed to be appropriately selected. Several interviewees were obtained through 'snowball sampling'; that is, participants were asked at the conclusion of their interview to suggest other people who would be appropriate for the research in question.[11] A small number of well-known people working in the relevant areas were contacted directly, the project explained to them, and their assistance requested to identify other potential interviewees. Most people responded quickly and were extremely helpful with referrals, and offered to provide a range of additional assistance, including invitations to

[7] Kirk and Miller cited in Lisa Webley, 'Qualitative Approaches to Empirical Legal Research' in Cane and Kritzer (eds), *The Oxford Handbook of Empirical Legal Research* (n 5) 927.

[8] One aspect of research design suggested by Webley, taking into account whether the research should be conducted alone or in a team, was irrelevant to the process and therefore is not discussed: *ibid* 932.

[9] *ibid* 932.

[10] See discussion in Sonia Thompson, *Paying Respondents and Informants* (University of Surrey Social Research Update, 1999) regarding paying non-professional respondents for their time and input. This is a particular concern when interviewing people in financial difficulties, such as people struggling with problem debt.

[11] Webley, 'Qualitative Approaches to Empirical Legal Research' (n 7) 934.

attend consumer events, and providing access to research and resources that had not been published.

Third, the data collection method was 'interacting', that is using the interviews and surrounding communications to gain an in-depth understanding of the high-cost credit market and the motivations of people who use these products.[12] The interviewees were questioned both about their experiences with borrowers and the general characteristics of people who needed to access this type of lending. Finally, the relevant ethical issues were considered.[13] All empirical research undertaken was reviewed and approved by the University of Oxford Central University Research Ethics Committee, using the resources relevant for the Social Sciences and Humanities. The Committee was provided with copies of the interview questions, information sheet given to interviewees, process for interviewing, and the consent form.

A total of 26 interviews were completed. The interviewees were:

- four researchers – two at University-based research centres, one based at a 'Think Tank', and one who worked with a number of research institutes;
- four consumer advocates – all of whom worked for different not-for-profit organisations;
- four debt advisors – all of whom worked for different not-for-profit organisations;
- four lenders or trade associations – one short-term only lender, one short- and medium-term lender, and two trade associations;
- four consumer lawyers – all of whom worked for not-for-profit organisations;
- four government parties – one policy advisor, one person from a regulator, one Member of Parliament, and one Parliamentary Assistant; and
- two miscellaneous – representatives from a credit reporting agency and a credit union.

The interview process did not attempt to produce results that would be statistically significant, nor to provide statistical quantification of the circumstances of high-cost credit borrowers – it was to 'capture and categorise' the social experiences.[14]

Considering the relatively limited number of consumer advocacy and debt advice organisations in the UK, the number of interviews conducted was considered sufficient to draw solid conclusions from the information obtained in the process.[15] In the words of Webley, the findings

[12] Kim Scheppele, 'Counting, Reading, Interacting: Focusing on the Activities of the Researcher in Thinking about Methods' paper presented at the Law and Society Association Early Career Workshop 2009, Denver, referred to in Laura Nielson, 'The Need for Multi-Method Approaches in Empirical Legal Research' in Cane and Kritzer, *The Oxford Handbook of Empirical Legal Research* (n 5) 954.

[13] Webley, 'Qualitative Approaches to Empirical Legal Research' (n 7) 932.

[14] *ibid* 928.

[15] *ibid* 933.

> … capture a broad range of experiences rather than those from only a few people or situations. The findings will be representative in the sense of capturing the range or variation in a phenomenon, but not in the sense of allowing for the estimation of the distribution of the phenomenon in the population as a whole.[16]

There were significant difficulties obtaining access to high-cost credit firms and trade associations, which is perhaps not surprising. This category of interviewee has a vested interest in denying or downplaying any problems associated with high-cost credit, and they generally challenge any calls for increased consumer protection. This also indicates that additional interviews in this category would be unlikely to provide any further assistance.

Despite the ability to draw solid conclusions from the current data, the information obtained from the interview process would be strengthened by the findings being confirmed with quantitative analysis.[17] Further research in this area would therefore be of great benefit and utility.

The interview participants were asked a set number of open-ended questions.[18] The main question was '*what were, in the interviewee's experience, the five most common scenarios where people use high-cost credit loans?*' For each of the five scenarios identified, the interviewee was asked about:

- the connection between the lending and bankruptcy;
- the legal protection available to the borrower;
- whether they believed the creditors were engaging in responsible lending; and
- how frequently borrowers accessed legal or financial advice.

Finally, the interviewee was asked a small number of general questions including '*whether, in their experience, borrowers read and understand consumer credit contracts*' and '*where they believe the balance should lie between freedom of contract and consumer protection?*'.

The questions generally stayed the same across all interviews, although there were slight variations within the different categories of interviewees. The focus of the interviews was on the different scenarios where borrowers accessed short-term loans, and the reasons they needed the credit. Additional information came to light during the interview process that raised other potentially relevant questions, and these were pursued.[19] The questioning varied on occasions, depending on the

[16] *ibid* 934.

[17] Sally Engle Merry, 'Getting Justice and Getting Even' in Halliday and Schmidt (eds), *Conducting Law and Society Research: Reflection on Methods and Practices* (Cambridge University Press, 2009).

[18] Webley, 'Qualitative Approaches to Empirical Legal Research' (n 7) 937.

[19] Hazel Genn, 'Paths to Justice' in Halliday and Schmidt (eds), *Conducting Law and Society Research: Reflection on Methods and Practices* (Cambridge University Press, 2009); Herbert Kritzer, '"Research is a Messy Business" – An Archaeology of the Craft of Sociological Research' in Halliday and Schmidt (eds), *Conducting Law and Society Research: Reflection on Methods and Practices* (Cambridge University Press, 2009) 266–67.

answers and focus of the interviewees. The interview responses were reviewed and collated as they were completed. This provided the opportunity to reflect on the information received, and to amend the questioning process in light of the knowledge already obtained. To encourage honesty and freedom of discussion, the interviews were not recorded and instead detailed short-hand notes were taken during the interview process. All interviewees were then sent the interview transcript shortly after it had been prepared and finalised. Provided that the interviewee had time to consider the transcript and gave consent, they are identified by name in the footnote. Some interviewees did not have time to consider the transcript or did not consent to being named, and these responses have been kept anonymous. When discussing the results received by the research, the interviewees will be referred to by their 'category' as this provides guidance on the background and perspectives of the specific respondent.

6.1.2. Methodology of Borrower Interviews

The process and questions for the borrower interviews were developed by the author, Karen Rowlingson and Lindsey Appleyard. The interviews were undertaken by the author and Lindsey Appleyard, in pairs whenever possible. Both interviewers are fully trained and experienced in carrying out interviews with vulnerable parties and covering potentially sensitive issues. The interview recruitment, process and questions received full ethical approval from the University of Birmingham. They were in-depth semi-structured interviews with 44 individuals who had borrowed from a range of alternative lenders in the 12 months prior to the interviews, this included payday lenders (both in person and online), doorstop lending, pawn brokers and credit unions. The interviews lasted between 45 minutes and two hours and took place in person at a venue of the interviewee's choice, with the majority being conducted in their own home but some in public venues such as cafes.

The interviewees were from the West Midlands and Oxfordshire region and were recruited by a specialist company who identified people from various public arenas, such as shopping centres and high-street venues. A screening questionnaire developed by Appleyard, Gardner and Rowlingson was used to determine appropriate interviewees, and to ensure an appropriate mix of people in terms of gender, age, employment and family situation. Informed consent was obtained for each interview. Interviewees were provided with detailed information about the project, the nature of the research, and how their data would be used.

It is recognised that the payment of interview respondents is a controversial matter. However, after the matter was discussed and debated by the interview team, it was decided that all participants would be given £30 cash to both thank them for their help and compensate for their time.[20] Participants were also given an

[20] See discussion in Thompson, *Paying Respondents and Informants* (n 10).

information sheet with the details of different organisations that can provide free and confidential advice on any money difficulties that they may be experiencing. Interviews were digitally recorded and transcribed in full by a professional transcription company. The transcripts were anonymised to protect the interviewees' personal data and pseudonyms were used during discussion and later reporting. The interviews were then analysed using a thematic 'framework' analysis[21] and with the assistance of Nvivo computer software.

The interviews were divided into two substantive sections. The first was designed to explore the consumer's experience with credit and involved asking them information on the different borrowing sources they had utilised over the previous year. This included where they borrowed from, what the funds were for and whether they considered other options for borrowing. The participants were also asked why they decided to use that particular lender/type of loan and information about the loan, such as its fees, charges and interest and length of the agreement. The interviewee was also asked if they were able to repay the loan on time and without financial difficulties. The potential for 'buyer's remorse' was considered, so the participant was asked whether they felt that the expense in question was necessary – at the time of getting the loan, when paying off the loan and at the time of the interview. Finally, the borrower was asked whether they would have gotten the same loan from the same lender with the benefit of hindsight and what they would have done had they not accessed the loan in question.

The second section of the borrower interview was focused on responsible lending and borrowing. The participant was given several scenarios and asked whether this was an example of responsible or irresponsible lending and/or borrowing. They were then asked generally about the concepts of responsible borrowing including what the Government should do to encourage people to borrow responsibly and to promote savings. The focus was then turned to responsible lending and what it means for businesses to lend responsibly. This included a discussion on government regulation and whether limits on fees and interest would be useful. The third section was based on difficult services available to borrowers who are struggling with problem debt. The participants were asked what they would do if they were unhappy with their lender and wanted to make a complaint. There was then a discussion on whether the participant was aware of different services, such as the Financial Ombudsman Service, Citizens Advice Bureau, StepChange Debt Charity and credit unions.

The results of the borrower interviews provide an exceptionally valuable and engaging insight into the lived experience of people using alternative credit sources in the UK. The interviews have already been the basis for a number of academic and policy publications by the academics involved in the *FinCris* grant.[22] They

[21] Jane Ritchie and others, *Qualitative Research Practice A Guide for Social Science Students and Researchers* (Sage Publishing, 2013).

[22] For example, Karen Rowlingson, Lindsey Appleyard and Jodi Gardner, 'Payday Lending in the UK: The Regul(aris)ation of a Necessary Evil?' (2016) 45 *Journal of Social Policy* 527; Lindsey Appleyard, Karen Rowlingson and Jodi Gardner, 'The Variegated Financialization of Sub-prime Credit Markets' (2016)

have not yet however been considered from a legal and/or regulatory approach, which is the basis for the current discussion. The focus of the analysis will be on the purpose in which the borrowers used funds obtained from the loan, however other aspects of the interviews may be discussed if relevant.

6.1.3. Interview Results

Despite the differing opinions of the stakeholders about the utility of high-cost credit, it became clear quite quickly that there was a surprising level of agreement as to when and why people use these products from both the stakeholder and borrower interviews. Three different classes of borrowers, encompassing six separate lending scenarios, clearly stood out as the most frequently referred to in the interviews. These classes have been further analysed for a greater understanding of the high-cost credit market, and to provide the basis for a more targeted regulatory response to the current challenges. The borrower classes and lending scenarios are as follows:

- Financially Secure Borrowers, who use the funds obtained:
  i. for discretionary expenses – including for travel or luxury items; and
  ii. for one-off or emergency expenses – for example, a larger than expected bill or an unexpected expense.
- Financially Insecure Borrowers, who use the funds obtained:
  i. for essential expenses – including rent, food and costs related to children; and
  ii. to meet existing financial obligations – mainly repaying interest on loans already incurred.
- Significantly Impaired Borrowers, including:
  i. people with mental health conditions; and
  ii. people who are compulsive gamblers.

Whilst there was a general level of agreement, some responses combined two of the scenarios together or broke the above scenarios down into further detailed sub-categories.[23]

The borrower interviews were then analysed on the basis of the borrower classes and lending scenarios developed from the stakeholder interviews. There were understandably some differences in emphasis, as many respondents were

20 *Competition & Change* 297; Jodi Gardner, Karen Rowlingson and Lindsey Appleyard, 'Responsible Borrowing and Lending' (2018) 2 *Journal of International Consumer Law and Practice* 16; Full details of outputs are available at Coventry University, 'FinCris: Responsibilities, Ethics and the Financial Crisis', available at www.coventry.ac.uk/research/research-directories/current-projects/2016/fincris-responsibilities-ethics-and-the-financial-crisis/ (all websites cited in this chapter were last accessed on 24 January 2022).

[23] This detailed information is available in the tables of interview results included in the Appendices.

unlikely to openly discuss gambling and mental health conditions. The borrowers themselves did however generally support the classes and scenarios and highlighted the wide variety of ways that funds from high-cost credit loans were used. Despite the assumed homogeneous nature of the high-cost credit market,[24] each of these borrower classes has a very different relationship to the financial products and the lending market. The next three sections focus on the different classes, applying the empirical research findings to the concepts of freedom, regulation and the provision of a social minimum and to the current legal approach to high-cost credit.

6.2. Financially Secure Borrowers

Financially Secure Borrowers use funds from high-cost credit loans for discretionary expenses or one-off purchases. These consumers are utilising the financial products in a responsible manner that does not create long-term financial hardship. They are not financially excluded or vulnerable, and could obtain credit from other mainstream (and probably less expensive) providers. These borrowers, however, value the speed and convenience of high-cost credit,[25] so choose to use these products over the less expensive options. This borrower class also corresponds very strongly with the types of borrowers touted by lenders as 'standard' consumers.

6.2.1. Lending Scenarios

The first scenario of borrowing (use of loans for discretionary expenses) was discussed to the largest extent by the lenders and trade associations. These interviewees highlighted that young people are increasingly using high-cost credit because of the convenience and technology factors. One stakeholder interviewee stated:

> It is a cultural thing as much as anything else. Young people like new products; their social interactions are increasingly online, so it makes sense that their financial requirements would move this way. There is also the generational focus on 'instant gratification'.[26]

Purchasing items on 'flash sales' was an example of a discretionary expense, where it could be cheaper for the consumer to obtain a high-interest loan and buy the item on sale than to wait until they had saved the funds themselves.[27] This type of activity

[24] See discussion in chapter two, section 2.2.2.
[25] Competition & Markets Authority (CMA), *Research into the Payday Lending Market* (2014) 84.
[26] Anonymous Interview, Trade Association. Telephone interview.
[27] Anonymous Interview, Lender. Telephone interview.

is supported by the findings of the Competition & Markets Authority (CMA) quantitative research on the high-cost credit market, which stated that four per cent of borrowers used the funds for holidays, two per cent for presents, and two per cent for going out or socialising.[28] Later research from the FCA also referred to borrowers purchasing a holiday, but this was not cited as one of the main uses of high-cost credit.[29] Furthermore, the CMA research highlighted that seven per cent of borrowers stated that they could have 'easily' gone without the loan and 32 per cent stated that they could 'possibly' have gone without it,[30] indicating that there is a reasonable amount of discretionary borrowing and spending associated with the high-cost credit market.

This category was also discussed by the researcher and debt advisor interviewees, and to a lesser extent by consumer lawyers and government parties. The emphasis on convenience and young people with access to technology were reinforced by a number of interviewees, including the regulator.[31] The credit referencing agency highlighted that people may use high-cost credit because they see it as 'short-term', whereas other credit products are viewed as 'long-term' debt, which they wanted to avoid.[32] One consumer advocacy organisation that had undertaken client surveys of loan expenditure reported that approximately ten per cent of high-cost credit borrowers used all or part of the funds received from the loan for discretionary spending.[33] A researcher stated that while this was previously a significant category, it was now decreasing in contrast to other rationales for borrowing.[34] Moreover, one of the debt advisor interviewees stated that, whilst some borrowers may use loan funds for these purposes, it would be uncommon owing to the exceptionally high interest rates of the loans. These borrowers are coping financially and are likely to have incomes at or above the national average; people who are already experiencing financial difficulties would generally not be able to afford this type of discretionary expenditure.[35]

A small but not insignificant number of borrower interviewees stated that the funds were used for discretionary expenses. For example, one younger borrower would often use online payday companies so that he could go out drinking at the weekend with his friends. Another participant went into debt to get the funds for plastic surgery and another got a loan to purchase a camper van. Both admitted that the purchase was a luxury for them, with one commenting 'It wasn't necessary … we just thought, well, it'd be nice'. The most common example of discretionary purchases is holidays. One participant obtained a loan because the flights were on a special deal and they did not want to miss out, another wanted to take their family

[28] CMA, *Research into the Payday Lending Market* (n 25) 68.
[29] FCA, *Financial Lives 2020 Survey* (n 2) 44.
[30] *ibid.*
[31] Anonymous Interview, Regulator. Telephone interview.
[32] James Jones, Experian. Telephone interview.
[33] Martyn Saville, Which?. Telephone interview.
[34] Sharon Collard, Personal Finance Research Centre. Telephone interview.
[35] Anonymous Interview, Debt Advisor. Telephone interview.

on a holiday but couldn't afford the money from their week to week living expenses so needed to get a loan. Another two participants saved for the actual holiday, but then needed to borrow for the spending money. Whilst holidays may seem like an extravagant purchase, if a household is unable to go on holiday for a week once a year, this is an indication of 'severe material deprivation'.[36] Almost 30 per cent of families in the UK are unable to afford to go on holiday, a significant increase from pre-austerity times, where it was 21.4 per cent of families being unable to afford this.[37] Despite this, the importance of holidays is actually decreasing in the eyes of the general public. In the 'Breadline Britain' surveys, in 2012 only 42 per cent of people thought that a holiday away from home was considered a 'necessity' to live a socially acceptable life.[38] This is a significant decrease from 1983, where 63 per cent of people thought it was a necessity.

There were other common examples that are more difficult to classify but are most appropriately considered in this category, namely children's birthdays, Christmas celebrations and important personal events, such as christenings. They are not technically 'unexpected' expenses but cannot easily be defined as either luxury purchases or everyday expenses. They are however 'discretionary' expenses if considered outside of the social and family pressures that are so often placed on people, particularly women.[39] There were many examples of this type of borrowing, including a memorable interview with a single mother who talked about the overbearing guilt she felt separating from her child's father and the subsequent desire to make this a very special birthday. There can also be a significant amount of regret with these types of loans, particularly by parent borrowers. One commented that 'looking back it wasn't [a necessary expense], because then, when they got up Christmas morning, they'd got too much stuff anyway. So at the time I did think it was necessary, but then afterwards I thought it really wasn't'. Another borrower stated 'now it does seem a bit like a waste of time, but it was for Christmas and the pressures of buying the kids Christmas presents'. One interviewee talked about how borrowing for Christmas had become a cycle, she takes the entire year to repay the loan and then almost straight away takes another loan out to pay for next year's celebrations.

The second lending scenario for Financially Secure Borrowers was using funds on a one-off basis for unexpected expenses. In advertisements and media representations of high-cost credit, this is by far the most common example of the use of borrower funds. The stakeholder interview responses for this scenario were in line with the responses received for discretionary expenses. These borrowers could

[36] Office for National Statistics, 'Poverty and Social Exclusion in the UK and EU, 2005–2011', available at https://webarchive.nationalarchives.gov.uk/ukgwa/20160105214433/http://www.ons.gov.uk/ons/rel/household-income/poverty-and-social-exclusion-in-the-uk-and-eu/2005-2011/rpt--poverty-and-social-exclusion.html.

[37] *ibid* 6.

[38] See Breadline Britain Tables discussed in chapter five, section 5.1.

[39] For a fascinating analysis of the gendered nature of high-cost credit, see Amy J Schmitz, 'Females on the Fringe: Considering Gender in Payday Lending Policy' (2014) 89 *Chicago-Kent Law Review* 65.

afford to repay the loans without financial hardship and choose to use high-cost credit owing to the ease and convenience of obtaining the money when compared with more mainstream credit products. Several interviewees across the categories combined these two scenarios together, labelling them as situations where borrowers used high-cost credit 'appropriately and responsibly'.[40] The most common examples of expenditure in this scenario were a temporary financial crisis or shock that could not be absorbed into the regular income stream, an unexpected bill, or something breaking and needing repair. The loan obtained could, however, easily be repaid without any long-term financial harm.

The lenders/trade association category emphasised that the expenditure for this category of borrower was generally quite practical, and one even noted that they had not seen funds spent on anything 'frivolous'.[41] A researcher highlighted that many people can use loans appropriately and have personal reasons for wanting to access high-cost credit – generally irregularly and on a one-off basis.[42] The consumer lawyer and government party categories also referred to this scenario, agreeing that, in certain circumstances, high-cost credit can be used responsibly and appropriately. As discussed in chapter two,[43] these views are supported by academic research outlining the potential benefits of these financial products.

Using funds for one-off and unexpected expenses was a frequent reason cited by borrowers. The interviewees provided a range of situations, including a house being flooded, a washing machine, a boiler needing repair, a new cooker, an expectedly high telephone bill and a rental deposit. The borrowers in this category regularly highlighted that, because of their personal situation, they did not have any real choice but to get a loan. They generally emphasised the one-off nature of the expense or, as stated by one of the interviewees, a 'last resort kind of thing'. For example, the person who borrowed to get their boiler fixed stated,

> Winter was coming and it was – after last winter and some other winters, we had to get it [the boiler] done. So it wasn't an option really. When we first moved in we didn't have heating; it was freezing, really, really cold. So it wasn't an option really. We just had to.

Another person highlighted the temporary nature of needing a loan, stating that the funds were used

> to put a [rental] deposit down on a flat, and it was one of those that's just like I need to secure it quick because it might go quick, so it was more, I don't have the money now, on this particular day, but it was more of a cash flow problem.

[40] For example, Donald Hirst, Consumer Focus. Telephone interview.

[41] Anonymous Interview, Trade Association. Telephone interview.

[42] Donald Hirst, Consumer Focus. Telephone interview.

[43] See discussion in chapter two, section 2.2.2 regarding research from Karen Rowlingson, *Moneylenders and their Customers* (Policy Studies Institute, 1994) and Andrea Finney, Sharon Collard and Elaine Kempson, *Easy Come, Easy Go: Borrowing Over the Life-Cycle* (Personal Finance Research Centre, 2007).

6.2.2. Application to High-Cost Credit Concepts

Freedom has inherent value for all classes of borrowers; it is, however, the most important concept for Financially Secure Borrowers. These consumers appreciate being able to exercise their financial freedom and are choosing to use high-cost credit because of its speed and convenience. This is a valuable choice that the law should protect. Interference with the credit choices of Financially Secure Borrowers creates the risk of unwarranted 'infantilisation' of consumers. This infantilisation removes or restricts the ability for people to make their own choices, an important aspect of psychological development.[44] As outlined by Sunstein,

> It is true that people err and that their errors can impair their welfare. But mistakes are often productive. Life is a movie, not a snapshot, and people can learn from what goes wrong. We should not freeze people's frames … [the] government ought not to short-circuit the valuable process of learning-by-doing. The process greatly increases human welfare. A paternalistic government infantilizes people; it treats them like children and makes it less likely that they will grow up.[45]

There is value in taking risks, making mistakes, and learning from the process. If the State is overly paternalistic in its approach to regulation, it 'robs [people] of the opportunity to genuinely flourish'.[46]

The concern of infantilisation applies to all contracts, including high-cost credit agreements. There should therefore be strong justifications for undermining borrowers' freedom. The State needs to balance the damage of interfering in high-cost credit contracts (ie, the infantilisation of borrowers) against the damage of taking a negative freedom approach (eg potential harm to borrowers). Loans to Financially Secure Borrowers generally do not cause ongoing harm; they occur on a one-off or irregular basis, and borrowers have the capacity to repay without suffering undue financial hardship. The balance is therefore in favour of freedom and non-interference; the focus on consent and non-exploitation by lenders will generally be a sufficient and appropriate way to respond to the needs of Financially Secure Borrowers.

The aim of regulation, namely stopping substantively unfair agreements and coercion from lack of choice, is not relevant to most Financially Secure Borrowers. These consumers have access to financial alternatives, so lack of choice is not a concern. Considering the long historical and religious concern with usury and general dislike of usurious agreements in our society,[47] there is some justification

[44] Sunstein, 'The Storrs Lecture' (n 4) 95.

[45] *ibid* 94.

[46] Jonathan Klick and Greg Mitchell, 'Infantilization by Regulation' (2016) 39 *Regulation* 32, 32. See also Richard Thaler and Cass Sunstein, *Nudge: Improving Decisions about Health, Wealth, and Happiness* (Yale University Press, 2008).

[47] Discussed in chapter four, section 4.2.1.

that – regardless of the lack of borrower vulnerability – prevention of a substantially unfair agreement may still be relevant to Financially Secure Borrowers. This is focused on preventing a harmful outcome to society, as opposed to protecting specific borrowers.[48] There is also one group of Financially Secure Borrowers that may benefit from further regulation, particularly by stopping unfair agreements. As discussed above, there are increasing numbers of younger Financially Secure Borrowers,[49] who are attracted to these products for the speed and engagement with technology. These individuals are likely to be more vulnerable due to their lack of financial experience, which may be a justification for taking a more protective approach.[50]

Financially Secure Borrowers, by definition, should not need social minimum provision or maintenance. They use the funds obtained for discretionary purposes or for one-off expenses, and are at or above the social minimum when they enter into the credit transaction. These borrowers have financial alternatives and use high-cost credit because they value the speed and ease of these products. There were some concerns from interviewees about the overlap between Financially Secure and Financially Insecure Borrowers. In particular, it is possible that Financially Secure Borrowers could easily obtain a loan for a discretionary or one-off expense, be unable to afford the repayments, and 'slip off the edge' into the next class.[51] An example of this was the borrower interviewee who needed a new washing machine. They could not make the repayments associated with the purchase and had a three-month-old baby, which put them into ongoing financial difficulties. This was a common issue when loans were for birthday presents or costs related to Christmas. If this happens, the social minimum is more likely to be a concern. One interviewee borrowed £200 for her daughter's christening that she was unable to pay and which snowballed into nearly £1,000 in a matter of months. She commented

> I'm, in a way it is, like, I should have been on top of the payments but then … the interest [is] very, very hard to pay off and it just keeps building up and like building up, but I would never do it, I would never go back to another payday loan again.

These types of borrowers are no longer classified as Financially Secure, as they cannot make ongoing repayments without suffering undue financial hardship and/or falling below the social minimum. They are therefore more appropriately classed as Financially Insecure Borrowers, and the relevant social minimum concerns will be discussed below.

[48] Discussed in chapter four section 4.3.1.
[49] See discussion in chapter six, section 6.2.1.
[50] Anonymous Interview, Lender. Telephone interview.
[51] Yvonne Fovargue MP. In-person interview.

6.2.3. Application to Current Legal Approach

The legal approach currently taken to high-cost credit is generally appropriate for the needs of Financially Secure Borrowers. As outlined in chapter two, the high-cost credit market has a strong focus on freedom with consent, disclosure and procedural fairness all being important aspects of the legal regime.[52] These mechanisms are extremely well suited to Financially Secure Borrowers, as they ensure choice and non-exploitation whilst avoiding infantilisation. There are, however, two potential concerns. First, the effectiveness of the current disclosure regime has been subject to significant criticism.[53] Second, there is the potential for some Financially Secure Borrowers (particularly younger, less experienced consumers) to be exploited by unscrupulous lenders or unfair business models.[54] How these issues should be addressed will be discussed in the next chapter.

6.3. Financially Insecure Borrowers

Financially Insecure Borrowers utilise high-cost credit in a manner that is likely to create long-term financial harm or hardship. These consumers use the funds from loans for everyday expenses or to repay existing financial obligations. They are often vulnerable, financially excluded, and cannot obtain credit from mainstream providers. The FCA's *High-Cost Credit Review* outlined how these projects are often used by people who are already the most vulnerable – with low credit scores, limited incomes and minimal financial security.[55] There was significant apprehension about this class of borrowers amongst many interviewees; they were generally considered to be at significant financial risk. Lending to Financially Insecure Borrowers often results in an 'untenable financial situation',[56] and the creation of a debt spiral[57] where 'borrowers are in perpetual loans'.[58]

6.3.1. Lending Scenarios

There are two lending scenarios relevant to Financially Insecure Borrowers. The first is loans for essential expenses (for example rent, food, council tax and utilities).

[52] Rowlingson, *Moneylenders and their Customers* (n 43) 13.

[53] See discussion in chapter three, section 3.5.1. It is recognised that this would however negatively impact the law's interaction with all borrowers.

[54] See discussion of cognitive biases in *ibid.*

[55] OFT, *Review of High-Cost Credit* (n 2); discussed and confirmed in FCA, *The Woolard Review* (n 2) para 1.15.

[56] Matt Bland, Association of British Credit Unions Limited. Telephone interview.

[57] Carl Packman, Author and Consumer Advocate. Telephone interview; Sharon Collard, Personal Finance Research Centre. Telephone interview.

[58] Anonymous Interview, Debt Advisor. Telephone interview.

This was discussed by each of the interviewee categories. This scenario has become an increasingly common category owing to the economic downturn, reduction of the Welfare State, and stagnating wages.[59] Many households are struggling financially, and high-cost credit has become part of these borrowers' routine; 'people are in a desperate situation – the ends just don't meet'.[60] Borrowers on low incomes generally have little or no savings, and are highly vulnerable to financial shocks from even small additional expenses.[61] One stakeholder interviewee highlighted these 'loans can be the only choice of credit for everyday expenses for a large number of vulnerable people who are overstretched and need access to funds'.[62] This scenario was also recognised by all of the government parties, with the regulator stating that high-cost credit has 'become a way of life' for many people who need access to additional funds to get through the month's usual expenses.[63]

This was a common scenario talked about in the interviews with borrowers. Many people borrowed just to make ends meet during times of increased expenses or income decreases. Examples included paying rent, putting money in electricity meters, TV licence costs and paying general utilities. The situation can become so bad that multiple interviewees admitted to using high-cost credit just to buy food. One interviewee stated, 'I buy food with [the money], you know if my cupboards are bare than I borrow a pay day loan just to fill up my cupboards', and another commented 'What I have to make sure of, I've got plenty of food in my house, I have to make sure of that because of my children'.

The individual circumstances also played an important role in this scenario. Some interviewees provided specific reasons why they needed to borrow funds for these kinds of expenses, with situations such as moving house, changing jobs, being made redundant, suddenly becoming a single parent and, in the case of a self-employed individual, a slowdown in provision of work. Other people had no specific life event, but were just generally trying to make ends meet. For example, one borrower commented

> I'm a single parent and sometimes, you know, I struggle on the finances that I already have and that's why I go for a payday loan because I need it there and then, I can't wait until another payday to come and I'm really, really struggling.

Another borrower received an unexpectedly high electricity bill due to the extra use over winter and was so concerned that the electricity might be turned off, they borrowed money to ensure the bill was paid on time. There was a significant link

[59] Sharon Collard, Personal Finance Research Centre. Telephone interview; Matt Bland, Association of British Credit Unions Ltd. Telephone interview. This is also discussed in Packman, *Loan Sharks* (n 3) 38–39 and highlighted by the London Assembly's Economy Committee investigation into low pay in London and London's living wage (final report available at www.london.gov.uk/sites/default/files/london_assembly_-_economy_committee_-_low_pay_and_in-work_poverty_.pdf)

[60] David Barclay, The Contextual Theology Centre. Telephone interview.

[61] Matt Bland, Association of British Credit Unions Ltd. Telephone interview.

[62] Anonymous Interview, Researcher. In-person interview.

[63] Anonymous Interview, Regulator. Telephone interview.

between life events and high-cost credit use reported in the FCA's *2020 Financial Lives* survey, with 23 per cent of people who used high-cost credit in the previous 12 months going through a divorce or separation and 19 per cent losing their job or experiencing a reduction in hours.[64]

The use of funds in this way, and the resultant harm, is strongly supported by other research. As an example, one consumer advocacy organisation interviewed had undertaken client surveys of loan expenditure, and found that 38 per cent of clients reported using funds from high-cost credit for household essentials (such as food and children's needs), 32 per cent had used the funds for regular household bills, and 20 per cent had used the funds for rent or mortgage repayments.[65] Shelter reported that after the global financial crisis almost one million people took out high-cost credit in order to pay their rent or mortgage.[66] Quantitative data from the CMA highlights the significant role that this category plays in the provision of high-cost credit, with 53 per cent of respondents stating that the money was used for everyday expenses (including groceries, utility or household bills or food). A further ten per cent said that the funds were used for general shopping, including clothes and household items, and 59 per cent used the money for something they 'definitely' could not have gone without.[67] The FCA's *2020 Financial Lives* survey reports that when asked why borrowers took out a high-cost credit product, 'by far the most common reason was to cover day-to-day expenses such as food, transport, bills'.[68]

There was general agreement between the stakeholder interviewees that high-cost credit was used by borrowers in this class to just 'get by'. There was, however, disagreement as to whether these loans were beneficial or detrimental for borrowers. One lender acknowledged that there may be a few customers who needed money for everyday expenses, but argued that this was 'quite rare'.[69] A different lender commented that high-cost credit is an important source of lending to people who cannot access mainstream financial services, or have self-excluded from mainstream lending, such as people who do not have bank accounts or do not trust High Street banks.[70] A trade association interviewee also commented that, if high-cost credit were not available for people to cover these types of expenses, there would be a significant problem with financial exclusion, which could make consumers' situations worse.[71]

Other categories of interviewees argued that the use of such high-interest loans for everyday expenses was generally dangerous, with one researcher declaring it an

[64] FCA, *Financial Lives 2020 Survey* (n 2) 44.
[65] Martyn Saville, Which?. Telephone interview.
[66] See discussion in Hilary Osborne, 'Millions Use Payday Loans to Cover Mortgage and Rental Costs' The Guardian (4 January 2012), available at www.theguardian.com/money/2012/jan/04/payday-loans-cover-mortgage-costs?CMP=twt_gu.
[67] CMA, *Research into the Payday Lending Market* (n 25).
[68] FCA, *Financial Lives 2020 Survey* (n 2) 44.
[69] Anonymous Interview, Lender. Telephone interview.
[70] *ibid.*
[71] Anonymous Interview, Trade Association. Telephone interview.

initial sign of financial distress.[72] The credit reference agency interviewee declared that, if high-cost credit lenders were being responsible, borrowers in this situation would be turned away.[73] A consumer lawyer interviewee commented that 'people do not have enough money to live on day to day and any sort of commercial credit is merely deepening their situation'.[74] There were also references to these borrowers being 'on the margins', with this type of loan 'push[ing] them over the edge'.[75]

Financially Insecure Borrowers also use funds to repay existing financial obligations. This is highly concerning, as approving loans for this purpose is prima facie irresponsible lending, and will often result in the creation of a debt spiral.[76] A number of interviewees provided case studies of consumers who had used high-cost credit for the repayment of existing financial obligations and become stuck in a harmful debt spiral, sometimes taking years to repay the loans in question.[77] They were often unable to improve the situation, and spent their lives 'ducking and diving' to make ends meet.[78] These types of borrowers are in an 'untenable financial situation', having exhausted existing credit options. The lender therefore becomes the last resort when existing debts become unmanageable.[79] Borrowers are generally struggling on a very low income, often on benefits or tax credits, and uses high-cost credit loans because they 'are easy to obtain and people can get sucked in … they might think it is bailing them out, but it is actually escalating the problem'.[80]

Unsurprisingly, this is the lending scenario that has attracted the most divergent views. The lender/trade association interviewees strongly believed that lending of this type did not occur. This, they argued, was because it was against the Irresponsible Lending Guidance (ILG) and/or because the software that they used would prevent loans of this type being approved. This contrasts starkly with the other categories of interviewees, who believed that (a) lending of this sort occurs to a concerning extent, and (b) is generally on the rise.[81] One consumer advocacy organisation stated that 24 per cent of clients reported using the loan funds to repay existing credit obligations.[82] Paying off a debt was one of the key reasons for

[72] Sharon Collard, Personal Finance Research Centre. Telephone interview. Similar comments were made by Carl Packman, Author and Consumer Advocate. Telephone interview.

[73] James Jones, Experian. Telephone interview.

[74] Joanna Kennedy, Consumer Lawyer. In-person interview.

[75] Helen McCarthy, Citizen Advice Bureau. Telephone interview.

[76] Sharon Collard, Personal Finance Research Centre. Telephone interview.

[77] Carl Packman, Author and Consumer Advocate. Telephone interview; David Barclay, The Contextual Theology Centre. Telephone interview.

[78] Niall Cooper, Christians Against Poverty. Telephone interview.

[79] Matt Bland, Association of British Credit Unions Ltd. Telephone interview. Supported by findings from CMA, *Research into the Payday Lending Market* (n 25) where 23% of borrowers stated that the high-cost loan was their 'last resort' (71) and one in four said that they had no other financial option (80–81).

[80] Anonymous Interview, Debt Advisor. Telephone interview.

[81] For example, John Ludlow, Parliamentary Assistant. In-person interview. Carl Packman, Author and Consumer Advocate. Telephone interview; Yvonne Fovargue MP. In-person interview.

[82] Martyn Saville, Which?. Telephone interview.

obtaining a high-cost credit product reported in the FCA's *2020 Financial Lives* survey.[83]

Despite the lender/trade association interviewees stating that lending in this manner does not occur, a number of the borrowers interviewed stated that they borrowed from high-cost credit providers to repay existing financial obligations. Examples of this occurring included to cover shortfalls in mortgage payments, paying an expensive unplanned overdraft, ensuring there were funds for outgoing direct debits or to pay off other general debt commitments. The borrowers who used funds in this way were generally fearful of losing their house or being visited by bailiffs, so thought that going into further debt was a better option. One individual however commented that borrowing to pay off debts was going to help 'boost' their credit rating, yet they could not explain how or why this would occur. Using high-cost credit in this way is therefore clearly not a rare or exceptional circumstance. The relative frequency of this scenario is confirmed by the CMA, where 36 per cent of people needed to repay an existing high-cost credit loan in the month before taking out the loan in question. Two per cent of people also used the funds to directly repay an existing high-cost loan.[84] Unfortunately, no figures were obtained for the number of borrowers who used the funds to repay other types of existing financial obligations (such as credit card bills, pawnbroking costs or door-stop credit). The full extent of the problem therefore remains unknown.

6.3.2. Application to High-Cost Credit Concepts

Freedom has inherent value for all borrowers, including Financially Insecure ones. Infantilisation is therefore still a potential concern for these consumers, although the factors to balance are quite different from those for the previous class. Financially Insecure Borrowers are generally vulnerable and lack adequate financial alternatives – high-cost credit has 'become a way of life'.[85] These borrowers are usually already in financial distress, and the loan can often push them into a debt spiral. Use of credit in this manner may provide temporary relief but exacerbates future financial difficulties; 'people think that accessing [high-cost credit] loans will generally help the situation, but it almost inevitably makes it worse – it is like throwing petrol onto a fire to put it out'.[86] This situation provides significantly stronger justification for government intervention, limiting borrowers' short-term choices to avoid long-term harm. An analogy can be drawn between Financially Insecure Borrowers and bankruptcy. In terms of individual financial control, being under a bankruptcy agreement is highly infantilising and takes away the bankrupt's freedom to a significant extent, as their income and expenditure choices

[83] FCA, *Financial Lives 2020 Survey* (n 2) 44.
[84] CMA, *Research into the Payday Lending Market* (n 25) 69.
[85] Anonymous Interview, Regulator. Telephone interview.
[86] Niall Cooper, Consumer Advocate. Telephone interview.

are extremely limited. This situation is widely accepted and justified on a range of bases, including protection of a social minimum, ensuring future autonomy, and rehabilitation.[87] A higher level of infantilisation can therefore be accepted in these circumstances, as it is important for financial rehabilitation.

Financially Insecure Borrowers need regulation, from both substantively unfair agreements and coercion that arises from a lack of choice. These consumers are at a significant disadvantage when contracting, and there is a real risk that they will agree to unconscionable terms and conditions because they have no other legal credit options. This is effectively summarised by Satz, who comments that 'when a person enters a contract from a position of extreme vulnerability he is likely to agree to almost any terms that are offered'.[88] It is, however, important to be aware of the potential consequences of regulation.[89]

Regulation – in the form of limitations on access to credit – can provide some assistance but, as outlined in chapter three, section 3.5, financial exclusion and the impact of poverty means that government intervention can leave these borrowers in a worse financial position. The provision and maintenance of a social minimum is therefore the most important factor for Financially Insecure Borrowers, as their reliance on high-cost credit often arises from pre-existing financial difficulties and ongoing poverty. The State must take some responsibility for this situation, as opposed to leaving it to private law mechanisms. Fried discussed these challenges in *Contract as Promise*, stating that courts can theoretically refuse to enforce contracts with highly disadvantaged people on this basis. He comments that the lack of real choice *and* substantively unfair terms may be considered sufficient to hold a contract unenforceable, especially if poverty or relatively powerlessness are pertinent factors.[90] However, he goes on to explain that lack of choice and substantive unfairness are not the fault of the contracting party. If the options are limited or inadequate, such as for Financially Insecure Borrowers, this is not the lender's fault.[91] Fried further comments that refusing to uphold these contracts may be tempting, as the law wants to protect vulnerable parties. He questions 'why should just this one representative of the more fortunate classes be made to bear the burden of our redistributive zeal?', arguing instead that the State should be responsible for the welfare of these parties.[92]

Fried's comments on substantive unfairness are no longer an accurate representation of our approach to high-cost credit. As discussed above, there are a

[87] Charles Fried, *Contract as Promise: A Theory of Contractual Obligation* (Harvard University Press, 1981) 108.

[88] Debra Satz, *Why Some Things Should Not be For Sale: The Moral Limits of Markets* (Oxford University Press, 2010) 97.

[89] See discussion in chapter four, section 4.5 (which refers to the relevant discussion in chapter three, section 3.5).

[90] Fried, *Contract as Promise* (n 87) 104. Fried clearly disagreed with this reasoning and with the 'no real choice' theory: 104–106.

[91] *ibid* 105.

[92] *ibid.*

variety of legal mechanisms in place, under both the common law and government regulation, to limit or prevent unfair bargains.[93] These are piecemeal and arguably inadequate, but there has been some movement to address issues of substantive unfairness. Fried's insight into the relationship between private law mechanisms and State duties does however have real value for the current high-cost credit situation, particularly for Financially Insecure Borrowers. This is about poverty and redistribution of resources. The key concern for these borrowers is the provision and maintenance of a social minimum, and this is far beyond the power of the private law.

6.3.3. Application to Current Legal Approach

High-cost credit is generally marketed as being for discretionary purchases or one-off expenses, and trade association websites use a range of statements to that effect. For example, the now defunct Consumer Finance Association commented that '[l]oans are not designed for longer-term borrowing, but to improve short-term personal cash flow', stated that the products are 'designed for short-term borrowing, not long-term debt' and '[p]ayday lending … helps consumers to avoid long-term debt'.[94] High-cost credit is extremely expensive, and therefore not designed to be used on a regular or even semi-regular basis. If this type of lending is limited to a rare one-off occasion, there is some level of justification for the exceptionally high cost of the credit. Based on the definition discussed in chapter four, section 4.5.3, the use of high-cost credit by Financially Insecure Borrowers is a strong indicator of financial exclusion. These borrowers are not accessing or using financial services in a mainstream market in a way that is appropriate to their needs.[95]

The legal system is not responding to the needs of Financially Insecure Borrowers. The procedural fairness approach of freedom allows these individuals to be exploited by lenders and business models designed to keep them trapped in expensive debt that they struggle to repay. A regulatory approach, which addresses the substantive fairness of the transaction, does improve the welfare of some borrowers by removing the most harmful aspects of these contracts. Many other consumers are, however, pushed out of the legal market, and risk financial exclusion and possibly moving into the illegal lending market. The law is unlikely to provide the answer; we need to move beyond the private legal system and consider the role

[93] See discussion in chapter four, section 4.4.

[94] These phrases appeared on the Consumer Finance Association website when the organisation was the main trade association for high-cost credit providers.

[95] Sharon Collard, Elaine Kempson and Claire Whyley, *Tackling Financial Exclusion: An Area-Based Approach* (The Policy Press, 2001); Nicola Howell and Therese Wilson, 'Access to Consumer Credit: The Problem of Financial Exclusion in Australia and the Current Regulatory Framework' (2005) 5 *Macquarie Law Journal* 127; Elaine Kempson and Sharon Collard, *Developing a Vision for Financial Inclusion* (Friends Provident Foundation, 2012).

of government services and social security in addressing the needs of Financially Insecure Borrowers.

6.4. Significantly Impaired Borrowers

The final class, Significantly Impaired Borrowers, use high-cost credit as a result of being under the influence of either a mental health condition or compulsive gambling. Whilst some of these borrowers may be financially included and adequately resourced, research highlights that they – as a class – are more likely to suffer from financial exclusion and poverty than average consumers.[96] The ability of these borrowers to understand the implications of high-cost credit contracts has been impaired to a concerning degree. This results in a lack of valid choices, as these borrowers can be coerced by both the lending environment and their personal impairment.

6.4.1. Lending Scenarios

The first lending scenario is when people with mental health conditions access high-cost credit. Many stakeholder interviewees stated that they had concerns about people without adequate understanding or capacity using high-cost credit products. One consumer advocate interviewed had spoken with an ex-lender who had been concerned about the company he worked for lending to people with capacity issues, and this was one of the reasons he left the position.[97] Two debt advisor interviewees also reported potential issues with high-cost credit and mental health; they expressed concern that there was no ability to question the client about this issue specifically.[98] Similar concerns were voiced by interviewees in the consumer lawyer and government categories. One lawyer commented that there was 'very much' a link between the two, especially as a large number of borrowers are vulnerable people with reduced capacity who do not adequately understand the contracts associated with high-cost credit.[99] Lending to borrowers with mental health concerns was also raised by one of the lenders interviewed, who acknowledged that whilst it may be a problem, they were not sure how to deal with the situation.[100]

[96] See below for discussion in relation to mental health conditions. In relation to gambling, see Matt Barnard and others, 'Exploring the Relationship between Gambling, Debt and Financial Management in Britain' (2014) 14 *International Gambling Studies* 82 and Heather Wardle and others, *Debt and Problem Gambling: Evidence from the Adult Psychiatric Morbidity Survey: Briefing Paper 1* (NatCen: Social Research That Works for Society, July 2012).

[97] David Barclay, The Contextual Theology Centre. Telephone interview.

[98] Anonymous Interview, Debt Advisor. Telephone interview; Anonymous Interview, Debt Advisor. Telephone interview.

[99] Helen McCarthy, Citizens Advice Bureau. Telephone interview; Anonymous Interview, Citizens Advice Bureau. In-person interview.

[100] Anonymous Interview, Lender. Telephone interview.

The relationship between debt and mental health difficulties was a common theme raised by borrowers in their interviews. Due to privacy restrictions, borrowers could not be asked directly whether they had an existing mental health condition or the impact that the loan in question had on their mental health. This topic did however arise frequently during the discussion. Some interviewees openly discussed their conditions, with a number of people having conditions such as depression, Obsessive Compulsive Disorder and/or anxiety, and another stated they had a long history of suffering from an eating disorder. It was often unclear the exact relationship between mental health and borrowing, and whether the interviewee had mental health conditions before entering the loan, or if it arose afterwards. Many had existing challenges that were exacerbated by the financial situation and difficulties repaying their debt obligations. It is clearly a significant problem – despite not asking questions specifically raising the issues, a third of borrowers talked about mental health challenges during the interview.

Many interviewees talked about stress, anxiety, depression and panic attacks brought on by financial difficulties and the subsequent debt. One interviewee commented that every month when they received a statement of their outstanding debt they 'nearly committed suicide' because of the stress. Others talked about how the situation made them 'sleep deprived', 'physically ill' or turn to anti-depressants to cope, with two interviewees also having to take time off work due to the stress they were experiencing. Another interviewee highlighted how significant the link between debt and mental health has been with people in their community, stating 'I've just found out my mate committed suicide last week … they stopped all his dole money and rent money and one my mates went round to find him … He was obviously in debt, wasn't he?'. Another said that the stress from constant visits by doorstop lenders wanting repayment exacerbated a pre-existing eating disorder, and she became anorexic.

Despite the widespread awareness of the potential problems, there appears to be little if any research on Significantly Impaired Borrowers. The Money Advice Liaison Group (MALG) has produced guidelines on providing credit to people with mental health conditions.[101] One interviewee reported, however, that these are completely voluntary and generally not adhered to, so provide little additional protection to borrowers.[102] The complexity of the situation has also been recognised by the Financial Ombudsman Service (FOS), which published a case study on high-cost credit where a loan was given to someone with a mental health condition shortly before he was sectioned. The Ombudsman specifically commented on the difficulties of the borrower (or another party acting on their benefit) providing proof of the situation to lenders, especially in light of the (very valid) confidentiality requirements associated with mental health. This makes it difficult for lenders

[101] Money Advice Liaison Group, *Good Practice Awareness Guidelines For Consumers with Mental Health Problems and Debt*, 2nd edn (Money Advice Liaison Group, 2009).

[102] Joanna Kennedy, Consumer Lawyer. In-person interview.

to respond to concerns adequately and promptly, with FOS finding that the firm had not 'acted very sensitively, and that there was more they could have done', such as proactively stopping interest from accruing and not sending overdue payment messages when the borrower was hospitalised. The complaint was therefore upheld, and the lender was not entitled to the interest and charges associated with the loan in question.[103]

The links between mental health and debt in general have been considered, with the Royal College of Psychiatrists undertaking an in-depth review of the complex way in which debt and mental health interact.[104] Focus on Mental Health also completed a quantitative study of 556 people with mental health concerns, with 72 per cent of respondents defining themselves as low income and 66 per cent having difficulties making their income last through the week.[105] The FCA's *2020 Financial Lives* survey reaffirmed this link. Of the people who had used high-cost credit products in the 12 months preceding, 31 per cent had a mental health condition or illness and 38 per cent had a social or behavioural condition – figures much higher than the general population.[106]

The Money and Mental Health Policy Institute report an even worse situation, with 46 per cent of people in problem debt having a mental health condition, and 86 per cent of people with existing mental health conditions stating that their financial difficulties have exacerbated their health problems. The Institute refers to a vicious cycle of money and mental health problems. The existing mental health problems make it difficult to earn and manage money, which then results in financial difficulty. The financial difficulties experienced then lead to increased mental health problems.[107] The situation becomes so severe that 13 per cent of people in problem debt reported suicidal thoughts.[108] Whilst it is very difficult to work out figures, the Money and Mental Health Policy Institute estimates that over 100,000 people in problem debt attempt suicide in England each year.[109] Unsurprisingly, the people with multiple debt problems are at a significantly higher risk of suicidal thoughts and attempts than those with one problem debt.[110]

[103] The Financial Ombudsman Service (FOS), *Ombudsman News Issue 119 (August 2014): Short-Term Credit* (2014) Case Study 119/9.

[104] Chris Fitch and others, *Debt and Mental Health: What Do We Know? What Should We Do?* (Royal College of Psychiatrists, 2011).

[105] Focus on Mental Health, 'An Uphill Struggle: A Survey of the Experiences of People Who Use Mental Health Services and are on a Low Income', available at www.ontheside.org/focus/fpovsur.htm. Further discussion in Chris Fitch and Ryan Davey, *Debt Collection and Mental Health: Ten Steps to Improve Recovery* (The Royal College of Psychiatrists and The Money Advice Trust, 2010).

[106] FCA, *Financial Lives 2020 Survey* (n 2) 44.

[107] Money and Mental Health Policy Institute, *Money and Mental Health: The Facts* (2019).

[108] Nikki Bond and Merlyn Holkar, *A Silent Killer: Breaking the Link between Financial Difficulty and Suicide* (Money and Mental Health Policy Institute, 2018) 13.

[109] *ibid* 13.

[110] *ibid* 14.

There is limited literature specifically focused on the impact of high-cost credit.[111] This is of significant concern, considering the high levels of mental health problems in our society (one in four people in the UK will experience mental illness at some point during their lifetime[112]) and the interactions between mental health concerns and poverty.[113] The Glasgow Centre for Population Health (GCPH) highlighted the link between high-cost credit and mental health. It determined that these types of credit products increased susceptibility to mental health disorders (and worsened physical health in the longer term) among borrower populations, through four cumulative mechanisms:

- Low income and existing adverse socioeconomic conditions.
- Existing personal debt and financial difficulties.
- Exhausted or excluded access to low interest credit.
- Worsened debt burden through unmanageable … loans, high interest and fees.[114]

The GCPH recommended that further work be undertaken into the complex relationship between high-cost credit and borrower vulnerability/disadvantage, particularly in relation to mental health concerns.[115]

The connection between mental health and credit goes both ways. First, people with existing mental health concerns are more likely to fall into problem debt. Second, financial difficulties (especially those related to debt) can be a trigger or cause for the development of mental health concerns. Half of adults in problem debt also have a mental health problem, and people in problem debt are twice as likely to develop mental health conditions as those not in financial difficulties.[116] This two-way relationship was also reflected in the interviews with the borrowers. Without further research it is impossible to determine the number of borrowers who fall into this category, although the initial figures – and the results from both sets of interviews – indicate that a significant number of people are likely to be affected.

The second scenario to consider is people with compulsive gambling problems accessing high-cost credit. The potential link between debt and gambling has been recognised to some degree, and there is an increasing academic and charitable focus on this topic.[117] One of the debt advisors interviewed discussed

[111] For further research on general debt and mental health see, Jane Sharpe and Janet Bostock, *Supporting People with Debt and Mental Health Problems* (Community Psychology, 2002).

[112] Money Advice Liaison Group, *Good Practice Awareness Guidelines* (n 101) 2.

[113] This issue was also discussed with Damon Gibbons, Centre for Responsible Lending. Telephone interview.

[114] Glasgow Centre for Population Health, *Public Health Implications of Payday Lending* (Briefing Paper 48, 2016) 17.

[115] *ibid* 19.

[116] Money and Mental Health Policy Institute, *Money and Mental Health: The Facts* (n 107).

[117] For example, Gerda Reith, *Research on the Social Impacts of Gambling* (Scottish Executive Social Research, 2006); Carolyn Downs and Ryan Woolrych, *Gambling and Debt Pathfinder Study* (Research Institute for Health and Social Change, GamCare and the Money Advice Trust, 2009).

how, due to privacy issues, it can be difficult for people working with high-cost credit borrowers to determine if there are any addiction problems, including those around gambling.[118] One of the consumer lawyers had seen several cases where addicts accessed high-cost credit to fund their gambling.[119] One interviewee had seen a large number of clients with gambling problems, and stated that if lenders conducted proper affordability assessments they should pick up on the issue (indicated for example by high income, minimal expenses, significant money unaccounted for) and refuse any further loans.[120]

Existing research shows a strong link between compulsive gambling and debt issues,[121] although there has been minimal consideration of the specific relationship with high-cost credit. The stakeholder interviews highlighted two potential issues. First, the increased use of both online gambling and online lending by consumers (and the potential interaction between these two),[122] and second, the close physical proximity of gambling venues and physical high-cost credit shops in disadvantaged communities.[123] A consumer advocate interviewee stated that this proximity can result in 'a very profitable business when directed at desperate people with a high risk of being tempted into gambling'.[124] There are obvious concerns about the potential for gambling to create a need for high-cost credit, as there have been ongoing calls for planning laws to prevent lenders from opening in close proximity to bookmakers.[125] A Town Centre Planning Pilots Programme from West Dunbartonshire found that 82 per cent of survey respondents had concerns about the proximity of payday lenders and betting offices.[126] One researcher interviewee highlighted 'gambling has not been such a big piece of the picture, but that could be because we are lagging behind in our understanding'.[127] This comment

[118] Daniel Tansey, Christians Against Poverty. Telephone interview.

[119] Helen McCarthy, Citizens Advice Bureau. Telephone interview.

[120] Yvonne Fovargue MP. In-person interview.

[121] Reith, *Research on the Social Impacts of Gambling* (n 117); Downs and Woolrych, *Gambling and Debt Pathfinder Study* (n 117).

[122] This was supported by comments from Sharon Collard, Personal Finance Research Centre. Telephone interview.

[123] Martyn Saville, Which?. Telephone interview. See also Dave Clements, 'Payday Loans and Gambling: Protecting the Poor from Themselves' *The Huffington Post* (23 March 2013), available at www.huffingtonpost.co.uk/dave-clements/payday-loans-gambling-protecting-the-poor_b_2949481.html; and Heather Wardle and others, '"Risky Places?": Mapping Gambling Machine Density and Socio-Economic Deprivation' (2014) 30 *Journal of Gambling Studies* 201.

[124] Niall Cooper, Christians Against Poverty. Telephone interview.

[125] Peter Jones, Daphne Comfort and Tim Hall, 'Betting Shops in the Public Eye: A Commentary' 21 (2021) *Journal of Public Affairs* e2153; Simon Read, 'Lenders Shouldn't Target Gamblers' *The Independent* (14 April 2013), available at www.independent.co.uk/money/loans-credit/simon-read-lenders-shouldnt-target-gamblers-8570508.html; Nell Lewis, 'Can Councils Stop Bookmakers' Push Into Poor Areas? Don't Bet On It' *The Guardian* (21 November 2017), available at www.theguardian.com/society/2017/nov/21/councils-bookmakers-poor-fixed-odds-betting-terminals-planning-permission.

[126] West Dunbartonshire Council, *Town Centre Planning Pilots Programme: West Dunbartonshire, England: Planning Guidance on Pay Day Loan and Betting Shops, How to Guide* (2016), available at www.gov.scot/binaries/content/documents/govscot/publications/advice-and-guidance/2016/06/town-centre-planning-pilot-west-dunbartonshire-planning-guidance-pay-day/documents/00501612-pdf/00501612-pdf/govscot%3Adocument.

[127] Sharon Collard, Personal Finance Research Centre. Telephone interview.

aligns with the existing research, which highlights the relationships between gambling and problem debt, but also states that 'we do not have the rich understanding needed to fully assess the relationships observed'.[128] Considering that high-cost credit is generally marketed on the ease and speed with which the borrower can obtain money, there is significant potential for the product to detrimentally impact people desperate for funds to feed compulsive gambling, and it is an area ripe for further investigation.

Unsurprisingly, few of the borrowers interviewed openly admitted to using the funds obtained from high-cost credit loans for gambling purposes. One younger male interviewee admitted to, on occasions, getting a loan to put 'a good few quid on a horse', another admitted to getting a loan to go 'clubbing and gambling' on a night in town. The FCA's *2020 Financial Lives* survey reports that 27 per cent of people who used high-cost credit products had some sort of addiction, namely drugs, alcohol or gambling. It did not however break this figure down any further.

Initial research supports the finding that there is a significant link between gambling and high-cost credit. The Responsible Gambling Strategy Board (RGSB) undertook a survey of people who had participated in online gambling in the previous 12 months, and reported that 25 per cent of respondents had taken out high-cost credit and a further 27 per cent had taken out a personal loan (which is likely to include some high-cost credit loans).[129] Evidence from the Adult Psychiatric Morbidity Survey highlights as many as 44 per cent of problem gamblers have definite or severe money problems.[130] Since the pandemic, the nature of gambling has understandably changed – with a notable increase in the use of online gambling services.[131] The situation therefore seems analogous to that of mental health discussed above; whilst there is no empirical evidence specifically identifying the number of people impacted by the connection between gambling and high-cost credit, it is likely to be affecting a large number of already vulnerable individuals.

6.4.2. Application to High-Cost Credit Concepts

Addressing the requirements of this class of borrowers is exceptionally complex; the need for assistance can vary quite widely between different Significantly Impaired Borrowers, and for the same borrower at different points in time. As with all consumers, freedom is still an important concept for Significantly

[128] Wardle and others, '"Risky Places?"' (n 123) 4.

[129] Personal correspondence provided by Katherine Jackson of the RGSB based on figures provided to them by the Gambling Commission's online gambling behaviour surveys (December 2015 and March 2016).

[130] Wardle and others '"Risky Places?"' (n 123) 2.

[131] Zoe Clarke and others, *The Impact of COVID-19 on Gambling Behaviour and Associated Harms* (Public Health England, 2021).

Impaired Borrowers. Intervention should only occur when the harm caused by the contract outweighs the risk of undue infantilisation. However, owing to the impact that the impairment in question has on the ability for these borrowers to validly consent to the contract, there will often be more than adequate justification for intervention beyond ensuring procedural fairness.

The most important concept for Significantly Impaired Borrowers is regulation. Both aspects of high-cost credit regulation, avoidance of substantively unfair agreements and coercion from lack of choice, are relevant for these consumers. There needs to be mechanisms in place to stop these borrowers from accessing agreements at extortionate interest rates. The impairment in question can prevent the consumer from understanding or appreciating the nature of the transaction, and how it may impact them in the long-term. The challenges of mental health conditions and compulsive gambling raise real questions about the validity of existing legal mechanisms of disclosure, cooling-off periods, and advertising restrictions. This is a particular concern for contracts relating to the provision of credit. These challenges highlight the limited role that freedom and procedural fairness can and should play when addressing the needs of Significantly Impaired Borrowers, and the importance of moving beyond this approach to prevent substantively unfair agreements. In addition, Significantly Impaired Borrowers need regulation that protects them against coercion arising from a lack of choice. As discussed in chapter three, this goes beyond coercion of lenders and looks at the social structures and environment in which the party is transacting. If people are entering into potentially harmful credit contracts because of a mental health condition or urges arising from compulsive gambling, there are real concerns of coercion through lack of meaningful choice.

Significantly Impaired Borrowers come from a range of financial backgrounds and use the high-cost credit funds in a variety of ways. The law needs to intervene not because of the coercive effect of poverty, but because of the coercive impact of the impairment in question. Whilst evidence shows that people who suffer from gambling additions or mental health conditions are more likely to struggle financially, this is by no means uniform. Significantly Impaired Borrowers are, however, more likely to suffer from financial exclusion and poverty, and if so be categorised as Financially Insecure Borrowers.[132] Due to the potential links between these two classes, the social welfare responses identified for Financially Insecure Borrowers should also apply to Significantly Impaired Borrowers when they use funds from high-cost credit for everyday expenses or to repay existing financial obligations.

[132] In relation to mental health conditions, see Focus on Mental Health, 'An Uphill Struggle' (n 105) and Fitch and Davey, *Debt Collection and Mental Health* (n 105). In relation to gambling, see Barnard and others, 'Exploring the Relationship between Gambling, Debt and Financial Management in Britain' (n 96) and Wardle and others, *Debt and Problem Gambling* (n 96).

6.4.3. Application to Current Legal Approach

There is a strong connection between gambling, mental health issues and consent. This connection is particularly relevant in the context of high-cost credit, and highlights the important role of legal regulation. When not impaired, these borrowers may not want or need to use this type of financial product. The impact of 'passions' on an individual's decision-making ability has long been recognised as an important factor. Kant in *Anthropology* defined these passions as an 'illness of the mind'.[133] These borrowers could be in a situation where they are 'knowingly acting against one's better judgment'.[134] Elster gives the example of a compulsive gambler who knows he is ruining his life and tries to quit, but relapses.[135] Significantly Impaired Borrowers can know what they are doing when they enter into high-cost credit contracts, but their condition may be overwhelming. Mental health conditions and gambling can undermine an individual's ability to control their actions to such an extent that they are no longer able to provide valid consent. The existing legal mechanisms of procedural fairness are insufficient. There is a need to prevent Significantly Impaired Borrowers from entering potentially harmful high-cost credit contracts.

There are three potential ways the law currently responds to Significantly Impaired Borrowers; the common law, the Mental Capacity Act 2005 (MCA), and inherent jurisdiction. The common law of contract provides limited protection for these borrowers through capacity requirements and vitiating factors.[136] Contracting parties must have the capacity to enter into binding agreements.[137] Unsoundness of mind, even to the extent of lunacy, historically did not constitute a valid defence, and these agreements were enforceable against parties and their estate.[138] The law was however modified by Pollock CB in *Moulton v Camroux*.[139] The result is that if a borrower does not have capacity when entering a high-cost

[133] Immanuel Kant, *The Philosophy of Law* (Morrison and Gibb, 1887) 7–251. Similar discussion also occurred in Immanuel Kant, *Metaphysical Elements of Justice* (Translated with Introduction and Notes by Ladd (ed), Hackett Publishing Company, 1999). For further discussion on this topic see Paul Formosa, 'A Life Without Affects and Passions: Kant on the Duty of Apathy' (2011) 13 *Parrhesia* 96.

[134] Jon Elster, 'Weakness of Will and Preference Reverals' in Elster and others (eds), *Understanding Choice, Explaining Behaviour* (UniPub ForLag Oslo Academic Press, 2006) 58.

[135] *ibid* 58. He uses the particularly vivid description of Euripides's *Medea*; when the protagonist attempts to kill her children declaring 'I know indeed what evil I intend to do. But stronger than all my after thoughts is my fury'.

[136] Insanity may also be considered a contract law 'defence', but this is highly controversial: see Andrew Dyson, James Goudkamp and Wilmot-Smith, 'Thinking in Terms of Contract Defences' in Dyson, Goudkamp and Wilmot-Smith (eds), *Defences in Contract* (Hart Publishing, 2017) 8.

[137] See *Hart v O'Connor* [1985] AC 1000, [1985] UKPC 1.

[138] For a discussion of this background, see *Moulton v Camroux* (1847) 2 Ex 487 (CA) 500–501; Joseph Chitty, *A Treatise on the Law of Contracts* (Sweet and Maxwell, 1912) 190.

[139] His Honour stated that the rule had 'in modern times been relaxed, and unsoundness of mind (as also intoxication) would now be a good defence to an action upon a contract, if it could be shown that the defendant was not of the capacity to contract, and the plaintiff knew it': *Moulton v Camroux* (n 138) 501.

credit contract, it cannot be enforced against them.[140] The requirements for incapacity are, however, quite high. In *Irvani v Irvani*, the Court of Appeal held that a serious ongoing alcohol addiction was insufficient grounds to void an arbitration agreement.[141] Only the most serious of mental health conditions will be sufficient to hold high-cost credit contracts unenforceable. It is unlikely that any sort of gambling addiction would be accepted by the courts as an adequate reason. Society's disapproval of compulsive gambling, and general refusal to recognise it as a legitimate medical condition, is likely to create a lack of sympathy for gamblers and in turn will impact the approach taken by the courts.[142]

If the impairment is so great that the borrower did not understand the nature of the transaction *and* the lender was aware of the impairment, the contract is voidable by the borrower[143] and there is a strong case of irresponsible lending.[144] In the context of high-cost credit transactions, it is very unlikely that there would be a sufficient relationship between the parties to provide the lender with an awareness of the impairment. The nature of the loan will often prevent the lender from obtaining this information; the transactions are quick, there is minimal disclosure, and often no direct contact between the lender and borrower. In addition, lenders cannot enquire about the borrower's physical or mental health or condition[145] as this is 'sensitive personal data'.[146] Even if they obtained this information, the lender cannot treat the borrower less favourably on the basis of the condition.[147] It is unclear how these competing legal obligations should be approached whilst also ensuring that lenders are fulfilling their duties under the ILG.

The second common law protection for Significantly Impaired Borrowers is vitiating factors. These factors were initially quite restrictive, but have expanded to address issues of procedural unfairness, substantive unfairness, and (arguably) maintenance of a social minimum. There are a number of vitiating factors, such as undue influence, unconscionability and economic duress, which may be relevant

[140] There are, however, certain requirements that the other party be aware of the mental incapacity: *Hart v O'Connor* (n 137) 1018–19.

[141] *Irvani v Irvani* [2000] 1 Lloyds LR 412 (CA), see esp comments at 424.

[142] Jeffrey J Marotta, Judy A Cornelius and William R Eadington, *The Downside: Problem and Pathological Gambling* (University of Nevada Press, 2002) 430.

[143] *Moulton v Camroux* (n 138) 501; *Irvani v Irvani* (n 141) 424; *Pitt v Smith* (1811) 3 Camp 33, 170 ER 1296 (NP); *Matthews v Baxter* (1873) LR 8 Exch 132 (ExCh).

[144] Subject to a potential claim for unjust enrichment of the original amount loaned. See *Blomley v Ryan* (1956) 99 CLR 362 ((HCA)); Peter Hall, *Unconscionable Contracts and Economic Duress* (CCH Australia Ltd, 1985); David Harland, 'Unconscionable and Unfair Contracts: An Australian Perspective' in Brownsword, Hird and Howells (eds), *Good Faith in Contract: Concepts and Context* (Ashgate Dartmouth, 1999); Malcolm Cope, *Duress, Undue Influence and Unconscientious Bargains* (The Law Book Company Ltd, 1985); Malcolm Cope, 'The Review of Unconscionable Conduct Bargains in Equity' (1983) 57 *The Australian Law Journal* 279.

[145] Data Protection Act 1998 (UK), Equality Act 2010 (UK) and Mental Capacity Act 2005 (UK).

[146] Data Protection Act 1998 (UK) s 2(e).

[147] Equality Act 2010 (UK) s 4 which states that 'disability' is a protected characteristic. 'Disability' is defined in s 6 as a 'physical or mental impairment'. See also Mental Health (Discrimination) Act 2013 (UK).

to high-cost credit contracts.[148] Significantly Impaired Borrowers still have to prove the elements of a vitiating factor; merely having a mental health condition or compulsive gambling problems will not be sufficient to find a high-cost credit contract voidable.[149] Thus, while vitiating factors have the potential to provide some assistance to Significantly Impaired Borrowers, it is a piecemeal approach that is insufficient to respond to the current challenges.

The MCA also provides limited protection for Significantly Impaired Borrowers. The profile identified two key scenarios for these borrowers. First, mental health concerns cover a range of conditions including schizophrenia, bipolar disorder, depression and anxiety, and these are all clearly recognised health conditions or disorders.[150] The second scenario is problem gambling, which, according to the World Health Organisation's *International Statistical Classification of Diseases and Related Health Problems*, is defined as 'pathological gambling' and is also a recognised mental and behavioural disorder.[151] Both scenarios are therefore associated with recognised health conditions.

The MCA creates a distinction between people who have capacity (and therefore are deemed to be able to consent) and those who do not have capacity (and therefore cannot consent). The threshold test for capacity is whether the person is able, at the material time, to decide for him or herself.[152] This is further explained in section 3, which states that a person is unable to make a decision if they are unable to:

- understand the information relevant to the decision;
- retain that information; and

[148] Jack Beatson and Daniel Friedman, 'Introduction: From "Classical" to Modern Contract Law' in Beatson and Friedman (eds), *Good Faith and Fault in Contract Law* (Oxford University Press, 1997) 12–14.

[149] See, eg, the discussion of unconscionable bargains and mental incapacity in *Hart v O'Connor* (n 137).

[150] These are divided into two categories in World Health Organisation, *International Statistical Classification of Diseases and Related Health Problems*, 10th edn (World Health Organisation, 2016). The first is Schizophrenia, schizotypal and delusional disorders (F20-F29), described as 'This block brings together schizophrenia, as the most important member of the group, schizotypal disorder, persistent delusional disorders, and a larger group of acute and transient psychotic disorders'. The second is Mood [affective] disorders (F30-F39), described as 'This block contains disorders in which the fundamental disturbance is a change in affect or mood to depression (with or without associated anxiety) or to elation. The mood change is usually accompanied by a change in the overall level of activity; most of the other symptoms are either secondary to, or easily understood in the context of, the change in mood and activity. Most of these disorders tend to be recurrent and the onset of individual episodes can often be related to stressful events or situations'.

[151] *ibid* F63.0 defines pathological gambling as 'The disorder consists of frequent, repeated episodes of gambling that dominate the patient's life to the detriment of social, occupational, material, and family values and commitments'.

[152] Mental Capacity Act 2005 (UK) s 2(1). For criticisms of the capacity test, see Jonathan Herring and Jesse Wall, 'Autonomy, Capacity and Vulnerable Adults: Filling the Gaps in the Mental Capacity Act' (2015) 35 *Legal Studies* 698 and Nancy Knauer, 'Defining Capacity: Balancing the Competing Interests of Autonomy and Need' (2003) 12 *Temple Political & Civil Rights Law Review* 321.

- use or weigh that information as part of the process of making the decision; or
- communicate the decision (whether by talking, using sign language or any other means).[153]

Significantly Impaired Borrowers may not have adequate capacity when entering into high-cost credit contracts. They are particularly likely to experience difficulties with adequately weighing the short-term benefits against the long-term implications. At other times, they may have the ability to make decisions, and therefore have full capacity. Most of these borrowers will, however, have fluctuating incapacity, meaning that they have periods of lucidity. This makes it difficult to create a regulatory response that adequately addresses the needs of these consumers. As outlined by Herring and Wall, the MCA 'typically seeks to determine the minimum necessary for autonomy and treats the person as autonomous once they cross that threshold'.[154] It is therefore a blunt instrument and cannot respond adequately to the needs of these borrowers.

There will be instances where an individual will not meet the threshold of the common law or MCA, but their decision-making abilities remain substantially impacted. A third potential approach has been developed, namely the inherent jurisdiction of the court. This is a common law doctrine that could 'plug' this gap, and create a situation where the law can intervene on behalf of vulnerable people.[155] The court has gradually increased the scope and application of inherent jurisdiction.[156] As outlined by the Court of Appeal in *DL v Local Authority*, inherent jurisdiction applies when 'other factors … combine with his borderline capacity to remove his autonomy to make an important decision'.[157] This definition highlights the potential relevance of inherent jurisdiction to Significantly Impaired Borrowers. Many of these individuals will have capacity under the MCA 2005, but other factors will 'remove [their] autonomy to make an important decision' (namely enter into a high-cost credit contract). The application of inherent jurisdiction was further discussed in *Re SA (vulnerable adult with capacity: marriage)*, where Munby J held it applicable to:

> A vulnerable adult who, even if not incapacitated by mental disorder or mental illness, is, or is reasonably believed to be, either (i) under constraint or (ii) subject to coercion

[153] Mental Capacity Act 2005 (UK) s 3(1).

[154] Herring and Wall, 'Autonomy, Capacity and Vulnerable Adults' (n 152) 702.

[155] The most frequently arising example of this situation is in relation to 16- and 17-year-olds being pressured into marriage: see, eg, *Re SA (vulnerable adult with capacity: marriage)* [2006] 1 FLR 867, [2005] EWHC 2942 (Fam).

[156] The key cases extending inherent jurisdiction are *ibid*; *Re SK* [2005] 2 FLR 230, [2004] EWHC 3202 (Fam); *Re G (An Adult)* [2004] EWHC 2222 (Fam).

[157] The quote in full states 'where, on a strict mental health appraisal, such an individual does not lack capacity in the terms of the MCA 2005 and therefore falls outside the statutory scheme, but other factors, for example coercion and undue influence, may combine with his borderline capacity to remove his autonomy to make an important decision, why, one may ask, should that individual not be able to access the protection now afforded to adults whose mental capacity puts them on the other side of that borderline?': *DL v A Local Authority* [2012] EWCA 253 [65].

> or undue influence or (iii) for some other reason deprived of the capacity to make the relevant decision, or disabled from making a free choice, or incapacitated or disabled from giving or expressing a real and genuine consent.[158]

The final comments in (iii) on being disabled from making a free choice and exercising real and genuine consent can be applied to (at least some) Significantly Impaired Borrowers. Inherent jurisdiction clearly goes beyond mere issues of capacity, and looks for genuine consent, taking a long-term view on autonomy and freedom. While not providing a comprehensive list of the people covered by inherent jurisdiction, Munby J comments that

> many … circumstances that may so reduce a vulnerable adult's understanding and reasoning powers as to prevent him forming or expressing a real and genuine consent, for example, the effects of deception, misinformation, physical disability, illness, weakness (physical, mental or moral), tiredness, shock, fatigue, depression, pain or drugs. No doubt there are others.[159]

This broad discussion highlights the wide spectrum of situations covered by inherent jurisdiction, indicating that mental health conditions and gambling addictions (falling short of what is required for the MCA) may be covered. The essential purpose of inherent jurisdiction is to respect and protect the autonomy of the individual;[160] their negative freedom can be limited to provide them with greater positive freedom. Whilst the inherent jurisdiction powers of the court have potential to assist high-cost credit borrowers with impacted capacity, its ability to invalidate private law contracts is unclear. There have been cases where marriage has been held invalid through inherent jurisdiction,[161] but the court has yet to consider its impact on commercial contracts. If, however, there were a process in place whereby people could be excluded from the market, such as the creation of a 'do-not-lend registry', it would be relatively uncontroversial for the court to exercise its powers under inherent jurisdiction and utilise this process for the benefit of the Significantly Impaired Borrower.

6.5. Conclusion

This chapter has highlighted the importance of recognising and responding to the underlying circumstances of borrowers and their specific needs. It has engaged with qualitative empirical research in the forms of interviews with both stakeholders

[158] *Re SA (vulnerable adult with capacity: marriage)* [2006] 1 FLR 867, [2005] EWHC 2942 (Fam) [79].

[159] *ibid* [78]. Munby J does not attempt to provide an exhaustive list of situations, stating this would be 'unwise, and indeed inappropriate' [77].

[160] See discussion in Herring and Wall, 'Autonomy, Capacity and Vulnerable Adults' (n 152) 702.

[161] See, eg, *A Local Authority v SY* [2013] EWHC 3485 (COP) and *XCC v AA & Ors* [2012] EWHC 2183 (COP).

and borrowers themselves to provide an insight into the lived experience of people utilising high-cost credit. The result of these interviews highlighted that there are multiple and complicated reasons why people use these financial products. It was however possible to distil these uses to identify three distinct classes of consumers; Financially Secure Borrowers, Financially Insecure Borrowers and Significantly Impaired Borrowers. All three of the concepts previously considered – freedom, regulation and a social minimum – are important, but in varying ways for the different borrower classes. The law has responded to the situation through various methods, but it is clear that more work needs to be done to address the challenges of high-cost credit. The next chapter will therefore provide a range of recommendations in light of the profile and taxonomy of borrowers developed.

7

Future Directions

> Good political principles must spell real changes in the real lives of real people: otherwise they are dust and ashes.
>
> — Barbara Wootton, Baroness Wootton of Abinger[1]

The previous chapters have identified the borrower taxonomy, assessed the needs of each class, and analysed the current and past legal processes relevant to the borrowers. These steps have raised a number of further questions. This final chapter therefore makes a range of recommendations for how to utilise the taxonomy to address the ongoing concerns in the high-cost credit industry, identifying what steps are necessary to take each recommendation forward. It is first and foremost a plea for further research and policy analysis. As much as a regulatory-based solution would be ideal, this is unfortunately not possible. The private law alone cannot solve the problems identified – we need to go beyond the existing legal structures and look at how they interact with the social welfare system. The recommendations in this chapter will therefore be divided into three separate headings; law reform recommendations, social welfare responses, and further research.

7.1. Law Reform Recommendations

The regulation of high-cost credit has received significant attention since the global financial crisis, and some of the most concerning aspects of the industry can be (and to some extent have been) addressed through law reform. As outlined by the Financial Conduct Authority (FCA) in *The Woolard Review*, 'regulation has a vital role to play in delivering a healthy credit market. This involves acting where poor and harmful practices are identified and to help rebalance incentives where there are conflicts of interest'.[2] This section therefore outlines some potential law reform recommendations. It is recognised that there has been considerable attention paid to reviewing the high-cost credit market and multiple rounds of reform. The recommendations discussed in this section however arise in relation to the

[1] Thank you to the Special Collections at The Keep for permission to use this quote; reference number SxMs9/2/13/2/3.

[2] Financial Conduct Authority (FCA), *The Woolard Review – A Review of Change and Innovation in the Unsecured Credit Market*, 2021) para 5.1.

three borrower classes identified in the previous chapter, focusing on enhanced disclosure, responsible lending obligations, and opt out processes.

7.1.1. Enhanced and Meaningful Disclosure

Disclosure is a central aspect of high-cost credit regulation; it is crucial that all borrowers understand the financial transaction into which they have entered or are about to enter. Information provision is one of the key ways that the State can assist people to make better decisions without the need for active paternalistic involvement.[3] Even a freedom-based approach supports disclosure obligations on lenders. Despite the limitations of disclosure, it is important to get it right. There needs to be an increased focus on transparent and effective disclosure. The current approach has been subject to trenchant criticism on its failure to engage with the lending reality of borrowers.[4] For example, during the debates on advertising of high-cost credit products, the former Consumer Minister Jo Swinson called for additional regulation and enhanced disclosure.[5]

During the 2014/2015 reforms, the FCA acknowledged the limitations with the existing disclosure regime in relation to high-cost credit transactions. As part of its reforms, the regulator included a requirement for a financial warning on all advertisements. Originally the warning was:

> Think! Is this loan right for you? Over 2 million short-term loans were not paid off on time in 2011/12. This can lead to serious money problems. If you're struggling, go to www.moneyadviceservice.org.uk for free and impartial help.[6]

This was however 'downgraded' to 'Warning: Late repayment can cause you serious money problems. For help, go to moneyadviceservice.org.uk'.[7]

Whilst the former recommendation is clearly superior to the one that was used in the end, both provide insufficient information to benefit borrowers. As an example, the UK obligations can be contrasted with the equivalent warning in Australia, which is required to be included on both lender websites[8] and business premises.[9] The Australian warning states:

> WARNING – Do you really need a loan today?

[3] Cass R Sunstein, 'The Storrs Lecture: Behavioral Economics and Paternalism' (2013) 122 *The Yale Law Journal* 1826, 1856.

[4] It is important to identify the limits associated with disclosure, namely the minimum impact that information disclosure has on the decision-making process of many individuals: see discussion in chapter three, section 3.5.1.

[5] Rupert Jones and Hilary Osborne, 'Crackdown on Payday Loans Advertising' *The Guardian* (2 July 2013), available at www.theguardian.com/money/2013/jul/01/crackdown-payday-loans-advertising (all websites cited in this chapter were accessed on 25 January 2022).

[6] FCA, *Detailed Proposals for the FCA Regime for Consumer Credit* (Consultation Paper CP13/10, 2013) 69.

[7] FCA, *FCA Handbook, Consumer Credit Sourcebook (CONC)* 3.4.1.

[8] National Consumer Credit Protection Regulations 2010 (Cth) r 28XXA referring to Schedule 7 for the wording of the warning.

[9] *ibid* r 28XXB referring to Schedule 9 for the wording of the warning.

> It can be expensive to borrow small amounts of money and borrowing may not solve your money problems.
>
> Check your options before you borrow:
>
> For information about other options for managing bills and debts, ring 1800 007 007 from anywhere in Australia to talk to a free and independent financial counsellor.
>
> Talk to your electricity, gas, phone or water provider to work out a payment plan.
>
> If you are on government benefits, ask if you can receive an advance from Centrelink: www.humanservices.gov.au/advancepayments.
>
> The Government's MoneySmart website shows you how small amount loans work and suggests other options that may help you.

This Australian wording is obviously focused specifically on the assistance provided in that country. This type of disclosure approach is however likely to be more effective as it provides readers with concrete alternatives to high-cost credit as opposed to merely a warning. A similar model could be implemented in the UK, especially as the downgrading of the originally proposed warning was not discussed or justified by the regulator.

Providing all borrower classes with clear, easy to understand information about high-cost credit is a necessity. It will be particularly relevant for Financially Secure Borrowers who often have other financial options and are using this financial source because of the ease and convenience associated with high-cost credit products. Reminding these borrowers of the high costs associated with the loan in question and the fact that there are other more affordable options could help to 'nudge' them to make more appropriate financial choices.[10] If they continue to choose the high-cost credit product and it is not going to cause them financial hardship, these borrowers should be entitled to make this decision.

An increased focus on disclosure may also be useful for Financially Insecure Borrowers, as it will provide these individuals with the opportunity to seek assistance instead of turning to expensive and potentially harmful credit products. The wording of the Australian warning provides these borrowers with information on their alternatives and could help people who feel like they have no other options realise that there is easy to access, free of charge assistance to deal with problem debt. When asked about their options and general support available, most of the high-cost borrowers interviewed were unaware of the plethora of support services available for people who were financially struggling, or unsure of what support the different organisers could provide. Ensuring enhanced and meaningful disclosure will mean that people who feel they have no option but to turn to high-cost credit are armed with this important information *before* they can agree to an expensive and potential harmful financial product. It is a simple, effective, and important way to respond to some of the root causes of the ongoing problem.

[10] Richard Thaler and Cass Sunstein, *Nudge: Improving Decisions about Health, Wealth, and Happiness* (Yale University Press, 2008).

7.1.2. Responsible Lending Obligations

The laws on responsible lending obligations were discussed in chapter four, section 4.4.3.[11] Despite the 2006 amendments to the responsible lending regime and the transition to the FCA, the UK system continues to put the onus on consumers to ensure that the loan is suitable for their needs. This is not appropriate, as Financially Insecure Borrowers often have few financial options and can be easily exploited.[12] There is also a lack of adequate detail about what amounts to responsible lending; in particular, what specific obligations lenders have regarding financial hardship, inappropriate lending models, and documentation required to prove repayment ability. This creates a situation where borrowers are not given adequate protection, and can be exploited by lenders who take advantage of the lack of proscriptive detail in the guidelines.

This relatively passive approach to responsible lending can be contrasted with the Australian regime. The responsible lending obligations in Australia comprise an entire chapter of legislation[13] with over 70 pages of text, as well as a Regulatory Guide[14] produced by the national regulator.[15] The core obligation on lenders in Australia is to ensure that the credit contract is 'not unsuitable' for the borrower. There are two aspects to this determination: whether the consumer can meet the financial obligations under the contract without substantial financial hardship,[16] and whether the product meets the consumer's requirements and objectives.[17] The lender has an obligation to take 'reasonable steps to verify information' provided by the consumer about their financial position to ensure that the credit is 'not unsuitable'. The lender is required to 'understand the purpose for which the credit

[11] See also Karen Fairweather, 'Apples and Oranges? Responsible Mortgage Lending in the UK and Australia' in O'Shea, Fairweather and Grantham (eds), *Credit, Consumers and the Law: After the Global Storm* (Routledge (Markets and the Law Series) 2016).

[12] This is further discussed in Jodi Gardner, Karen Rowlingson and Lindsey Appleyard, 'Responsible Borrowing and Lending' (2018) 2 *Journal of International Consumer Law and Practice* 16.

[13] National Consumer Credit Protection Act 2009 (Cth).

[14] Australian Securities and Investment Commission (ASIC), *Credit Licensing: Responsible Lending Conduct* (Regulatory Guide 209, 2013).

[15] The Australian Securities and Investment Commission (ASIC). The National Consumer Credit Protection Act 2009 (Cth) (NCCPA) and the National Credit Code (NCC) regulate the provision of consumer credit. In 2013, the Consumer Credit Legislation Amendment (Enhancements) Act 2012 (Cth) (CCLAEA) was enacted, providing for a national interest rate cap and additional protections for borrowers of high-cost credit. For more details, see Jodi Gardner, *The Challenges of Regulating High-Cost Short-Term Credit: A Comparison of UK and Australian Approaches* (Centre on Household Assets and Savings Management, 2014).

[16] A detailed list of what is potentially relevant for determining whether a consumer can repay their financial obligations without suffering substantial financial hardship is set out in ASIC, *Credit Licensing: Responsible Lending Conduct* (n 14) 32–37. There are also presumptions of substantial financial hardship for small-amount loans under the National Consumer Credit Protection Act 2009 (Cth) ss 118, 123, 131, 133.

[17] A detailed list of what should be considered when determining whether the credit product meets the consumer's requirements and objectives is set out in *ibid* 40–42. The ASIC guide however explicitly states that the contract is not unsuitable merely because another product would be more suitable for the consumer, highlighting that the product does not have to be the most suitable loan available.

is sought and determine if the type, length, rate, terms, special conditions, charges and other aspects of the proposed contract meet this purpose'.[18] This is a very different approach to that adopted in the UK. It puts additional obligations on lenders to ensure that the loan is appropriate and suited to the borrower's needs. It also fulfills the requirement of ensuring that the borrower will be at or above the social minimum when the loan is taken out and during all scheduled repayments.

Furthermore, for people who access 'small-amount credit' in Australia, the Consumer Credit Legislation Amendment (Enhancements) Act 2012 (Cth) (CCLAEA) in combination with the National Consumer Credit Protection Act 2009 (Cth) (NCCPA) imposes additional responsible lending requirements in relation to Small Amount Credit Contracts (SACCs). The borrower will be presumed to be unsuitable for additional loans if (a) they are currently in default under a SACC or (b) have had two or more SACCs in the past 90 days. If the borrower already has an account in an authorised deposit-taking institution, the lender must as part of the assessment of loan suitability, obtain *and consider* statements from their account over the previous 90 days before approving a loan. This ensures that the lender is aware of – and considers – the financial situation of the borrower before a loan is granted. The CCLAEA dictates that if 50 per cent or more of the borrower's income is from government benefits or pension, the SACC repayments can only be a maximum of 20 per cent of the borrower's income. If the loan is paid back under a Continuous Payment Authority (CPA),[19] the lender cannot attempt to debit the borrower's account until the borrower is advised that the debit has been unsuccessful. This is an attempt to stop the 'drip feeding' of money out of borrowers' accounts, and to ensure that there is sufficient money to pay priority debts.

The UK would benefit from taking a more detailed approach to lender obligations. This would be particularly relevant for the class of Financially Insecure Borrowers, as these types of lending restrictions are designed to ensure that borrowers can afford to repay their credit obligations without going below the social minimum or suffering financial hardship. They therefore assist with the maintenance of the borrower's social minimum. Whilst the specific details would need to be determined in the light of the unique social and legal culture in the UK,[20] helpful guidance for responsible lending obligations can be drawn from the Australian approach.

7.1.3. Opt Out Processes

Proactive mechanisms could be put in place to prevent consumers, particularly Significantly Impaired Borrowers, from accessing harmful high-cost credit by

[18] Explanatory Memorandum, National Consumer Credit Protection Act 2009 (Cth) para 379.

[19] See chapter one, n 35 for the definition.

[20] For an interesting analysis of applying doctrines from one country to another, see Mindy Chen-Wishart, 'Legal Transplant and Undue Influence: Lost in Translation or a Working Misunderstanding' (2013) 62 *International & Comparative Law Quarterly* 1.

developing an 'opt out' process. An analogy can be drawn to Ulysses and the Sirens, where Ulysses asks to be tied up when passing the Sirens to avoid succumbing to the temptation. From a regulatory perspective, this is 'pre-commitment'; the notion of constraining the rights and actions of an individual when they are in a rational state, to protect them from choices they may make when acting in a less rational manner.[21] Significantly Impaired Borrowers could voluntarily remove their access to high-cost credit during times of lucidity, and this would be binding on them when impacted by the impairment in question. If a loan were given in breach of the pre-commitment, the lender would not be able to recover the funds. When high-cost credit usage impacts people beyond the borrower (ie family members reliant on funds for living expenses), those affected could also request that the borrower be excluded from the market. The opt out could then be imposed on the borrower. This would not, however, be an automatic process, and would require further regulatory hurdles (such as court or regulatory approval) to ensure that the borrower's freedom was not unduly undermined. This type of interventionalist approach is already available in the gambling industry, but on an optional basis. Considering the strong links between gambling and problem debt, the extension of the process to high-cost credit is easily justified.

The regulatory approach to Significantly Impaired Borrowers may raise potential issues of discrimination, ie people with mental health conditions or compulsive gamblers are being treated unfavourability compared to the remaining population. Negative discrimination against vulnerable groups is prohibited,[22] although positive discrimination (or more accurately 'protection') should be encouraged on the basis that these groups need additional assistance from the State. There are examples of positive discrimination for both borrower categories. Consumer credit contracts in Scotland are unenforceable if the borrower did not have adequate capacity, irrespective of whether the lender had constructive notice of the situation.[23] Singapore recognised the need for specific protection of people with gambling problems, and has excluded from gambling institutions citizens who have a poor credit record or are financially vulnerable.[24] Whilst Singapore is a more authoritarian society and there is less concern for freedom of contract, such limitations are also justifiable in the UK, as the 'freedom' to become indebted because of compulsive gambling is not a worthwhile freedom that the law should facilitate.[25]

[21] See further discussion in Jon Elster, *Ulysses Unbound: Studies in Rationality, Precommitment, and Constraints* (Cambridge University Press, 2000); Jon Elster, 'Weakness of Will and Preference Reverals' in Elster and others (eds), *Understanding Choice, Explaining Behaviour* (UniPub ForLag Oslo Academic Press, 2006).

[22] Equality Act 2010 (UK) s 4 which states that 'disability' is a protected characteristic. 'Disability' is defined in s 6 as a 'physical or mental impairment'. See also Mental Health (Discrimination) Act 2013 (UK).

[23] See discussion in the Office of Fair Trading, *Mental Capacity – OFT Guidance for Creditors* (2011) 3.

[24] Social standards implemented under Casino Control Act 2006 (Sg).

[25] Joseph Raz, *The Morality of Freedom* (Oxford University Press, 1988) see esp 15, 156.

7.2. Social Welfare Responses

This section discusses the need for a welfare-based response in conjunction with the legal reforms discussed above. As considered in the previous section, the challenges of lending – particularly to Financially Insecure Borrowers – cannot be solved merely by looking at the legal regime for high-cost credit. Chapter five described how the concept and application of a social minimum has developed quickly in the UK. There is, however, more work to be done in the area before the social minimum can be applied to meet the current high-cost credit challenges. These financial products require people, many of whom are already on low incomes, to repay loans at exceptionally high interest rates. *Even if* people are provided with an adequate social minimum, high-cost credit repayments have the potential to push them back below this level. This section will therefore discuss both the provision and maintenance of a social minimum in relation to high-cost credit.

7.2.1. Providing a Social Minimum

Providing a social minimum involves tackling the underlying issues of poverty by the redistribution of resources. This is particularly important for Financially Insecure Borrowers, as they often turn to high-cost credit to make ends meet. Regulation will therefore not solve the problem, as (a) redistribution will only occur on an ad hoc basis between specific lenders and borrowers and (b) borrowers will still have limited financial means and choices. The problems go beyond the private law realm and needs a response from the State.[26] The redistribution should come from an effective and proactive social welfare system. The importance of this was highlighted by Fried:

> Redistribution is not a burden to be borne in a random, ad hoc way by those who happen to cross paths with persons poorer than themselves. Such a conception, heartwarmingly spontaneous though it may be, would in the end undermine our ability to plan and live our lives as we choose. Liberal democracies have chosen to effect redistribution (to assure a social minimum) by welfare benefits on one hand and by general taxation based on overall ability to pay on the other. In this way government, as it seeks contributions to remove inequalities, remains neutral about the ways in which the better-off acquire their greater wealth, exacting (in principle, at least) the same contribution from everyone who enjoys the same level of wealth … The provision of a social minimum should be society's general responsibility.[27]

[26] We must however recognise the role of responsible borrowing and lender obligations. As has been discussed above, if loans are given when borrowers cannot afford to make repayments without suffering financial hardship, this is an issue with lender's exploitative actions and the contracts should not be upheld by the courts.

[27] Charles Fried, *Contract as Promise: A Theory of Contractual Obligation* (Harvard University Press, 1981) 106. Similar comments were made by Atiyah; 'During the past decade or so the view has been

The UK is a developed Welfare State, and it is accepted that citizens have a right to a basic standard of living. There is an expectation that the State will provide a minimal level of support for vulnerable and low-income citizens.[28] Since the 2008 global financial crisis and economic downturn, there has been a shift towards a more conservative approach to social security and away from the Welfare State. This decreasing government support coincides with stagnated wages, increased unemployment, and higher costs of living, occurring at a time when people most need the extra support.[29] Increasing numbers of low-income consumers are using high-cost credit to pay for life's necessities, raising the question of whether 'mainstream society is failing these people'.[30] Financially Insecure Borrowers are becoming more common amongst high-cost credit users. They have been forced to turn to high-cost credit for everyday expenses or existing financial obligations. These types of purchases are 'not something we should be relying on credit for', and the State should ensure people have access to these basic essentials without resorting to high-cost credit.[31]

It is beyond the purpose and scope of this book to enter a detailed debate about how adequate levels of welfare should be calculated.[32] What is important to note is that if the State wants to tackle high-cost credit, it must address the links with poverty and therefore the need to provide an adequate social minimum. The current Government, however, is taking steps to reduce the welfare safety net for many vulnerable people at the same time as regulating the high-cost credit market. The positive impact of the latter is likely to be greatly overshadowed by the negative impact of the former. Individuals, whether employed or not, must be provided with their basic needs without resorting to credit. The Government needs to take welfare provision seriously and raise the social minimum. Research from the Child Poverty Action Group highlights the failure of the current system.

gaining ground, certainly in England, that these contracts should still be left to the market, while we should try and control or handle the externalities by other government actions. If a tenant is too poor to pay an open market rent, then the tenant should receive some state financial benefit, but the market should be left to operate freely': Patrick Atiyah, *Essays on Contract Law* (Oxford University Press, 1990) Essay 12, 360.

[28] For discussion of the causes of poverty and role of the Government, see Tracy Shildrick and others, *Poverty and Insecurity: Life in "Low-Pay, No-Pay" Britain* (Policy, 2012); Jonathan Cribb and others, *Living Standards, Poverty and Inequality in the UK 2013* (Institute for Fiscal Studies distributed by Central Books Ltd, 2013); Dalia Ben-Galim and Tess Lanning, *Strength Against Shocks: Low-Income Families and Debt* (Institute for Public Policy Research, 2010).

[29] See Karen Rowlingson, Lindsey Appleyard and Jodi Gardner, 'Payday Lending in the UK: The Regul(aris)ation of a Necessary Evil?' (2016) 45 *Journal of Social Policy* 527.

[30] Carl Packman, Author and Consumer Advocate. Telephone interview. This was discussed numerous times in the interviews; Packman stated, 'I have to question the use of the term "civil society" … [it is] a drastic and scary situation which is undermining people's financial security' (Carl Packman, Author and Consumer Advocate. Telephone interview). This is supported by James Jones from the credit reference agency Experian, who states that the widespread use of high-cost credit for everyday expenses 'suggests other things are not working well in society and welfare in general' (James Jones, Experian. Telephone interview).

[31] James Jones, Experian. Telephone interview.

[32] For an excellent collection of essays discussing these issues, see Kotkas, Leijten and Pennings (eds), *Specifying and Securing a Social Minimum in the Battle Against Poverty* (Hart Publishing, 2019).

Two parents working full-time on the *national living wage* earn £49 less per week than they need to live in what society defines as an 'acceptable, no-frills living standard'. The situation is significantly worse for parents who are unemployed or part-time workers, in minimum wage jobs, on zero hour contracts or are lone parents.[33] Until the importance of providing a decent social minimum is acknowledged and addressed, history will continue to repeat itself, and the high-cost credit market will remain an ongoing source of regulatory frustration and failure.

7.2.2. Maintaining a Social Minimum

Whilst the *provision* of a social minimum is clearly important, the *maintenance* of this minimum is also critical. There is no use providing people with adequate resources if they then have such limited financial choices that, when unexpected expenses arise, they need to resort to high-cost credit contracts with repayments that push them below the social minimum. The majority of people using high-cost credit (over seven out of ten) are doing so because of an unforeseen change in circumstances.[34] Even if people are initially provided with a social minimum, exploitative high-cost credit contracts have the potential to push borrowers below the level of resources needed to live a meaningful life.[35]

To truly tackle the problems of high-cost credit, the Government needs to develop a financial system that not only provides but also maintains the social minimum of vulnerable borrowers. There are two aspects to this approach. The first is to ensure that lenders are prohibited from giving high-cost credit if the repayments are going to push people into financial hardship (discussed above in relation to responsible lending requirements), and the second is to create a social security system where people do not need to turn to these loans in times of need. This second step requires a range of responses, including:

- increasing financial control when borrowers experience problem debt;
- providing affordable credit options for low income consumers;
- establishing financial hardship regulations that give people flexibility when they suffer temporary financial difficulties; and
- encouraging a savings culture.

[33] See Donald Hirsch, *The Cost of a Child in 2018* (Child Poverty Action Group, 2018) and analysis in Child Poverty Action Group, 'The Cost of a Child in 2018' (*Child Poverty Action Group*, 20 August 2018), available at http://cpag.org.uk/content/cost-child-2018. As COVID-19 has had an unprecedented impact on these issues, the pre-pandemic figures are used here to get a picture of the situation without the additional burdens caused by the pandemic.

[34] Competition & Markets Authority, *Research into the Payday Lending Market* (2014) 70.

[35] This is discussed in The Rt Hon Frank Field MP and The Rt Revd Tim Thornton, *Feeding Britain: A Strategy for Zero Hunger in England, Wales, Scotland and Northern Ireland* (All-Party Parliamentary Inquiry into Hunger in the United Kingdom, 2014) particularly Recommendation 24 on page 26.

Each of these responses will be briefly discussed. First, the Government should be given more financial control over borrowers with unacceptable levels of problem debt. If Financially Insecure Borrowers are using high-cost credit for everyday expenses or to repay existing obligations, their credit position is highly precarious, and it is likely they will need an intervention to get their finances under control. An analogy can be drawn between Financially Insecure Borrowers and people in bankruptcy. Their financial obligations have become overly detrimental, and they need external control from the State for the sake of their future autonomy. This control could, for example, consist of the Government (or a not-for-profit organisation) receiving any income from the borrower and making the necessary payments on their behalf.

There are currently a number of debt management companies providing this service.[36] These are likely to do more harm than good as it costs the borrower money – and at a time they can least afford further expenses.[37] These companies often exploit the vulnerabilities of people who use them, and concerns about their services have been raised by Which?,[38] the Citizens Advice Bureau[39] and the Office of Fair Trading.[40] Providing borrowers in problem debt with private market solutions is not the answer; it merely creates opportunities for business to further exploit the vulnerability of these consumers. We should instead institute a government-based solution. Some initial comments can be made here. StepChange is a not-for-profit organisation that is already providing advice and assistance to people struggling under the weight of problem debt. The scope of its services, or of other similar not-for-profit organisations, could be extended to include financial control services for people, similar to those offered in the private market. Once people have gone through financial education, akin to a rehabilitation programme, they can gradually regain control of their own finances.

The second recommendation is to provide borrowers with increased financial options. The Government is currently focusing on reforms to regulate the high-cost credit industry and to provide increased protection. Attention must also be

[36] A quick internet search reveals a wide range of paid for debt management companies, including eg CreditFix (www.creditfix.co.uk/about-us); Debt Support Direct (https://debtsupportdirect.co.uk/) and Debt Advice Line (https://debtadviceline.co.uk/). These often use paid for advertising and therefore will come up in search results before free debt services or government advice.

[37] See analysis (from an Australian perspective) in Greg Hoy, 'Financial Counsellors Urge Caution over New Industry Offering Help for Budget Difficulties' *ABC News* (Australia, 9 December 2013), available at www.abc.net.au/news/2013-12-09/financial-counsellors-urge-caution-over-new-industry-offering-h/5145550.

[38] Which? News, 'Debt Management Companies Exploit the Vulnerable, says Charity' (Which?, 16 September 2011), available at www.which.co.uk/news/2011/09/debt-management-companies-exploit-the-vulnerable-says-charity-265956/.

[39] Citizens Advice Bureau, 'People in Debt being "exploited"' by Rogue Advice Companies' (Citizens Advice Bureau, 2011), available at www.cas.org.uk/news/people-debt-being-exploited-rogue-advice-companies.

[40] See the Office of Fair Trading, *Debt Management Guidance Compliance Review* (Compliance Review: OFT1274, September 2010) and the Office of Fair Trading, 'OFT Refuses to Licence Three Debt Management Companies in Ongoing Drive to Push Up Standards', available at www.oft.gov.uk/news-and-updates/press/2013/13-13#.URj3H2fz6So.

paid to preventing the need for loans in the first place. Consumers should have valuable options, and the Government should ensure that there are robust, efficient and widely available alternative credit products for low-income consumers. Steps have already been taken in this direction; the UK has invested £35.6 million into the credit union sector to provide a viable alternative to high-cost loans. It is estimated that this will save consumers almost £1 billion in interest repayments.[41] In the light of the size of the high-cost credit market and the (understandable) limits of credit unions, the amount of money provided by the Government is disproportionate, and further reforms are required. This could include an increased role for Community Development Finance Institutions[42] or reinvigoration of the dismantled Social Fund.[43] Again, lessons can be learnt from Australia. The country's No-Interest and Low-Interest Lending Schemes provide affordable loans for hundreds of thousands of low-income Australian consumers,[44] thereby removing their reliance on high-cost credit during their time of need.

The third response is to give consumers more leeway when they suffer temporary financial difficulties. Financially Insecure Borrowers use the funds obtained for everyday expenses and existing financial obligations. A considerable portion of these loans could be resolved by the implementation of financial hardship requirements, which legally require businesses (or other creditors, such as government bodies) to enter into penalty-free repayment plans when consumers suffer temporary financial difficulties. Such programmes could easily be instituted for the payment of utilities, council tax and existing financial obligations. Widespread financial hardship obligations of this nature are already implemented in Australia,[45] and consumers there can deal directly with the issues causing the need for funds rather than entering into expensive and potentially harmful high-cost credit contracts.

The final suggestion is an increased focus on encouraging low-income consumers to save money, providing them with a financial 'safety net'. The credit needs of Financially Insecure Borrowers show how many consumers do not have sufficient savings to deal with these issues, and therefore turn to credit. This is strongly linked with the shortage of consumer savings and the lack of a 'savings culture' in the UK. As outlined by Packman, 'The UK has a very severe savings problem

[41] Jodi Gardner 'High-Cost Credit in the UK: A Philosophical Justification for Government Intervention' in O'Shea, Fairweather and Grantham (eds), *Credit, Consumers and the Law: After the Global Storm* (Routledge 2016) 150.

[42] An example of this is the funding that the Australian Government has given to CDFIs. See Department of Families Housing Community Services and Indigenous Affairs, 'Community Development Financial Institutions (CDFI) Pilot Project', available at www.fahcsia.gov.au/our-responsibilities/communities-and-vulnerable-people/programs-services/financial-management-program/community-development-financial-institutions-cdfi-pilot-project.

[43] See Gardner, 'High-Cost Credit in the UK' (n 41) 150.

[44] See Jordan Grace 'Partnering to Address Financial Exclusion in Australia' in Gardner, Gray and Möser (eds), *Debt and Austerity* (Edward Elgar, 2020) 260.

[45] See, eg, National Credit Code (Cth) s 72 and Energy Legislation (Hardship, Metering and Other Matters) Act 2006 (Vic).

which becomes particularly problematic for low-income households. The issue for many people is not that they aren't saving enough, but that they are not saving at all'.[46] The impact of COVID-19 has exacerbated these issues. Whilst overall savings increased significantly during the pandemic, it was exceptionally uneven. Particularly during the lockdown periods, low-income households were less able to save and more likely to utilise any money that had been saved, exacerbating existing inequalities.[47] Some research has already been conducted on this topic, with a joint report by Toynbee Hall and JP Morgan into low-income savings. This report outlined a wide range of recommendations for increasing the savings rates amongst those who have the greatest need.[48] By encouraging and rewarding low-income consumers to save, we are providing them with a safety net and avoiding the need to access high-cost credit in the first place.

7.3. Further Research

It is always useful for an academic to justify their existence by recommending further research, and that is exactly what this final section is going to do. The profile developed provided a new taxonomy of high-cost credit borrowers, and a means to approach the ongoing problems caused by these financial products. Further research is, however, needed on a range of topics related to high-cost credit. First, the borrower profile and taxonomy developed was obtained through qualitative empirical research with stakeholders in the industry and borrowers themselves. This should be supported and complemented by further research, including quantitative empirical research to confirm the profiles and provide an idea of the commonality of the different classes. Whilst there is considerable agreement from interviewees about the existence of the borrower classes, there is disagreement – particularly between various stakeholders – as to the sizes of the different classes and scenarios. In addition, borrowers themselves were unlikely to be forthcoming about issues such as gambling, during discussion as part of an in-person interview. Some steps have been taken in this regard,[49] but more research and consumer engagement are clearly necessary.

[46] Carl Packman, *Savings for the Future: Solving the Savings Puzzle for Low Income Households* (Toynbee Hall and JP Morgan, 2017) 18.

[47] Brigid Francis-Devine, *Coronavirus: Impact on Household Debt and Savings* (House of Commons Library Research Briefing, 2021) 3.1. This is also discussed in Jodi Gardner and Mia Gray, *Covid-19, Inequality and Council Tax: A Perfect Storm* (Insights into Policy Development Priorities for a Post Covid-19 Environment: Briefing Paper BP8/2020, 2020).

[48] See Packman, *Savings for the Future* (n 46) especially 64–82.

[49] See the research based on consumer interviews in Rowlingson, Appleyard and Gardner, 'Payday Lending in the UK: The Regul(aris)ation of a Necessary Evil?' (n 29); Lindsey Appleyard, Karen Rowlingson and Jodi Gardner, 'The Variegated Financialization of Sub-Prime Credit Markets' (2016) 20 *Competition & Change* 297; Gardner, Rowlingson and Appleyard, 'Responsible Borrowing and Lending' (n 12). See also Lindsey Appleyard and Carl Packman, *Payday Futures: Sub-Prime Credit Markets in Transition?* (Centre for Business in Society, Toynbee Hall and Barrow Cadbury Trust, 2018).

Second, we need to understand the impact of the FCA's 2014/2015 reforms on the 160,000 people who are no longer able to access high-cost credit. It has been assumed that these consumers are 'better off' because they are no longer accessing potentially harmful credit products, but there is no evidence either way. In 2013, the Personal Finance Research Centre bemoaned the lack of empirical evidence on the overall impact of a cap in the UK.[50] There has been limited research on this specific issue conducted since, so our awareness and understanding of the situation has not improved. Appleyard, Packman and Lazell highlighted the complexity of the result of the cap, emphasising that the most common outcome is that the person denied a loan often turned to family and friends instead. Alternatively, the individual was successful with another high-cost lender, went without, went into arrears or sought assistance from a debt management plan.[51] It is unclear what long-term impact this had on them and whether this cap enhanced or harmed their overall financial welfare. Until a longer-term empirical study can be conducted, it will be difficult to make evidence-based recommendations on the best way to approach these difficult questions. One particularly important question that should be specifically considered is the impact that these reforms had on the illegal loan industry and whether there was more demand for 'loan shark' services.[52]

Third, further work is needed to understand the connections between high-cost credit, gambling and mental health. We know there is a major problem with Significantly Impaired Borrowers accessing high-cost credit, but it is unclear how many people are impacted and how the legal and social welfare system could most effectively respond to these challenges. This is, at least partly, the result of a lack of organisational interaction. People on the financial side (lenders, regulators and debt advisors) are aware of the problems associated with mental health and gambling. Those working in the specialist organisations (not-for profit and government organisations, Gambling Commission, etc) are aware of the problems associated with high-cost credit. There appears, however, to be limited discussion between the two groups. These bodies need to work together to undertake targeted research on this complicated relationship, further identifying the specifics of the problem as well as potential solutions.

Some initial steps have been taken, particularly the excellent initiatives of the Responsible Gambling Strategy Board, but there is clearly scope for further work. If this does not happen, it is unlikely that any regulatory proposals will be utilised successfully. For example, if the 'opt out' process discussed above were implemented, support organisations for people with mental health conditions

[50] Personal Finance Research Centre, *The Impact on Business and Consumers of a Cap on the Total Cost of Credit* (Department of Business and Innovation Skills, 2013). This was also supported by Sharon Collard, Personal Finance Research Centre. Telephone interview.

[51] Lindsey Appleyard, Carl Packman and Jordon Lazell, *Payday Denied: Exploring the Lived Experience of Declined Payday Loan Applicants* (2018) 20.

[52] This is particularly important in light of the Centre for Social Justice's March 2022 report showing that over 1 million people potentially use illegal lending, a 700,000 increase from previous estimates: Centre for Social Justice, *Swimming with Sharks* (2022).

and compulsive gambling would need to be aware of the processes so they could assist their clients to access the service. Significantly Impaired Borrowers present a particularly complex range of challenges; a multi-faceted and multi-party response is therefore needed. In addition, as highlighted in chapter six, section 6.4.3 above, further research on the relationship between lending, privacy and non-discrimination law is required to clarify what information lenders are allowed to ask borrowers during the application process, and what they can do with this information once it is received.

This chapter concludes with a plea for further policy analysis and additional research into the challenges posed by the provision and regulation of high-cost credit. These are not meant to be detailed policy recommendations but are designed to act as guidance for where we should go next to tackle the ongoing problems caused by these financial products. There are three main types of recommendations – law reform, social welfare responses and further research. The fact that law reform recommendations are only one aspect of a multi-pronged approach to these challenges highlights the complex nature of the high-cost credit situation. This book has provided a new taxonomy of borrowers and highlighted the important role of a social minimum to the debate. More work is, however, required to understand the high-cost credit market, and to respond to the needs of the different classes of people using these financial products.

Conclusion

> Most people are not in debt because they live beyond their means; they are in debt because they have been denied the means to live.
>
> — Astra Taylor[1]

To quote a friend and mentor, the fabulous Sarah Green, when concluding her book *Causation in Negligence* – 'there is little more to be said'.[2] I feel the same. This book has engaged with the challenges of regulating the high-cost credit market as a case study on both the limits of private law concepts and the important role of the State when responding to these issues. The solution to these problems is far from clear; but it is obvious that the existing contract law principles are insufficient to respond to vulnerable borrowers in desperate need of funds. There are several challenges in the current high-cost credit market. First, people who use these products are too often blamed for their own financial problems. This victim-blaming has occurred throughout history, starting with debtors' prisons, and continuing until the present day. People with financial difficulties are too often the subject of disparaging and offensive commentary in political and media debates on poverty and welfare. Second, there is inadequate engagement in the high-cost credit market. During a time of intense scrutiny, we do not have an accurate understanding of the concepts relevant to high-cost credit, or the needs and circumstances of borrowers. The way to respond to both these challenges is through high-quality, objective research into the high-cost credit market and the people using these products. The book has started to fill this information gap.

The analysis in this book was based on three key concepts relevant to high-cost credit – freedom, regulation, and a social minimum. The first concept, freedom, is associated with non-intervention and procedural fairness, including ensuring consent and avoiding exploitation by lenders. There are several explanations why the law values freedom – the importance of consent, human rights approaches, responsibilisation, and the different approaches to financial and physical products. The law related to high-cost credit has several examples of freedom, including lender restrictions, disclosure obligations, advertising restrictions, cooling off rights, the unfair relationship test and vitiating factors. Despite the historical explanations for freedom, this approach has its limitations, such as the failure of disclosure, lack of meaningful choice and inability to address underlying borrower poverty. Freedom therefore does not address the ongoing concerns or underlying

[1] Thank you to Astra Taylor and the Debt Collective for permission to use this quote.
[2] Sarah Green, *Causation in Negligence* (Hart Studies in Private Law, Hart Publishing, 2015) 173.

unfairness of the agreement and allows consumers to continue accessing potentially harmful credit products.

Owing to these failings, many people advocate a movement away from the freedom focus, and instead towards regulation, which is a more protective-based approach to high-cost credit. The second concept, regulation, is associated with government intervention. It aims to protect consumers against substantively unfair agreements and coercion arising from lack of choice. Regulation has a strong historical basis in the religious prohibition on usury; it aims to prevent harmful outcomes, stop unconscionable conduct and defend the vulnerable. There are many ways the law on high-cost credit has embraced a regulatory-focused approach, including prohibition on contract terms, interest rate restrictions, unfair terms legislation, and various common law mechanisms. As high-cost credit borrowers often have restricted financial choices, regulation also has limitations. The procedural fairness approach of freedom can only work if disclosure is effective and meaningful, and borrowers have valuable choices. Regulation and substantive fairness restrict access to legal credit, creating a risk of financial exclusion and potentially pushing already desperate people to illegal lending. Responding to the fairness of the agreement is not sufficient. The coercion often does not arise from a borrower impairment or the lending environment – the underlying issues are poverty and a lack of affordable credit options.

These concerns are strongly connected with the State's obligation to provide and maintain a social minimum, the third concept raised in this book. There are many justifications for a social minimum, including equality and liberal democracy, government obligations and societal happiness. At the present time, the social minimum is provided through welfare and maintained by bankruptcy relief. The law related to vitiating factors is also beginning to recognise and address social minimum maintenance. Despite the strong justifications, there are some limitations on the utility of a social minimum and its ability to address ongoing challenges, including undermining property rights, uncertainty about who is responsible for the provision of a social minimum, and the potential development of moral hazards.

It is crucial to have an accurate understanding of the high-cost credit market and who is utilising these types of products. The book therefore used qualitative empirical research to identify three classes of borrowers – Financially Secure Borrowers, Financially Insecure Borrowers and Significantly Impaired Borrowers. Each of these classes have different needs, and values the concepts of freedom, regulation and a social minimum in varying ways. The three classes of borrowers also have different relationships with the current legal approach to high-cost credit. This recognises the heterogeneity of the borrowers, thus appreciating and responding to the lending reality. The final chapter provided a range of recommendations, including further research, law reform suggestions and social welfare proposals. The borrower taxonomy created and overall analysis, whilst specific to the high-cost credit situation, can be applied more broadly. The general philosophical debate on freedom, regulation and provision of a social minimum is widely applicable – particularly during a period of austerity, pandemic restrictions and political conservatism. The underlying framework and findings of the book therefore have a wider utility and are relevant to a range of consumer products and financial challenges.

If the State wishes to tackle high-cost credit, it must address the links with poverty. The Government is regulating the high-cost credit market but, paradoxically, at the same time is taking steps to reduce the safety net for many vulnerable people. The positive impact of the former is likely to be greatly overshadowed by the negative impact of the latter. We cannot address issues of vulnerable borrowers merely through the lens of private law obligations and contract law rules. This challenge goes much deeper and raises issues of government obligations to its citizens. The primary obligation of the State should be to promote and protect the *real* autonomy of all people; it should encourage self-authorship, with all people pursuing meaningful goals and relationships.[3] This is a richer comprehension of freedom and autonomy. In the context of high-cost credit, the law should move away from the concepts of 'freedom versus regulation' or 'procedural versus substantive fairness'. Instead, we need to look for a richer, more meaningful concept of autonomy, yielding a social welfare system that allows people to pursue a good life.[4]

The collapse of the notorious high-cost credit provider, Wonga, was met with mixed responses. Whilst many were tempted to celebrate the death of Wonga and dance on the company's metaphorical grave, we – as a society – need to ask ourselves a few hard questions. That company, whilst flawed and based on an exploitative business model, was only allowed to thrive because of an inadequate legal regime, the desperate need of financially excluded borrowers, the lack of adequate social minimum maintenance, and harmful austerity measures. The powerful combination of these factors sent millions of people into the arms of commercial high-cost credit providers, including Wonga. It is quite possible however that many of Wonga's clients will be worse off without access to the company's very expensive products. If we care about the welfare of these individuals, we must ensure that their basic needs are met without resorting to potentially harmful credit. Until this is acknowledged and addressed, history will repeat itself – the demand for high-cost credit will continue, a new company will rise, phoenix-like, from Wonga's ashes, and the market will remain an ongoing source of regulatory frustration and failure.

[3] Joseph Raz, *The Morality of Freedom* (Oxford University Press, 1988).

[4] This concept is discussed in a range of sources: Mindy Chen-Wishart, 'The Nature of Vitiating Factors in Contract' in Saprai, Letsas and Klass (eds), *Philosophical Foundations of Contract Law* (Oxford University Press, 2014); Joseph Raz, 'Promises in Morality and Law' (1982) 95 *Harvard Law Review* 916; Mindy Chen-Wishart, 'In Defence of Consideration' (2013) 13 *Oxford University Commonwealth Law Journal* 209.

APPENDIX 1: STAKEHOLDER INTERVIEW RESPONSES

Scenarios	Using funds for discretionary expenses	Using funds on a one-off basis	Using funds for essential purposes (rent, bills, food)	Using funds to repay existing financial obligations	People with mental health conditions accessing loans	People with compulsive gambling problems accessing loans	Other scenarios arising from interview
Researchers							
Researcher at a University-based research centre	Young people usually using online lending for discretionary spending. Eight years ago a major group, but it is now decreasing.	Not discussed.	Increasing scenario due to the economic downturn and reduction in Welfare State. People in this scenario are usually showing signs of financial distress.	These borrowers are already in financial stress. Loans of this type result in a 'debt spiral'.	No specific research links, but strong links with general debt.	Research shows strong link between debt and gambling. Increasing concerns about online gambling and online lending.	General concerns about lead generators and lack of regulation.
Researcher at various centres	People who use high-cost credit loan appropriately and responsibly and have personal reasons for wanting to use high-cost credit, usually only irregularly.		Borrowers are desperate, locked in and have a lack of information or understanding; high-cost credit lending 'becomes a way of life for many people'.		Not discussed.	Not discussed.	Nil.

Researcher at Think Tank	This has nothing to do with vulnerability, but is related to how loans are marketed. Students and younger people use the service because it is a convenient way to get large sums of money quickly.	For example, appliance repairs.	Borrowers who urgently need money to pay general bills, usually utility bills.	People who have 'maxed out' existing mainstream credit options, and therefore need high-cost credit loans to cover interest on previous loans.	Not discussed.	Not discussed.	People who have some decrease in income causing financial difficulties to such an extent that they cannot access mainstream credit.
Researcher at a University-based research centre	Not discussed.	Usually related to an unexpected expense.	High-cost credit loans can be the only choice of credit for everyday expenses for vulnerable people who are overstretched.	Not discussed.	The links go both ways and it is hard to see what the direct causal effect is.	Has not come across any links but there is significant research on the links between general debt and gambling problems.	Nil.
Consumer Advocates							
Consumer Advocate	Not discussed.	Using high-cost credit loans in a 'quick and easy' manner.	Separated on the basis of (a) previous borrowing from mainstream credit and (b) previous borrowing from family and friends.		Discussion with ex-lender who expressed concerns about lending to people with capacity issues.	Heard stories of people with gambling addictions accessing high-cost credit loans for gambling.	Nil.

(continued)

(Continued)

Scenarios	Using funds for discretionary expenses	Using funds on a one-off basis	Using funds for essential purposes (rent, bills, food)	Using funds to repay existing financial obligations	People with mental health conditions accessing loans	People with compulsive gambling problems accessing loans	Other scenarios arising from interview
Consumer Advocate & Author	Not discussed.	Not discussed.	Two categories: (a) People needing large amounts of money for rent/ mortgage/ bills. (b) People needing smaller amounts of money for immediate needs.	People get into 'debt spiral' – provided case examples.	General concerns about lending to people who may not have adequate capacity.	Not discussed.	Nil.
Consumer Advocate	Not discussed.	When borrower has a financial shock that cannot be absorbed into income stream, no savings and they urgently need to access funds.	High-cost credit loans become part of the individual's routine, there are multiple loans with different lenders and life involves 'ducking and diving' to make ends meet.	Not discussed.	Not discussed.	Concerned with increasing numbers of betting shops in small, poor communities often close to high-cost credit lending outlets. 'It is a very profitable business when directed at desperate people with a high risk of being tempted into gambling'.	Borrowers self-excluded from mainstream lenders – for example, they do not have a bank account or trust banks.

Consumer Advocate	Not discussed.	Obtaining loans for unexpected expenses – ie something breaks, unexpected bills.	Increasing use in this way. 'People are in a desperate situation – the ends just don't meet'.	Provided two relevant case studies.	Provided a relevant case study.	Provided a relevant case study.	Increasing problem of borrowing money from family and friends.
Debt Advisors							
Debt Advisor	Not dealing with these categories of borrowers.		Generally these borrowers have a sudden drop in income – losing job, redundancy, sickness, divorce, losing overtime, etc.	Borrowers are struggling with very low incomes for long periods, often people on benefits or tax credits. High-cost credit loans 'are easy to obtain and people can get sucked in … they might think it is bailing them out but it is actually escalating the problem'.	There is a large body of research on this connection. Debt advisors have witnessed this issue but do not have the ability to explicitly record it.	There is a body of research showing the connections between debt and mental health issues.	Nil.

(continued)

(Continued)

Scenarios	Using funds for discretionary expenses	Using funds on a one-off basis	Using funds for essential purposes (rent, bills, food)	Using funds to repay existing financial obligations	People with mental health conditions accessing loans	People with compulsive gambling problems accessing loans	Other scenarios arising from interview
Debt Advisor	Not discussed.	People in a difficult financial place, have significant debts and are 'cash hungry'.	People already in considerable trouble and using high-cost credit loans to make ends meet. 'These people think that accessing payday loans will generally help the situation, but it almost inevitably makes it worse – it is like throwing petrol onto a fire to put it out.'	These borrowers 'are in perpetual loans due to credit difficulties.'	There is significant qualitative evidence on the link and there is evidence of high-cost credit borrowers with capacity issues.	There is anecdotal evidence of a link.	Nil.
Debt Advisor	Increase in loans through 'apps'; tend to be younger people who have access to technology.	Not discussed.	Not discussed.	People get into a 'debt spiral' and may use high-cost credit loans for existing financial obligations.	It is hard to measure as most people do not disclose this information and all clients suffer from some level of stress.	Clients include people recovering from addictions, including gambling. They are getting back on their feet. Due to privacy, it is difficult to determine the number of people affected.	People in a relationship breakdown or who have lost their job.

Debt Advisor	10–11% of clients use funds for discretionary purposes.	34% of clients use funds for household emergencies.	38% of clients use funds for household essentials; 32% of clients use funds for regular household bills; 20% of clients use funds for rent or mortgage payments.	24% of clients use funds for existing credit obligations. This group is 'low income in crisis' and have given up trying to service their existing debts, often borrowing from family and friends.	Not on survey and therefore no focus group information.	Not on survey, but there was a recent round-table on whether to ban high-cost credit lenders from operating close to gambling venues.	Broke up high-cost credit loan users into seven different categories based on income levels and coping abilities.
Lenders / Trade Associations							
Lender Trade Association	Young people and technology, generally using funds for discretionary purposes to supplement inconsistent income.	The most important basis for loans – people need access to credit for unexpected, one-off financial needs.	Showed concerns about financial exclusion for these people if high-cost credit loans were not available.	ILG should prevent these people from accessing loans.	Covered by the Code of Practice.	Not discussed.	Nil.

(continued)

(Continued)

Lender	For example, if there was a 'flash sale' and it is cheaper to get a loan and buy the item on sale.	In tough economic times there is increasing use of payday loans in this manner.	Not discussed.	Lending of this type is not allowed and should not be occurring.	This may be a problem but unsure of what the lender does in this regard, there is no specific question to borrowers.	Not discussed.	There is a wide variety of reasons and we should not assume borrowers are ignorant or misinformed, payday borrowing can be a completely reasonable course of action.
Lender Trade Association	'It is a cultural thing. Young people like new products; their social interactions are increasingly online, so it makes sense that their financial requirements would move this way. There is also a generational focus on "instant gratification"'.	People who have financial stress, no bank account but a good salary. They have adapted their standard of living to their income but need quick access to cash.	Not discussed.	Not discussed.	Not discussed.	Not discussed.	'We must regulate for the lowest common denominator, but must also recognise that it is a broad, more varied market'.

Lender	A very common situation, people want to make a large discretionary purchase but do not have the funds.	The primary use of funds, ie car/appliance repair, health needs, etc – expenses 'which are quite practical.' They have never come across anything 'frivolous.'	Very few customers access loans for everyday expenses, primarily for one-off, unexpected expenses.	The software program used would not allow this type of lending.	Covered by the lender's Code of Conduct.	Not discussed.	Nil.
Consumer Lawyers							
Consumer Lawyer	Not discussed.	Not discussed.	Concerns about the crippling cost of mainstream banking fees.	Not discussed.	Had seen this connection in theory and practice.	Not discussed.	A large portion of clients were Muslim and borrowed from family/friends, not commercial lending.
Consumer Lawyer	Have noticed an increase in young single men aged 25–34 using high-cost credit loans, largely through increased use of technology. Lenders are marketing using the internet, smart phones, 'apps', etc.	Not standard circumstances of the interviewee clients.	A large number of people take out payday loans for general living expenses.	People take out a loan for emergency expenses, including paying existing financial expenses.	Frequently hear stories of people with mental health conditions obtaining large inappropriate loans, therefore 'would not be surprised' if this link also existed with payday loans.	Do not see a big link, however there are concerns about the number of gambling venues in close proximity to payday lenders.	People who take high-cost credit loans are generally on very low incomes or benefits.

(continued)

(Continued)

Consumer Lawyer	Not discussed.	Some clients were just managing financially, but any unexpected expenditure pushes them 'over the edge'.	High-cost credit loans are used for a range of things, including general household expenses.	Not discussed.	There is 'very much' a link. A large number of people do not understand the credit contract and are vulnerable with reduced capacity.	Has seen a couple of cases of gambling addicts using the funds for their addiction.	Nil.
Consumer Lawyer	People who want to buy a luxury item but do not have the funds.	People suffering a financial shock or unexpected expenses arising.	An unexpected financial burden associated with everyday expenditures.	Not discussed.	Not discussed.	Not discussed.	There is a general lack of research identifying the characteristics of high-cost credit borrowers.
Government Parties							
Policy Advisor	Young people use loans for discretionary purchases, they tend to be on lower wages and need money on a one-off basis.		People need loans on a regular basis and do not have access to alternative, mainstream credit.		Problems with high-cost credit loans also run into other areas, including mental health.	Not discussed.	Nil.
Regulator	Some people find it easy and convenient, particularly for online transactions and younger borrowers.	Used by people who experience unexpected financial shocks, for example, unplanned or larger than expected bills.	Increasing numbers of people are not just using high-cost credit loans for temporary one-off issues, 'it has become a way of life' and they need it to get through the month's usual expenses.		Not discussed.	Not discussed.	The regulator did not undertake consumer surveys – only anecdotal evidence available.

Member of Parliament	Did not see any evidence of this – why would people pay high interest if they did not have to?	People are 'on the margins' and any small event can tip them over the edge. These are small expenses, but the borrowers have no savings to cushion the blow.		This sees borrowers going into a 'debt spiral'.	Large numbers of borrowers are obviously suffering from low level depression due to financial difficulties.	Saw a number of people who had obtained loans for gambling addictions. If the lenders had conducted affordability assessments, they should have picked up the issue and not provided the loan.	The situation will become worse as access to the Social Fund decreases.
Parliamentary Assistant	Not discussed.	The use of high-cost credit loans used to be mainly associated with an unexpected income decrease or expenses increase, but this scenario is decreasing.	Cost of living means that people have increasingly turned to high-cost credit loans to cover the gap.	Interviewee reported seeing increased instances of this scenario.	Not discussed.	Did not see much evidence of this.	Nil.

(continued)

(Continued)

Other							
Credit Referencing Agency	Some people use loans because they want quick, convenient credit without long-term implications. These people may have savings and overdraft facilities. They are making an educated decision as payday loans are 'short-term' debt, whereas other products are 'long-term'.		These people generally have no savings and are using loans as a last resort. They cannot get mainstream credit, are financially struggling and probably should not be given credit. If high-cost credit lenders were being responsible, these borrowers should be turned away.		Not discussed.	Not discussed.	Recognised that 'there is a kaleidoscope of people accessing high-cost credit lending products'.
Credit Union	Not discussed.	Incomes have stagnated and the cost of living is consistently increasing, people are using loans for any reasonably large costs they incur, such as rent or unexpected bills.	Often relevant for people on low fixed incomes, including benefits. These people have little or no savings and are very vulnerable to small financial shocks.	Borrowers are in an untenable financial situation, payday loans are the 'last resort' when the debts become unmanageable.	Not discussed.	Not discussed.	Since the sub-prime crisis, lenders have become more risk adverse and more people need access to high-cost credit loans.

APPENDIX 2: BORROWER INTERVIEW RESPONSES

Scenarios	Using funds for discretionary expenses	Using funds on a one-off basis	Using funds for essential purposes (rent, bills, food)	Using funds to repay existing financial obligations	People with mental health conditions accessing loans	People with compulsive gambling problems accessing loans
Consumer 1	Not discussed.	Not discussed.	Borrowed in order to purchase food, pay electricity bills and a TV licence.	Not discussed.	Not discussed.	Not discussed.
Consumer 2	Borrowed in order to pay for their daughter's third birthday party.	Not discussed.	Not discussed.	Not discussed.	Not discussed.	Not discussed.
Consumer 3	Not discussed.	Not discussed.	Not discussed.	Not discussed.	Borrower demonstrated clear mental health difficulties exacerbated by their struggle with sustaining themselves on welfare benefits.	Not discussed.
Consumer 4	Not discussed.	Not discussed.	Not discussed.	Borrowed in order to boost their credit rating.	Suffered symptoms of depression for over a year as a result of debt.	Not discussed.

(continued)

(Continued)

Scenarios	Using funds for discretionary expenses	Using funds on a one-off basis	Using funds for essential purposes (rent, bills, food)	Using funds to repay existing financial obligations	People with mental health conditions accessing loans	People with compulsive gambling problems accessing loans
Consumer 5	Not discussed.	Not discussed.	Payday loans a normal part of the consumer's routine in order to meet everyday utilities.	Not discussed.	Not discussed.	Not discussed.
Consumer 6	Borrowed in order to buy their children Christmas presents.	Not discussed.	Not discussed.	Not discussed.	Discusses how the borrowing made them ill such that time was required off work due to stress.	Not discussed.
Consumer 7	Borrowed in order to pay for cosmetic surgery.	Not discussed.	Not discussed.	Not discussed.	Not discussed.	Not discussed.
Consumer 8	Not discussed.	Not discussed.	Borrowed in order to pay everyday bills.	Not discussed.	Not discussed.	Not discussed.
Consumer 9	Not discussed.	Not discussed.	Borrowed in order to pay gas and electricity bills.	Not discussed.	Not discussed.	Not discussed.
Consumer 10	Not discussed.	Not discussed.	Not discussed.	Borrowed in order to meet shortfalls in mortgage repayments.	Not discussed.	Not discussed.

Consumer 11	Not discussed.	Borrowed in order to pay for works on their house following a major flood.	Not discussed.	Not discussed.	Not discussed.	Not discussed.
Consumer 12	Borrowed in order to pay for Christmas presents.	Not discussed.	Not discussed.	Not discussed.	Not discussed.	Not discussed.
Consumer 13	Not discussed.	Not discussed.	Borrowed in order to pay gas and electricity bills.	Not discussed.	Not discussed.	Not discussed.
Consumer 14	Not discussed.	Not discussed.	Borrowed in order to pay for food, gas and electric bills.	Not discussed.	Not discussed.	Not discussed.
Consumer 15	Not discussed.	Borrowed in order to fix an urgent boiler problem.	Not discussed.	Not discussed.	Not discussed.	Not discussed.
Consumer 16	Not discussed.	Not discussed.	Not discussed.	Borrowed in order to pay off financial commitments.	Borrowing brought on symptoms of severe stress.	Not discussed.
Consumer 17	Borrowed funds to help with a house move.	Not discussed.	Not discussed.	Not discussed.	Not discussed.	Not discussed.
Consumer 18	Not discussed.	Not discussed.	Not discussed.	Not discussed.	Borrower suffers depression following a friend's suicide as a result of his outstanding debts.	Borrower used funds in order to bet on horse races.

(continued)

(Continued)

Scenarios	Using funds for discretionary expenses	Using funds on a one-off basis	Using funds for essential purposes (rent, bills, food)	Using funds to repay existing financial obligations	People with mental health conditions accessing loans	People with compulsive gambling problems accessing loans
Consumer 19	Loan was for general Christmas expenses.	Loan was also for a new cooker.	Not discussed.	Not discussed.	Not discussed.	Not discussed.
Consumer 20	Loan taken to help with repairs of a camper van.	Not discussed.	Not discussed.	Not discussed.	Not discussed.	Not discussed.
Consumer 21	Borrowed funds to take their children on holiday.	Not discussed.	Not discussed.	Not discussed.	Not discussed.	Not discussed.
Consumer 22	Not discussed.	Not discussed.	Not discussed.	Borrowed in order to pay off an unplanned overdraft.	Not discussed.	Not discussed.
Consumer 23	Borrowed in order to buy a car.	Not discussed.	Not discussed.	Not discussed.	Not discussed.	Not discussed.
Consumer 24	Not discussed.	Not discussed.	Borrowed in order to pay for everyday bills. Struggled particularly as a result of being a single parent.	Borrowed also due to concerns about their credit rating.	Not discussed.	Not discussed.
Consumer 25	Not discussed.	Not discussed.	Used to pay existing phone bills, water bills and rent.	Not discussed.	Suffered from extreme stress.	Not discussed.

Consumer 26	Not discussed.	Not discussed.	Loan used to pay everyday bills.	Not discussed.	Not discussed.	Not discussed.
Consumer 27	Borrowed to renovate their house.	Not discussed.	Not discussed.	Not discussed.	Not discussed.	Not discussed.
Consumer 28	Not discussed.	Borrowed in order to have her car fixed after a break-down.	Loan used also for food.	Not discussed.	Borrower was concerned she was facing a 'depressing future'.	Not discussed.
Consumer 29	Loan used to pay for Christmas expenses.	Not discussed.	Loan used to pay for bills.	Not discussed.	Not discussed.	Not discussed.
Consumer 30	Loan was to put a rental deposit down on a flat.	Not discussed.	Not discussed.	Not discussed.	Not discussed.	Not discussed.
Consumer 31	Not discussed.	Not discussed.	Not discussed.	Loan to pay direct debits and outstanding credit.	Not discussed.	Not discussed.
Consumer 32	Not discussed.	Not discussed.	Loan used to pay bills after being made redundant.	Not discussed.	Describes being put under immense pressure that affected their health.	Not discussed.
Consumer 33	Not discussed.	Not discussed.	Not discussed.	Not discussed.	Borrowing made the consumer 'quite ill for a while'.	Not discussed.

(continued)

(Continued)

Scenarios	Using funds for discretionary expenses	Using funds on a one-off basis	Using funds for essential purposes (rent, bills, food)	Using funds to repay existing financial obligations	People with mental health conditions accessing loans	People with compulsive gambling problems accessing loans
Consumer 34	Not discussed.	Not discussed.	Borrowed in order to pay bills after work as a self-employed electrician slowed down.	Not discussed.	Not discussed.	Not discussed.
Consumer 35	Not discussed.	Not discussed.	Borrowed for everyday bills and rent.	Not discussed.	Borrower described feeling in a cycle of negativity and stress.	Not discussed.
Consumer 36	Borrowed money in order to pay for an upcoming holiday.	Not discussed.	Not discussed.	Not discussed.	Discussed feeling intensely miserable and depressed. Borrower also suffered severe weight loss as a result of the depression.	Not discussed.
Consumer 37	Borrowed money in order to pay for Christmas presents.	Not discussed.	Not discussed.	Not discussed.	Not discussed.	Not discussed.
Consumer 38	Borrowed in order to have a little extra 'spending money'.	Not discussed.	Not discussed.	Not discussed.	Not discussed.	Not discussed.

Consumer 39	Not discussed.	Not discussed.	Electricity bill as the cost had gone up due to extra use in winter.	Not discussed.	Borrower describes feeling miserable and how debt had 'ruined his life.'	Not discussed.
Consumer 40	The cost of her daughter's christening.	Not discussed.	Not discussed.	Not discussed.	Borrower describes suffering extreme stress resulting in frequent trips to the hospital.	Not discussed.
Consumer 41	The costs associated with Christmas.	Not discussed.	Not discussed.	Not discussed.	Consumer describes spending significant amounts of time worrying and stressed.	Not discussed.
Consumer 42	Not discussed.	Not discussed.	Changed jobs and had a short period of time without income, so needed money for general bills.	Not discussed.	Borrower was receiving medical treatment for OCD and anxiety.	Not discussed.
Consumer 43	Not discussed.	Telephone bill from time spent abroad.	Not discussed.	Not discussed.	Not discussed.	Borrower would also use the money for gambling and clubbing.
Consumer 44	Not discussed.	A new tumble dryer as it was in the middle of winter.	Not discussed.	Not discussed.	Borrower suffered anxiety and depression and felt 'struck in this unbreakable cycle.'	Not discussed.

BIBLIOGRAPHY

Adams J and Brownsword R, *Understanding Contract Law*, 5th edn (Sweet & Maxwell, 2007)

Aitken L, 'A "Duty to Lend Responsibly" – A New Terror for Lenders in a Consumer's World?' (2007) 18 *Journal of Banking and Finance Law and Practice* 18

Alighieri D, *The Inferno*, Canto XVII

Allgoewer E, *Underconsumption Theories and Keynesian Economics: Interpretations of the Great Depression* (University of St. Gallen, Department of Economics: Research Paper 2002–14, 2002)

Appleyard L and Packman C, *Payday Futures: Sub-Prime Credit Markets in Transition?* (Centre for Business in Society, Toynbee Hall and Barrow Cadbury Trust, 2018)

Appleyard L, Packman C and Lazell J, *Payday Denied: Exploring the Lived Experience of Declined Payday Loan Applicants* (2018)

Appleyard L, Rowlingson K and Gardner J, 'The Variegated Financialization of Sub-Prime Credit Markets' (2016) 20 *Competition & Change* 297

Aquinas ST, *Aquinas ethicus, or, The Moral Teaching of St Thomas: A Translation of the Principal Portions of the Second Part of the "Summa Theologica"*, 2nd edn (edited by Rickaby J) (Burns and Oates, 1896)

Artemieva T and Mikeshin M (eds), *The Philosophical Age, The Science of Morality: J Bentham and Russia* (St Petersburg Center for History of Ideas, 1999)

Atiyah P, *The Rise and Fall of Freedom of Contract* (Oxford University Press, 1985)

——, 'Contract and Fair Exchange' (1985) 35 *University of Toronto Law Journal* 1

——, *Essays on Contract Law* (Oxford University Press, 1990)

——, 'Contracts, Promises and the Law of Obligations' in Atiyah PS (ed), *Essays on Contract* (Oxford University Press, 1990)

——, 'The Liberal Theory of Contract' in Atiyah PS (ed), *Essays on Contract* (Oxford University Press, 1990)

Atkinson AB, *The Economics of Inequality* (Oxford University Press, 1975)

Australian Securities and Investment Commission, *Credit Licensing: Responsible Lending Conduct* (Regulatory Guide 209, 2013)

——, *Report 426: Payday Lenders and the New Small Amount Lending Provisions* (2015)

Bacon F, *The Essayes or Covnsels Civill and Morall of Francis Bacon: Baron of Verulam, Viscount St. Alban, and Lord High Chancellor of England* (1998 JBi tr, Renascence Editions, 1625)

Badger E, 'Are Economic Rights Fundamental Human Rights?' (*Pacific Standard*, 12 May 2009) https://psmag.com/are-economic-rights-fundamental-human-rights-524ede71ed88#.3wmf7jymh

Baker J, *The Oxford History of the Laws of England. Volume VI: 1483–1558* (Oxford University Press, 2003)

Ball R, 'The Global Financial Crisis and the Efficient Market Hypothesis: What Have We Learned?' (2009) 21 *Journal of Applied Corporate Finance* 8

Banks M and others, *Caught Short. Exploring the Role of Small, Short-Term Loans in the Lives of Australians* (Social Policy Unit, The University of Queensland, 2012)

Barnard M and others, 'Exploring the Relationship between Gambling, Debt and Financial Management in Britain' (2014) 14 *International Gambling Studies* 82

Barnett RE, 'A Consent Theory of Contract' (1986) 86 *Columbia Law Review* 269

Barry N, *An Introduction to Modern Political Theory*, 3rd edn (The MacMillan Press Ltd, 1995)

——, 'Neoclassicism, the New Right and British Social Welfare' in Page RM (ed), *British Social Welfare in the Twentieth Century* (Palgrave, 1999)

Beale HG and Chitty J, *Chitty on Contracts*, 34th edn (Sweet & Maxwell, 2021)

Beatson J, *The Use and Abuse of Unjust Enrichment* (Clarendon Press, 1991)

——, *Has the Common Law a Future? Inaugural Lecture Delivered 29 April 1996* (Cambridge University Press, 1996)

Beatson J and Friedman D, 'Introduction: From 'Classical' to Modern Contract Law' in Beatson J and Friedman D (eds), *Good Faith and Fault in Contract Law* (Oxford University Press, 1997)

Beddows S and McAteer M, *Payday Lending: Fixing a Broken Market* (Association of Chartered Certified Accountants, 2014)

Bellot H, *The Law Relating to Unconscionable Bargains with Money-Lenders: Including the History of Usury to the Repeal of the Usury Laws* (Stevens & Haynes, 1898)

——, 'The Money Lenders Act 1900' (1901) 26 *Quarterly Review of Jurisprudence* 456

Ben-Galim D and Lanning T, *Strength Against Shocks: Low-Income Families and Debt* (Institute for Public Policy Research, 2010)

Bennett F and Millar J, 'Social Security: Reforms and Challenges' in Millar J (ed), *Understanding Social Security: Issue for Policy and Practice* (Policy Press, 2003)

Ben-Shahar O and Scheider CE, 'The Failure of Mandated Disclosure' (2011) 159 *University of Pennsylvania Law Review* 647

Benson P, 'The Unity of Contract Law' in Benson P (ed), *The Theory of Contract Law* (Cambridge University Press, 2001)

Bentham J, *Defence of Usury; shewing the impolicy of the present legal restraints on the terms of pecuniary bargains. In a series of letters to a friend. To which is added, a letter to Adam Smith, Esq; LL.D. on the discouragements opposed by the above restraints to the progress of inventive industry* (Messrs D Williams, Colles, White, Byrne, Lewis, Jones, and Moore, 1788)

——, *A Manual of Political Economy* (McMaster University Archive for the History of Economic Thought, 1843)

Berlin I, 'Two Concepts of Liberty' in Berlin I (ed), *Four Essays on Liberty* (Oxford University Press, 1958)

Bernstien H, 'Civil Liability for Pure Economic Loss under American Tort Law' (1998) 46 *American Journal of Comparative Law* 111

Bertrand M and Morse A, *Information Disclosure, Cognitive Biases and Payday Borrowing* (Chicago Booth Research Paper No 10-01, 2009)

Beveridge SW, *Social Insurance and Allied Services* (HMSO London, 1942)

Bigwood R, 'Curbing Unconscionability: *Berbatis* in the High Court of Australia' (2004) 28 *Melbourne University Law Review* 203

Bix B, 'Contracts' in Miller F and Wertheimer A (eds), *The Ethics of Consent: Theory and Practice* (Oxford University Press, 2009)

Blair T, 'My Vision for Britain: by Tony Blair' *The Observer* (10 November 2002) www.guardian.co.uk/politics/2002/nov/10/queensspeech2002.tonyblair?CMP=email

Block-Lieb S and others, 'Disclosure as an Imperfect Means for Addressing Overindebtedness: An Empirical Assessment of Comparative Approaches' in Niemi J, Ramsay I and Whitford WC (eds), *Consumer Credit, Debt and Bankruptcy* (Hart Publishing, 2009)

Bond N and Holkar M, *A Silent Killer: Breaking the Link between Financial Difficulty and Suicide* (Money and Mental Health Policy Institute, 2018)

Bramstead EK and Melhuish KJ (eds), *Western Liberalism: A History in Documents from Locke to Croce* (Prentice Hall Press, 1978)

Branford I and Gardner J, 'Cause I Gotta' Have (Bad) Faith: *Times Travel v Pakistan International Airlines Corporation*' [2022] LMCLQ 64–69

Bridges S and Disney R, 'Use of Credit and Arrears on Debt among Low-Income Families in the United Kingdom' (2004) 25 *Fiscal Studies* 1

Bright S, 'Winning the Battle Against Unfair Contract Terms' (2000) 20 *Legal Studies* 331

Bright S and Whitehouse L, 'The Opportunities and Challenges of Empirical Work: Housing Possession in Theory and in Practice' in Akkermans B, Ramaekers E and Marais E (eds), *Property Law Perspective II* (Intersentia, 2013)

Broadcasting Committee of Advertising, *BCAP Payday Loans Consultation Regulatory Statement* (2015)
Brook Y, 'The Morality of Moneylending: A Short History' (*The Objective Standard*, 20 August 2007) www.theobjectivestandard.com/issues/2007-fall/morality-of-moneylending/
Brownsword R, *Contract Law: Themes for the Twenty-First Century* (Oxford University Press, 2006) vol 2
——, 'Chapter 1: General Considerations' in Furmston M and Adams J (eds), *The Law of Contract: Butterworths Common Law Series*, 4th edn (Butterworths, 2010)
Buckley F, *Just Exchange: A Theory of Contract* (Routledge, 2005)
Burton M, *Keeping the Plates Spinning: Perceptions of Payday Loans in Great Britain* (Consumer Focus, 2010)
Bussani M and Palmer VV (eds), *Pure Economic Loss in Europe* (Cambridge University Press, 2003)
Cadywould C, *Banking for All* (Demos, 2016)
Camerer C and others, 'Regulation for Conservatives: Behavioral Economics and the Case for "Asymmetric Paternalism"' (2003) 151 *University of Pennsylvania Law Review* 1211
Cameron D, *Speech on the Big Society* (A Speech Delivered in Liverpool on 18 July 2010)
Cane P and Kritzer H, 'Introduction' in Cane P and Kritzer H (eds), *The Oxford Handbook of Empirical Legal Research* (Oxford University Press, 2010)
Caplovitz D, *The Poor Pay More* (Free Press, 1967)
Carr H and others, *The Housing Act 2004: A Practical Guide* (Jordan Publishing Ltd, 2005)
Carter I, 'Positive and Negative Liberty' (*Stanford Encyclopedia of Philosophy*, 2003)
Cartwright J, *Unequal Bargaining: A Study of Vitiating Factors in the Formation of Contracts* (Oxford University Press, 1991)
Cayne D and Treblicock M, 'Market Considerations in the Formulation of Consumer Protection Policy' (1973) 23 *University of Toronto Law Journal* 396
Centre for Research in Social Policy, 'Minimum Income Standards' (Department of Social Sciences, Loughborough University)
Charlesworth M and Williams N, *The Myth of the Undeserving Poor: A Christian Response to Poverty in Britain Today* (Grosvenor House Publishing Ltd, 2014)
Chen-Wishart M, 'The O'Brien Principle and Substantive Unfairness' (1997) 56 *Cambridge Law Journal* 60
——, 'Undue Influence: *Beyond* Impaired Consent and Wrongdoing towards a Relational Analysis' in Burrows A and Rodger A (eds), *Mapping the Law: Essays in Memory of Peter Birks* (Oxford University Press, 2006)
——, 'In Defence of Consideration' (2013) 13 *Oxford University Commonwealth Law Journal* 209
——, 'Legal Transplant and Undue Influence: Lost in Translation or a Working Misunderstanding' (2013) 62 *International & Comparative Law Quarterly* 1
——, 'The Nature of Vitiating Factors in Contract' in Saprai P, Letsas G and Klass G (eds), *Philosophical Foundations of Contract Law* (Oxford University Press, 2014)
——, 'Regulating Unfair Terms' in Gullifer L and Vogenaur S (eds), *English and European Perspectives on Contract and Commercial Law: Essays in Honour of Hugh Beale* (Hart Publishing, 2015)
——, *Contract Law*, 7th edn (Oxford University Press, 2021)
Chesterton GK, *St. Thomas Aquinas* (Hodder & Stoughton, 1943)
Child Poverty Action Group, 'The Cost of a Child in 2018' (Child Poverty Action Group, 20 August 2018) http://cpag.org.uk/content/cost-child-2018
Chitty J, *A Treatise on the Law of Contracts* (Sweet and Maxwell, 1912)
Christians Against Poverty, 'The CAP Story: How it All Started' (Christians Against Poverty) https://capuk.org/about-us/the-cap-story
Citizens Advice Bureau, *Consultation Document on the Study of Interest Rate Restrictions in the EU: Response by Citizens Advice to the European Commission* (2011)
——, 'People in Debt being "Exploited" by Rogue Advice Companies' (Citizens Advice Bureau, 2011) www.cas.org.uk/news/people-debt-being-exploited-rogue-advice-companies
——, 'Citizens Advice Urges Payday Loan Customers to Fight Back against Unscrupulous Lenders' Citizens Advice Bureau www.citizensadvice.org.uk/index/pressoffice/press_index/press_office-20130805.htm

Clarke J, Langan M and Williams F, 'Remaking Welfare: The British Welfare Regime in the 1980s and 1990s' in Cochrane A, Clarke J and Gewirtz S (eds), *Comparing Welfare States*, 2nd edn (Sage, 2001)

Clarke Z and others, *The Impact of COVID-19 on Gambling Behaviour and Associated Harms* (Public Health England, 2021)

Coco G and Meza DD, 'In Defense of Usury Laws' (2009) 41 *Journal of Money, Credit & Banking* 1691

Colin Morgan-Cross and Marieka Klawitter, *Effects of State Payday Loan Price Caps & Regulation* (2008)

Collard S, *Understanding Financial Difficulty: Exploring the Opportunities for Early Intervention* (Personal Finance Research Centre & Money Advice Trust, 2011)

Collard S, Finney A and Crosswaite K, *Facing the Squeeze: A Qualitative Study of Household Finances and Access to Credit in a 21st-Century Recession* (Personal Finance Research Centre, 2009)

Collard S, Finney A and Davies S, *Working Households' Experiences of Debt Problems* (A Research Report Prepared for StepChange Debt Charity, 2012)

Collard S and Kempson E, *Affordable Credit: The Way Forward* (The Policy Press, 2005)

Collard S, Kempson E and Whyley C, *Tackling Financial Exclusion: An Area-Based Approach* (The Policy Press, 2001)

Collins H, *The Law of Contract*, 4th edn (LexisNexis, 2003)

Committee of Advertising Practice, *Trivialisation in Short-Term, High-Cost Credit Ads* (2015) www.london.gov.uk/sites/default/files/london_assembly_-_economy_committee_-_low_pay_and_in-work_poverty_.pdf

Competition & Markets Authority, *Payday Lending Market Investigation: Provisional Decision on Remedies* (2014)

——, *Payday Lending Market Investigation: Provisional Findings Report* (2014)

——, *Research into the Payday Lending Market* (2014)

——, *Payday Lending Market Investigation: Final Report* (2015)

——, *Unfair Contract Terms Guidance: Guidance on the Unfair Terms Provisions in the Consumer Rights Act 2015* (2015)

Competition Commission, *Home Credit Market Investigation* (2006)

Consumer Action Law Group, 'Consumer Action Group Fraud Warning: Toothfairy Finance Limited' (2013)

——, 'About the Industry' (2013)

——, 'Home Web Page' (2013)

Coons C and Weber M (eds), *Paternalism: Theory and Practice* (Cambridge University Press, 2013)

Cope M, 'The Review of Unconscionable Conduct Bargains in Equity' (1983) 57 *The Australian Law Journal* 279

——, *Duress, Undue Influence and Unconscientious Bargains* (The Law Book Company Ltd, 1985)

Corlett A and Clarke S, *Living Standards 2017: The Past, Present and Possible Future of UK Incomes* (Resolution Foundation, 2017)

Cribb J and others, *Living Standards, Poverty and Inequality in the UK 2013* (Institute for Fiscal Studies distributed by Central Books Ltd, 2013)

Crimmins J, 'Political Economy and Projectors: Bentham's Defence of Usury' in Artemieva T and Mikeshin M (eds), *The Philosophical Age, The Science of Morality: J Bentham and Russia* (St Petersburg Center for the History of Ideas, 1999)

Crowther SG, *Consumer Credit: Report of the Committee* (Department of Trade and Industry, 1971)

Davies G, *A History of Money: From Ancient Times to the Present Day* (University of Wales Press, 1994)

Davis A and others, *A Minimum Income Standard for the UK in 2016* (Joseph Rowntree Foundation, 2016)

Deeming C, Collard S and Hayes D, *Affordable Credit: Lessons from Overseas* (Personal Finance Research Centre, 2011)

Dennis L, 'The Squirrel Cage of Debt' (1933) *Saturday* 661

Department of Business Innovation and Skills, *Making Consumer Credit Fairer: BIS Report on Surveys of the Payday Lending Good Practice Charter and Codes of Practice* (2013)

——, *Making Consumer Credit Markets Fairer: Payday Lending Advertising Research Conducted for BIS by Ipsos MORI Social Research Institute* (2013)
Department of Energy and Climate Change, *Annual Fuel Poverty Statistics Report*, 2021 (2019 data)
Department of Trade and Industry, *Reform of the Law on Consumer Credit* (1973)
——, *Fair, Clear and Competitive: The Consumer Credit Market in the 21st Century – White Paper* (2003)
——, *A Fair Deal for All – Extending Competitive Markets: Empowered Consumers, Successful Businesses* (2005)
Department of Work and Pensions, *DWP Quarterly Statistical Summary, First Release* (2014)
——, *Raising Expectations and Increasing Support: Reforming Welfare for the Future* (2008)
DiMatteo L and others, *Visions of Contract Theory: Rationality Bargaining and Interpretation* (Carolina Academic Press, 2007)
Directorate General Internal Market and Services, *Summary of Responses to the Public Consultation on the Study on Interest Rate Restrictions in the EU* (European Commission, 2011)
Directorate-General for Employment SAaEOI, Social Policy Aspects of Migration, Streamlining of Social Policies, *Financial Services Provision and the Prevention of Financial Exclusion* (European Commission, 2008)
Directorate-General for Employment SAaEO, *Towards a Common Operational European Definition of Over-Indebtedness* (European Communities, 2008)
Dobson J, *Measuring Social Class* (Bright Blue, 2016)
Downs C and Woolrych R, *Gambling and Debt Pathfinder Study* (Research Institute for Health and Social Change, GamCare and the Money Advice Trust, 2009)
Dubbink W, *Assisting the Invisible Hand: Contested Relations Between Market, State and Civil Society* (Kluwer Academic Publishers, 2003)
Duncan J and Derrett M, 'Law in the New Testament: The Parable of the Talents and Two Logia' (1965) 56 *Zeitschrift für die neutestamentliche Wissenschaft* 184
Dworkin G, 'Moral Paternalism' (2005) 24 *Law and Philosophy* 305
——, 'Paternalism' (Stanford Encyclopedia of Philosophy, 2016)
Dworkin R, *Sovereign Virtue: The Theory and Practice of Equality* (Harvard University Press, 2000)
Dwyer P, 'Making Sense of Social Citizenship: Some User Views on Welfare Rights and Responsibilities' (2002) 22 *Critical Social Policy* 273
Dyson A, Goudkamp J and Wilmot-Smith F, 'Thinking in Terms of Contract Defences' in Dyson A, Goudkamp J and Wilmot-Smith F (eds), *Defences in Contract* (Hart Publishing, 2017)
Ehrenreich B, 'Time to Wake Up: Stop Blaming Poverty on the Poor' in Shriver M (ed), *The Shriver Report: A Woman's Nation Pushes Back from the Brink* (Center for American Progress, 2014)
Einhorn H and Hogarth R, 'Behavioural Decision Theory: Processes of Judgment and Choice' (1981) 19 *Journal of Accounting Research* 1
Eisenberg M, 'The Theory of Contracts' in Benson P (ed), *The Theory of Contract Law* (Cambridge University Press, 2001)
Ellison A and others, *Interim Evaluation of the National Illegal Money Lending Projects* (Department of Business, Innovation & Skills and Policis, 2010)
Elster J, *Ulysses Unbound: Studies in Rationality, Precommitment, and Constraints* (Cambridge University Press, 2000)
——, 'Weakness of Will and Preference Reverals' in Elster J and others (eds), *Understanding Choice, Explaining Behaviour* (UniPub ForLag Oslo Academic Press, 2006)
Epstein R, *Scepticism and Freedom: A Modern Case for Classical Liberalism* (University of Chicago Press, 2003)
Ernst K, Bocian D and Li W, *Steered Wrong: Brokers, Borrowers, and Subprime Loans* (Centre for Responsible Lending, 2008)
Erskine J, *The Principles of the Law of Scotland: In the Order of Sir George Mackenzie's Institutions of that law* (Bell & Bradfute, 1754)
Essene R and Apgar W, *Understanding Mortgage Market Behaviour: Creating Good Mortgage Options for All Americans* (Joint Centre for Housing Studies, Harvard University, 2007)

Europe Economics, *A New Consumer Credit Regime: Benefits, Compliance Costs and Firm Behaviour* (2013)
Evans D, 'The Behavioral Economics of Paying and Borrowing' (2010) *The Lydian Payments Journal* http://pymnts.com/assets/Lydian_Journal/LydianJournalJanuaryEconomics.pdf
Experian, *The Fraud Report 2013* (2013)
Fairweather K, 'Apples and Oranges: Responsible Lending in the UK and Australia' (Consumers, Credit and the Law Symposium, Brisbane, 7 July 2012)
——, Fairweather K and Grantham R (eds), *Credit, Consumers and the Law: After the Global Storm* (Routledge (Markets and the Law Series) 2016)
Falconer A and Lane J, *Debt on Your Doorstep: Problem Debt in the Home Credit Market* (Citizen Advice, 2017)
Farber D, 'Contract Law and Modern Economic Theory' (1983) 78 *Northwestern University Law Review* 303
Finlayson A, 'Financialisation, Financial Literacy and Asset-Based Welfare' (2009) 11 *The British Journal of Politics and International Relations* 400
Finney A, Collard S and Kempson E, *Easy Come, Easy Go: Borrowing Over the Life-Cycle* (Personal Finance Research Centre, 2007)
Fitch C and Davey R, *Debt Collection and Mental Health: Ten Steps to Improve Recovery* (The Royal College of Psychiatrists and The Money Advice Trust, 2010)
Fitch C and others, *Debt and Mental Health: What Do We Know? What Should We Do?* (Royal College of Psychiatrists, 2011)
Fleet K and others, *Encyclopedia of Islam (Third Edition)* (Brill, 2007)
Focus on Mental Health, 'An Uphill Struggle: A Survey of the Experiences of People who use Mental Health Services and Are on a Low Income' www.ontheside.org/focus/fpovsur.htm
Formosa P, 'A Life Without Affects and Passions: Kant on the Duty of Apathy' (2011) 13 *Parrhesia* 96
Foxall G, 'A Behaviouralist Perspective on Purchase and Consumption' (1993) 27 *European Journal of Marketing* 8
Francis K, 'Rollover, Rollover: A Behavioral Law and Economics Analysis of the Payday-Loan Industry' (2010) 88 *Texas Law Review* 611
Francis-Devine B, *Coronavirus: Impact on Household Debt and Savings* (House of Commons Library Research Briefing, 2021)
Fredman S, *Human Rights Transformed: Positive Rights and Positive Duties* (Oxford University Press, 2007)
Freeman RB, 'The Minimum Wage as a Redistributive Tool' (1996) 106 *The Economic Journal* 639
Freeman S, *Rawls* (Routledge, 2007)
Fried C, *Contract as Promise: A Theory of Contractual Obligation* (Harvard University Press, 1981)
Friedman M, *Capitalism and Freedom* (University of Chicago Press, 1963)
Galbraith J, *The Affluent Society* (Penguin, 1958)
Gans J, 'Protecting Consumers by Protecting Competition: Does Behavioural Economics Support this Contention?' (2005) 13 *Competition and Consumer Law Journal* 1
Gardner J, *The Challenges of Regulating High-Cost Short-Term Credit: A Comparison of UK and Australian Approaches* (Centre on Household Assets and Savings Management, 2014)
——, *Regulating Moneylending in Singapore: Looking at All Side: Research Policy Paper* (Centre for Banking & Finance Law, 2015)
——, 'Responsible Lending and Borrowing' (2018) 6 2 *Journal of International Consumer Law and Practice* 14
——, 'Being Conscious of Unconscionability in Modern Times: *Heller v Uber Technologies*' (2021) 84 *The Modern Law Review* 874
—— 'High-Cost Credit in the UK: A Philosophical Justification for Government Intervention' in O'Shea P, Fairweather K and Grantham R (eds), *Credit, Consumers and the Law: After the Global Storm* (Routledge (Markets and the Law Series) 2016)
Gardner J and Tham CH, 'Debt Collection and Assignment of Debts: Navigating the Legal Maze' in Davies P and Tan C (eds), *Intermediaries in Commercial Law* (Hart Publishing, 2022)

Gardner J and Gray M, *Covid-19, Inequality and Council Tax: A Perfect Storm* (University of Birmingham, 2020)
Gardner J, Rowlingson K and Appleyard L, 'Responsible Borrowing and Lending' (2018) 2 *Journal of International Consumer Law and Practice* 16
Gardner J and Uhr C, *Financial Counselling in Queensland* (Centre for Credit and Consumer Law, 2008)
Garthwaite K, "The Language of Shirkers and Scroungers?' Talking about Illness, Disability and Coalition Welfare Reform' (2011) 26 *Disability & Society* 369
Geisst CR, *Beggar Thy Neighbor: A History of Usury and Debt* (University of Pennsylvania Press, 2013)
Gelpi R-M and Julien-Labruyere F, *The History of Consumer Credit: Doctrines and Practice* (Palgrave McMillan, 2000)
Genn H, 'Paths to Justice' in Halliday S and Schmidt P (eds), *Conducting Law and Society Research: Reflection on Methods and Practices* (Cambridge University Press, 2009)
Gentleman A, 'Wonga: The Real Cost of a Payday Loan' *The Guardian* (1 March 2012) www.theguardian.com/business/2012/mar/01/wonga-real-cost-payday-loan
Genworth Financial, *The Genworth Index: Measuring Consumer Financial Vulnerability and Security in 18 Countries* (Genworth Financial, 2010)
Gibbons D, *Taking on the Money Lenders: Lessons from Japan* (Centre for Responsible Credit, 2012)
——, *Where Now for Local Welfare Schemes?* (Centre for Responsible Credit, 2015)
Gilbert N, *Transformation of the Welfare State: The Silent Surrender of Public Responsibility* (Oxford University Press, 2002)
Gladstone D, 'Welfare before the Welfare State' in Gladstone D (ed), *Before Beveridge: Welfare before the Welfare State* (IEA Health and Welfare Unit, 1999)
Glasgow Centre for Population Health, *Public Health Implications of Payday Lending* (Briefing Paper 48, 2016)
Good Shepherd Microfinancing, 'What is NILS?' (*NILS: Good Shepherd Microfinancing*, 2017) http://nils.com.au/
Goodin RE, *Protecting the Vulnerable: A Reanalysis of Our Social Responsibility* (The University of Chicago Press, 1985)
Gordon D and others, *The Impoverishment of the UK; PSE UK First Summary Report* (Economic & Social Research Council, 2013)
Grace J, 'Partnering to Address Financial Exclusion in Australia' in Gardner J, Gray M and Möser K, *Debt and Austerity* (Edward Elgar, 2020) 260
Graeber D, *Debt: The First 5,000 Years* (Melville House Publishing, 2012)
Grant J, *Money of the Mind: Borrowing and Lending in America from the Civil War to Michael Milken* (Farrar Straus Giroux, 1992)
Gray M, Möser K and Gardner J, 'Understanding Low-Income Debt in a High-Income Country' in Gardner J, Gray M and Möser K, *Debt and Austerity* (Edward Elgar, 2020)
Green DG, 'The Friendly Societies and Adam-Smith Liberalism' in Gladstone D (ed), *Before Beveridge: Welfare before the Welfare State* (IEA Health and Welfare Unit, 1999)
Green S, *Causation in Negligence* (Hart Publishing, 2015)
Green TH, 'Liberal Legislation and Freedom of Contract' in Harris P and Morrow J (eds), *Lectures on the Principles of Political Obligation and Other Writings* (Cambridge University Press, 1986)
Greenway D, 'Economic Aspects of Minimum Wages' (1996) 106 *Economic Journal* 637
Griggs L, 'The [Ir]rational Consumer and Why We Need National Legislation Governing Unfair Contract Terms' (2005) 13 *Competition and Consumer Law Journal* 1
Gunn M, 'The Meaning of Incapacity' (1994) 2 *Medical Law Review* 8
Gunningham N and Rees J, 'Industry Self-Regulation: An Institutional Perspective' (1997) 19 *Law & Policy* 363
Guthrie F, *Too Poor to go Bankrupt: The Impact of the New Fee for Lodging a Debtor's Petition* (Financial Counselling Australia, 2014)
Habib I, 'Usury in Medieval India' (1964) 6 *Comparative Studies in Society and History* 393

Hadfield G, 'An Expressive Theory of Contract: From Feminist Dilemmas to a Reconceptualisation of Rational Choice in Contract Law' (1998) 146 *University of Pennsylvania Law Review* 1235
Hall P, *Unconscionable Contracts and Economic Duress* (CCH Australia Ltd, 1985)
Hamblin-Boone R, *Industry Response to FCA Regulation* (Consumer Finance Association, 2014)
Harland D, 'Unconscionable and Unfair Contracts: An Australian Perspective' in Brownsword R, Hird N and Howells G (eds), *Good Faith in Contract: Concepts and Context* (Ashgate Dartmouth, 1999)
Harris J, 'Political Thought and the Welfare State 1870–1940: An Intellectual Framework for British Social Policy' in Gladstone D (ed), *Before Beveridge: Welfare Before the Welfare State* (IEA Health and Welfare Institute, 1999)
Harrison JL, 'Quality of Consent and Distributive Fairness: A Comparative Perspective' in DiMatteo L and Hogg M (eds), *Comparative Contract Law: British and American Perspectives* (Oxford University Press, 2016)
Hawkes D, *The Culture of Usury in Renaissance England* (Palgrave Macmillan, 2010)
Hawkins W, *A Treatise of the Pleas of the Crown, or, A System of the Principal Matters Relating to that Subject, Digested under Proper Heads*, vol 1 (Printed by Eliz Nutt, (executrix of J Nutt, assignee of E Sayer) for J Walthoe, 1721)
——, *A Treatise of the Pleas of the Crown, or, A System of the Principal Matters Relating to that Subject, Digested under Proper Heads*, vol 2 (Printed by Eliz Nutt, (executrix of J Nutt, assignee of E Sayer) for J Walthoe, 1721)
Hayek F, *The Constitution of Liberty* (University of Chicago Press, 1960)
Helliwell J, Layard R and Sachs J, *World Happiness Report 2012* (United Nations Sustainable Development Solutions Network, 2012)
——, *World Happiness Report 2013* (Sustainable Development Solutions Network, 2013)
——, *World Happiness Report 2015* (Sustainable Development Solutions Network, 2015)
——, *World Happiness Report 2016, Update* (Sustainable Development Solutions Network, 2016)
——, *World Happiness Report 2018* (Sustainable Development Solutions Network, 2018)
——, *World Happiness Report 2020* (Sustainable Development Solutions Network, 2020)
Hellman D, 'Indirect Discimination and the Duty to Avoid Compounding Injustice' in Collins H and Khaitan T (eds), *Foundations of Indirect Discrimination Law* (Hart Publishing, 2018)
Helmholz RH, *The Oxford History of the Laws of England. Volume I: The Canon Law and Ecclesiastical Jurisdiction from 597 to the 1640s* (Oxford University Press, 2004)
Herring J and Wall J, 'Autonomy, Capacity and Vulnerable Adults: Filling the Gaps in the Mental Capacity Act' (2015) 35 *Legal Studies* 698
Hirsch D, *The Cost of a Child in 2018* (Child Poverty Action Group, 2018)
Hirsch W, *Law and Economics: An Introductory Analysis*, 3rd edn (Academic Press, 1999)
HM Treasury, *Promoting Financial Inclusion* (2004)
——, *Spending Review 2010* (Cm Paper 7942, 2010)
HM Treasury and Department of Business Innovation and Skills, *A New Approach to Financial Regulation: Transferring Consumer Credit Regulation to the Financial Conduct Authority* (2013)
Hodge FD, Kennedya JJ and Maines LA, 'Does Search-Facilitating Technology Improve the Transparency of Financial Reporting?' (2004) 79 *The Accounting Review* 687
Hodges C, 'Unlocking Justice and Markets: The Promise of Consumer ADR' in Zekoll J, Bälz M and Amelung I (eds), *Dispute Resolution: Alternatives to Formalization Formalization of Alternatives?* (Brill, 2014)
——, *Law and Corporate Behaviour: Integrating Theories of Regulation, Enforcement, Compliance and Ethics* (Hart Publishing, 2015)
——, 'Consumer Redress: Implementing the Vision' in Cortés P (ed), *The New Regulatory Framework for Consumer Dispute Resolution* (Oxford University Press, 2017)
Hoecke MV, 'Methodologies of Legal Research: Which Kind of Method for What Kind of Discipline?' in Hoecke MV (ed), *Methodologies of Legal Research: Which Kind of Method for What Kind of Discipline?* (Hart Publishing, 2011)

Howell N, 'Small Amount Credit Contracts and Payday Loans' (2016) 41(3) *Alternative Law Journal* 174
Howell N and Wilson T, 'Access to Consumer Credit: The Problem of Financial Exclusion in Australia and the Current Regulatory Framework' (2005) 5 *Macquarie Law Journal* 127
Huckstep A, 'Payday Lending: Do Outrageous Prices Necessarily Mean Outrageous Profits?' (2007) 12 *Fordham Journal of Corporate & Financial Law* 203
Hudson M, *The Lost Tradition of Biblical Debt Cancellations* (Hentry George School of Social Science, 1992)
Hume D, *The Philosophical Works of David Hume* (Adam Black and William Tait, 1826)
Hunt C, 'Unconscionability in the Supreme Court of Canada: *Uber Technologies Inc v Heller*' (2021) 80 *Cambridge Law Journal* 25
Jones N, *God and the Moneylenders: Usury and the Law in Early Modern England* (Basil Blackwell, 1989)
Jones P, Comfort D and Hall T, 'Betting Shops in the Public Eye: A Commentary' 21 (2021) *Journal of Public Affairs* e2153
Kant I, *The Philosophy of Law* (edited by Hastie TbW) (Morrison and Gibb, 1887)
——, *Metaphysical Elements of Justice* (edited by Ladd TwIaNbJ) (Hackett Publishing Company, 1999)
——, *Anthropology from a Pragmatic Point of View* (Cambridge University Press, 2006)
Kelly JB, *A summary of the history and law of usury: with an examination of the policy of the existing system and suggestions for its amendment, together with an analysis of the Parliamentary proceedings relative to the subject up to the present time and a collection of statutes* (RJ Kennett, 1835)
Kempson E, *Independent Review of the Banking Code: Report to Code Sponsors* (Personal Finance Research Centre, 2004)
——, *Looking Beyond Our Shores: Consumer Protection Regulation Lessons from the UK* (Joint Center for Housing Studies, Harvard University, 2008)
Kempson E and Collard S, *Developing a Vision for Financial Inclusion* (Friends Provident Foundation, 2012)
Kempson E, Collard S and Moore N, *Fair and Reasonable: An Assessment of the Financial Ombudsman Service* (Personal Finance Research Centre, 2004)
Kempson E and others, *Is a Not-For-Profit Home Credit Business Feasible?* (Joseph Rowntree Foundation, 2009)
Kenway P and others, *Monitoring Poverty and Social Exclusion in Scotland 2015* (Joseph Rowntree Organisation, 2015)
Keynes JM, *The General Theory of Employment, Interest and Money* (MacMillan Cambridge University Press, 1936)
——, 'Economic Possibilities for our Grandchildren' in Keynes JM (ed), *Essays in Persuasion* (W. W. Norton & Company, 1963)
Kimel D, 'Neutrality, Autonomy, and Freedom of Contract' (2001) 21 *Oxford Journal of Legal Studies* 473
——, *From Promise to Contract: Towards a Liberal Theory of Contract* (Hart Publishing, 2003)
——, 'The Choice of Paradigm for Theory of Contract: Reflections on the Relational Model' (2007) 27 *Oxford Journal of Legal Studies* 233
King James Bible, *Authorised Version* (Cambridge Edition)
Kinsby B, 'The Big Society: Power to the People?' (2010) 81 *The Political Quarterly* 484
Klick J and Mitchell G, 'Infantilization by Regulation' (2016) 39 *Regulation* 36
Klimes M, 'CoE Bolsters Crusade Against Payday Loans with Hector Sants Hire' *International Business Times* (16 January 2014) www.ibtimes.co.uk/coe-eyes-crusade-against-payday-loans-hector-sants-hire-1432514
Knauer N, 'Defining Capacity: Balancing the Competing Interests of Autonomy and Need' (2003) 12 *Temple Political & Civil Rights Law Review* 321
Kokas T and others, *Specifying and Securing a Social Minimum in the Battle Against Poverty* (Hart Publishing, 2019)

Kritzer H, '"Research is a Messy Business" – An Archaeology of the Craft of Sociological Research' in Halliday S and Schmidt P (eds), *Conducting Law and Society Research: Reflection on Methods and Practices* (Cambridge University Press, 2009)

Kronman AT, 'Contract Law and Distributive Justice' (1980) 89 *Yale Law Journal* 472

Lane P, 'The Working Class and State 'Welfare' in Britain, 1880-1914' in Gladstone D (ed), *Before Beveridge: Welfare Before the Welfare State* (IEA Institute of Health and Welfare, 1999)

Lansley S and Mack J, *Breadline Britain: The Rise of Mass Poverty* (OneWorld Publications, 2015)

Lawson R, *Exclusion Clauses and Unfair Contract Terms* (Sweet & Maxwell, 1998)

Levitas R and others, *The Multi-Dimensional Analysis of Social Exclusion* (University of Bristol, 2007)

Lewalski BK, 'Biblical Allusion and Allegory in "The Merchant of Venice"' (1962) 13 *Shakespeare Quarterly* 327

Lewis J, 'The Voluntary Sector in the Mixed Economy of Welfare' in Gladstone D (ed), *Before Beveridge: Welfare Before the Welfare State* (IEA Health and Welfare Unit, 1999)

London Assembly, 'Low Pay and In-Work Poverty' (Economy Committee, March 2020), www.london.gov.uk/sites/default/files/london_assembly_-_economy_committee_-_low_pay_and_in-work_poverty_.pdf

Long I, *Consumer Rights* (Thomson Round Hall Ltd, 2004)

Lowe R, *The Welfare State in Britain since 1945*, 2nd edn (MacMillan Press Ltd, 1999)

Luther M, *Von Kauffshandlung vnd Wucher (On Trading and Usury)* (Durch Hans Lufft, 1524)

Macey JM and Miller GP, 'An Economic Analysis of Conflict of Interest Regulation' (1997) 82 *Iowa Law Review* 965

Machin S and Manning A, 'Employment and the Introduction of a Minimum Wage in Britain' (1996) 106 *The Economic Journal* 667

Mack E, 'Individualism and Libertarian Rights' in Christiano T and Christman J (eds), *Contemporary Debates in Political Philosophy* (Blackwell Publishing, 2009)

Macmillan L, 'While there is Evidence that Workless Spells are Associated Across Generations, the "Culture of Welfare Dependency" Argument does not Hold' (*LSE British Politics and Policy*, 2 April 2014) http://blogs.lse.ac.uk/politicsandpolicy/intergenerational-worklessness-the-unexplored-curse/

Malbon J, 'Shopping for Credit: An Empirical Study of Consumer Decision-Making' (2001) 29 *Australian Business Law Review* 44

——, 'Predatory Lending' (2005) 33 *Australian Business Law Review* 224

Mann R, 'Nudging from Debt: The Role of Behavioral Economics in Regulation' [2011] *The Lydian Payments Journal*, www.pymnts.com/assets/Lydian_Journal/LydianJournalFebLawReg.pdf.

Manning I and Jonge A, *Regulating the Cost of Credit* (Consumer Affairs Victoria, 2006)

Marotta JJ, Cornelius JA and Eadington WR, *The Downside: Problem and Pathological Gambling* (University of Nevada Press, 2002)

Marston G and Shevellar L, 'In the Shadow of the Welfare State: The Role of Payday Lending in Poverty Survival in Australia' (2014) 43 *Journal of Social Policy* 155

Marx K, *Capital Volume III: The Process of Capitalist Production as a Whole* (Institute of Marxism-Leninism, translated by Marxists Internet Archive, 1894)

Matthews JB, *The Law of Money-Lending, Past and Present: Being a Short History of the Usury Laws in England, Followed by a Treatise upon the Money-lenders Act, 1900* (Sweet & Maxwell, 1906)

——, *The Money-Lenders Act, 1900 (63 and 64 Victoria, Chapter 51), The Law of Money-Lending, Past and Present* (Sweet & Maxwell, 1908)

May T, *The Shared Society: Prime Minister's Speech at the Charity Commission Annual Meeting on 9 January 2017* (Gov.UK, 2017)

McCartney TRHI and Gibbons D, *Protecting Low Income Borrowers in the Credit Crisis* (2008)

McCrudden C, 'Legal Research and the Social Sciences' (2006) 122 *Law Quarterly Review* 632

McDermott T, *Consumer Credit Regulation: The Journey so Far: Speech Delivered at the Credit Summit 2016 on 7 April 2016* (2016)

McKeand R, 'Economic Duress – Wearing the Clothes of Unconscionable Conduct' (2001) 17 *Journal of Contract Law* 1

Mead LM, 'The Rise of Paternalism' in Mead LM (ed), *The New Paternalism: Supervisory Approaches to Poverty* (Brookings Institution Press, 1997)
Meislin BJ and Cohen ML, 'Backgrounds of the Biblical Law against Usury' (1964) 6 *Comparative Studies in Society and History* 250
Mercuro N and Medema S, *Economics and the Law: From Posner to Post-Modernism and Beyond*, 2nd edn (Princeton University Press, 2006)
Merry SE, 'Getting Justice and Getting Even' in Halliday S and Schmidt P (eds), *Conducting Law and Society Research: Reflection on Methods and Practices* (Cambridge University Press, 2009)
Merton RK, 'The Matthew Effect in Science' (1968) 159 *Science* 56
Messer E and Cohen MJ, *Approaches to Food and Nutrient Rights, 1976–2008* (World Hunger Education, 2009)
Mill JS, *On Liberty* (Longman, Roberts & Green, 1859)
——, *Principles of Political Economy* (Longmans, Green & Co, 1891)
——, *On Socialism* (Feuer LS ed, Prometheus Books, 1987)
——, *Principles of Political Economy, and, Chapters on Socialism* (edited by Riley J) (Oxford University Press, 1994)
Miller AD and Perry R, 'The Reasonable Man' (2012) 87 *New York University Law Review* 323
Money Advice Liaison Group, *Good Practice Awareness Guidelines For Consumers with Mental Health Problems and Debt*, 2nd edn (Money Advice Liaison Group, 2009)
——, *Money and Mental Health: The Facts* (Money Advice Liaison Group, 2019)
Morgan F, Drue S and Stoltman J, 'A Framework for Examining the Legal Status of Vulnerable Consumers' (1995) 14 *Journal of Public Policy & Marketing* 267
Morris RA, 'Consumer Debt and Usury: A New Rationale for Usury' (1988) 15 *Pepperdine Law Review* 151
Mulhall S and Swift A, *Liberals and Communitarians*, 2nd edn (Blackwell Publishers, 1996)
Mullainathan S and Shafir E, *Scarcity: Why Having Too Little Means So Much* (Allen Lane, 2013)
Murray C, 'The Emerging British Underclass' in Lister R (ed), *Charles Murray and the Underclass: The Developing Debate* (IEA Health and Welfare Unit in association with *The Sunday Times*, 1996)
National Audit Office, *Office of Fair Trading: Regulating Consumer Credit* (2012)
National Health Service Choices, 'The History of the NHS in England' (*National Health Service*, 2015) www.nhs.uk/NHSEngland/thenhs/nhshistory/Pages/NHShistory1948.aspx
National Trading Standards, 'Manchester Loan Shark Sentenced to Twelve Months in Prison' (*National Trading Standards*, 30 September 2015) www.nationaltradingstandards.uk/news/manchester-loan-shark-sentenced-to-twelve-months-in-prison/
NHS England, 'New Research – Public NHS Satisfaction Levels Rise with Dissatisfaction Levels at all Time Low' (*NHS England*, 29 January 2015) www.england.nhs.uk/2015/01/nhs-satisfaction-levels-rise/
Nielson L, 'Counting, Reading, Interacting: Focusing on the Activities of the Researcher in Thinking about Methods' in Cane P and Kritzer H (eds), *The Oxford Handbook of Empirical Legal Research* (Oxford University Press, 2010)
——, 'The Need for Multi-Method Approaches in Empirical Legal Research' in Cane P and Kritzer H (eds), *The Oxford Handbook of Empirical Legal Research* (Oxford University Press, 2010)
Niemi J, Ramsay I and Whitford WC, 'Introduction' in Niemi J, Ramsay I and Whitford, WC (eds), *Consumer Credit, Debt and Bankruptcy* (Hart Publishing, 2009)
Nottage L, 'Innovating for 'Safe Consumer Credit': Drawing on Product Safety Regulation to Protect Consumers of Credit' in Wilson T (ed), *International Responses to Issues of Credit and Over-indebtedness in the Wake of Crisis* (Ashgate Publishing Ltd, 2013)
Now: Pensions, 'Britian's Savings Culture in Crisis' www.nowpensions.com/wp-content/uploads/2013/07/Britains-savings-culture-now-pensions.pdf
Nozick R, *Anarchy, State and Utopia* (Basic Books, 1974)
Nussbaum M, 'Women and Cultural Universals' in Nussbaum M (ed), *Sex and Social Justice* (Oxford University Press, 1999)
O'Connell S, *Credit and Community: Working-Class Debt in the UK since 1880* (Oxford University Press, 2009)
Ofcomf, *Trends in Advertising Activity – Payday Loans* (2013)

Office for National Statistics, 'Poverty and Social Exclusion in the UK and EU, 2005–2011' https://webarchive.nationalarchives.gov.uk/ukgwa/20160105214433/http://www.ons.gov.uk/ons/rel/household-income/poverty-and-social-exclusion-in-the-uk-and-eu/2005-2011/rpt--poverty-and-social-exclusion.htm
Ogus A, *Regulation: Legal Form and Economic Theory* (Clarendon Law Series, 1994)
——, *Costs and Cautionary Tales: Economic Insights for the Law* (Hart Publishing, 2006)
Ord M, *An Essay on the Laws of Usury* (Hartford, 1808)
Organisation for Economic Co-operation and Development Data, 'Income Inequality: Chart' (*Organisation for Economic Co-operation and Development*, 2016) https://data.oecd.org/inequality/income-inequality.htm
——, 'Poverty Rate: Chart' (*Organisation for Economic Co-operation and Development*, 2016) https://data.oecd.org/inequality/poverty-rate.htm#indicator-chart
O'Shea P, 'All is Fair in Love and War – but not Contract' (2004) 23 *The University of Queensland Law Journal* 226
Owen CL, Staudt RW and Pedwell EB, *Access to Justice: Meeting the Needs of Self-Represented Litigants* (Institute of Design and Chicago-Kent College of Law, Illinois Institute of Technology, 2002)
Oxfam, *The Perfect Storm: Economic Stagnation, the Rising Cost of Living, Public Spending Cuts, and the Impact on UK Poverty* (2012)
Oxford English Dictionary, '"Usury, n"', 2nd edn (Oxford University Press, 1989)
Packman C, *Loan Sharks: The Rise and Rise of Payday Lending* (Searching Finance, 2012)
——, *Savings for the Future: Solving the Savings Puzzle for Low Income Households* (Toynbee Hall and J.P. Morgan, 2017)
Page RM, 'The Prospects for Social Welfare' in Page RM and Silburn R (eds), *British Social Welfare in the Twentieth Century* (Palgrave, 1999)
Paterson J and Brody G, 'Targeting Business Models that Prey on Vulnerable Consumers: The Role of Prohibition on Unfair and Unconscionable Conduct' [International Association of Consumer Law Conference, Sydney, 4 July 2013]
Pattison M, *Payday Lending a Top Obstacle for Financial Independence for the Poor* (The Boston Pilot, 2015)
Pearson G, 'Finance Brokers – A Regulatory Anomaly' (2003) 14 *Journal of Banking and Finance Law & Practice* 200
——, 'The Ambit of Unconscionable Conduct in Relation to Financial Services' (2005) 23 *Companies and Securities Law Journal* 105
Peel E and Treitel GH, *The Law of Contract*, 13th edn (Sweet & Maxwell, 2011)
Pennycook M and Wittaker M, *Low Pay Britain 2012* (Resolution Foundation, 2012)
Persky J, 'From Usury to Interest' (2007) 21 *Journal of Economic Perspectives* 227
Personal Finance Research Centre, *Easy Come, Easy Go: Borrowing over the Lifecycle* (Standard Life, 2007)
——, *The Impact on Business and Consumers of a Cap on the Total Cost of Credit* (Department of Business and Innovation Skills, 2013)
Personal Finance Research Centre and Policis, *Illegal Lending in the UK: Research Report* (2006)
Plowden F, *A Treatise upon the Law of Usury and Annuities by Francis Plowden of the Middle Temple, Barrister at Law* (Printed for J Butterworth, Fleet-Street, 1797)
Polanyi K, *The Great Transformation: The Political and Economic Origins of Our Time* (Beacon Press, 2001)
——, 'The Idea of Usury: From Tribal Brotherhood to Universal Otherhood, by Benjamin N. Nelson' (*Commentary*, 1950) www.commentary.org/articles/karl-polanyi/the-idea-of-usury-from-tribal-brotherhood-to-universal-otherhood-by-benjamin-n-nelson/
Pollard W and Mitchell T, 'Decision Theory Analysis of Social Power' (1972) 78 *Psychological Bulletin* 433
Porres E, *Bubbles and Contagion in Financial Markets: An Integrative View* (Palgrave Macmillan, 2016)
Posner EA, 'Contract Law in the Welfare State: A Defense of the Unconscionability Doctrine, Usury Laws, and Related Limitations on the Freedom to Contract' (1995) 24 *The Journal of Legal Studies* 283

Posner R, 'Economics, Politics, and the Reading of Statutes and the Constitution' (1982) 49 *University of Chicago Law Review* 263

——, 'Rational Choice, Behavioral Economics, and the Law' (1997) 50 *Stanford Law Review* 1551

Powell R, 'The Unreasonableness of the Reasonable Man' (157) 157 *Current Legal Problems* 104

Public Accounts Committee, *8th Report – Regulating Consumer Credit* (2013)

Quigley WP, 'Five Hundred Years of English Poor Laws, 1349–1834: Regulating the Working and Nonworking Poor' (1997) 30 *Akron Law Review* 73

Radin M, 'Market-Inalienability' (1987) 100 *Harvard Law Review* 1849

——, *Boilerplate: The Fine Print, Vanishing Rights, and the Rule of Law* (Princeton University Press, 2012)

Rajapaske P and Gardner J, 'Unconscionable Conduct and Consumer Protection in Subprime Lending in Australia' (2014) 29 *Banking & Finance Law Review* 485

Ramsay I, *Rationales for Intervention in the Consumer Marketplace* (The Office of Fair Trading, 1984)

——, 'Consumer Credit law, Distributive Justice and the Welfare State' (1995) 15 *Oxford Journal of Legal Studies* 177

——, 'Consumer Law, Regulatory Capitalism and the 'New Learning' in Regulation' (2006) 28 *Sydney Law Journal* 9

——, '"To Heap Distress Upon Distress": Comparative Reflections of Interest-Rate Ceilings' (2010) 60 *University of Toronto Law Journal* 707

——, 'Consumer Credit Regulation After the Fall: International Dimensions' (2011) 1 *Zeitschrift fur Europaisches Unternehmens – und Verbraucherrecht* 24

——, *Consumer Law and Policy*, 3rd edn (Hart Publishing, 2012)

——, '"Wannabe WAGS" and "Credit Binges": The Construction of Overindebtedness in the UK' in Niemi J, Ramsay I and Whitford WC (eds), *Consumer Credit, Debt and Bankruptcy* (Hart Publishing, 2009)

Rawls J, *A Theory of Justice* (Harvard University Press, 1971)

Raz J, 'Liberalism, Autonomy, and the Politics of Neutral Concern' (1982) 7 *Midwest Studies in Philosophy* 89

——, 'Promises in Morality and Law' (1982) 95 *Harvard Law Review* 916

——, *The Morality of Freedom* (Oxford University Press, 1988)

Reeder J (ed), *Brice on Maritime Law of Salvage*, 5th edn (Sweet & Maxwell, 2012)

Reeves MP and Wilson C, *Round About A Pound A Week* (G Bell & Sons, 1913 (reprinted in 1994 by Virago Books))

Reifner U, *Responsible Credit in the EU* (Institute of Financial Services, 2008)

——, *Responsible Bankruptcy* (Institute of Financial Services, Hamburg, 2011)

——, '"A Call to Arms" – For Regulation of Consumer Lending' in Niemi J, Ramsay I and Whitford WC (eds), *Consumer Credit, Debt and Bankruptcy* (Hart Publishing, 2009)

Reifner U and others, *Harmonisation of Cost Elements of the Annual Percentage Rate of Charge* (Institute for Financial Services, Hamburg, 1998)

Reifner U, Clerc-Renaud S and Knobloch RM, *Study on Interest Rate Restrictions in the EU, Final Report for the EU Commission DG Internal Market and Services* (Institute for Financial Services, Hamburg, 2010)

Reith G, *Research on the Social Impacts of Gambling* (Scottish Executive Social Research, 2006)

Report by the Comptroller and Auditor-General, *The Office of Fair Trading: Protecting the Consumer from Unfair Trading Practices* (HC57 Session 1999–20, 2000)

Rethink, 'Mental Health and Debt: Knowing the Facts and Where to Seek Help' (*Rethink Mental Illness*, 2015) www.rethink.org/news-views/2015/08/debt

Ritchie J and others, *Qualitative Research Practice: A Guide for Social Science Students and Researchers* (Sage Publishing, 2013)

Roberts J, *Routledge Philosophy Guidebook to Aristotle and the Politics* (Routledge, 2009)

Roosevelt FD, 'First Inugural Address' (*History Tools*, 4 March 1933) www.historytools.org/sources/froosevelt1st.html

Rougeau VD, 'Rediscovering Usury: An Argument for Legal Controls on Credit Card Interest Rates' (1996) 67 *University of Colorado Law Review* 1

Rowlingson K, *Moneylenders and their Customers* (Policy Studies Institute, 1994)

Rowlingson K, Appleyard L and Gardner J, 'Payday Lending in the UK: The Regul(aris)ation of a Necessary Evil?' (2016) 45 *Journal of Social Policy* 527

Rowlingson K and McKay S, *Financial Inclusion Annual Monitoring Report 2015* (University of Birmingham, 2015)

——, *Financial Inclusion Monitor 2020* (University of Birmingham, 2021)

Rowntree BS, *Poverty: The Study of Town Life* (MacMillan and Co Ltd, 1908)

——, *Poverty and Progress: A Second Social Survey of York* (Longmans, Green and Co, 1941)

Rt Hon Lord Hunt of Wirral MBE, *Opening Up, Reaching Out and Aiming High: An Agenda for Accessibility and Excellence in the Financial Ombudsman Service* (2008)

Rubin J, 'Bills of Exchange, Interest Bans, and Impersonal Exchange in Islam and Christianity' (2010) 47 *Explorations in Economic History* 213

Saintier S, 'Defects of Consent in English Law' in DiMatteo L and Hogg M (eds), *Comparative Contract Law: British and American Perspectives* (Oxford University Press, 2016)

Sandel M, *Liberalism and the Limits of Justice*, 2nd edn (Cambridge University Press, 1998)

——, *What Money Can't Buy: The Moral Limits of Markets* (Penguin, 2013)

Satz D, *Why Some Things Should Not be For Sale: The Moral Limits of Markets* (Oxford University Press, 2010)

Schmitz AJ, 'Females on the Fringe: Considering Gender in Payday Lending Policy' (2014) 89 *Chicago-Kent Law Review* 65

Schnuk PH, 'Rethinking Informed Consent' (1994) 103 *Yale Law Journal* 899

Schwartz A and Scott R, *Contract Theory and the Limits of Contract Law* (John M Olin Center for Studies in Law, Economics, and Public Policy Working Papers, 2003)

Scottish Parliament, *Measuring Social Exclusion Research Paper 99/11* (Scotland Information Centre, 1999)

Scoular J and O'Neill M, 'Regulation Prostitution: Social Inclusion, Responsibilisation and the Politics of Prostitution Reform' (2007) 47 *British Journal of Criminology* 764

Sefa M Franken, 'The Political Economy of the EC Consumer Credit Directive' in Niemi J, Ramsay I and Whitford WC (eds), *Consumer Credit, Debt and Bankruptcy* (Hart Publishing, 2009)

Selwyn W, *An Abridgment of the Law of Nisi Prius* (W Clarke and Sons, 1812)

Sen A, 'Rational Fools: A Critique of the Behavioral Foundations of Economic Theory' (1977) 6 *Philosophy & Public Affairs* 317

——, *The Standard of Living* (Cambridge University Press, 1987)

——, *Inequality Reexamined* (Harvard University Press, 1992)

——, *Development as Freedom* (Oxford University Press, 1999)

Shakespeare W, *The Merchant of Venice* (Printed by IR for Thomas Heyes, 1600)

Sharpe J and Bostock J, *Supporting People with Debt and Mental Health Problems* (Community Psychology, 2002)

Shildrick T and others, *Poverty and Insecurity: Life in 'Low-Pay, No-Pay' Britain* (Policy, 2012)

Sleeman JF, *The Welfare State: Its Aims, Benefits and Costs* (George Allen & Unwin Ltd, 1973)

Slocock C, Hayes R and Harker D, *Whose Society? A Final Big Society Audit* (Civil Exchange and DHA, in conjunction with Joseph Rowntree Charitable Trust and the Barrow Cadbury Trust, 2015)

Smalley B, *The Study of the Bible in the Middle Ages*, 3rd edn (Blackwell, 1983)

Smith A, *Lectures on Justice, Police, Revenue and Arms* (edited by Cannan E) (Clarendon Press, 1896)

——, *An Inquiry into the Nature and Causes of the Wealth of Nations* (The Modern Library, 1937)

Smith C and Cooper-Martin E, 'Ethics and Target Marketing: The Role of Product Harm and Consumer Vulnerability' (1997) 61 *Journal of Marketing* 1

Smith J and McCalla S, *Consumer Credit Act 2006: A Guide to the New Law* (Law Society (Great Britain) 2006)

Smith S, 'In Defence of Substantive Unfairness' (1996) *Law Quarterly Review* 138

——, *Contract Theory* (Oxford University Press, 2004)

Spengler JJ, 'Economic Thought of Islam: Ibn Khaldun' (1964) 6 *Comparative Studies in Society and History* 268
Spooner J, 'Seeking Shelter in Personal Insolvency Law: Recession, Eviction and Bankruptcy's Social Safety Net' (2017) 44 *Journal of Law and Society* 374
Squires GD, 'Inequality and Access to Financial Services' in Niemi J, Ramsay I and Whitford WC (eds), *Consumer Credit, Debt and Bankruptcy* (Hart Publishing, 2009)
Stepchange Debt Charity, *Life on the Edge: Our Major New Report on the State of the Nation's Family Finances* (2014)
——, *Life on the Edge: Towards More Resilient Family Finances* (2014)
——, *StepChange Debt Charity Response to the Financial Conduct Authority Consultation: CP10/14: Proposals for a Price Cap on High-Cost Short-Term Credit* (2014)
Stern K, 'Procedural Fairness – Its Scope and Practical Obligation' (2008) 56 *AIAL Forum* 2
Stewart J, 'The Twentieth Century: an Overview' in Page RM and Silburn R (eds), *British Social Welfare in the Twentieth Century* (Palgrave, 1999)
Straus RR, 'Almost Half of Payday Lenders Quit the Market Rather than Face OFT Probe' (*This is Money*, 15 August 2013) www.thisismoney.co.uk/money/cardsloans/article-2393291/19-payday-lenders-quit-market-face-OFT-probe.html
Summers LH, 'Some Simple Economics of Mandated Benefits' (1989) 79 *The American Economic Review* 177
Sunstein CR, 'The Storrs Lecture: Behavioural Economics and Paternalism' (2013) 122 *The Yale Law Journal* 1826
Temin P, *Did Monetary Forces Cause the Great Depression?* (Norton, 1976)
Thal S, 'The Inequality of Bargaining Power Doctrine: The Problem of Defining Contractual Unfairness' (1988) 8 *Oxford Journal of Legal Studies* 17
Thaler R, 'Toward a Positive Theory of Consumer Choice' (1980) 1 *Journal of Economic Behaviour and Organisation* 39
Thaler R and Sunstein C, *Nudge: Improving Decisions about Health, Wealth, and Happiness* (Yale University Press, 2008)
The Archbishop of Canterbury JW, *Payday Loans: Archbishop's Speech in the House of Lords on 20 June 2013* (2013)
The Association for Qualitative Research, 'Mystery Shopping Definition' (2017) www.aqr.org.uk/glossary/mystery-shopping
The Baptist Union of Great Britain and others, *The Lies We Tell Ourselves: Ending Comfortable Myths about Poverty* (2013)
The Center for Responsible Lending, *Modern Day Usury: The Payday Loan Trap* (2010)
The Centre for Social Justice, *Swimming with Sharks* (2022)
The Commission on Social Justice, 'The UK in a Changing World' in Franklin J (ed), *Social Policy and Social Justice* (Polity Press published in Association with the Institute for Public Policy Research, 1998)
The Economist Newspaper Ltd, 'Towards the End of Poverty' *The Economist* (1 June 2013) www.economist.com/news/leaders/21578665-nearly-1-billion-people-have-been-taken-out-extreme-poverty-20-years-world-should-aim
The Financial Conduct Authority, *2012 Annual Review of Consumer Complaints* (2012)
——, *Journey to the FCA* (2012)
——, *Detailed Proposals for the FCA Regime for Consumer Credit* (Consultation Paper CP13/10, 2013)
——, 'Ombudsman News: Issue 109, April/May 2013 – Payday Lending' www.financial-ombudsman.org.uk/publications/ombudsman-news/109/109-payday-lending.html
——, *Consumer Credit and Consumers in Vulnerable Circumstances* (2014)
——, *Consumer Credit Firms Must Raise Advertising Standards, Says FCA* (2014)
——, *Detailed Rules for the Price Cap on High-Cost Short-Term Credit; Including Feedback on CP14/10 and Final Rules* (2014)
——, *FCA Confirms Price Cap Rule for Payday Lenders* (2014)

——, *Media Release: Wonga to Make Major Changes to Affordability Criteria Following Discussions with the FCA* (2014)
——, *Media Release: Wonga to Pay Redress for Unfair Debt Collection Practices* (2014)
——, *Ombudsman News Issue 119 (August 2014): Short-Term Credit* (2014)
——, *Proposals for a Price Cap on High-Cost Short-Term Credit: Consultation Paper* (2014)
——, *FCA Handbook, COND Threshold Conditions*
——, *FCA Handbook, Consumer Credit Sourcebook (CONC)*
——, *Consumer Credit: Authorisations Data Bulletin Published June 2015* (2015)
——, *Press Release: Payday Lender Dollar to Provide £15.4 million Redress to Over 147,000 Customers* (2015)
——, *Press Release: Payday Lenders Failing Customers in Arrears, says FCA* (2015)
——, *Financial Ombudsman Service Annual Review 2015/2016* (2016)
——, *FCA Regulation of High-Cost Short-Term Credit (HCSTC)* (2017)
——, *Enforcement Guide, Chapter 20: Enforcement of the Consumer Credit Act 1974* (2018)
——, *High-Cost Credit Review – Update* (2018)
——, *Financial Ombudsman Service Annual Review 2017/2018* (2018)
——, *Financial Lives 2020 Survey: The Impact of Coronavirus* (2020)
——, *Annual Complaints Data and Insight 2020/21* (2021)
——, *The Woolard Review – A Review of Change and Innovation in the Unsecured Credit Market* (2021)
The Financial Conduct Authority's Practitioner Panel, 'High-Level Proposals for an FCA Regime for Consumer Credit' www.fs-pp.org.uk/docs/inquiry_responses/PP%20Consumer%20Credit%20FCA%20consultation%20response%2020130501%20.pdf
The Financial Stability Board, *Consumer Finance Protection with Particular Focus on Credit* (2011)
The Law Commission and The Scottish Law Commission, *Consumer Redress for Misleading and Aggressive Practices* (Law Com No 332 & Scot Law Com No 226, 2013)
The Office of Fair Trading, *Consumer Credit Deregulation: A Review by the Director General Of Fair Trading of the Scope and Operation of the Consumer Credit Act 1974* (1994)
——, *Consumer Credit Licensing: General Guidance for Licensees and Applicants on Fitness and Requirements* (2008)
——, *Irresponsible Lending – OFT Guidance for Creditors* (2010)
——, 'OFT Acts to Improve Lending Practices' (Press Release, 9 November 2010), www.oft.gov.uk/news-and-updates/press/2010/116-10#.UjsIuj8ygmY
——, *Review of High-Cost Credit* (2010)
——, *Mental Capacity – OFT Guidance for Creditors* (2011)
——, *Unfair Relationships: Enforcement Action under Part 8 of the Enterprise Act 2002* (2011)
——, *Payday Lending Compliance Review – Interim Report* (The Office of Fair Trading, 2012)
——, *Payday Lending: Final Compliance Review* (The Office of Fair Trading, 2013)
The Rt Hon Frank Field MP and The Rt Revd Tim Thornton, *Feeding Britain: A Strategy for Zero Hunger in England, Wales, Scotland and Northern Ireland* (All-Party Parliamentary Inquiry into Hunger in the United Kingdom, 2014)
The Select Committee on Money Lending, *1897 Report from the Select Committee on Money Lending; Together with the Proceedings of the Committee, Minutes of Evidence, Appendix, and Index* (19th Century House of Commons Sessional Papers, No 364, 1897)
——, *1898 Report from the Select Committee on Money Lending; Together with the Proceedings of the Committee, Minutes of Evidence, Appendix and Index* (House of Commons Papers; Report of Committees, No 260, 1898)
The UK Cards Association, *Summary of Key Payments Statistics: September 2013* (2013)
Thiel V, *Doorstop Robbery: Why the UK Needs a Fair Lending Law* (New Economics Foundation, 2009)
Thompson S, *Paying Respondents and Informants* (University of Surrey Social Research Update, 1999)
Townsend P, 'The Meaning of Poverty' (1962) 13 *British Journal of Sociology* 225
Traynor R, 'The Ways and Meanings of Defective Products and Strict Liability' (1965) 32 *Tennessee Law Review* 363

UK Government and Parliament: Petitions, *End Legal Loan Sharking: Cap the Total Cost of Credit Petition* (2012)
Vaillant GE, *Poverty and Paternalism: A Psychiatric Viewpoint* (edited by Mead L) (Brookings Institution Press, 1997)
Vincent AW, 'The Poor Law Reports of 1909 and the Social Theory of the Charity Organisation Society' in Gladstone D (ed), *Before Beveridge: Welfare before the Welfare State* (IEA Health and Welfare Unit, 1999)
Visser WA and Macintosh A, 'A Short Review of the Historical Critique of Usury' (1998) 8 *Accounting, Business & Financial History* 175
Waldron J, 'John Rawls and the Social Minimum' (1986) 3 *Journal of Applied Philosophy* 21
Walker A, 'Blaming the Victims' in Lister R (ed), *Charles Murray and the Underclass: The Developing Debate* (IEA Health and Welfare Unit in association with The Sunday Times, 1996)
Walker C, '"Responsibilizing" a Healthy Britain: Personal Debt, Employment and Welfare' (2011) 41 *Neoliberalism and Health* 525
Wardle H and others, *Debt and Problem Gambling: Evidence from the Adult Psychiatric Morbidity Survey: Briefing Paper 1* (NatCen: Social Research That Works for Society July, 2012)
Wardle H and others, '"Risky Places?": Mapping Gambling Machine Density and Socio-Economic Deprivation' (2014) 30 *Journal of Gambling Studies* 201
Warren E, 'Unsafe at Any Rate' [2007] *Democracy: A Journal of Ideas* 8
Warwick-Booth L, *Social Inequality* (Sage Publishing, 2013)
Waymann C, *Lessons from the Past, Ambitions for the Future: Our 2019/20 Complaints Data Analysis* (Financial Ombudsman Service, 2020)
Webber D and Clark C, *Persistent Poverty in the UK and EU* (Office of National Statistics, 2017)
Webley L, 'Qualitative Approaches to Empirical Legal Research' in Cane P and Kritzer H (eds), *The Oxford Handbook of Empirical Legal Research* (Oxford University Press, 2010)
Wheatley M, *Consumer Credit and the FCA: One Year On: A Speech Delivered by Martin Wheatley on 11 March 2015* (Financial Conduct Authority, 2015)
Which?, 'Half of People with Payday Loans Cannot Afford to Pay Back their Debts' *Which?*, 8 November 2012) http://press.which.co.uk/whichstatements/half-of-people-taking-out-payday-loans-cannot-afford-to-pay-them-back/#.UYyyvMrsxn4
——, Which? *Credit Britain: Making Lending Work for Consumers* (Which?, 2013)
—— News, 'Debt Management Companies Exploit the Vulnerable, says Charity' (Which?, 16 September 2011) www.which.co.uk/news/2011/09/debt-management-companies-exploit-the-vulnerable-says-charity-265956/Which?
—— News, 'Payday Loans and Bank Overdrafts Compared' (*Which?*, 30 September 2011) www.which.co.uk/news/2011/09/payday-loans-and-bank-overdrafts-compared-266802/
White JB, 'Economics and Law: Two Cultures in Tension' (1987) 54 *Tennessee Law Review* 161
White M, 'Personal Bankruptcy under the 1978 Bankruptcy Code: An Economic Analysis' (1988) 63 *Indiana Law Journal* 1
White S, 'Social Minimum' (*Stanford Encyclopedia of Philosophy*, 2004) http://plato.stanford.edu/entries/social-minimum/
Whiteside N, 'Private Provision and Public Welfare: Health Insurance Between the Wars' in Gladstone D (ed), *Before Beveridge: Welfare Before the Welfare State* (IEA Health and Welfare Unit, 1999)
Wiener R and others, 'Consumer Credit Card Use: The Roles of Creditor Disclosure and Anticipated Emotion' (2007) 13 *Journal of Experimental Psychology* 32
Williams S, 'The Rise and Rise of Affordability Complaints' in Gardner J, Gray M and Möser K (eds), *Debt & Austerity: Implications of the Financial Crisis* (Edward Elgar, 2020)
Wilkinson R and Pickett K, *The Spirit Level: Why Equality is Better for Everyone* (Penguin, 2010)
Wilson T, 'The Bank and Customer Relationship, and *Australian Competition and Consumer Commission v Oceana Commercial Pty Ltd*' (2004) 25 *Queensland Lawyer* 2
——, 'The Inadequacy of the Current Regulatory Response to Payday Lending' (2004) 32 *Australian Business Law Review* 193

——, 'Values Driven Innovation or Inadequate Self-Regulation? The Effective Regulation of Australian Banks as Service Providers to Low Income Consumers' (2008) 21 *Australian Journal of Corporate Law* 258

Wolf S, 'Happiness and Meaning: Two Aspects of the Good Life' (1997) 14 *Social Philosophy and Policy* 207

Wolff J, *An Introduction to Political Philosophy* (Oxford University Press, 2016) vol 3

World Health Organisation, *International Statistical Classification of Diseases and Related Health Problems*, 10th edn (World Health Organisation, 2016)

YouGov, *Consumer Finance Association: Attitudes Towards Payday Loans Amongst Payday Customers & Policymakers* (Sponsored by Consumer Finance Association, 2012)

Zamir E, 'The Efficiency of Paternalism' (1998) 84 *Virginia Law Review* 229

Zuckerman A, *Zuckerman on Civil Procedure: Principles of Practice*, 3rd edn (Sweet & Maxwell, 2013)

INDEX

www.ingramcontent.com/pod-product-compliance
Ingram Content Group UK Ltd.
Pitfield, Milton Keynes, MK11 3LW, UK
UKHW020802290926
15470UKWH00003B/916

9 781509 939350